British Foreign Policy, 1918–1945
A Guide to Research and Research Materials

Guides to European Diplomatic History
Research and Research Materials

Series Editor
Christoph M. Kimmich
Brooklyn College
The City University of New York

British Foreign Policy, 1918-1945
Revised Edition
By Sidney Aster
ISBN: 0-8420-2310-0

European International Economic Relations, 1918-1945
By Harold James and Diane B. Kunz
ISBN: 0-8420-2370-4

French Foreign Policy, 1918-1945
Revised Edition
By Robert J. Young
ISBN: 0-8420-2308-9

German Foreign Policy, 1918-1945
Revised Edition
By Christoph M. Kimmich
ISBN: 0-8420-2311-9

International Organizations, 1918-1945
Revised Edition
By George W. Baer
ISBN: 0-8420-2309-7

Italian Foreign Policy, 1918-1945
Revised Edition
By Alan Cassels
ISBN: 0-8420-2307-0

Soviet Foreign Policy, 1918-1945
By Robert H. Johnston
ISBN: 0-8420-2312-7

Available from Scholarly Resources Inc.
Wilmington, Delaware

British Foreign Policy
1918–1945

A Guide to Research and Research Materials

*Compiled and Edited
by
Sidney Aster*

Revised Edition

SR *Scholarly Resources Inc.*
Wilmington, Delaware

©1991 by Scholarly Resources Inc.
All rights reserved
First edition published 1984
Revised edition published 1991
Printed and bound in the United States of America

Scholarly Resources Inc.
104 Greenhill Avenue
Wilmington, DE 19805-1897

Library of Congress Cataloging-in-Publication Data

Aster, Sidney, 1942–
    British foreign policy, 1918–1945 : a guide to research and research materials / compiled and edited by Sidney Aster. — Rev. ed.
        p.   cm. — (Guides to European diplomatic history research and research materials)
    Includes bibliographical references and index.
    ISBN 0-8420-2310-0
    1. Great Britain—Foreign relations—1910–1936—Library resources. 2. Great Britain—Foreign relations—1936–1945—Library resources. 3. Great Britain—Foreign relations—1910–1936—Archival resources. 4. Great Britain—Foreign relations—1936–1945—Archival resources. 5. Library resources—Great Britain. 6. Archival resources—Great Britain. I. Title. II. Series.
Z6465.G7A85 1991
[DA578]
016.32741—dc20   90-46466
                                                                                          CIP

To my children
Andrea Zoe and Dylan Mark

ABOUT THE EDITOR

Sidney Aster, formerly a lecturer in the University of Glasgow and a free-lance historian, is currently an associate professor of history at Erindale College, University of Toronto. He is the author of 1939, The Making of the Second World War (London, 1973; New York, 1973; Paris, 1974) and Anthony Eden (London, 1976; New York, 1976), and the editor of A.P. Young, The "X" Documents: The Secret History of Foreign Office Contacts with the German Resistance, 1937-1939 (London, 1974; Munich, 1989) and The Second World War as a National Experience (Ottawa, 1981). He has also contributed to Lloyd George: Twelve Essays, edited by A.J.P. Taylor (London, 1970), and Paths to War: New Essays on the Origins of the Second World War, edited by Robert Boyce and Esmonde M. Robertson (London, 1989).

INTRODUCTION TO THE SERIES

The reception accorded this series when it first appeared confirmed the editors in their belief that these research guides would meet a genuine need. It seems appropriate, therefore, since new material, published and unpublished, has become available over the last decade, that the series be brought up to date. A second edition is also an opportunity to add further volumes to the series. The series now consists of revised volumes on France, Germany, Great Britain, Italy, and International Organizations, and new volumes on the Soviet Union and on International Economic Relations.

The series is intended for scholars doing research for seminar papers, dissertations, and books dealing with European diplomatic history between 1918 and 1945. It provides information to assist them in their researches and to guide them on their visits to libraries and archives. It will enable them to find their way quickly and efficiently through the voluminous research and research materials that have become available in recent years and will point them toward solutions to the problems they will encounter in the course of their work.

The individual handbooks in this series are organized to serve the researcher's needs. Each has its own distinctive features, for the archival holdings and the research based on these holdings vary considerably. They are, however, meant to be complementary. They focus on materials relevant to different subject areas and, within the limits set by the history of international relations, avoid unnecessary repetition. They are organized along similar lines, and researchers who need to consult several volumes will have no trouble finding their way.

The first chapter will help the reader understand the nature and significance of the sources and allow him to determine where to concentrate his research, how to allot research time, and, not least, how best to approach the materials in the archives. It describes how foreign policy was made - how the foreign ministry was organized and how it functioned, how it affected the conduct of foreign affairs and diplomacy, and how it was influenced by bureaucratic politics, domestic developments, and public opinion.

The second chapter brings together the most current information on public and private archives, libraries, research institutes, and newspaper collections. It indicates what work can be undertaken on this side of the Atlantic and what has to be left for a visit to Europe, and further, what repository will be most useful and rewarding.

The remainder of the volume is bibliography. Sections on general and bibliographical reference works are followed by a survey of the literature in the field, ranging from documentary series to memoirs to significant secondary sources. Arranged topically within a broadly chronological framework, largely annotated, this bibliography permits ready reference to specific books and articles, historical personalities, and diplomatic events. Together with the archival information, the bibliography will suggest areas for further research or reassessment.

Each volume is edited by an authority in the field. Each reflects experience gained on the spot in archives and libraries as well as knowledge shared by colleagues, archivists, and librarians. The volumes therefore are as current and reliable as possible. They will be valuable companions to all who are interested in international affairs and diplomacy.

Christoph M. Kimmich
Series Editor

CONTENTS

PREFACE

"I have not read all these books myself, but I have read more of them than it would be good for any one to read again," was how John Maynard Keynes prefaced a bibliography in 1921. Such sentiment is certainly dear to the heart of any bibliographer. However, there are others. It is equally pertinent, for example, that any bibliography is obsolete the moment compilation ends. But that is not a definition of despair. For the function of bibliography, among many others, is to act as an occasional sieve. The outdated, the irrelevant and the slipshod are discarded, hopefully without too many errors of judgement. It must also be acknowledged that the problem of selection is personal. It is one individual's attempt to take stock, assess the best, indicate the gaps, and point to the road ahead.

The process of gathering information, selecting and annotating was an individual one. Consequently, my few acknowledgements are deeply intended. Over a period of many months, Kathie Hill typed the manuscript on a word processor. She carried out this exacting task with enormous skill, patience and even good humour. In the latter stages, she was joined by Clara Stewart, who applied her expertise at a crucial time. Together they saw the manuscript through to completion. I am very grateful and indebted to them. Stella Gora and Margaret Byrne of Erindale College Library never baulked at my massive requests for interlibrary loans. Wolfgang Arnold very kindly gave of his time to proofread some of the foreign-language titles. As always, Joyce deserves more thanks than I can possibly offer in print.

Erindale College   Sidney Aster
University of Toronto
December 1983

PREFACE TO THE REVISED EDITION

Since the publication of the first edition, the subject of British foreign policy from 1918 to 1945 has continued to be an area of the most intensive research. Books and articles have proliferated. In order to update the present edition, substantial and very extensive revisions have been made. This has required the addition of another 233 annotated entries.

I had the dubious pleasure, shared increasingly by authors in the last part of this century, of processing the entire manuscript, from draft stage to final copy, on my own. This also includes the index. My debts of gratitude during the preparation of this second edition, therefore, are even fewer but no less meaningful. The staff of Erindale College Library have proved themselves once more true friends of the bibliographer. In particular, Stella Gora, Margaret Byrne and, at a later stage, Roberta McCarthy cheerfully filled my quite unreasonable requests for books through the interlibrary loan system. Again, my thanks to Joyce for incorporating bibliography into our lives.

Erindale College   Sidney Aster
University of Toronto
December 1990

I. INTRODUCTION

Nothing succeeds like failure as far as the historian of international history is concerned. And nowhere is this more applicable than in the case of British foreign policy from 1918 to 1945. At the end of the second world war, Britain did of course emerge as a member of a victorious coalition of major powers. But to prescient observers, few as they were, Britain's former great power status and prestige were in question, and her resources seriously depleted. The dynamics of decline and failure, therefore, form the themes of British foreign policy in the first half of the twentieth century.

This experience has proved naturally to be a windfall for the historian. Rarely can a similar span of about twenty-five years have been subjected to such scalpellike dissection by both the scholar and the popular historian, not to speak of the media. And the corpse continues to invite further attention and examination.

While some of the mystery of why this should be so remains, given the obsession with failure, there are some possible explanations. One must begin with the fact that the archival documentation for the period is massive, to say the least. In May 1967 the Labour government of Prime Minister Harold Wilson reduced the rule of secrecy governing British state records from fifty to thirty years. Two years later, he announced that the records for the second world war, occupying nearly seven miles of shelving, would be released as a whole in 1972. In a very short time, therefore, the available material surpassed the ability of any one historian to examine in an entire working lifetime. In other words, there is adequate documentation and research topics for generations of historians to come.

Another possible suggestion is that the period under consideration contains questions about the conduct of foreign policy which might never be conclusively answered. For example, were there alternative and viable policies which British diplomats, politicians and the military could have pursued? A final suggestion, closely related, is largely historiographical. The first commentators on the interwar period set up an inviting target. British foreign policy makers, pursuing a policy of appeasement, were passionately condemned as "guilty men." The attempt to undo that verdict became the raison d'être of virtually every historian entering the Public Record Office in London. The effort to set the record straight, therefore, and with the evidence available to reopen the trial, emerged as the obsession of historians from the early 1960s to the 1980s. The net result of almost thirty

1

years of historical investigation, if generalisation is possible, has been fragmentation rather than synthesis, analysis without perspective, comment instead of value judgement.

The process of returning to the archives for intensive investigation has had certain beneficial effects. The monodimensional view of diplomatic history as a recital of correspondence between the Foreign Office and embassies abroad has mercifully been abandoned. Instead, investigation has focused on vital, but previously neglected areas. For example, publicity, propaganda and the media are proving of increasing interest. Wartime intelligence, particularly relating to Ultra matters, has found abundant investigators. Despite clever conclusions based on insufficient evidence, interwar intelligence matters will always be problematic until the relevant material is released, if ever. The military and strategic dimension, and its close relationship to diplomatic discussions, has drawn numerous students, as has foreign economic policy. Diplomacy during the second world war is continuing to attract considerable attention. Finally, there has been no scarcity of contributors to the continuing debate about appeasement. The discussion has now widened to include the research methodology of the social sciences in an attempt to produce a model-oriented approach to the problem. Other investigators insist on the necessity of relating domestic political, cultural, financial and social considerations to foreign policy. Still others search for the roots of appeasement in a "tradition of appeasement" in British foreign policy. While the area of debate and research has no doubt widened, the great breakthrough, let alone the final word, remains as elusive as ever. Perhaps it is about time to return to the "guilty men" thesis.

For the historian looking to the future, the requirement must surely be synthesis. No doubt studies of particular events and issues will continue. But the preliminary research, combined with the available documents, has adequately prepared the ground for a new generation of works of synthesis. Possible areas include a thorough history of Britain's relation with the League of Nations, a survey of foreign economic policy, a comprehensive analysis of public opinion, and a history of the Foreign Office. Broad area or bilateral studies still show gaps, particularly with regard to Eastern Europe, Scandinavia and South America as a whole, or Portugal, Spain, Czechoslovakia, Greece and South Africa to name but a few. The 1920s remain relatively unexplored. While it lacks the perverse glamour of the 1930s, the post-Versailles decade has yet to find its historian. Last but not least, it is indicative that there exists no satisfactory history of British foreign policy from 1918 to 1945.

Such are the considerations that have moulded the shape of this bibliography. Its objective, among many others, is to point the way towards greater synthesis in future research. Following an account of the development of the Foreign Office, chapter three has been designed to present, as clearly as possible, the major British resources for research in libraries and archives. Chapter four begins with a breakdown of the rich, existing reference guides and bibliographies. One section in this chapter, a

INTRODUCTION

rather long one, is intended to emphasise the extensive range of British memoirs and biographies. The following section specifically highlights various dimensions of foreign policy, bilateral and area studies, and the appeasement debate. The concluding section takes a chronological approach to the entire period, indicating research accomplished and specific aspects yet to be explored.

In the final analysis, the burden of bibliography is about selection. The materials considered in this volume are merely a sampling from a vast field. But those choices have been deliberately fashioned by several particular guidelines. Emphasis has been placed on monographs and articles produced with the benefit of documents released under the thirty-year rule of secrecy. As a result, work produced prior to the 1960s is generally underrepresented. Secondly, it has not been considered feasible to divorce entirely foreign from imperial policy. The interaction of both areas was a pressing problem at the time. While not emphasised as strongly as foreign policy, therefore, imperial questions form part of the bibliography. For the same reason, military, foreign economic policy, foreign service, propaganda and media, intelligence, resistance, and League of Nations aspects are also included. Thirdly, annotations have been designed to provide information of value to the researcher. They indicate sources used, contents, where this is unclear, and sometimes other works of a closely related nature. Judgemental comments have been omitted, despite the obvious temptation, on the assumption that one historian's dross is another's gold. Lastly, the emphasis throughout has been on British and British-related research. That in itself is more than enough for the lifetime, or interest, of any one historian.

II. THE FOREIGN OFFICE AND FOREIGN POLICY

A. HISTORY AND BACKGROUND

The Foreign Office, as so many other British departments of state, enjoyed no orderly line of historical development.[1] Until 1640 the fiction was maintained that foreign policy, like religion, marriage and the succession in the previous century - "matters of state" as Elizabeth I's lord keeper described them - was a subject suitable for treatment by the crown alone. The office of secretary of state for Foreign Affairs dates only from 1782, as does the formation of a separate department for the subject. The term "Foreign Office" does not occur before 1807. It was not until 1868 that the Foreign Office building in Downing Street, occupied to this day, was opened. An amalgamated Foreign Office and foreign service at long last became a reality in 1943. In many ways, the Foreign Office and foreign policy have been a prisoner of this evolution, a combination of "organic development and conscious planning."[2]

Although foreign policy had traditionally been regarded as a matter of royal prerogative, advice on the subject, in particular from the Privy Council, was not viewed as below the dignity of the crown. As early as 1253, during the reign of Henry III, there is evidence of a secretary to the crown. The expansion of royal business, occasioned in no small part by the reformation, led to the appointment of two secretaries between 1539 and 1540. A hundred years later, a division of foreign business was arranged. The "King's Principal Secretary" had his work divided with one other colleague. A rough line appears to have been drawn across the map of Europe, separating a more protestant north from a largely catholic south. Generally, by the eighteenth century the senior secretary presided over the southern department, that is, France, Spain, Italy, Portugal and Turkey. The other concerned himself with the northern department which covered the rest of Europe. This dual secretariat, a very flexible operation, worked efficiently, though hardly as a system. Foreign affairs were limited in terms of geography and capable of being handled by one or two individuals, while the sovereign, as previously, was still powerful enough to impart overall coherence and unified direction.

Implementation, as distinct from formulation, of foreign policy required a diplomatic service. A memorable comment, from an otherwise unmemorable diplomat, defined for posterity the role of the early

5

ambassador. Sir Henry Wooton, ambassador of James I, once wrote in a hotel visiting book while on his way to Vienna, "an Ambassador is a honest man sent to lie abroad for the good of his country." That observation, when reported to James I, led to the dismissal of Wooton. Nonetheless, it effectively epitomised the status and function of the earliest diplomats. "They lied, they spied, they stole," Sir Harold Nicolson aptly noted.[3]

Membership of this early diplomatic coterie, for it was not yet a service, was very much a family affair. There was no system of training, selection or promotion. Crown patronage usually guaranteed appointment to a foreign post, and politics led to a recall. Ambassadors were without privileges, except the sometimes useful one of immunity from arrest for excessive debt abroad. They tended to be professional meddlers in the internal affairs of their host state, dispensing bribery, planning internal opposition, and ferreting out what little intelligence was available. Staff at the British embassy, a privately rented home with the royal coat of arms hanging over the door, was recruited by the ambassador himself, dispensing largesse to relatives or cronies. This imprint of a family embassy was to survive with little change until the first world war.

Crown prerogative, rudimentary organisation and an aristocratic diplomatic class served the purposes of state until the late eighteenth century. Then, on 29 March 1782, Charles James Fox sent a circular to British diplomats abroad. It informed them that George III had appointed him as "One of His Majesty's Principal Secretaries of State" entrusted "with the sole Direction of the Department for Foreign Affairs." The exact functions of the new department were thus described three years later:

> The business of the Secretary of State's Office for the Foreign Department consists in conducting the correspondence with all Foreign Courts, negotiating with the Ambassadors or Ministers of all the Foreign Courts in Europe, as well as of the United States of America, and receiving and making representations and applications to and from the same, and in corresponding with other principal Departments of the State thereupon.[4]

Few subsequent definitions have so succinctly summarised the nature of the work entrusted to the newly created Foreign Office.

Throughout the course of the nineteenth century the Foreign Office expanded structurally, yet at the same time successfully resisted external pressure to change. The number of despatches received and sent, for example, swelled from 6,193 in 1821 to 101,515 in 1900. In the course of the century, too, the number and size of the "political" departments tended to increase. By 1899 there was a Western, Far Eastern, American and Eastern department handling respective geographic areas. Yet the staff responsible for this work hardly expanded, numbering forty-three in 1858 compared to forty-one in 1902-03.[5] One possible explanation was sounded in a typically Victorian note of self-deprecation by a Foreign Office official who observed: "The immense number of despatches which come from agents to Foreign Courts are piled up in large presses, but no note of them is taken, nor is there even an index to them; so that, if anything is wanted, the whole year's accumulation must be rummaged over before it can be found."[6]

The autonomy of the nineteenth-century Foreign Office, zealously guarded by a series of influential foreign secretaries, did not go unchallenged. In the 1850s the entire civil service came under the scrutiny of the Treasury. Recruitment and organisation were the focus of attention, emphasis being placed on the need for competitive entrance examinations and for a distinction between intellectual and mechanical functions for officials. During the next forty years the Foreign Office successfully fought the Treasury, maintaining that the nature of its work, largely confidential, and the necessity for absolute integrity among its officials obviated large-scale reforms. The maximum concession allowed by the Foreign Office was the introduction by 1871 of a system of limited competitive examination. For the most part, however, the nineteenth-century Foreign Office remained a "family system." The need for nomination continued to ensure that candidates came from families known to the foreign secretary, usually from the aristocratic and gentry ranks. And all candidates were still required to have a guaranteed personal income of £400 a year for the initial two years of service.

While the Foreign Office resisted the demands of its critics, the diplomatic service did in fact respond to the mid-Victorian trend towards professionalism in the civil service.[7] Senior diplomatic appointments were gradually removed from the realm of political patronage. The amateur was replaced by the career diplomat, with a salary, allowances, rank, promotion and from 1883 a competitive entrance examination. The £400-a-year income qualification remained. The Ridley Commission on the Civil Service, which sat between 1886 and 1890, recommended the amalgamation of the Foreign Office with the diplomatic service, and the removal of the income qualification. Both suggestions met with complete disapproval. Nonetheless, temporary exchanges between the two, permitted from the early 1860s, resulted in some movement at the lower levels. By 1914 such changeovers were beginning to appear at the higher ranks. In most ways, however, the Foreign Office and the diplomatic service retained the imprint of the family system. Both were socially exclusive, drawn from the titled and the political elite, and with the persisting aura of patronage. John Bright's view in 1858 that foreign affairs was "a gigantic system of outdoor relief for the aristocracy of Great Britain" still rang true.

By the turn of the twentieth century, the Foreign Office was more prepared to admit that its critics might be talking sense. In quick succession a series of reforms were phased in between 1900 and 1907. The so-called mechanical functions, which included clerical work, cyphering and decyphering, registering correspondence and filing, were handed over to junior clerks. Senior clerks began the practice of writing minutes for the consideration of the foreign secretary, a task which has proved to be the contemporary historian's great delight. Boards of selection were introduced to assist the foreign secretary on individual nominations. The diplomatic service was left relatively untouched by these reforms.

On the eve of the first world war, therefore, the Foreign Office was opening its corridors to the winds of change. The cobwebs and dust of the Victorian regime may have been partially shaken off. But it was indeed a minimum concession. For it was still an imperfect machine on the verge of an era where Britain's competitive advantage was no longer automatic.

B. INTERWAR, 1919-1939

"In war . . . diplomacy is the handmaid of the necessities of the War Office and the Admiralty," Sir Edward Grey noted in his memoirs. Another foreign secretary, Anthony Eden, echoed this view, writing that "in War . . . diplomacy is strategy's twin."[8] Such a loss of influence by the Foreign Office was to some extent inevitable in wartime. It was worsened by a streamlined war cabinet, a prime minister, David Lloyd George, with independent views on foreign policy, and a private secretariat which had his ear. This decline was one from which the Foreign Office was never to recover.

The prewar momentum for continued structural reforms had been sidetracked, as so much else in British life, by the outbreak of the war. By 1918 the pressure returned, more in the form of a public crusade than an in-house quarrel. A vociferous, if not entirely accurate, case was made that the "old diplomacy" had contributed to the outbreak of war. It was alleged that secret negotiations monopolised by an irresponsible elite should be replaced in a postwar world by "open diplomacy," with "open covenants, openly arrived at." Part of this "open diplomacy," it was argued, should be a foreign policy structure which was more responsive to parliamentary control and more representative of all sections of British society.

The 1919-20 reforms of the Foreign Office were only in part a response to the public mood. In essence, they implemented some of the recommendations of the Macdonnell Commission on the Civil Service which had reported in December 1914. The Foreign Office and the diplomatic service were amalgamated into a single "foreign service." A promotions committee was established to advise the foreign secretary. The private-means qualification was abolished and new recruits were to be placed on a joint seniority list.

It was grandly proclaimed at the time that these reforms were an admission that "diplomacy, once a question between Court and Court, had now become a question between People and People."[9] In practice, the reforms were not quite so sharp a break with the past. Recruitment still tended to come from the aristocracy. Interchangeability encouraged some transfer, at the lower level, between Foreign Office desk jobs and foreign posts. But senior Foreign Office positions were still zealously coveted, and supply and demand worked to disastrous effect. While there were perhaps three senior Foreign Office jobs, at least forty to fifty ambassadors and ministers could easily qualify. The impediments to democratisation still remained. In the Foreign Office, at least, there was no lasting impression made of any difference between the 'old" and the "new" diplomacy.

Far more serious were the problems which the 1919-20 reforms failed to resolve. It is surprising, but not untypical, that for a nation of shopkeepers foreign economic policy had suffered from inadequate attention and a divided command structure. Prior to the first world war commercial affairs obeyed different masters in London. There existed a commercial department of the Board of Trade, a separate commercial department of the Foreign Office since 1872, commercial attachés abroad appointed in the 1880s, separate trade commissioners for the dominions overseas, and from 1917 a Department of Overseas Trade. Instead of a massive rationalisation, a new commercial diplomatic service was established in 1920, under the joint control of the Foreign Office and the Board of Trade. In a period when the economic and financial dimensions of diplomacy were to become as important a battlefield as foreign policy, the Foreign Office was left without its own commercial service.

The problem of British consuls overseas, it could hardly be termed a service, was also not resolved. In the early nineteenth century, it had been intended to convert this hotchpotch of semipublic officials into salaried civil servants, paid by parliamentary vote. None of these intentions were realised by the turn of the twentieth century. Consuls remained a mixture of independent individuals, without systematic recruitment, with inadequate prospects or rewards, and socially ostracised by their diplomatic colleagues. Periodic suggestions for amalgamation were always rejected. At the end of 1936, the three consular branches, the General, Levant and Far Eastern, were finally integrated with the Foreign Office and diplomatic service, at least as far as new entrants were concerned. Complete integration lay in the not-too-distant future.

Propaganda, publicity and news information was the last difficulty swept under the carpet in 1919-20. The prewar Foreign Office cultivated very little press contact, with the exception of employees of The Times. Under the impact of the war, however, the British proved resilient and even innovative, building up sophisticated propaganda and information services. The entire structure, in which Britain had a commanding lead, was unfortunately dismantled after 1918. Temporary wartime departments and ministries, such as for political intelligence and information, were wound up. They were regarded as a regrettable and temporary expedient. The sole survivor was the news department. It was reconstituted, severely restricted in scope, and delegated to maintain peacetime contacts with the press. The prevailing attitude, which so handicapped British foreign policy in the interwar years, was that publicity and propaganda were "diplomatically dangerous and anyhow quite unworthy of Great Britain."[10]

The consequences of this limited reorganisation became increasingly apparent as the influence of the Foreign Office continued to decline from 1919 to 1939. With regard to structure and organisation, personnel remained fairly static. After the recruitment explosion of the war, the number of civil servants in the foreign service in 1938 stood at 902, a very small increase over the 1920 figure of 885. Yet the sheer physical demands sharply increased. The number of despatches handled by the Foreign Office, for example in 1926, had been 145,169. In 1938 the comparable figure was 223,879.[11] The political departments tried to accommodate this increased pressure of work. Between 1920 and 1939 these comprised the following: American and African (from 1930 American); Far Eastern; Eastern; Central; Western (from 1922 League of Nations and Western); Northern; Egyptian (formed in 1924); and Southern (formed in 1933). It is little wonder that in 1939 the permanent under-secretary of state for Foreign Affairs complained in his diary, "Life is hell."[12]

The news department of the Foreign Office continued to struggle for recognition in its own little backwater. Only in the mid-1930s, with the establishment of the British Council, the appointment of a chief press liaison officer at No. 10, and increased funding, did the "projection of Britain" finally begin to recover some ground. Even then the suspicion remained that somehow publicity, not to speak of propaganda, was incompatible with appeasement.

Foreign economic policy fared little better in the 1919-39 period. Throughout that time the Foreign Office and the Treasury were at loggerheads. One aspect of the difficulty concerned the degree of control, if not outright interference, exercised by the secretary to the Treasury and head of the civil service upon the Foreign Office and foreign policy. The other concerned the question of reparations in the 1920s. The Foreign Office and the Treasury held diametrically opposing views on this most difficult aspect of foreign economic policy. The former argued the case for linking reparations and disarmament; the latter contended that reparations and war debts posed the greater threat to stability. The fact, too, that the Foreign Office had to communicate its policy to the Bank of England via the Treasury led to an almost complete breakdown of coordination.

The foreign economic problems of the 1930s changed, but the structural ones persisted. There existed no single department with overall control over the collection, assessment and dissemination of politico-economic intelligence. In December 1930 precisely such a proposal was floated in the Foreign Office. It evoked little reaction. What resulted was neither a compromise nor a concession, but a token gesture. An economic section within the Western department was formed. Frank Ashton-Gwatkin, a former consular official, was put in charge of what he later described as "a one-man liaison bureau."[13] In its overall aim of sharpening the appreciation of foreign economic policy, the experiment proved an almost complete failure.

Structural and organisational weaknesses, vital as they were, do not in the final analysis illuminate the course of British foreign policy in the interwar years. It is highly doubtful whether a fully amalgamated and democratised foreign service, effective news and propaganda organs, a less authoritarian Treasury, and effective politico-economic intelligence would have made any great difference, other than timing, in the final outcome of the period, that is, a renewal of war with Germany. Of far greater importance, for example, was the failure to distinguish between Weimar and Nazi Germany, the constraints imposed on foreign policy by domestic economic problems, the stark realities of military weakness peddled by the chiefs of staff, and profound divisions of opinion within the Foreign Office itself about policy towards the dictators. Equally relevant is the lead given by strong prime ministers and avoided by ineffective foreign secretaries. Of the five interwar prime ministers, only David Lloyd George, James Ramsay MacDonald and Neville Chamberlain held decisive views, right or wrong, on foreign affairs. Only Sir Austen Chamberlain, of the eight interwar foreign secretaries, served long and effectively enough to return the Foreign Office temporarily to a position of some influence. These then are some of the factors one must examine for the continuing eclipse of the Foreign Office and the diplomatic failures of the interwar years.

C. THE SECOND WORLD WAR AND THE EDEN REFORMS

The second world war proved to be among the greatest tests ever faced by the Foreign Office, but it was thoroughly met. In common with other ministries, there was the experience of the previous world war to draw upon. In addition, the foreign secretary was invited to join the war cabinet, and from December 1940 the Anthony Eden-Winston Churchill relationship must be taken into account. While not as special as both later pretended, it guaranteed a pivotal role for the Foreign Office in wartime diplomatic negotiations, particularly involving the grand alliance.

What served further to reinvigorate the Foreign Office was the introduction of the most daring reorganisation of the foreign services ever attempted. Anthony Eden's Proposals for the Reform of the Foreign Service, the White Paper (Cmd. 6420) of January 1943, declared that it was the intention of the government to create a new service which, by its composition, recruitment, training and organisation,

> shall be better able not merely to represent the interests of the nation as a whole, but also to deal with the whole range of international affairs, political, social and economic, and so constitute an adequate instrument for the maintenance of good relations and mutual understanding between the United Kingdom and other countries.[14]

This statement, in essence, acknowledged the failures of the Foreign Office and overseas services since 1919, if not earlier. At the heart of the proposals was the recommendation to amalgamate completely the Foreign Office and the diplomatic, commercial and consular services into a new foreign service. Subsidiary proposals included grants and allowances for complete mobility, proper personnel management and control, power to retire, on pension, unsuitable officers before the age of sixty, complete interchangeability, and consideration for the question of recruiting women. The Eden reforms became law through an order-in-council on 20 May 1943.

By the mid-1950s most of these recommendations had been implemented. The ideal of a generalist service, with mobility, interchangeability and open recruitment, was at last realised. But the Foreign and Commonwealth Office, as the Foreign Office was renamed in 1968, continued to invite investigation. The 1964 Plowden report had been followed by the 1969 Duncan report, the 1977 cabinet think tank (Central Policy Review Staff) report, and the resignation of the foreign secretary and his two senior Foreign Office ministers in the wake of the Falkland Islands war of 1982. In that year, too, on the 200th anniversary of its foundation, the Foreign and Commonwealth Office stood accused of acting as a "spokesman in Britain for foreign governments rather than for Britain to foreign governments."[15]

D. APPENDIX

1. The Foreign Office

Secretaries of State for Foreign Affairs

Dec. 1916	Arthur James Balfour, 1st Earl of Balfour
Oct. 1919	1st Earl Curzon, Marquess Curzon of Kedleston
Jan. 1924	James Ramsay MacDonald
Nov. 1924	Sir Austen Chamberlain
June 1929	Arthur Henderson
Aug. 1931	Sir Rufus D. Isaacs, 1st Marquess of Reading
Nov. 1931	Sir John Simon, 1st Viscount Simon
June 1935	Sir Samuel Hoare, 1st Viscount Templewood
Dec. 1935	Anthony Eden, 1st Earl of Avon
Mar. 1938	Sir Edward F. Lindley Wood, 1st Earl of Halifax
Dec. 1940	Anthony Eden, 1st Earl of Avon
July 1945	Ernest Bevin

Permanent Under-Secretaries of State for Foreign Affairs

1916-20	Charles Hardinge, 1st Baron Hardinge of Penshurst
1920-25	Sir Eyre Crowe
1925-28	Sir William G. Tyrrell, 1st Baron Tyrrell
1928-30	Sir Ronald C. Lindsay
1930-38	Sir Robert Vansittart, Baron Vansittart
1938-46	Sir Alexander G.M. Cadogan

2. The Diplomatic Service

Ambassadors, Ministers, etc. to Select Powers

Argentina
Sir R.T. Tower, 1911-20
Sir J.W.R. Macleay, 1920-22, 1930-33
Sir B.F. Alston, 1923-25
Sir M.A. Robertson, 1925-30
Sir H.G. Chilton, 1933-35
Sir N.M. Henderson, 1935-37
Sir E. Ovey, 1937-42
Sir D.V. Kelly, 1942-46.

Austria
Sir F.O. Lindley, 1919-20
Sir A. Akers-Douglas, 2nd Viscount Chilston, 1921-27
Sir E.C.E. Phipps, 1928-33
Sir W.H.M. Selby, 1933-37
Sir C.M. Palairet, 1937-38

Belgium
Sir F.H. Villiers, 1911-20
Sir G.D. Grahame, 1920-28
Sir G.G.L. Gower, 3rd Earl Granville, 1928-33
Sir G.R. Clerk, 1933-34
Sir E. Ovey, 1934-37
Sir R.H. Clive, 1937-39
Sir L. Oliphant, 1939-40, 1941-44
A.F. Aveling, 1940-41
Sir H.M. Knatchbull-Hugessen, 1944-47

Brazil
Sir A.R. Peel, 1915-19
Sir R.S. Paget, 1919-20
Sir J.A.C. Tilley, 1921-25
Sir B.F. Alston, 1925-29
Sir W. Seeds, 1930-35
Sir H. Gurney, 1935-39
Sir G.G. Knox, 1939-41

Sir N.H.H. Charles, 1941-44
Sir D.St.C. Gainer, 1944-47

Bulgaria
Sir H.G. Dering, 1919-20
Sir A.R. Peel, 1920-21
Sir W.A.F. Erskine, 1921-27
Sir R.A.C. Sperling, 1928-29
Sir S.P. Waterlow, 1929-33
Sir C.H. Bentinck, 1934-36
Sir M.D. Peterson, 1936-38
Sir G.W. Rendel, 1938-41
Sir W.E. Houstoun-Boswall, 1944-46

Chile
Sir F.W. Stronge, 1913-19
Sir J.C.T. Vaughan, 1919-22
Sir A.C. Grant-Duff, 1923-24
Sir T.B. Hohler, 1924-27
Sir A.J.K. Clark Kerr, 1st Baron Inverchapel, 1928-30
Sir H.G. Chilton, 1930-33
Sir R.C. Michell, 1933-37
Sir C.H. Bentinck, 1937-40
Sir C.W. Orde, 1940-45

China
Sir J.N. Jordan, 1906-20
Sir B.F. Alston, 1920-22
Sir J.W.R. Macleay, 1922-26
Sir M.W. Lampson, 1st Baron Killearn, 1926-33
Sir A.G.M. Cadogan, 1933-36
Sir H.M. Knatchbull-Hugessen, 1936-38
Sir A.J.K. Clark Kerr, 1st Baron Inverchapel, 1938-42
Sir H.J. Seymour, 1942-46

Czechoslovakia
Sir G.R. Clerk, 1919-26
Sir J.W.R. Macleay, 1927-29
Sir J. Addison, 1930-36
Sir C.H. Bentinck, 1936-37
Sir B.C. Newton, 1937-39
Sir R. H. Bruce Lockhart, 1940-41
Sir F.K. Roberts, 1941
Sir P.B.B. Nichols, 1941-47

Denmark
Sir R.S. Paget, 1916-18
Sir C.M. Marling, 1919-21
Sir G.G.L. Gower, 3rd Earl
  Granville, 1921-26
Sir M. Cheetham, 1926-28
Sir T.B. Hohler, 1928-33
Sir H. Gurney, 1933-35
Sir P.W.M. Ramsay, 1935-39
C.H. Smith, 1939-40
Sir A.W.G. Randall, 1945-52

Egypt
Gen. Sir F.R. Wingate, 1917-19
Field-Marshal 1st Viscount
  Allenby, 1919-25
Sir G.A. Lloyd, 1st Baron Lloyd of
  Dolobran, 1925-29
Sir P.L. Loraine, 1929-33
Sir M.W. Lampson, 1st Baron
  Killearn, 1934-46

France
Sir F. Bertie, 1st Viscount Bertie of
  Thame, 1905-18
Sir E.G.V. Stanley, 17th Earl
  of Derby, 1918-20
Sir C. Hardinge, 1st Baron
  Hardinge of Penshurst,
  1920-22
Sir R.O.A. Crewe-Milnes, 1st
  Marquess of Crewe, 1922-28
Sir W.G. Tyrrell, 1928-34
Sir G.R. Clerk, 1934-37
Sir E.C.E. Phipps, 1937-39
Sir R.H. Campbell, 1939-40

A. Duff Cooper, 1st Viscount
  Norwich, 1944-48

Germany
Baron Kilmarnock, 21st Earl of
  Erroll, 1920
Sir E. Vincent, 1st Viscount
  D'Abernon, 1920-26
Sir R.C. Lindsay, 1926-28
Sir H.G.M. Rumbold, 1928-33
Sir E.C.E. Phipps, 1933-37
Sir N.M. Henderson, 1937-39

Greece
Sir G.G.L. Gower, 3rd Earl
  Granville, 1917-21
Sir F.O. Lindley, 1921-23
Sir M. Cheetham, 1924-26
Sir P.L. Loraine, 1926-29
Sir P.W.M. Ramsay, 1929-33
Sir S.P. Waterlow, 1933-39
Sir C.M. Palairet, 1939-43
Sir R.W.A. Leeper, 1943-46

Hungary
Sir T.B. Hohler, 1920-24
Sir C.A. Barclay, 1924-28
Sir A. Akers-Douglas, 2nd
  Viscount Chilston, 1928-33
Sir P.W.M. Ramsay, 1933-35
Sir G.G. Knox, 1935-39
Sir O.St.C. O'Malley, 1939-41
Sir A.D.F. Gascoigne, 1945-46

Iran (Persia)
Sir P.Z. Cox, 1918-20
H.C. Norman, 1920-21
Sir P.L. Loraine, 1921-26
Sir R.H. Clive, 1926-31
Sir R.H. Hoare, 1931-34
Sir H.M. Knatchbull-Hugessen,
  1934-36
Sir H.J. Seymour, 1936-39
Sir R.W. Bullard, 1939-46

Iraq
Sir H.W. Young, 1932

Sir F.H. Humphrys, 1932-35
Sir A.J.K. Clark Kerr, 1st Baron
Inverchapel, 1935-38
Sir M.D. Peterson, 1938-39
Sir B.C. Newton, 1939-41
Sir K. Cornwallis, 1941-45

Italy
Sir J. Rennell Rodd, 1st Baron
Rennell of Rodd, 1908-19
Sir G.W. Buchanan, 1919-21
Sir R.W. Graham, 1921-33
Sir J.E. Drummond, 16th Earl
of Perth, 1933-39
Sir P.L. Loraine, 1939-40
Sir N.H.H. Charles, 1944-47

Japan
Sir W. Conyngham Greene,
1912-19
Sir C.N.E. Eliot, 1920-26
Sir J.A.C. Tilley, 1926-31
Sir F.O. Lindley, 1931-34
Sir R.H. Clive, 1934-37
Sir R.L. Craigie, 1937-41

Mexico
H.A.C. Cummins, 1917-24
Sir N. King, 1925
Sir E. Ovey, 1925-29
Sir E.St.J.D.J. Monson,
1929-34
J. Murray, 1935-37
Sir O.St.C. O'Malley, 1937-38
T.I. Rees, 1941
Sir C.H. Bateman, 1941-47

Netherlands
Sir W.B. Townley, 1917-19
Sir R.W. Graham, 1919-21
Sir C.M. Marling, 1921-26
Sir G.G.L. Gower, 3rd Earl
Granville, 1926-28
Sir O.W.T. Russell, 1928-33
Sir C.H. Montgomery, 1933-38
Sir G.N.M. Bland, 1938-48

Norway
Sir M.de C. Findlay, 1911-23
Sir F.O. Lindley, 1923-29
Sir C.J.F.R. Wingfield, 1929-34
Sir C.F.J. Dormer, 1934-40
Sir L. Collier, 1941-50

Poland
Sir H.G.M. Rumbold, 1919-20
Sir W.G. Max-Muller, 1920-28
Sir W.A.F. Erskine, 1928-34
Sir H.W. Kennard, 1935-41
Sir C.F.J. Dormer, 1941-43
Sir O.St.C. O'Malley, 1943-45

Portugal
Sir L.D. Carnegie, 1913-28
Sir C.A. Barclay, 1928-29
Sir F.O. Lindley, 1929-31
Sir C.F.W. Russell, 1931-35
Sir C.J.F.R. Wingfield,
1935-37
Sir W.H.M. Selby, 1937-40
Sir R.H. Campbell, 1940-45

Rumania
Sir G.H. Barclay, 1912-19
Sir A.R. Peel, 1919-20
Sir. H.G. Dering, 1920-26
Sir R.H. Greg, 1926-29
Sir C.M. Palairet, 1929-35
Sir R.H. Hoare, 1935-41
Sir J.H. Le Rougetel, 1944-46

Russia, and the Soviet Union
Sir G.W. Buchanan, 1910-18
Sir R.M. Hodgson, 1924-27
Sir E. Ovey, 1929-33
Sir A. Akers-Douglas, 2nd
Viscount Chilston, 1933-38
Sir W. Seeds, 1939-40
Sir R. Stafford Cripps,
1940-42
Sir A.J.K. Clark Kerr, 1st Baron
Inverchapel, 1942-46

Saudi Arabia
W.L. Bond, 1929-30
Sir A. Ryan, 1930-36
Sir R.W. Bullard, 1936-39
Sir F.H.W. Stonehewer-Bird, 1939-43
S.R. Jordan, 1943-45

Spain
Sir A.H. Hardinge, 1913-19
Sir E.W. Howard, 1st Baron Howard of Penrith, 1919-24
Sir H.G.M. Rumbold, 1924-28
Sir G.D. Grahame, 1928-35
Sir H.G. Chilton, 1935-38
Sir O.St.C. O'Malley, 1938-39
Sir R.M. Hodgson, 1939
Sir M.D. Peterson, 1939-40
Sir S. Hoare, 1st Viscount Templewood, 1940-44

Sweden
Sir E.W. Howard, 1st Baron Howard of Penrith, 1913-19
Sir C.A. Barclay, 1919-24
Sir A.C. Grant-Duff, 1924-27
Sir J.C.T. Vaughan, 1927-29
Sir H.W. Kennard, 1929-31
Sir A.J.K. Clark Kerr, 1st Baron Inverchapel, 1931-35
Sir C.M. Palairet, 1935-37
Sir E.St.J.D.J. Monson, 1938-39
Sir V.A.L. Mallet, 1940-45

Switzerland
Sir H.G.M. Rumbold, 1916-19
Sir O.W.T. Russell, 1919-22
Sir M. Cheetham, 1922-24
Sir R.A.C. Sperling, 1924-27

Sir C.F.W. Russell, 1928-31
Sir H.W. Kennard, 1931-35
Sir G.R. Warner, 1935-39
Sir D.V. Kelly, 1940-42
Sir C.J. Norton, 1942-46

Turkey
Sir H.G.M. Rumbold, 1920-24
Sir R.C. Lindsay, 1924-26
Sir G.R. Clerk, 1926-33
Sir P.L. Loraine, 1933-39
Sir H.M. Knatchbull-Hugessen, 1939-44
Sir M.D. Peterson, 1944-46

United States of America
Sir C.A. Spring Rice, 1913-18
Sir R.D. Isaacs, 1st Marquess of Reading, 1918
Sir E. Grey, 1st Viscount Grey of Falloden, 1919
Sir A.C. Geddes, 1st Baron Geddes, 1920-24
Sir E.W. Howard, 1st Baron Howard of Penrith, 1924-30
Sir R.C. Lindsay, 1930-39
P.H. Kerr, 11th Marquess of Lothian, 1939-40
Sir E.F.L. Wood, 1st Earl of Halifax, 1941-46

Yugoslavia
Sir C.A. Young, 1919-25
Sir H.W. Kennard, 1925-29
Sir N.M. Henderson, 1929-35
Sir R.H. Campbell, 1935-39
Sir R.I. Campbell, 1939-41
Sir G.W. Rendel, 1941-43
Sir R.C.S. Stevenson, 1943-46

3. The Foreign Office circa 1930

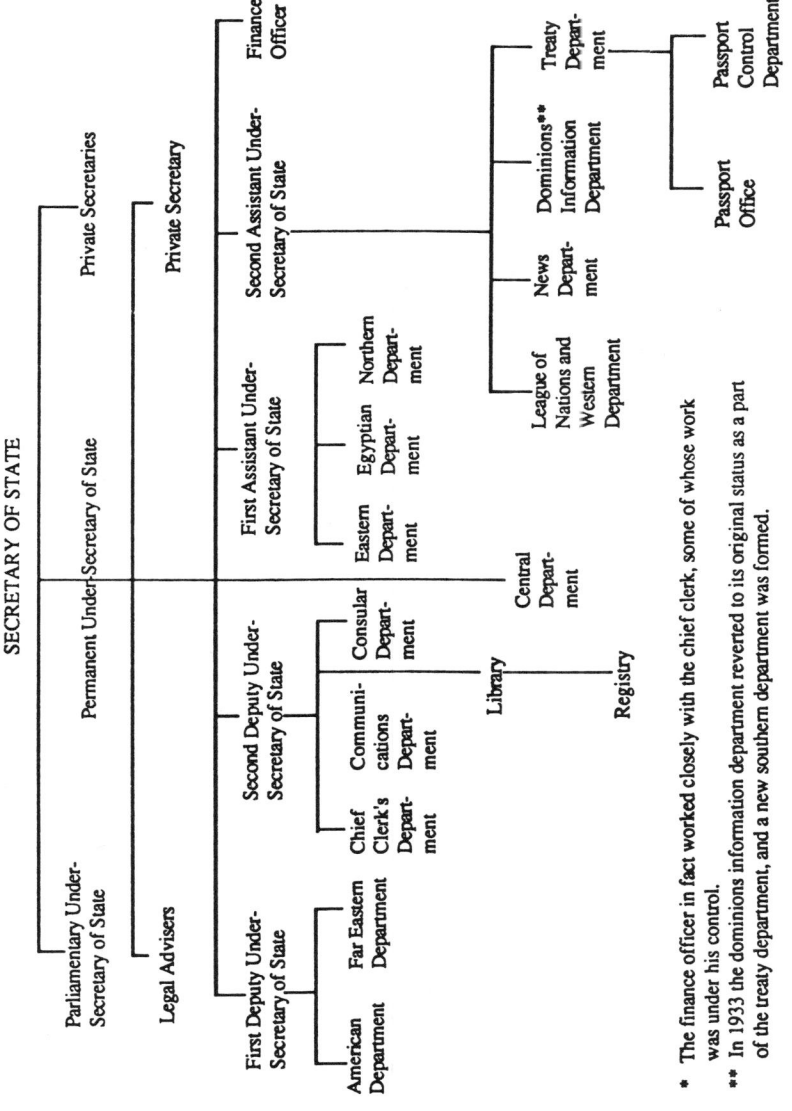

* The finance officer in fact worked closely with the chief clerk, some of whose work was under his control.
** In 1933 the dominions information department reverted to its original status as a part of the treaty department, and a new southern department was formed.

END NOTES

1. This analysis of the Foreign Office and foreign policy is based on the sources indicated in the section below entitled "The Foreign Office"; additional material on the pre-1919 period has been gathered from British Foreign Secretaries and Foreign Policy: From Crimean War to First World War, edited by Keith Wilson (London, 1986); Charles Ronald Middleton, The Administration of British Foreign Policy, 1782-1846 (Durham, NC, 1977); Raymond A. Jones, The Nineteenth Century Foreign Office: An Administrative History (London, 1971); his The British Diplomatic Service, 1815-1914 (Waterloo, Ontario, 1983); and Zara Steiner, The Foreign Office and Foreign Policy, 1898-1914 (London, 1969); and D.B. Horn, The British Diplomatic Service, 1689-1789 (London, 1961).

2. Lord Plowden, Report of the Committee on Representational Services Overseas, Cmd. 2276 (London, 1964), 1.

3. Sir Harold Nicolson, Diplomacy (London, 1963), 20-21.

4. Quoted in The Records of the Foreign Office, 1782-1939, Public Record Office Handbooks, no. 13 (London, 1969), 2-3.

5. Frank T.A. Ashton-Gwatkin, The British Foreign Service (Syracuse, NY, 1950), 11-12; Sir John A.C. Tilley and Stephen Gaselee, The Foreign Office (London, 1933), 48-49; Valerie Cromwell, "The Foreign and Commonwealth Office," in 'The Times' Survey of Foreign Ministries of the World, edited by Zara Steiner (London, 1982), 546.

6. Quoted in Tilley and Gaselee, 34-35.

7. Cf. Horn, 13; and Jones, British Diplomatic Service, 215.

8. Viscount Grey, Twenty–Five Years, 1892-1916, vol. 2 (London, 1925), 166; Earl of Avon, The Eden Memoirs, vol. 3, The Reckoning, 183.

9. Algernon Cecil, "The Foreign Office," in The Cambridge History of British Foreign Policy, 1783-1919, vol. 3, edited by Sir Adolphus Ward and G.P. Gooch (London, 1923), 619.

10. Ashton–Gwatkin, British Foreign Service, 20.

11. David Butler and Gareth Butler, British Political Facts, 1900-1985, 6th ed. (London, 1986), 291; Documents on British Foreign Policy, 1919-1939, 1st Series, vol. 1, edited by Sir Llewellyn Woodward et al., iii.

12. Sir Alexander Cadogan, The Diaries of Sir Alexander Cadogan, O.M., 1938-1945, edited by David Dilks (London, 1971), 86.

13. Frank Ashton-Gwatkin, "Thoughts on the Foreign Office, 1918-1939," Contemporary Review, 188 (1955), 378.

14. Proposals for the Reform of the Foreign Service, Cmd. 6420 (London, 1953), xi.

15. Quoted in "Britain's Foreign Office," The Economist, 27 Nov. 1982, 20.

III. RESEARCH LIBRARIES AND ARCHIVES

A. INFORMATION AND PUBLICATIONS

The material for the study of British foreign policy from 1918 to 1945 is scattered throughout the United Kingdom. There is hardly a national or local record office and library, university library, or special archive supported by a privately endowed society which does not contain some relevant material. Record Repositories in Great Britain: A Geographical Directory (8th ed., London, 1987), compiled by the Royal Commission on Historical Manuscripts, lists no less than 248 repositories "whose objectives include the systematic collection and preservation of written records, other than those of its own administration, and which also make regular provision for their public use." A comprehensive list therefore is impossible. What follows is a selection of libraries, record offices and archives which are known to contain useful material for the study of British foreign policy.

1. BANK OF ENGLAND, Archive Section HO-M, Corporate Services Department, Threadneedle Street, London EC2R 8AH (M-F 10-4.45). Three separate sections within the Bank deal with reference materials dating from the foundation of the Bank of England in 1694 to the present. The Archive houses the Bank's own records and handles the administration of researchers. The record groups cover the principal activities, including the Administration Department which contains the papers of such senior officials as Montagu Norman, and the Economic Intelligence Department. Descriptive lists of records transferred to the archive are stored on a data base which can be accessed by researchers. Most records are open to research after 30 years. The Library holds published materials dealing with banking and finance, such as trade statistics, acts of parliament, etc. The Museum and Historical Research section is responsible for the Bank of England Museum, which opened in 1988.

2. BIRMINGHAM UNIVERSITY, The Library, Special Collections Department, Main Library, PO Box 363, Birmingham B15 2TT (M-F 9-5). The main library of the University of Birmingham,

›|

opened in 1960 and extended in 1971, houses more than one million volumes and 7,700 current periodicals. The political archives are centred around the Chamberlains' papers and those of Anthony Eden.

University of Birmingham, The Library. Guide to the Chamberlain Collection. Compiled by B.S. Benedikz. Birmingham, 1978.

For the papers of Joseph, Austen and Neville Chamberlain and their families.

3.   BRITISH BROADCASTING CORPORATION, Written Archives Centre, Caversham Park, Reading RG4 8TZ (T-F, 9.45-1, 2-5.15, by appointment only). The BBC written archives, established at Caversham in 1970, contain material relevant to history, politics, biography and broadcasting. Beside internal BBC documentation, there are files on contributors, radio and television scripts, audience research, programme indexes, and various BBC publications. There is additionally an extensive and classified collection of press cuttings relating to broadcasting and broadcasters, 1922-62.

BBC. Written Archives. Reading, 1980.

4.   BRITISH LIBRARY. The British Library was formed in July 1973 with the amalgamation of the British Museum Library, the National Central Library, the National Lending Library for Science and Technology, the British National Bibliography and, in 1974, the functions of the Office of Scientific and Technical Information. Subsequently, the Library took responsibility for the India Office Library and Records, and the National Sound Archive. The British Library is the United Kingdom's national library and occupies the central position in the library and information network. It enjoys the privilege of copyright deposit, that is, it has the legal right to receive any book, music, or map published in the United Kingdom. Its services are based on collections which include over 18 million volumes (books, manuscripts, maps, newspapers and other serials, stamps and music), one million discs, 55,000 hours of tape recordings in more than 18 buildings in London and one complex at Boston Spa, Wetherby, West Yorkshire LS23 7BQ amounting to over 328 miles of shelving growing at a rate of eight miles every year. There are ten reading rooms, most of which require an admission pass available on application to the respective reader admission office. The British Library, which is independent of the British Museum, is organised into two main divisions: Humanities and Social Sciences; and Science, Technology and Industry. The former, Great Russell Street, London WC1B 3DG (M,F,Sat. 9-5, T,W,Th 9-9) includes the West European, Slavonic and East

European, English language, and Western Manuscripts Collections. The British Library will be moving to purpose-built accommodation at St. Pancras, London NW1 in 1991 (open to the public in 1993). The Newspaper Library, Colindale Avenue, London NW9 5HE (M-Sat. 10-5), established in 1905 as a storage library for post-1800 newspapers, is the principal legal deposit library for newspapers in the United Kingdom. It contains over half a million volumes and parcels of British daily and weekly newspapers and periodicals, as well as a vast collection of Commonwealth and foreign newspapers.

British Library. Catalogue of Additions to the Manuscripts in the British Museum, 1916-1920. London, 1933-.

Supplements for 1921-45, 5 vols. (1950-70); 1946-50, 3 vols. (1980); 1951-55, 2 vols. (1982).

―――. Index of Manuscripts in the British Library. 11 vols. London, 1984-86.

An amalgamated person and place name index to all collections of Western manuscripts acquired to 1950; no subject index.

―――. Catalogue of Additions to the Manuscripts in the British Library: The Cecil of Chelwood Papers. Compiled by A.N.E.D. Schofield. London, 1989.

―――. Register of Microfilms and Other Photocopies in the Department of Manuscripts. London, 1976.

Published by the List and Index Society for the British Library; vol. 9 of the "Special Series."

―――. General Catalogue of Printed Books to 1975. 360 vols. London, 1980-87.

Supersedes Photolithographic Edition to 1955, 263 vols. (London, 1976); the published version of the catalogue of the British Library Humanities and Social Sciences in all languages except those of the Library's Oriental Collections; basically an author catalogue; an indispensable bibliographical source both to the Library's holdings and means of verifying titles, etc.; available on CD-ROM; subject indexes published in five- or ten-year cumulations, 1946-60, 10 vols. (1961-70), 1961-70, 12 vols. (1982), 1971-75, 15 vols. (1986); post-1975 material is available to subscribers to BLAISE, the Library's online service; General Catalogue of Printed Books, 1976-1985 (1986), supplements for

1982-85 (1986), 1986-87 (1988), and Subject Catalogue of Printed Books, 1975-1985 (1985) are available in microform.

————. Index of Conference Proceedings Received. Boston Spa, 1964-.

Monthly, with annual cumulations; 18-year cumulation, 1964-81 available in microform.

————. Catalogue of Books and Periodicals on Estonia in the British Library Reference Division. Compiled by Salme Pruuden. London, 1981.

————. Catalogue of Printed Maps, Charts and Plans. 15 vols. London, 1967.

Volume of "Corrections and Additions" (1968); ten-year supplement, 1965-74 (1977); the supplement is continued by the Catalogue of Cartographic Materials in the British Library: Accessions from 1975 in microform.

British Library, Newspaper Library. Catalogue of the Newspaper Library, Colindale. 8 vols. Compiled by P.E. Allen. London, 1975.

Vols. 1-4 by place of publication; vols. 5-8 for alphabetical listing by titles; see also Microfilm of Newspapers and Journals for Sale, 1985-1986 (London, 1986); and Newspapers and Periodicals for Sale on Microfilm: Foreign and Commonwealth Countries (London, 1988).

British Library, Official Publications and Social Sciences Service. Checklist of British Official Serial Publications. 12th ed. London, 1983.

Adkins, R.T., ed. Guide to Government Department and Other Libraries. 28th ed. London, 1988.

Day, Alan Edwin. The British Library: A Guide to Its Structure, Publications, Collections and Services. London, 1988.

Nickson, M.A.E. The British Library: Guide to the Catalogues and Indexes of the Department of Manuscripts. 2nd ed. London, 1982.

Also of use is T.C. Skeat, The Catalogues of the Manuscript Collections, rev. ed. (London, 1962).

Taylor, P.J., comp. Information Guides: A Survey of Subject Guides to Sources of Information Produced by Library and Information Services in the United Kingdom. London, 1978.

4a.   India Office Library and Records, Orbit House, 197 Blackfriars Road, London SE1 8NG (M-F 9.30-6, Sat. 9.30-1). The basis of the Library is an amalgamation in 1967 of the India Office Records and the India Office Library. The main collection of documents, derived from the India Office (1858-1947) and the Burma Office (1937-48), comprises over 170,000 volumes and files. Departmental records include the "Political and Secret, 1778-1950" and the "Private Ofice, c. 1916-1947." The latter contains the private files of the secretaries of state for India.

Ashtiany, Julia. The Arabic Documents in the Archives of the British Political Agency, Kuwait, 1904-1949. London, 1982.

Baxter, Ian A. A Brief Guide to Biographical Sources. London, 1979.

Farrington, A.J. Guide to the Records of the India Office Military Department. London, 1982.

Griffin, Andrew. A Brief Guide to Sources for the Study of Burma in the India Office Records. London, 1979.

See also Lesley Hall, A Brief Guide to Sources for the Study of Afghanistan (London, 1981).

India Office Library. Catalogue of European Printed Books. 10 vols. Boston, MA, 1964.

———. Index of Post-1937 European Manuscript Accessions, India Office Library. Boston, MA, 1964.

India Office Records. Accessions of Private Collections, 1937-1977. Compiled by Rosemary Seton. London, 1978.

For manuscripts received before 1937 see Catalogue of Manuscripts in European Languages, edited by C.O. Blagden et al., 2 vols. (London, 1916-37).

Lancaster, Joan C. A Guide to the Lists and Catalogues of the India Office Records. London, 1966.

See also her "The India Office Records," Archives, 9(1970), 130-41; and "The Scope and Uses of the India Office Library and

Records with Particular Reference to the Period 1600-1947," Asian Affairs, 9(1978), 31-43.

Moir, Martin. A General Guide to the India Office Records. London, 1988.

Sims, John. A List and Index of Parliamentary Papers Relating to India, 1908-1947. London, 1981.

Singh, Amar Kaur Jasbir. A Guide to Source Materials in the India Office Library and Records for the History of Tibet, Sikkim and Bhutan, 1765-1950. London, 1988.

Sutton, S.C. A Guide to the India Office Library, with a Note on the India Office Records. 2nd ed. London, 1971.

Tuson, Penelope. The Records of the British Residency and Agencies in the Persian Gulf. London, 1979.

Walker, Dorothy. Catalogue of the Newspaper Collection in the India Office Library. London, 1977.

5. BUSINESS ARCHIVES COUNCIL, Library, 185 Tower Bridge Road, London SE1 2VF (M-F 10-4). The Council, formed in 1934, is concerned with the preservation and location of business records for historical research. It houses a collection of business histories, some privately printed, and a register of business archives. Its biannual Business Archives contains articles in the field, reviews, information about accessions and bibliographies. The Council also publishes a quarterly Newsletter. Similar functions are performed by the Business Archives Council of Scotland, Glasgow University Archives, The University, Glasgow G12 8QQ.

Business Archives Council. Shipping: A Survey of Historical Records. Edited by Peter Mathias and A.W.H. Pearsall. London, 1971.

———. A Guide to the Historical Records of British Banking. Edited by L.S. Pressnell and John Orbell. London, 1985.

The records, locations, etc. of 639 banking institutions.

———. Directory of Corporate Archives. Edited by Lesley Richmond and Alison Turton. 2nd ed. London, 1987.

————. The Shipbuilding Industry: A Guide to Historical Records. Edited by Alex Ritchie. London, 1990.

6.   CAMBRIDGE UNIVERSITY, University Library, West Road, Cambridge CB3 9DR (M-F 9-7.15, Sat. 9-1). The University Library serves the needs of the University and visiting scholars. Since 1709 it has had the privilege of copyright deposit. It contains nearly 4,530,000 monographs and bound serials, 996,000 maps and 91,000 manuscripts. The Official Publications Room contains British and Commonwealth publications, as well as being the depository for United Nations and other international agency publications. The department was also a depository for League of Nations publications and contains one of the best collections of Foreign Office Confidential Prints available. Unpublished handlists of the papers of Lords Crewe and Templewood are available in the Department of Manuscripts.

Munby, A.N.L. Cambridge College Libraries: Aids for Research Students. 2nd ed. Cambridge, 1962.

University Library. Cambridge University Archives: A Classified List. Compiled by D.M. Owen. Cambridge, 1988.

————. A Catalogue of the German Naval Archives Microfilmed at the Admiralty, London, for the University of Cambridge and the University of Michigan. Directed by F.H. Hinsley and H.M. Ehrmann. London, 1959.

Additional catalogue of selected files (1964).

————. Handlist of the Hardinge Papers at the University Library Cambridge. Compiled by N.J. Hancock, Cambridge, 1968.

————. Handlist of the Political Papers of Stanley Baldwin, First Earl Baldwin of Bewdley. Compiled by A.E.B. Owen. Cambridge, 1973.

————. Libraries Directory. Cambridge, 1988.

————. List of Serials. Microfiche, six-monthly updates.

————. Microfilm Series. Cambridge, 1977.

————. Summary Guide to Accessions of Western Manuscripts Other than Medieval, since 1867. Compiled by A.E.B. Owen. Cambridge, 1966.

6a.   Centre of South Asian Studies, University of Cambridge, Laundress Lane, Cambridge CB2 1SD (M-F 9.30-5). The Centre of South Asian Studies, established in 1964, promotes study and research in south Asian subjects, including southeast Asia. The Cambridge South Asian Archive has a large subject-related collection of documentary materials, including private papers, film and tape recordings.

Centre of South Asian Studies. Cambridge South Asian Archive. 4 vols. Edited by Mary Thatcher and Lionel Carter. Cambridge, 1973-86.

Details of the holdings of the Centre.

————. Guide to South Asian Material in the Libraries of London, Oxford and Cambridge. Edited by Rajeshwari Datta. Cambridge, 1966.

————. Principal Collections of Papers in the Cambridge South Asian Archive. 2nd ed. Cambridge, 1987.

————. Union Catalogue of the Government of Pakistan Publications Held by Libraries in London, Oxford and Cambridge. Cambridge, 1967.

————. Brief Guide to Original Memoirs Held in the Cambridge South Asian Archive. Cambridge, 1989.

6b.   The Churchill College Archives Centre, Cambridge CB3 0DS (M-F 9-12.30, 1.30-5). The Churchill Archives Centre was purpose built to house the papers of Sir Winston Churchill and is situated in the grounds of Churchill College, the National and Commonwealth Memorial to Sir Winston. The Centre was opened in 1973 and now holds the papers of over 300 other personages covering all those fields of public life in which Churchill played a part. The heart of the collection remains the Sir Winston Churchill papers.

Churchill Archives Centre. Guide to the Holdings. Cambridge, 1980.

Alphabetical listing of holdings with brief annotations.

7.   CONSERVATIVE AND UNIONIST PARTY RESEARCH DEPARTMENT LIBRARY, 32 Smith Square, London SW1P 3HH. The Library contains much of the printed materials and archives of the Conservative Party since 1868. This includes periodicals, pamphlets and leaflets, candidates' general election

addresses since 1929 and press cuttings. As the working library of a political party, the collections are intended primarily for internal use. However, upon application, assistance is afforded to scholars and researchers.

8. DURHAM UNIVERSITY, Library, Palace Green Section, Palace Green, Durham DH1 3RN (M-F 9-5, Sat. 9-12.30). Among the University Library's special collections is the Sudan Archive. This research collection was established in 1957 as a repository principally for the private papers of former British officials, civil servants, soldiers, missionaries, businessmen and others who had lived or worked in the Sudan. Its main focus is on the Anglo-Egyptian Condominium, 1899-1955. As well as official and private papers, diaries and letters, it holds maps, photographs, cine films, newspapers and printed material. Papers relating to Egypt, Arabia, Ethiopia, and other Near Eastern and African countries are also preserved. The Centre for Middle Eastern and Islamic Studies, Documentation Unit, University of Durham, South End House, South Road, Durham City DH1 3TG was established in 1970. It is a freely accessible archive of primary documents on the Middle East and the Islamic world and forms one of the most important collections in Western Europe. The Unit, which holds some 200,000 publications, procures and makes available primary materials relating to all the countries of the Arab world, including Afghanistan, Iran, Israel, Pakistan and Turkey.

Centre for Middle Eastern and Islamic Studies. A Bibliography of Saudi Arabia. Compiled by J.H. Stevens and R. King. Durham, 1973.

See also the same authors' A Bibliography of Oman (Durham, 1973).

————. Current British Research in Middle Eastern and Islamic Studies, nos. 1-4. Durham, 1971-83.

————. Collections in British Libraries on Middle Eastern and Islamic Studies. Durham, 1982.

9. ECONOMIC AND SOCIAL RESEARCH COUNCIL, DATA ARCHIVE, University of Essex, Wivenhoe Park, Colchester, Essex CO4 3SQ. The ESRC Data Archive is the largest national repository of machine-readable social science data in Britain. It was set up in 1967 with a brief to collect, preserve and disseminate machine-readable data relating to social and economic affairs from academic, commercial and government sources. Over

3,500 data sets are currently held by the Data Archive. Acquisitions are listed in the triannual Data Archive Bulletin.

ESRC Data Archive. ESRC Data Archive Catalogue. Edited by Marcia Taylor. Cambridge, 1986.

Updates are produced on request.

10. FOREIGN AND COMMONWEALTH OFFICE LIBRARY, Cornwall House, Stamford Street, London SE1 9NS (M-F 9.30-4.30). The Foreign and Commonwealth Office Library is one of the five constituent branches of the Library and Records Department. The others are Records Branch, Historical Branch, Translation Branch and Registrar's Branch. The Library is based on the collections of the former Colonial Office, Foreign Office and Commonwealth Relations Office and is organised on three separate sites. The Cornwall House branch holds the historical collections. This includes books, photographs, journals and an indexed set of legislation of dependent territories and independent Commonwealth countries.

Colonial Office, Library. Catalogue of the Colonial Office Library, London. 15 vols. Boston, MA, 1964.

Supplement for 1963-67 (1967); 2nd supplement, 1968-71, 2 vols. (1972); 3rd supplement, 1971-77, 4 vols. (1979).

Foreign Office, The Library. Catalogue of the Printed Books in the Library of the Foreign Office. London, 1926.

Continued in Catalogue of the Foreign Office Library, 1926-1968, 8 vols. (London, 1972); after the merger in 1968 of the Foreign Office and the Commonwealth Office, accessions to the merged Library from 1969-71 were included in Second Supplement to the Catalogue of the Colonial Office Library (London, 1972); and then in Accessions to the Library, 1971-1977, 4 vols. (Boston, MA, 1979); and subsequently on microfiche, Fourth Supplement, 1977-1980 (Cambridge, 1981).

Parry, Clive. "The Foreign Office Archives." International Relations, 2(1961), 211-19.

11. HOUSE OF LORDS RECORD OFFICE, London SW1A OPW (M-F 9.30-5). The records of both houses of parliament are preserved in the Palace of Westminster. These records are accessible to the public in the search room of the House of Lords Record Office. Of major interest is the collection of modern

political papers acquired in 1975 after the closure of the Beaverbrook Library, especially the David Lloyd George and Lord Beaverbrook papers.

Bond, Maurice F. Guide to the Records of Parliament. London, 1971.

Includes printed and manuscript sources to 1970; subsequent accessions are published in the annual Reports.

House of Lords Record Office. A Guide to Historical Collections of the Nineteenth and Twentieth Centuries Preserved in the House of Lords Record Office. Memorandum no. 60. Compiled by H.S. Cobb. London, 1978.

————. A Guide to the Political Papers, 1874-1970, Deposited by the First Beaverbrook Foundation. Memorandum no. 54. Compiled by Katharine V. Wheeler. London, 1975.

————. The Political Papers of Herbert, 1st Viscount Samuel. Compiled by H.S. Cobb. 2nd ed. London, 1974.

12.   IMPERIAL WAR MUSEUM, Lambeth Road, London SE1 6HZ (M-F 10-5). The Imperial War Museum, founded in 1917, is concerned with documenting the two world wars and other military operations involving Britain and the Commonwealth since 1914. The Museum's organisation includes the Departments of Printed Books, Documents, Photographs, Film, Sound Records and Art. The Department of Printed Books is a national reference library with a very large collection of books, pamphlets, periodicals and maps. It issues monthly accessions lists by subject and compiles short bibliographies on some 600 aspects of military history. The Department of Documents collects military archives of the twentieth century. It contains some captured German material and a large collection of British private, military and political, papers. Established in 1972, the Department of Sound Records has an extensive oral history programme, about 12,000 hours of material, which includes taped reminiscences of service personnel and broadcast recordings. Catalogues of oral history recordings are available from the Museum.

Kavanagh, Gaynor. "Museum as Memorial: The Origins of the Imperial War Museum." Journal of Contemporary History, 23(1988), 77-98.

Imperial War Museum. A Catalogue of the Records of the Reichsministerium für Rüstung und Kriegsproduktion. London, 1969.

―――. List of Current Periodicals. London, 1989-.

Currently provides details of around 450 journals in the Museum's subject field; kept up to date on computer and printed on demand; as is Guide to Booklists and Information Sheets (London, 1989-), with about 700 reading lists, bibliographies and information sheets.

See also Subject Guide to Booklists, Corrected to the End of June 1976 (London, 1976).

Imperial War Museum, Foreign Documents Centre. Provisional Reports, no. 1-. London, 1966-.

Contents: no. 1 provides information on 13 British repositories holding unpublished records of former enemy powers; nos. 2-6 respectively describe various archives in the German Federal Republic, Italy, the German Democratic Republic, Austria and Poland.

Imperial War Museum. Handbook. London, 1976.

13.   LABOUR PARTY, Archives, 150 Walworth Road, London SE17 1JT (M-F 10-5). The Library contains resources covering party politics in all fields of home and foreign affairs. The archives of the Labour party include press cuttings from 1918, party and committee documents, such as the minutes of the National Executive Committee and the International department, and personal and special collections. The archives will eventually be lodged with the National Museum of Labour History, 103 Princess Street, Manchester 3.

Labour Party. Guide to the Archives. Compiled by Stephen Bird. London, 1982.

―――. Labour Party: A Bibliography. London, 1967.

14.   LEEDS UNIVERSITY, BROTHERTON LIBRARY. Leeds LS2 9JT (M-F 9-5). The Brotherton Library contains a major collection of materials for the study of international history. The Library continues to add to its extensive holdings of source materials, mainly published documents and extensive microfilms from the

PRO, but including an expanding collection of manuscripts relating to international history in the twentieth century.

Brotherton Library. Some Source Materials in the Brotherton Library of Interest to Students of International History. Leeds, 1989.

15. LONDON UNIVERSITY, Library, Senate House, Malet Street, WC1E 7HU (in term, M-Th 9.30-9, F 9.30-6.30, Sat. 9.30-5.30; vacation, M-Sat. 9.30-5.30). The Library has been designated an Arts, Humanities and Social Science library. It serves all the constituent institutions of the University of London and maintains some comprehensive research collections. Its holdings contain over one and a quarter million monographs and serials and about 5,000 periodical titles.

London University. Guide to Admission to Libraries in the University of London. London, 1989.

Percival, Janet. A Guide to Archives and Manuscripts in the University of London. Vol. 1-. London, 1984-.

Vol. 1 covers the six major institutions; vol. 2 will include material on other constituents of the University.

Garside, Kenneth, comp. Guide to the Library Resources of the University of London. London, 1983.

15a. British Library of Political and Economic Science, 10 Portugal Street, London WC2A 2HD (Main Library, in term, M-F 9.30-9.20, long vacation, 9.30-5; in term, Sat. 10-5; Manuscripts Department, M-F 10-5.30). Founded in 1896 on the initiative of Sidney Webb, the British Library of Political and Economic Science is both the working library of the London School of Economics and Political Science and a national collection of research materials. It covers the social sciences in the widest sense and holds an estimated two and a half million separate items. The Library is also a depository for United States federal documents, and materials from the United Nations and the Organisation of American States, as well as government publications from most other states. The Manuscripts Department is particularly rich in twentieth-century political and economic private papers.

British Library of Political and Economic Science. A London Bibliography of the Social Sciences. Compiled by B.M. Headicar and C. Fuller. 4 vols. London, 1931-32.

Based on the holdings to 1929 of the Library and several other London libraries; the largest subject bibliography of its kind; supplements, vols. 5-46, in progress (London, 1934-89); annual volumes record previous year's accessions.

————. Guide to the Library. London, 1989.

————. Publications of Sidney and Beatrice Webb: An Interim Check List. London, 1973.

Seldon, Anthony. " 'Elite' Oral History at the London School of Economics." Oral History Journal, 10(1982), 12-15.

15b.   Institute of Commonwealth Studies, 27-28 Russell Square, London WC1B 5DS (In term, M-W 10-7, Th-F 10-6; vacation, M-F 10-5.30). The Institute, established in 1949, promotes the study of Commonwealth history and political and social sciences. As a research centre of the University of London, it organises seminars, publishes, and contains a major reference library. Relevant documents and manuscripts are also actively acquired. The Library maintains a Register of Research, from which is produced Theses in Progress in Commonwealth Studies, and publishes a quarterly Accessions List.

Institute of Commonwealth Studies. Guide to Resources for Commonwealth Studies in London, Oxford and Cambridge, with Bibliographical and Other Information. Compiled by Arthur Reginald Hewitt. London, 1957.

15c.   Institute of Historical Research, Senate House, Malet Street, London WC1E 7HU (M-F 9-9, Sat. 9-5). The Institute functions as the University's centre for advanced research in history. The Library is for reference only. It contains about 140,000 volumes and emphasises such acquisitions as primary materials, reference works, bibliographies, and guides to archives and manuscripts. In 1987 the Institute of United States Studies amalgamated with the Institute. Lists of theses completed and in progress and of teachers of history in the universities and polytechnics of the United Kingdom are compiled annually.

Institute of Historical Research. A Guide to the Library. London, 1989.

15d.   Liddell Hart Centre for Military Archives, The Library, King's College, Strand, London WC2R 2LS (M-F 9.30-5.30; 9.30-4.30 vacation; closed last fortnight in August). Military affairs have been a subject of specialisation at King's College since 1927.

Facilities for study have been vastly intensified since 1953. In 1964 the Centre for Military Archives was established at the College to act as a repository for twentieth-century private papers relating to military matters. The Centre was renamed the Liddell Hart Centre for Military Affairs after the acquisition of his papers and library in 1973. It has a large collection of diaries, letters, etc. of statesmen, service officers, civil servants and others, all relating to defence policy since 1900 and the two world wars. There is also an extensive collection of microfilms of US official and semiofficial papers. A location register of the private papers of senior British defence personnel in this century is being compiled in the Centre.

Brooks, Stephen. "Liddell Hart and His Papers," in War and Society: A Yearbook of Military History. Vol. 2. Edited by Brian Bond and Ian Roy. London, 1977.

Liddell Hart Centre for Military Archives. Consolidated List of Accessions. London, 1986.

————. Supplement, 1 August 1985-31 March 1988 (London, 1988).

————. An Introduction for Readers. London, 1989.

15e.   School of Oriental and African Studies, Thornhaugh Street, Russell Square, London WC1E 0XG (M-Th 9-8, F 9-6.30, Sat. 9.30-12.30; vacations, M-F 9-5, Sat. 9-12.30). Founded in 1917, the Library has a major specialist collection of over 700,000 volumes, and 2,350 manuscripts, including 25 major archives, in 109 languages. It is the major lending Library for Asian and African materials. The British in India Oral Archive Committee has deposited a number of tapes and transcripts.

Gacek, Adam. Catalogue of the Arabic Manuscripts in the Library of the School of Oriental and African Studies. London, 1981.

School of Oriental and African Studies. Library Catalogue of the School of Oriental and African Studies. 28 vols. Boston, MA, 1963.

Supplements published in 1968, 1973, 1979 and 1984.

————. Papers Relating to the Chinese Maritime Customs, 1860-1943 in the Library. London, 1973.

————. Union Catalogue of Asian Publications, 1965-1970. 4 vols. Edited by David E. Hall. London, 1971.

Supplement (1973); lists Asian publications acquired by 64 British libraries since 1964.

Williams, Margaret Harcourt. Catalogue of the Papers of Sir Charles Addis. London, 1986.

Yasmura, Yoshiko. List of Japanese Periodicals in the Library of the School of Oriental and African Studies. London, 1974.

15f.   School of Slavonic and East European Studies, Senate House, Malet Street, London WC1E 7HU (M-F 10-7; vacation, 10-6). Founded in 1915 as a part of King's College, the School of Slavonic and East European Studies became a university institute in 1932. The Library supports teaching and research into the languages, literature, history and social conditions of the USSR and Eastern Europe. The library collection of over 280,000 monographs and 1,300 current periodicals also includes some manuscript materials.

School of Slavonic and East European Studies. Short Guide to the Library. London, 1989.

16.   MANCHESTER UNIVERSITY, John Rylands University Library, Special Collections Division, Deansgate, Manchester M3 3EH (M-F 10-5.30, Sat. 10-1). The John Rylands University Library was formed in 1972 by merging the John Rylands Library and the Manchester University Library. The immense resources of this merger include over two and a half million volumes and 8,000 current periodicals.

John Rylands University Library. Handlist of English Manuscripts . . . 1928; and Handlist of Additions . . . 1928-1935 Onwards. Manchester, 1928-.

17.   MINISTRY OF DEFENCE HEADQUARTERS LIBRARIES, 3-5 Great Scotland Yard, London SW1A 2HW (M-F 9.30-4.30). In January 1989 the three libraries holding the historical collections of the army, navy and royal air force - namely Whitehall Library, Old War Office Building, the Naval Historical Library, Empress State Building and the Air Library, Adastral House - were amalgamated in new premises. Limited access, for reference purposes, is available at the discretion of the Chief Librarian, on prior application. Excluded from the amalgamation is the Library, Royal United Services Institute for Defence Studies, Whitehall, London SW1A 2ET (M-F 9.30-5.30).

Ministry of Defence, Naval Library, London. Author and Subject Catalogue of the Naval Library. 5 vols. Boston, MA, 1967.

War Office, Library. Catalogue of the War Office Library. 3 vols. London, 1906-12.

Annual supplements, 1913-40.

18. NATIONAL ARMY MUSEUM, Royal Hospital Road, London SW3 4HT (T-Sat. 10-4.30). The Collections Division is divided into five departments: including Printed Books; Archives; Photographs; and Film and Sound. Emphasis is on materials relating to the British army and auxiliary forces from 1485 to the present day, the Commonwealth forces to their date of independence, and the Indian army until 1947.

Chandler, D.G. "The National Army Museum." History Today, 22(1972), 664-68.

19. NATIONAL LIBRARY OF SCOTLAND, Department of Manuscripts, George IV Bridge, Edinburgh EH1 1EW (M-F 9.30-8.30, Sat. 9.30-1). The Library is a national institution for research on all aspects of Scottish history, a copyright deposit library since 1710, and with special responsibility for Scottish bibliography. Its Lending Services are the result of a merger in 1974 between the Scottish Central Library and the National Library. The entire collection numbers over five million books, with additional periodicals and newspapers. There are over 20,000 manuscript volumes in the Library, many relevant to the wider context of British history. Accessions are noted in the Annual Report of the National Library of Scotland.

National Library of Scotland. Catalogue of Manuscripts Acquired since 1925. 7 vols. Edinburgh, 1938-89.

————. A Guide to the Reference Services. Compiled by J.R. Seaton. Edinburgh, 1976.

For the Encouragement of Learning: Scotland's National Library, 1689-1989. Edited by P.M. Cadell and Ann Matheson. Edinburgh, 1989.

20. NATIONAL LIBRARY OF WALES, Department of Manuscripts and Records, Aberystwyth, Dyfed SY23 3BU (M-F, 9.30-6, Sat. 9.30-5). The National Library of Wales was founded in 1907 by Royal Charter and opened in 1909. As well as a copyright deposit library, it is a national library specialising in Welsh materials, but

with a good collection of private papers of Welshmen prominent in British public life.

National Library of Wales. Handlist of Manuscripts in the National Library of Wales. 4 vols. Aberystwyth, 1943-86.

Supplementary listings in the National Library of Wales Journal, The Welsh Political Archive Newsletter, and the Annual Reports.

21. NATIONAL MARITIME MUSEUM, Manuscripts Section, Romney Road, Greenwich, London SE10 9NF (M-F 10-5, Sat. 10-1, 2-5). The Museum was established in 1934 for the study and illustration of British maritime history, art, literature, science and archaeology. Particular attention is paid to the areas of the administrative history of the Royal Navy, strategical and tactical developments, the economics of transportation and the management of merchant shipping in peace and war. As a recognised repository for public documents, the Manuscripts Section holds about 9,000 volumes of Admiralty records and maritime-related private papers. The Library also contains 80,000 volumes of printed material, 20,000 pamphlets and 15,000 bound volumes of periodicals. A microfiche catalogue is available.

National Maritime Museum. Guide to the Manuscripts in the National Maritime Museum. Edited by R.J.B. Knight. 2 vols. London, 1977-80.

Vol. 1 entitled: The Personal Collections; vol. 2: Public Records, Business Records and Artificial Collections.

22. OXFORD UNIVERSITY, Bodleian Library, Department of Western Manuscripts, Oxford OX1 3BG (M-F 9-10 term, 9-7 vacation, Sat. 9-1). The Bodleian Library, dating back to the seventeenth century, is a copyright library, second only in size to the British Library. The collection numbers about 5.2 million volumes, with particularly rich manuscript holdings, in the Department of Western Manuscripts, for twentieth-century politicians and public figures. A Summary Catalogue of manuscripts acquired 1916-1975, edited by Mary Clapinson and T.D. Rogers is forthcoming, as is a Guide to the modern political collections by Helen Langley.

Current Foreign and Commonwealth Periodicals in the Bodleian Library and in Other Oxford Libraries. London, 1953.

Supplemented by microfiches available in Oxford Libraries, Oxford Libraries Union Catalogue of Foreign Serials in the Humanities and Social Sciences, compiled by Georgina Cray and Diana Reese (Oxford, 1987).

Morgan, Paul, comp. Oxford Libraries outside the Bodleian: A Guide. 2nd ed. Oxford, 1980.

Listing by college, faculty, departmental and institute libraries; includes an appendix of manuscript collections.

22a.   Nuffield College, The Library, Oxford OX1 1NF (M-F 9.30-1, 2-6, Sat. 9.30-1). Nuffield College, endowed in 1937 by 1st Viscount Nuffield, concentrates on postgraduate research. The Library holds the private papers of some twentieth-century figures prominent in British political, economic and social life. Included are collections relevant to the study of foreign policy, such as the papers of Sir Stafford Cripps and F.A. Lindemann (1st Viscount Cherwell).

22b.   Rhodes House Library, South Parks Road, Oxford OX1 3RG (M-F 9-7, Sat. 9-1). Rhodes House Library concentrates on the history, politics, economics and social conditions of the Commonwealth (excluding the Indian subcontinent), the United States and Sub-Saharan Africa. Relevant British publications claimed by the Bodleian Library under the copyright privilege are deposited at the Library. The collection consists of about 350,000 books, some 15,000 units of manuscripts, as well as maps and microforms. Since the inception of the Oxford Colonial Records Project in 1963, the Library has been the principal recipient of the private papers of colonial administrators, over 3,000 of whom have contributed to the holdings. Organisations whose papers are held at Rhodes House Library include the Anti-Slavery Society and the Fabian Colonial Bureau.

Manuscript Collections of Africana in Rhodes House Library, Oxford. Compiled by Louis B. Frewer. Oxford, 1968.

Supplement. Oxford, 1971.

Manuscript Collections (Excluding Africana) in Rhodes House Library, Oxford. Compiled by Louis B. Frewer. Oxford, 1970.

Manuscript Collections (Africana and Non-Africana) in Rhodes House Library, Oxford. Supplementary Accessions to the End of 1977, and Cumulative Index. Compiled by Wendy S. Byrne. Oxford, 1978.

22c.   St. Antony's College, Middle East Centre, Oxford OX2 6JF (M-F 9.30-1, 2-5.15). Since 1962 the Library has collected the private papers of individuals who either served in the Middle East or whose main concern, as bankers, businessmen, etc., was with the Middle East.

Middle East Centre, St. Antony's College. A Catalogue of the Private Papers Collection in the Middle East Centre, St. Antony's College, Oxford. Edited by Diana Grimwood-Jones. London, 1979.

23.   PUBLIC RECORD OFFICE, (i) Chancery Lane, London WC2A 1LR; (ii) Ruskin Avenue, Kew, Richmond, Surrey TW9 4DU (M-F 9.30-5, closed on public holidays and first two weeks in October). The Public Record Office in Chancery Lane was established by an act of parliament in 1838. Prior to that time documents had been collected by individual government departments, but storage facilities were poor and limited. In order to establish some control over these numerous repositories of public records, the government appointed a royal commission in 1800. Then, in 1838, the Public Record Office Act provided for the centralisation of "all rolls records writs books proceedings decrees bills warrants accounts papers and documents whatsoever of a public nature" in one office. A new repository was erected in 1850-53 and records were gathered together, with terms of preservation and public access gradually defined.

The national archives preserved at the PRO, consisting of many millions of documents, derive from two main sources. The first are the nation's judicial and administrative records: those of Chancery, the Exchequer, the Courts of Common Law and other courts. The second are those of the public departments: the State Paper Office, the Admiralty, the Treasury, the Home, the Colonial, the Foreign Office and the War Office, among many others. The records now remaining at Chancery Lane comprise all those described in volume one of the Guide to the Contents of the Public Record Office (see below), except the Copyright Office, those of some other departments with quasi-legal or related functions, the records of the State Paper Office, the Probate and Census Records and some gifts and deposits. Most materials relevant to the study of foreign policy from 1918 to 1945 are stored at Kew. Records are available for consultation only in the building in which they are stored. It is also important to remember that not all official records are in the PRO. The lord chancellor has designated certain local repositories as places of deposit. Some government departments, such as the India Office Library and Records, maintain their own records. Others not covered by the Public Records Act include the House of Lords Record Office, the Office of Population Censuses and Surveys, and the record offices of Scotland and Northern

Ireland. Finally, some collections remain in private hands, or have been given, sold or lent to institutions, most notably the British Library. Departmental records are generally available for public inspection 30 years after their creation. A list of documents closed for longer periods or retained in the department of origin is available in the search rooms.

The records are arranged into major divisions, called 'classes.' Each class represents, at least in theory, an original series of documents created in relation to a particular function or activity of a government department, court of law or other agency. Each class is identified by its own 'class reference.' This consists of a letter code of between one and four capital letters, such as FO for Foreign Office. Generally, the same letter code is given to classes of common or related origin. Each separately orderable item in a class is known as a 'piece,' which represents a specific volume, box, bundle or file. This is identified by its own piece number. Thus FO371/23015 represents a volume in the class of Political Correspondence after 1906 in the Foreign Office records.

There is in fact no overall general index to the entire body of the records. However, the researcher is extremely fortunate in having a multiplicity of extensive finding aids. The Guide to the Contents of the Public Records, in its printed (1963 and 1968) and new computerised form, Current Guide, is the basic tool for research about a specific person, subject or place. The Current Guide is now held in-house on computer. Updated printouts are regularly provided for the search rooms. These describe records at the level of class and give readers the information needed to proceed to the class lists, which describe records at the level of the piece. The Current Guide is divided into three parts. Part one describes each government department or agency whose records are in the PRO. It outlines organisation, functions and identifies the classes of records it created. Part two contains a description of the nature and contents of each class of records. The third part serves as an alphabetical index. The Current Guide is available in binders in the PRO reading rooms, and on microfiche as part of Kew Lists: The Microfiche Edition, for sale by HMSO. Class lists and indexes are also widely available through the arrangements for reprints reached in 1972 between the PRO and the Kraus-Thomson Organisation. Photographic copies of many other unpublished lists are issued periodically to libraries and subscribers by the List and Index Society. As well, large collections of Foreign Office and other PRO documents have been reproduced in microform by such publishers as Scholarly Resources, Kraus Microform, Harvester Microform, University

Publications of America and Garland Publishing. Information about records thus microfilmed is available from the PRO.

Visitors to the Public Record Office may also avail themselves of an extensive array of Information Leaflets, including no. 22, "The Records of the Foreign Office from 1782." Finally, the PRO publishes an ongoing series of handbooks. These are very valuable research tools and every intending researcher should be thoroughly familiar with the relevant volumes to derive the greatest benefit from a visit to the PRO.

Galbraith, Vivian Hunter. Introduction to the Use of the Public Records. London, 1952.

A practical handbook for the beginner; contains a useful bibliography.

Public Record Office. The Cabinet Office to 1945. Compiled by S.S. Wilson. London, 1975.

PRO handbook, no. 17; an account of the evolution of the Cabinet Office and an explanation of surviving records in the various cabinet classes; 12 annexes of related information.

————. Classes of Department Papers for 1906-1939. London, 1966.

Alphabetical listing of government departments with classes of departmental records transferred to the PRO before the middle of 1965; in effect, an addendum to vol. 2 of the Guide to the Contents of the Public Record Office (London, 1963); superseded by the Current Guide.

————. Guide to the Contents of the Public Record Office. 3 vols. London, 1963-68.

Vol. 1 for legal records, etc.; vol. 2 for state papers and departmental records transferred before 31 Aug. 1960; vol. 3 describes records transferred up to 31 Dec. 1966, with corrections and additions to vols. 1-2; descriptions of classes added from Jan. 1967 are entered in typed supplements, known as the Current Guide, in the search rooms of the PRO; as are amendments to vols. 1-3 of the Guide to the Contents of the Public Record Office; brief details of new classes and additions to existing classes are given in the "Summary of Records Transmitted" as an appendix to the Annual Report of the Keeper of Public Records; for materials prior to 1923 see M.S. Giuseppi, Guide to the Manuscripts Preserved in the Public Record Office, 2 vols. (London, 1923-24).

—————. The Records of the Cabinet Office to 1922. London, 1966.

PRO handbook, no. 11; detailed description of the organisation of the Cabinet Office from 1916-22 and contents of 44 classes of records transferred to the PRO.

—————. The Records of the Colonial and Dominions Office. Compiled by R.B. Pugh. London, 1964.

PRO handbook, no. 3; section 1 describes the organisation of the Colonial Office since 1801 and the Dominions Office since 1925; section 2 analyses the records; section 3 gives an annotated list of record classes by colonies and subjects; revised edition forthcoming.

—————. The Records of the Foreign Office, 1782-1939. London, 1969.

PRO handbook, no. 13, an indispensable guide to research in the Foreign Office papers; introduces the researcher to about 900 classes of papers in the Foreign Office group and related records; part 1 provides a history of the administrative machinery of the Foreign Office between 1782 and 1939; part 2 analyses the records developed in this process; part 3 describes four specimen searches; part 4 is an annotated list of all the classes making up the Foreign Office group, including classes created after 1939; appendixes detail signs and codes used in the Foreign Office registers and indexes, private collections in the PRO bearing on foreign affairs, and the location of papers of secretaries of state for Foreign Affairs.

—————. Records of Interest to Social Scientists, 1919 to 1939; Introduction. Compiled by Brenda Swann and Maureen Turnbull. London, 1971.

PRO handbook, no. 14; includes sections on 'central direction,' finance, foreign affairs, industry and defence.

—————. The Second World War: A Guide to Documents in the Public Record Office. London, 1972.

PRO handbook, no. 15; covers the main military, political and administrative documents released to the public in 1972; explains the workings of government departments and other bodies that produced the records; describes classes, with glossaries of wartime code names, abbreviations and cabinet committees; revised edition forthcoming.

Public Record Office, Lists and Indexes. Alphabetical Guide to War Office and Other Military Records Preserved in the Public Record Office. London, 1931.

Vol. 53 of the PRO Lists and Indexes.

Public Record Office, Supplementary Lists and Indexes. List of Admiralty Records. Vols. 3-9. Millwood, NY, repr. 1975-80.

No. VI in the PRO Supplementary Lists and Indexes; reprinted by agreement between the PRO and the Kraus Reprint Division of Kraus-Thompson Organisation Ltd.; other series reprinted from the Supplementary Lists and Indexes include no. VIII, List of War Office Records, 2 vols. (1969-75); no. XIII, List of Foreign Office Records, 29 vols. (1964-85); these include General Correspondence (Political) volumes for 1914-46; and no. XVI, List of Colonial Office Records, 8 vols. (1976-77).

Foreign Office. Index to Foreign Office Correspondence, 1920-. Nendeln, 1969-.

Originally prepared and used within the Foreign Office, and not by the PRO; preserved in FO409, with reprints by Kraus International Publications available in the reference room at Kew; complete for 1920-45; not all papers identified have been selected for permanent preservation.

HMSO (Her Majesty's Stationery Office). Guide to the Records of the Lord Chancellor's Department. Compiled by Patrick Polden. London, 1988.

23a.   List and Index Society, c/o Public Record Office, Ruskin Avenue, Kew, Richmond, Surrey TW9 4DU. The Society was formed in 1965 to publish and distribute, to members only, previously unpublished PRO search room lists and indexes. The choice of volumes is made by the Council, which attempts to give equitable representation to all periods and interests. 237 volumes of PRO class lists and indexes have so far been published. About 15 of these volumes deal with the Cabinet Office and the prime minister's office. The 25 volumes of the "Special Series" reproduce lists in archives other than the PRO.

List and Index Society. Publications, 1966-1989. London, 1989.

24. READING UNIVERSITY, The Library, Department of Archives and Manuscripts, Whiteknights, PO Box 223, Reading RG6 2AE (M-F 9-1, 2-5). The Library contains about 880,000 volumes and 5,640 current periodicals, as well as housing the European Documentation Centre and a fairly extensive collection of foreign newspapers. The growing collection of manuscript material is divided into five main groups. The most relevant are the archive of modern political papers, including the papers of 2nd Viscount Astor and Lady Nancy Astor, and the archive of British publishing.

> Edwards, J.A. A Brief Guide to Archives and Manuscripts in the Library, University of Reading. Reading, 1930.

25. ROYAL AIR FORCE MUSEUM. The Archives/Library, Grahame Park Way, Hendon, London NW9 5LL (M-F 9.30-4.30). Established in 1963, the Royal Air Force Museum is concerned with aviation in all its aspects. In addition to displays, the museum is also a research centre with a growing collection of books, periodicals, manuscripts, etc. The Library contains over 70,000 volumes and subscribes to almost 300 periodicals. The Archives contains thousands of items, including flying log books, private papers of airmen, plans and drawings, and records of commercial aviation companies such as the British Airways Archive.

> Royal Air Force Museum. Periodicals Catalogue. London, 1975.

> ————. Royal Air Force Museum, 1972-1975. London, 1976.

26. ROYAL COMMISSION ON HISTORICAL MANUSCRIPTS: NATIONAL REGISTER OF ARCHIVES, Quality House, Quality Court, Chancery Lane, London WC2A 1HP (M-F 9.30-5). The Royal Commission on Historical Manuscripts, established in 1869, acts as a central clearinghouse for information about the nature and location of historical manuscripts and papers outside the public records. Since 1945 it has also maintained the National Register of Archives, a vital source of information on public and private records. The search room in Chancery Lane contains over 32,000 reports on collections of papers, accumulating at the rate of about 2,000 a year, including those of the National Register of Archives (Scotland). All these reports are numbered and catalogued and their contents are selectively indexed. The reports can be searched through various finding aids, including an index of persons, companies and subjects. Copies of the principal lists are distributed to the copyright libraries and the Institute of Historical Research, among other locations. However, the only complete set is maintained in the search room.

HMSO. Publications of the Royal Commission on Historical Manuscripts: Government Publications Sectional List, no. 17. London, 1985.

Ranger, Felicity. "The National Register of Archives, 1945-1969." Journal of the Society of Archivists, 3(1969), 452-62.

Royal Commission on Historical Manuscripts. The Manuscript Papers of British Scientists, 1600-1940. London, 1982.

Vol. 2 of Guides to Sources for British History.

————. Guide to the Location of Collections Described in the Reports and Calendars Series, 1870-1980. London, 1982.

Vol. 3 of Guides to Sources for British History.

————. Private Papers of British Diplomats, 1782-1900. London, 1985.

Vol. 4 of Guides to Sources for British History.

————. Papers of British Churchmen, 1780-1940. London, 1989.

Vol. 6 of Guides to Sources for British History.

————. A Guide to the Reports on Collections of Manuscripts of Private Families, Corporations and Institutions in Great Britain and Ireland Issued by the Royal Commissioners for Historical Manuscripts. 2 parts. London, 1914-73.

Part 1, 2 vols. for index of places; part 2, 5 vols., for index of persons.

————. Accessions to Repositories and Reports Added to the National Register of Archives, 1972. London, 1973-.

Previously published in the Bulletin of the Institute of Historical Research, 1923-54, and by the Commission in the Bulletin of the National Register of Archives, 1955-59 and as List of Accessions to Repositories, 1960-72.

27. ROYAL COMMONWEALTH SOCIETY, Library, Commonwealth Trust, Commonwealth House, 18 Northumberland Avenue, London WC2N 5BJ (M-F 10-5.30). The Royal Commonwealth Society, founded in 1868, has one of the largest collections of material on the Commonwealth. The Library, with a bookstock of

over 250,000 items, contains monographs, an extensive collection of periodicals, official publications, manuscripts, photographs, and the collections of the Royal African Society, the Kipling Society and the British Association of Malaysia among others. The bimonthly Library Notes includes a select accessions list, book reviews, library news and scholarly articles.

Reese, Trevor R. The History of the Royal Commonwealth Society, 1868-1968. London, 1968.

Royal Commonwealth Society. Biography Catalogue of the Library of the Royal Commonwealth Society. Compiled by Donald H. Simpson. London, 1961.

Royal Commonwealth Society, Library. The Manuscript Catalogue of the Library of the Royal Commonwealth Society. Compiled by Donald H. Simpson. London, 1975.

Entries arranged alphabetically by author within geographic areas; supplementary lists in the Society's Library Notes.

────. Subject Catalogue of the Royal Commonwealth Society. 7 vols. Boston, MA, 1971.

Extensive card catalogue arranged by geographical areas, subdivided by subject; within these headings the order is chronological; 1st supplement, 2 vols., for additions from 1971-76, published 1977.

28.   ROYAL INSTITUTE OF INTERNATIONAL AFFAIRS, Chatham House, 10 St. James's Square, London SW1Y 4LE (Library M-W 10-6, Th 10-7, Press Library M-F 10-6). The Royal Institute of International Affairs was established in 1920 to advance the study of international relations, economics and jurisprudence, and to provide information on these subjects. The Institute organises lectures, sponsors research projects, issues various publications and maintains two libraries. The main library is a leading specialist collection in the field with monographs, pamphlets and official documents. It also maintains a classified card index to periodicals since 1950 and issues monthly Articles in Periodicals, as well as a Classified List of Books and Pamphlets Added to the Library. The Chatham House Press Library, established in 1924, contains over ten million cuttings on all aspects of international affairs. Arrangement of this massive archive is by country and subject, with extensive subdivision and cross-referencing. Files for the 1920s and 1930s are microfilmed; those for the period 1940-71 have been transferred to the British

Library Newspaper Library. The libraries are open to members and to bona fide researchers at postgraduate level on payment of a fee. In 1976 the Council of the RIIA agreed that the Institute's archives, subject to certain exclusions, would be open for study after 30 years.

Morgan, Roger. " 'To Advance the Sciences of International Politics . . .': Chatham House's Early Research." International Affairs, 55(1979), 140-51.

Royal Institute of International Affairs. Index to Periodical Articles, 1950-1964, in the Library of the Royal Institute of International Affairs. 2 vols. Boston, MA, 1964.

Index to over 30,000 articles taken from the wide range of periodicals received by the Institute; supplements for periodical articles 1965-72 and 1973-78 published in 1973 and 1979 respectively.

————. Review of the Foreign Press, 1939-1945. 27 vols. Munich, 1980.

Originally prepared in collaboration with the Foreign Office, 1939-45, for restricted circulation; 10 series by geographic area.

29. SCOTTISH RECORD OFFICE, H.M. General Register House, Edinburgh EH1 3YY (M-F 9-4.45). Primarily a repository for the Public Records of Scotland, the Scottish Record Office also holds the private papers of individuals and organisations with a wider influence on British foreign affairs. The National Register of Archives (Scotland) is maintained at West Register House.

List of Gifts and Deposits in the Scottish Record Office. 2 vols. Edinburgh, 1971-76.

Source List of Manuscripts Relating to the USA and Canada in Private Archives Preserved in the Scottish Record Office. Edinburgh, 1970.

Special Series, vol. 3, from the List and Index Society.

30. SUSSEX UNIVERSITY, Library. Falmer, Brighton BN1 9QL (M-F 9-5.30). The University of Sussex Library contains over 500,000 volumes and 3,500 current periodicals. It houses the Tom Harrisson Mass-Observation Archive, established in 1974 as a charitable trust. Mass-Observation functioned between 1937 and 1950 as a social-survey movement.

Sussex University, Library, Manuscript Section. Leonard Woolf Papers, c. 1885-1969. Brighton, 1980.

————. Kingsley Martin Papers, 1897-1969. Brighton, 1976.

————. Vernon Bartlett Papers, 1913-1973. Brighton, 1975.

31.   THE TIMES, Record Office, 214 Gray's Inn Road, London WC1X 8EZ (M-F 10-1, 2-5). The collection includes information relating to the history of The Times within the context of British political, social and economic life. The holdings contain private papers, diaries and correspondence, official and private, of editors and correspondents.

Phillips, Gordon. "The Archives of 'The Times.' " Business Archives, 41(1976), 20-24.

32.   WARWICK UNIVERSITY LIBRARY, Modern Records Centre, Coventry CV4 7AL (M-Th 9-1, 1.30-5, F 9-1, 1.30-4). The Modern Records Centre is a national specialist repository for the archives of trade unions and employers' organisations. It also holds the business records of some British motor car manufacturers and some personal papers, including those of Sir Victor Gollancz. Descriptive lists are compiled for each accession, as soon as practicable. A set is available in the Centre and copies are supplied to the National Register of Archives.

Consolidated Guide to the Modern Records Centre, University of Warwick Library, Occasional Publications No. 2. Compiled by Richard Storey and Alistair Tough. Coventry, 1977.

New accessions are described in the Centre's annual reports.

33.   WIENER LIBRARY AND INSTITUTE OF CONTEMPORARY HISTORY, 4 Devonshire Street, London W1N 2BH (M-F 10-5.30). The Library is a major resource for the study of twentieth-century totalitarianism and antisemitism. It contains material on Nazism, fascism, Germany since 1914, Middle East history, and a large Nuremberg Trials collection. The press-cutting archive, organised by subject, holds over one million items.

Kehr, Helen, and Langmaid, Janet, comps. The Nazi Era, 1919-1945: A Select Bibliography of Published Works from the Early Roots to 1980. London, 1982.

Based on the holdings of the Wiener Library; see also the earlier From Weimar to Hitler: Germany, 1918-1933, 2nd ed. (London, 1964).

Wiener Library. Catalogue of Nuremberg Documents. London, 1961.

Supplements 1-2 (1962-63); register of documents related to the holocaust and index of persons interrogated.

————. Persecution and Resistance under the Nazis. Part 1. Edited by Ilse R. Wolfe. 2nd ed. London, 1978.

Part 2, New Materials and Amendments, edited by Helen Kehr (London, 1978).

B. GENERAL GUIDES, DIRECTORIES AND UNION LISTS

34.   ASLIB. Directory of Information Sources in the United Kingdom. Edited by Ellen M. Codlin. 5th ed. 2 vols. London, 1982-84.

Vol. 2 for the humanities and social sciences; see also her Shorter ASLIB Directory of Information Sources in the United Kingdom (London, 1986).

35.   Auchterlonie, Paul, and Safadi, Yasin H., eds. Union Catalogue of Arabic Serials and Newspapers in British Libraries. London, 1977.

36.   Bloomfield, Valerie. Guide to Resources for Canadian Studies in Britain. 2nd ed. London, 1983.

Subtitled: With Some Reference to Relevant Collections in Europe; see also her Resources for Australian and New Zealand Studies: A Guide to Library Holdings in the United Kingdom (London, 1986).

37.   Burkett, Jack. Special Library and Information Services in the United Kingdom. 3rd ed. London, 1979.

Vol. 2: Government and Related Library and Information Services in the United Kingdom.

38.   Clark, G. Kitson, and Elton, G.R. Guide to Research Facilities in History in the Universities of Great Britain and Ireland. 2nd ed. Cambridge, 1965.

39.   Collison, Robert Lewis. Published Library Catalogues: An Introduction to Their Contents and Use. London, 1973.

A subject guide to the many published library catalogues; see also his Directory of Libraries and Special Collections on Asia and North Africa (Hamden, CT, 1970).

40.   Datta, Rajeshwari, ed. Union Catalogue of the Government of Pakistan Publications Held by Libraries in London, Oxford and Cambridge. London, 1967.

See also his Union Catalogue of the Central Government of India Publications Held by Libraries in London, Oxford and Cambridge (London, 1970); and Teresa Macdonald, Union Catalogue of the Government of Ceylon Publications Held by Libraries in London, Oxford and Cambridge (London, 1970).

41.   Deering, Catherine M. Union List of American Studies Periodicals in United Kingdom Libraries. London, 1983.

42.   Directory of British Associations, and Associations in Ireland, 1965-. Beckenham, 1965-.

9th ed., 1988; brief listing of national associations, societies, organisations, institutes, etc.

43.   Downs, Robert Bingham, and Downs, Elizabeth C. British and Irish Library Resources: A Bibliographical Guide. London, 1981.

Library catalogues, checklists, guides and directories; arranged by subject.

44.   Guide to the Historical Publications of the Societies of England and Wales. 13 vols. London, 1930-48.

Supplements 1-13, 1929-42/46, to the Bulletin of the Institute of Historical Research; see also E.L.C. Mullins, A Guide to the Historical and Archaeological Publications of Societies in England and Wales, 1903-1933 (London, 1968); and Cyril Matheson, Catalogue of the Publications of Scottish Historical and Kindred Clubs and Societies . . . 1908-1927 (Aberdeen, 1928).

45.   Harcup, Sara E. Historical, Archaeological and Kindred Societies in the British Isles: A List. 2nd ed. London, 1968.

46.   Harrold, Ann, ed. Libraries in the United Kingdom and the Republic of Ireland 1990. 16th ed. London, 1990.

Annual listing of over 600 major libraries, with details of address, personnel, etc.; from the Library Association; to be supplemented by her Libraries in Colleges of Further and Higher Education in the United Kingdom (London, 1986).

47.   Hewitt, Arthur Reginald, comp. Union List of Commonwealth Newspapers in London, Oxford and Cambridge. London, 1960.

Based on the holdings of the British Library; details of 2,426 newspapers in 62 libraries and newspaper offices.

48.   HMSO. British National Archives: Government Publications Sectional List, no. 24. London, 1984.

A list of publications and microfilms of the Public Record Office, the Public Record Office of Northern Ireland, the Scottish Record Office and the House of Lords Record Office.

49.   Hudson, Kenneth, and Nicholls, Ann. The Cambridge Guide to the Museums of Britain and Ireland. London, 1987.

A comprehensive guide to contents, opening hours, etc. of 2,041 collections.

50.   Jackson, Paul. British Sources of Information: A Subject Guide and Bibliography. London, 1987.

A guide to texts, information and teaching resources on all aspects of British life, society and culture.

51.   Lambert, Jean. The Bibliography of Museum and Art Gallery Publications and Audio-Visual Aids in Great Britain and Ireland 1977. London, 1978.

52.   The Libraries Year Book, 1989. Cambridge, 1989-.

Previously Libraries, Museums and Art Galleries Year Book.

53.   The London Union List of Periodicals: Holdings of the Municipal and County Libraries of Greater London. Edited by H.J. Rengert. 3rd ed. London, 1969.

54.   Mandahl, S.M., and Carnell, R.W. Checklist of Japanese Periodicals Held in British University and Research Libraries. Sheffield, 1971.

55.   Moon, Brenda Elizabeth, comp. Periodicals for South-East Asian
        Studies: A Union Catalogue of Holdings in British and Selected
        European Libraries. London, 1979.

        See too Directory of South-East Asian Library Collections in the
        United Kingdom and Western Europe, edited by S. Gunasingam
        (London, 1988).

56.   Mullins, E.L.C. Texts and Calendars, vol. 1, An Analytical Guide
        to Serial Publications to 1957. London, 1958.

        As issued by various Public Record Offices and record societies;
        continued in Texts and Calendars, vol. 2, An Analytical Guide to
        Serial Publications, 1957-1982 (London, 1983); nos. 7 and 12
        respectively of Royal Historical Society Handbooks and Guides.

57.   Naylor, Bernard, et al. Directory of Libraries and Special
        Collections on Latin America and the West Indies. London,
        1975.

        Expanded in Roger Macdonald and Carole Travis, Libraries and
        Special Collections on Latin America and the Caribbean: A
        Directory of European Resources (London, 1988).

58.   Record Repositories in Great Britain: A Geographical Directory.
        8th ed. London, 1987.

        HMSO for the Royal Commission on Historical Manuscripts.

59.   Roberts, Stephen, et al., comps. Research Libraries and
        Collections in the United Kingdom: A Selective Inventory and
        Guide. London, 1978.

        Descriptions and detailed information on 247 institutions.

60.   Shaw, Graham W., and Quraishi, Salim. The Bibliography of
        South Asian Periodicals: A Union List of Periodicals in South
        Asian Languages. Brighton, 1982.

61.   Sims-Williams, Ursula, ed. Union Catalogue of Persian Serials
        and Newspapers in British Libraries. London, 1985.

62.   Snow, Peter, comp. The United States: A Guide to Library
        Holdings in the United Kingdom. London, 1982.

        A guide to printed and other materials in 350 libraries.

63. Standing Conference on Library Materials on Africa. Periodicals from Africa: A Bibliography and Union List of Periodicals Published in Africa. Compiled by Carole Travis and Miriam Alman. Boston, MA, 1977.

Holdings of 67 libraries, representing the major African collections in Britain; first supplement, compiled by David Blake and Carole Travis (1984).

64. ————. The SCOLMA Directory of Libraries and Special Collections on Africa in the United Kingdom and Western Europe. Compiled by Harry Hannam. 4th ed. London, 1983.

65. Tait, James A., and Tait, Heather, eds. Scottish Library and Information Resources. Glasgow, 1984.

See too Library Resources in Wales, edited by M. June Maggs, 2nd ed. (London, 1976).

66. Walker, Gregory, ed. Directory of Libraries and Special Collections on Eastern Europe and the U.S.S.R. London, 1971.

See also his Resources for Soviet, East European and Slavonic Studies in British Libraries (Birmingham, 1981).

67. World of Learning, 1947-. London, 1947-.

Annual; international listing, by country, of learned societies, research organisations and libraries.

C. MANUSCRIPT RESEARCH

68. Baldock, Robert W. A Survey of Southern African Manuscripts in the United Kingdom. London, 1976.

69. Bill, E.G.W. A Catalogue of Manuscripts in Lambeth Palace Library, MSS 2341-3119. London, 1983.

Including material on Anglo-German relations in the 1930s.

70. Cook, Chris, et al., comps. Sources in British Political History, 1900-1951. 6 vols. London, 1975-85.

The researcher's vade mecum; a project of the Political Archives Investigation Committee carried out under the auspices of the British Library of Political and Economic Science; vol. 1 subtitled:

A Guide to the Archives of Selected Organisations and Societies; vol. 2: A Guide to the Private Papers of Selected Public Servants; vol. 3: A Guide to the Private Papers of Members of Parliament, A-K; vol. 4: A Guide to the Private Papers of Members of Parliament, L-Z; vol. 5: A Guide to the Private Papers of Selected Writers, Intellectuals and Publicists; vol. 6: First Consolidated Supplement; numerous useful appendixes in each volume; of related interest is Sources in European Political History, vol. 1-, edited by Chris Cook et al. (London, 1987); vol. 1 subtitled The European Left; vol. 2, Diplomacy and International Affairs (London, 1989).

71.   Crick, Bernard R., and Alman, Miriam, eds. A Guide to Manuscripts Relating to America in Great Britain and Ireland. London, 1961.

Revised edition by John Raimo (1979); for the British Association for American Studies; see also Carnegie Institution, Washington, Guides to Manuscript Materials for the History of the United States, 23 vols. (Washington, DC, 1906-43); includes some volumes on British materials.

72.   Emmison, F.G., and Smith, W.J., comps. Material for Theses in Local Record Offices and Libraries. London, 1979.

Historical Association, Helps for Students, no. 87; a geographic listing, further subdivided by subject; useful for out-of-the-way manuscripts; persons and subject index.

73.   Foster, Janet, and Sheppard, Julia, eds. British Archives: A Guide to Archive Resources in the United Kingdom. 2nd ed. London, 1989.

1,048 entries listing repositories which hold archives and manuscript collections of historical interest; detailed indexes; essential for manuscript research.

74.   Guides to Materials for West African History in European Archives. Nos. 1-5. London, 1962-73.

No. 5 by Noel Matthews (1973) for British archives.

75.   Hartley, Janet M., comp. Guide to Documents and Manuscripts in the United Kingdom Relating to Russia and the Soviet Union. London, 1987.

Alphabetical listing by location and then repository; see too her The Study of Russian History from British Archival Sources (London, 1986).

76. Hazlehurst, Cameron, and Woodland, Christine. A Guide to the Papers of British Cabinet Ministers, 1900-1951. London, 1974.

For the Royal Historical Society; an indispensable research tool; alphabetical listing with detailed information as to career and papers, both in archives and privately held; index of collections in institutions; also useful for careers spanning the nineteenth and twentieth century is Royal Commission on Historical Manuscripts, Papers of British Cabinet Ministers, 1782-1900 (London, 1982); vol. 1 of Guides to Sources for British History.

77. Hepworth, Philip, ed. Select Biographical Sources: The Library Association Manuscripts Survey. London, 1971.

Alphabetical listing with brief notes on career and location of manuscripts; see also his Archives and Manuscripts in Libraries (London, 1964).

78. Jones, A. Philip, comp. Britain and Palestine, 1914-1948: Archival Sources for the History of the British Mandate. London, 1979.

For the British Academy; locates unpublished records and papers of organisations and individuals based in Britain, and involved in any manner with Palestine in this period.

79. Jones, Charles A. Britain and the Dominions: A Guide to Business and Related Records in the United Kingdom Concerning Australia, Canada, New Zealand and South Africa. Boston, MA, 1978.

Listing by location, with details of archives.

80. Keen, Rosemary. A Survey of the Archives of Selected Missionary Societies. London, 1968.

For the Royal Commission on Historical Manuscripts.

81. Lenz, Wilhelm, comp. Manuscript Sources for the History of Germany since 1500 in Great Britain. Boppard/R., 1975.

82. MacLeod, Roy, and Friday, James R. Archives of British Men of Science. London, 1972.

By a Sussex University study group; traces papers of 3,500 scientists who were active between 1850 and 1939; on microfiche, with accompanying index and guide.

83.   Mander-Jones, Phyllis, ed. Manuscripts in the British Isles Relating to Australia, New Zealand and the Pacific. Canberra, 1972.

Arranged by country, with London holdings analysed first.

84.   Matthews, Noel, and Wainwright, Mary Doreen. A Guide to Manuscripts and Documents in the British Isles Relating to the Middle East and North Africa. Edited by J.D. Pearson. London, 1980.

See also the same authors' A Guide to Manuscripts and Documents in the British Isles Relating to the Middle East and North Africa (London, 1980); A Guide to Manuscripts and Documents in the British Isles Relating to the Far East (London, 1977); A Guide to Manuscripts and Documents in the British Isles Relating to Africa (London, 1971); for Africa south of the Sahara; and A Guide to Western Manuscripts and Documents in the British Isles Relating to South and South East Asia (London, 1969); supplement in A Guide to Manuscripts and Documents in the British Isles Relating to South and South-East Asia, vol. 1, London, compiled by J.D. Pearson (London, 1989); continued in vol. 2, British Isles (Excluding London) (London, 1990).

85.   Mayer, Sydney L., and Koenig, William J. The Two World Wars: A Guide to Manuscript Collections in the United Kingdom. London, 1976.

Details of military, naval and diplomatic materials.

86.   The National Inventory of Documentary Sources in the United Kingdom and Ireland. Cambridge, 1985-.

In progress; reproduces on microfiche more than 12,000 unpublished finding aids to manuscript collections in libraries, public record offices, private hands, etc.; indexed by name, subject and repositories.

87.   Netton, Ian Richard, comp. Middle East Materials in United Kingdom and Irish Libraries: A Directory. London, 1983.

Brief descriptions of holdings, with hours of opening, etc.

88.   Oral History Society. Directory of British Oral History Collections. Colchester, 1981.

Information on the contents of 231 collections; see also British Library, Oral History (London, 1990); further details, with United States emphasis, in Allen Smith, Directory of Oral History Collections (Phoenix, AZ, 1988); and Alan M. Meckler and Ruth McMullin, Oral History Collections (New York, 1975).

89.   Pearson, J.D., comp. Guide to Manuscripts and Documents in the British Isles Relating to the Middle East and North Africa. London, 1980.

90.   Pemberton, John E. European Materials in British University Libraries: A Bibliography and Union Catalogue. London, 1972.

91.   Pritchard, R. John. "A Survey of Tokyo War Trial Records in Britain," in Proceedings of the British Association for Japanese Studies, vol. 1, part 1: History and International Relations. Edited by Peter Lowe. Sheffield, 1976.

For the Centre of Japanese Studies, Sheffield University.

92.   Sturges, R.P. Economists' Papers, 1750-1950: A Guide to Archive and Other Manuscript Sources for the History of British and Irish Economic Thought. London, 1975.

Alphabetical listing of over 150 prominent economists.

93.   Thomas, Daniel H., and Case, Lynn M. The New Guide to the Diplomatic Archives of Western Europe. Philadelphia, PA, 1975.

The chapter on Britain describes the history and content of various archives.

94.   Walne, Peter, ed. A Guide to Manuscript Sources for the History of Latin America and the Caribbean in the British Isles. London, 1973.

IV. BIBLIOGRAPHY

A. GENERAL

The information explosion which erupted in the middle of the twentieth century gathers speed as the century comes to a close. Word processing and computer printing have further served to increase the output of materials. Online bibliographic data bases and electronic publishing have also enhanced the flow. This has proved to be a very mixed blessing for the historian. The guides to this information are inordinately abundant and sometimes complex. But the benefits to be derived are likewise enormous, limited only by the enthusiasm of the researcher. What follows in this reference section can only be a mere sampling of such reference guides. The selection is designed on two basic principles. The first is to indicate the variety of guides that are available. The second principle is to cite, as far as possible, British-produced and British-related materials.

1. Bibliographies

Bibliographies of Bibliographies

95. Besterman, Theodore. <u>A World Bibliography of Bibliography and of Bibliographical Catalogues, Calendars, Abstracts, Digests, Indexes, and the Like</u>. 4th ed. 5 vols. Lausanne, 1965-66.

Standard and comprehensive work for bibliographies published to 1963; about 117,000 items divided by about 16,000 headings; decennial supplement, 1964-74, compiled by Alice F. Toomey (Totowa, NJ, 1977).

96. <u>Bibliographic Index: A Cumulative Bibliography of Bibliographies, 1937-</u>. New York, 1938-.

Subject list of bibliographies published separately or found in books and periodicals, including some foreign languages; online access available since 1984.

97.   Bibliographies in History. 2 vols. Santa Barbara, CA, 1988.

        Vol. 2 subtitled: An Index to Bibliographies in History Journals
        and Dissertations Covering All Countries of the World except the
        U.S. and Canada.

98.   Collison, Robert Lewis. Bibliographies, Subject and National: A
        Guide to their Contents, Arrangement and Use. 3rd ed. London,
        1968.

        About 500 annotated bibliographies; name and subject index.

99.   Gray, Richard A., and Villmow, Dorothy. Serial Bibliographies in
        the Humanities and Social Sciences. Ann Arbor, MI, 1969.

Reference Guides

100.   American Reference Books Annual, 1970-. Vol. 1-. Edited by
        Bohdan S. Wynar. Littleton, CO, 1970-.

        Annotated annual of reference books; five-year cumulative index.

101.   Conover, Helen F., comp. A Guide to Bibliographical Tools for
        Research in Foreign Affairs. 2nd ed. Washington, DC, 1958.

102.   Day, Alan Edwin. History: A Reference Handbook. London,
        1977.

        An alphabetical guide with 787 annotated entries.

103.   Higgens, Gavin, ed. Printed Reference Material. 2nd ed. London,
        1984.

        For the Library Association; a standard work with various
        contributors.

104.   Levine, Herbert M., and Owen, Dolores B. An American Guide to
        British Social Science Resources. Metuchen, NJ, 1976.

        Details of British information services in the United States, and
        major British libraries and archives.

105.   Mason, John Brown. Research Resources: Annotated Guide to
        the Social Sciences. 2 vols. Santa Barbara, CA, 1968-71.

        Vol. 1 for international relations and recent history.

BIBLIOGRAPHIES

106.   Poulton, Helen J. The Historian's Handbook: A Descriptive Guide
        to Reference Works. Norman, OK, 1972.

        Introductory bibliographic guide to reference works.

107.   Sheehy, Eugene P., comp. Guide to Reference Books. Chicago, IL,
        1976.

        Supplements (1980, 1982); large section on general reference
        books; special section on history; see also William H. Webb et al.,
        Sources of Information in the Social Sciences: A Guide to the
        Literature, 3rd ed. (Chicago, IL, 1986).

108.   Walford, Albert John. Guide to Reference Material. 3 vols. 4th
        ed. London, 1980-87.

        A standard reference guide, well annotated; emphasis on items
        published in Britain; vol. 2 for social and historical sciences;
        condensed version Walford's Concise Guide to Reference Material
        (London, 1981); 5th edition, vol. 1 (London, 1989-).

General Bibliographies

109.   Boehm, Eric H. Bibliographies on International Relations and
        World Affairs: An Annotated Directory. Santa Barbara, CA,
        1965.

        Lists 20 best bibliographies and 83 publications with regular
        bibliographies.

110.   Commonwealth National Bibliographies: An Annotated Directory.
        London, 1977.

        For the Commonwealth Secretariat; listing by country.

111.   Coulter, Edith M., and Gerstenfeld, Melanie.   Historical
        Bibliographies: A Systematic and Annotated Guide. Berkeley,
        CA, 1965.

112.   Council on Foreign Relations. Foreign Affairs Bibliography: A
        Selected and Annotated List of Books on International
        Relations, 1919/32-1962/72. 5 vols. New York, 1933-76.

        Revised and enlarged bibliography based on quarterly ones
        appearing in Foreign Affairs; see also Foreign Affairs 50-Year
        Bibliography: New Evaluations of Significant Books on

International Relations, 1920-1970, edited by Byron Dexter (New York, 1972).

113.   Leistner, Otto, ed. Internationale Bibliographie der Festschriften von den Anfängen bis 1979 mit Sachregister. 2 vols. 2nd ed. Osnabrück, 1984-86.

Continued in Internationale Jahresbibliographie der Festschriften, 1980, vol. 1- (Osnabrück, 1982-); with online research available; see also New York Public Library, Research Libraries, Guide to Festschriften, 2 vols. (Boston, MA, 1977); and International Committee of Historical Sciences, Bibliographie internationale des travaux historiques publiés dans les volumes de "Mélanges," 1880/1939-1940/50. 2 vols. (Paris, 1955-65).

114.   Roach, John, ed. A Bibliography of Modern History. London, 1968.

Intended as an independent reference work and companion to the New Cambridge Modern History, vol. 1- (London, 1957-).

Current Bibliographies

115.   Bibliography of Historical Works Issued in the United Kingdom, 1940/45-1966/70. 5 vols. London, 1947-72.

In progress; sponsor and editor varies; volumes exclude periodical articles; strong emphasis on British history.

116.   Bindoff, Stanley Thomas, and Boulton, James T. Research in Progress in English and History in Britain, Ireland, Canada, Australia and New Zealand. London, 1976.

117.   British Books in Print: The Reference Catalogue of Current Literature, 1874-. London, 1874-.

With alphabetical author and title sequence; available on CD-ROM.

118.   British Library. Current Research in Britain. 4th ed. 4 vols. London, 1989.

A register of current research in every university, polytechnic, etc.; separate volume for the humanities.

119.   British National Bibliography, 1950-. London, 1950-.

The basic national bibliography prepared by the Bibliographic Services Division of the British Library; periodical listings excluded; weekly with cumulations at intervals; cumulated subject volumes published every four years; since 1977 carries advance cataloguing information; Author-Title Cumulation, 1950-1984 available on microfiche; for publications before 1950, see The English Catalogue of Books (London, 1906-); and The Bookseller (London, 1858-), which cumulate annually into Whitaker's Cumulative Book List (1924-).

120.   Current Research in British Studies by North American Scholars. Edited by Robert Kent Donovan and Patricia Clark. 9th ed. Manhattan, KS, 1988.

Previous editions published irregularly since 1953; produced for the Conference on British Studies.

121.   Historical Association, London. Annual Bulletin of Historical Literature. Vol. 1-, 1911-. London, 1911-.

Survey articles by specialists on the annual publications of books and articles; mainly British emphasis.

122.   Institut für Zeitgeschichte München. Bibliographie zur Zeitgeschichte, 1953-1980. Edited by Thilo Vogelsang and Hellmuth Auerbach. 3 vols. Munich, 1982-83.

Retrospective cumulation of the quarterly supplement, Bibliographie zur Zeitgeschichte, to Vierteljahreshefte für Zeitgeschichte.

123.   International Bibliography of Historical Sciences. Edited for the International Committee of Historical Sciences. Vol. 1-, 1926-. Washington, 1930-.

Historical sciences widely interpreted to include international relations, political, economic and social aspects, etc.; no volumes for 1940-46; this gap partially remedied by Pier Fausto Palumbo, Bibliografia storica internazionale, 1940-1947 (Rome, 1950); see also from the same sponsor, Commission internationale d'histoire militaire comparée, Bibliographie internationale d'histoire militaire, Sélection 1974/1976-, vol. 1 (Berne, 1978-).

124.   Royal Historical Society. Writings on British History, 1901-1933: A Bibliography on the History of Great Britain from about 400 A.D. to 1914, Published during the Years 1901-1933 Inclusive,

with an Appendix Containing a Select List of Publications in These Years on British History since 1914. 5 vols. London, 1968-70.

Annual (irregular) series of same title thereafter, compiled by Alexander Taylor Milne et al. for years 1934-45, in 8 vols., published 1937-60; 1946/48-73/74, for the Institute of Historical Research, 12 vols. (1973-81); continued in Royal Historical Society, Annual Bibliography of British and Irish History: Publications of 1975-, edited by Geoffrey R. Elton et al. (Hassocks, 1976-); chronological approach with subject subdivisions; covers books and periodicals; author and subject indexes.

Subject Bibliographies

125.   Amstutz, Mark R. Economics and Foreign Policy: A Guide to Information Sources. Detroit, MI, 1977.

Annotated bibliography on the political economy of international relations; other such bibliographies relevant to this guide include Gerard L. Alexander, Guide to Atlases: World, Regional, National, Thematic: An International Listing of Atlases Published Since 1950 (Metuchen, NJ, 1971); supplement for 1971 to 1975 published in 1977; Hardin Craig, A Bibliography of Encyclopedias and Dictionaries Dealing with Military, Naval and Maritime Affairs, 1577-1971, 4th ed. (Houston, TX, 1971); Henry Oliver Lancaster, Bibliography of Statistical Bibliographies (London, 1968); S. Padraig Walsh, Anglo-American General Encyclopaedias, 1703-1967: A Historical Bibliography (New York, 1968); and Lora Jeanne Wheeler, International Business and Foreign Trade: Information Sources (Detroit, MI, 1968).

126.   Anderson, Martin, and Bloom, Valerie, comps. Conscription: A Select and Annotated Bibliography. Stanford, CA, 1976.

Includes 1,385 annotated entries; separate chapter on bibliographies.

127.   Atherton, Alexine L. International Organizations: A Guide to Information Sources. Detroit, MI, 1975.

1,532 English-language sources; extensive coverage of the League of Nations; likewise see International Organization: An Interdisciplinary Bibliography, compiled by Michael Haas (Stanford, CA, 1971); and Harold S. Johnson and Baljit Singh,

International Organization: A Classified Bibliography (East Lansing, MI, 1969).

128. Bayliss, Gwyn M. Bibliographic Guide to the Two World Wars: An Annotated Survey of English-Language Reference Materials. London, 1977.

Arranged by type of reference work; author, title and subject indexes; see also Bibliografia della seconda guerra mondiale, 1945-1975, edited by Enzo Fasanotti (Rome, 1980); J.L. Black et al., Origins, Evolution and Nature of the Cold War: An Annotated Bibliographic Guide (Santa Barbara, CA, 1986); E. David Cronon and Theodore Rosenof, The Second War and the Atomic Age, 1940-1973 (Northbrook, IL, 1975); A Subject Bibliography of the Second World War: Books in English, 1939-1974, compiled by A.G.S. Enser (Boulder, CO, 1977); continued in A Subject Bibliography of the Second World War: Books in English, 1975-1983 (Aldershot, 1985); World War II: An Account of Its Documents, edited by James E. O'Neill and Robert W. Krauskopf (Washington, DC, 1976); The Royal Navy in World War II: An Annotated Bibliography, compiled by Derek G. Law (London, 1988); Myron J. Smith, World War II at Sea: A Bibliography of Sources in English (Metuchen, NJ, 1976); supplement for 1974-89 (Metuchen, NJ, 1990); the same author's World War II: The European and Mediterranean Theatres, an Annotated Bibliography (New York, 1984); Marty Bloomberg and Hans H. Weber, World War II and Its Origins: A Select Annotated Bibliography of Books in English (Littleton, CO, 1975); Arthur L. Funk et al., A Select Bibliography of Books on the Second World War, in English, Published in the United States, 1966-1975 (Manhattan, KS, 1975); continued in his The Second World War: A Select Bibliography of Books in English Published since 1975 (Claremont, CA, 1985); and World War II: Books in English, 1945-1965, compiled by Janet Ziegler (Stanford, CA, 1971).

129. Biographical Books, 1876-1949. New York, 1983.

More than 40,000 entries, with vocation, name/subject, author and title indexes; continued in Biographical Books, 1950-1980 (New York, 1980); see also Diane J. Cimbala et al., Biographical Sources: A Guide to Dictionaries and Reference Works (Phoenix, AZ, 1986); ARBA Guide to Biographical Dictionaries, edited by Bohdan S. Wynar (Littleton, CO, 1986); Biographical Dictionaries and Related Works, edited by Robert B. Slocum, 2 vols., 2nd ed. (Detroit, MI, 1986); and Historical Biographical Dictionaries Master Index, edited by Barbara McNeil and Miranda C. Herbert (Detroit, MI, 1980).

130.   Böttcher, Winfried, et al. Britische Europaideen, 1940-1970: Eine
         Bibliographie. 2 vols. Düsseldorf, 1971-73.

         Vol. 1 is a chronological list of books published in Britain on
         integration; vol. 2 concentrates on individual European countries;
         see also the same authors' Das britische Parlament und Europa,
         1940-1972: Eine Fachbibliographie (Baden-Baden, 1975).

131.   Cargas, Harry James.   The Holocaust: An Annotated
         Bibliography. 2nd ed. London, 1985.

         Thorough annotations; see also Martin A. Sable, Holocaust
         Studies: A Directory and Bibliography of Bibliographies
         (Greenwood, FL, 1987); Anti-Semitism: An Annotated
         Bibliography, vol. 1-, edited by Susan Sarah Cohen (New York,
         1987-); David Szonyi, The Holocaust: An Annotated Bibliography
         and Resource Guide (New York, 1985); and more generally,
         Genocide: A Critical Bibliographic Review, edited by Israel W.
         Charney (London, 1988).

132.   Carroll, Berenice A., et al.   Peace and War: A Guide to
         Bibliographies. Santa Barbara, CA, 1983.

         Contains 1,398 entries, many annotated; subdivided into "Peace
         and War," "Peace" and "War"; see also Justus D. Doenecke, Anti-
         Intervention: A Bibliographical Introduction to Isolationism and
         Pacifism from World War I to the Early Cold War (London, 1987);
         Elise Boulding et al., Bibliography on World Conflict and Peace
         (Boulder, CO, 1979); and Bibliography on Peace Research in
         History, edited by Blanche Wiesen Cook (Santa Barbara, CA,
         1969).

133.   Chaloner, William Henry, and Richardson, R.C.   Bibliography of
         British Economic and Social History. 2nd ed. Manchester, 1984.

         Chronological approach, with subdivisions by subject.

134.   Christie, Ian R.   British History since 1760:   A Select
         Bibliography. London, 1970.

         Historical Association, Helps for Students of History, no. 81;
         about five pages devoted to the twentieth century.

135.   Elton, G.R. Modern Historians on British History, 1485-1945: A
         Critical Bibliography, 1945-1969. London, 1970.

A bibliographic essay, with a chapter devoted to the twentieth century; author and subject index.

136.   Flint, John E. Books on the British Empire and Commonwealth: A Guide for Students. London, 1968.

See also Historiography of the British Empire-Commonwealth: Trends, Interpretations and Resources, edited by Robin W. Winks (Durham, NC, 1966); and Recent Views on British History: Essays on Historical Writing since 1966, edited by Richard Schlatter (New Brunswick, NJ, 1984).

137.   Ghebali, Victor-Yves, comp. Bibliographical Handbook of the League of Nations. 3 vols. Geneva, 1980.

Special Bibliographies, Repertoires and Indexes, no. 3, of the United Nations Library, Geneva; comprehensive subject bibliography; provisional edition.

138.   Goehlert, Robert U., and Martin, Fenton S. The Parliament of Great Britain: A Bibliography. Lexington, MA, 1983.

Concentrates on the history, development and legislative process of parliament; see also John Palmer, Government and Parliament in Britain: A Bibliography (London, 1964).

139.   Goodall, Francis. A Bibliography of British Business Histories. London, 1987.

Alphabetical by author, with company-name index; see also Debrett's Bibliography of Business History, edited by Stephanie Zarach (London, 1987).

140.   Gunzenhäuser, Max, ed. Die Pariser Friedenskonferenz 1919 und die Friedensverträge, 1919-1920. Frankfurt/M., 1970.

Introductory essay with long bibliography; see also Nina Almond and Ralph H. Lutz, An Introduction to a Bibliography of the Paris Peace Conference (Stanford, CA, 1935).

141.   Havighurst, Alfred F. Modern England, 1901-1984: A Bibliography. 2nd ed. London, 1987.

For the Conference on British Studies; 2,670 entries divided by subject; separate chapter on foreign relations.

142. Havlice, Patricia Pate. Oral History: A Reference Guide and Annotated Bibliography. Jefferson, NC, 1985.

For more British-oriented materials, see Anthony Seldon and Joanna Pappworth, By Word of Mouth: 'Elite' Oral History (London, 1983).

143. Higgens, Gavin. British Broadcasting, 1922-1982: A Selected and Annotated Bibliography. London, 1983.

144. Higham, Robin, ed. A Guide to the Sources of British Military History. Berkeley, CA, 1971.

For the Conference on British Studies; six chapters on period 1918-45; detailed bibliographic essays; updated with a further 3,000 entries in British Military History: A Supplement to Robin Higham's "Guide to the Sources," edited by Gerald Jordan (London, 1988); see also Robert Greenhalgh Albion, Naval and Maritime History: An Annotated Bibliography, 4th ed. (London, 1973).

145. Hill, Richard Leslie. A Bibliography of the Anglo-Egyptian Sudan, from the Earliest Times to 1937 . . . . London, 1939.

Supplemented by Abdel Rahman el Nasri, A Bibliography of the Sudan, 1938-1958 (London, 1962).

146. Laska, Vera. Nazism, Resistance and Holocaust in World War II: A Bibliography. London, 1985.

See also Ulrich Cartarius, Bibliographie "Widerstand" (London, 1984); and Henri Michel, Bibliographie critique de la résistance (Paris, 1964); updated in Revue d'histoire de la deuxième guerre mondiale.

147. Lincove, David A., and Treadway, Gary R. The Anglo-American Relationship: An Annotated Bibliography of Scholarship, 1945-1985. London, 1988.

A collection of 1,953 titles, thoroughly annotated, on social, cultural, diplomatic and military aspects.

148. Linton, David, and Boston, Ray, eds. The Newspaper Press in Britain: An Annotated Bibliography. London, 1987.

Alphabetical arrangement by author, with annotations; see also Bibliography of British Newspapers, vol. 1, Wiltshire, edited by Charles A. Toase et al. (London, 1975-); a series intended to cover all the counties of Britain.

149.   Lloyd, Lorna, and Sims, Nicholas A.   British Writing on Disarmament from 1914 to 1978: A Bibliography. London, 1979.

See also Stephen E. Atkins, Arms Control and Disarmament, Defense and Military, International Security and Peace: An Annotated Guide to Sources, 1980-1987 (Santa Barbara, CA, 1989); Richard Dean Burns, Arms Control and Disarmament: A Bibliography (Santa Barbara, CA, 1977); and League of Nations, Annotated Bibliography on Disarmament and Military Questions (Geneva, 1931).

150.   Matthews, William.   British Diaries: An Annotated Bibliography of British Diaries Written between 1442 and 1942. Berkeley, CA, 1950.

Lists both published and manuscript diaries; author index; see also his British Autobiographies: An Annotated Bibliography of British Autobiographies Published or Written before 1951 (Berkeley, CA, 1955); updated in Patricia Pate Havlice, And So to Bed: A Bibliography of Diaries Published in English (Metuchen, NJ, 1987).

151.   Messick, Frederic M., comp.   Primary Sources in European Diplomacy, 1914-1945. London, 1987.

Published memoirs, diaries, etc., by primary participants; appendix lists 636 entries by nationality, including British; see also his "With Churchill: A Bibliography of His Associates," Bulletin of Bibliography, 46 (1989), 195-203.

152.   Mowat, Charles Loch.   British History since 1926: A Select Bibliography. Revised by Peter Lowe. London, 1977.

Historical Association, Helps for Students of History, no. 61; includes sections on biography, memoirs, foreign policy and defence; see also his Great Britain since 1914 (London, 1971); part of "The Sources of History: Studies in the Use of Historical Evidence" series.

153.   Olson, William J.   Britain's Elusive Empire in the Middle East, 1900-1921: An Annotated Bibliography. New York, 1982.

Introductory essay; lists both Middle East reference books and those dealing with British policy in particular; continued in Vincent Ponko, Britain in the Middle East, 1921-1956: An Annotated Bibliography (New York, 1986); and on related imperial subjects, see Robert Heussler, British Malaya: A Bibliographical and Biographical Compendium (New York, 1981); and Thomas P. Ofcansky, British East Africa, 1856-1963: An Annotated Bibliography (London, 1985).

154. Parker, James G., ed. Lord Curzon: A Bibliography. Westport, CT, 1989.

Part of a "Bibliographies of British Statesmen" series; see also Neville Chamberlain: A Bibliography, edited by Stephen Stacey (Westport, CT, 1990).

155. Rees, Philip. Fascism in Britain: An Annotated Bibliography. Brighton, 1979.

See also his Neo-Fascism in Western Europe from 1890 to 1945: A Bibliography (London, 1983); and Fascism and Pre-Fascism in Europe, 1890-1945: A Bibliography of the Extreme Right (Brighton, 1984).

156. Sainsbury, Keith. International History, 1939-1970: A Select Bibliography. London, 1973.

Historical Association, Helps for Students of History, no. 86; chronological listing, subdivided by areas.

157. Smith, Bruce Lannes, et al. Propaganda, Communication and Public Opinion: A Comprehensive Reference Guide. Princeton, NJ, 1946.

About 2,500 titles of books and articles appearing between 1934 and 1943; continued in Bureau of Social Science Research, International Communication and Public Opinion: A Guide to the Literature, compiled by Bruce Lannes Smith and Chitra M. Smith (Princeton, NJ, 1956).

158. Smith, Harold, comp. The British Labour Movement to 1970: A Bibliography. London, 1981.

Covers all aspects; almost 4,000 entries, arranged by subject, published between 1945 and 1970; see also Ruth and Edmund

Frow and Michael Katanka, The History of British Trade Unions: A Select Bibliography (London, 1969).

159.   Smith, Myron J. The Secret Wars: A Guide to Sources in English. 3 vols. Santa Barbara, CA, 1980-81.

Vol. 1 entitled: Intelligence, Propaganda and Psychological Warfare, Resistance Movements, and Secret Operations, 1939-1945; see also Bibliography of Intelligence Literature, edited by Walter Pforzheimer, 8th ed. (Washington, DC, 1985); George C. Constantinides, Intelligence and Espionage: An Annotated Bibliography (Boulder, CO, 1983); Scholar's Guide to Intelligence Literature: Bibliography of the Russell J. Bowen Collection, edited by Marjorie W. Cline et al. (Frederick, MD, 1983); Intelligence, Espionage, Counterespionage and Covert Operations: A Guide to Information Sources, edited by Paul W. Blackstock and Frank L. Schaf (Detroit, MI, 1978); William R. Harris, Intelligence and National Security: A Bibliography with Selected Annotations (Cambridge, MA, 1968); and Max Gunzenhäuser, Geschichte des geheimen Nachrichtendienstes (Spionage, Sabotage und Abwehr): Literaturbericht und Bibliographie (Frankfurt/M., 1968).

160.   Spiers, John, et al. The Left in Britain: A Checklist and Guide. Hassocks, 1976.

Subtitled: With Historical Notes to 37 Left-Wing Political Movements and Groupings Active in Britain between 1904-1972 Whose Publications Comprise the Harvester/Primary Sources Microfilm Collection.

161.   Tutorow, Norman E., ed. War Crimes, War Criminals and War Crimes Trials: An Annotated Bibliography and Source Book. New York, 1986.

Annotated sources and publications, European and Asian.

162.   Watson, Charles A. The Writing of History in Britain: A Bibliography of Post-1945 Writings about British Historians and Biographers. New York, 1982.

163.   Woods, Frederick. A Bibliography of the Works of Sir Winston Churchill. 2nd ed. London, 1979.

Similar works include Chris Wrigley, A.J.P. Taylor: A Complete Annotated Bibliography and Guide to His Historical and Other

Writings (Brighton, 1980); and Philip O'Brien, T.E. Lawrence: A Bibliography (Winchester, 1987).

164. Woolven, Gillian B. Publications of the Independent Labour Party, 1893-1932. Manchester, 1977.

571 entries, with a section on international affairs.

165. Wright, Moorhead, et al. Essay Collections in International Relations: A Classified Bibliography. New York, 1977.

Over 1,600 essays, from 240 books published between 1945 and 1975, listed by subject; author and subject index.

Dissertations

166. ASLIB. Index to Theses Accepted for Higher Degrees in the Universities of Great Britain and Ireland, vol. 1-, 1950/51-. London, 1953-.

Subject arrangement and alphabetically by university; from vol. 38, 1989 retitled Index to Theses with Abstracts; for previous period see Retrospective Index to Theses of Great Britain and Ireland, 1716-1950, edited by Roger R. Bilboul, 5 vols. (Santa Barbara, CA, 1975-77); vol. 1 for the social sciences and humanities.

167. Bloomfield, Barry Cambray. Theses on Asia Accepted by Universities in the United Kingdom and Ireland, 1877-1964. London, 1967.

Updated in the Bulletin of the Association of British Orientalists.

168. Dissertation Abstracts International, Section C: European Abstracts, vol. 37-, no. 1-. Ann Arbor, MI, 1976-.

Part of Dissertation Abstracts International (Ann Arbor, MI, 1938-); quarterly list of mainly western European theses on microfilm from University Microfilm, Inc.; online data base searching available; see also Comprehensive Dissertation Index, 1861-1972, 1973-77, 1978 (Ann Arbor, MI, 1973-); ten-year cumulation covering 1973-82 (1984).

169. Gabel, Gernot U., and Gabel, Gisela R. Theses on Germany Accepted for Higher Degrees by the Universities of Great Britain and Ireland, 1900-1975: A Bibliography. Hamburg, 1979.

BIBLIOGRAPHIES

170. Labour and Social History Theses: American, British and Irish
      University Theses and Dissertations in the Field of British and
      Irish Labour History, Presented between 1900 and 1978.
      Compiled by Victor F. Gilbert. London, 1982.

      Includes theses on labour and foreign policy.

171. London University, Institute of Commonwealth Studies. Theses in
      Progress in Commonwealth Studies: A Cumulative List.
      London, 1950-.

172. London University, Institute of Historical Research. Historical
      Research for University Degrees in the United Kingdom,
      1931/32-52. London, 1933-53.

      Bulletin of the Institute of Historical Research, Theses
      Supplement, no. 1-14; information on theses completed and in
      progress; follows on lists published annually in History, 1920-29;
      and in the Bulletin, 1930-32; superseded by the Institute's annual
      Theses Completed, 1953- (London, 1954-) and Theses in
      Progress, 1954- (London, 1954-); issues for 1954-66 published as
      Theses Supplement, no. 15-27 to the Bulletin; from 1967 lists
      appear as separate publications of the Institute; for a definitive
      retrospective list see History Theses, 1901-1970, compiled by
      Phyllis M. Jacobs (London, 1976); and History Theses, 1971-1980,
      compiled by Joyce M. Horn (London, 1984).

173. London University, Institute of Latin American Studies. Theses in
      Latin American Studies at British Universities in Progress and
      Completed, 1966/67-. London, 1967-.

      Annual listing by university; author and subject indexes.

174. Reynolds, Michael M. Guide to Theses and Dissertations: An
      International Bibliography of Bibliographies. Phoenix, AZ, 1985.

      A subject classification of bibliographies of theses and
      dissertations; see also Marc Chaveinc, Guide to the Availability of
      Theses (Groningen, 1978).

175. Sluglett, Peter. Theses on Islam, the Middle East and North-
      West Africa, 1880-1978, Accepted by Universities in the United
      Kingdom and Ireland. London, 1983.

See also American and British Doctoral Dissertations on Israel and Palestine in Modern Times, edited by F.J. Shulman (Ann Arbor, MI, 1973).

176. United Kingdom Publications and Theses on Africa, 1963. Cambridge, 1966-68.

Thesis section is supplement to Theses on Africa Accepted by Universities in the United Kingdom and Ireland (Cambridge, 1964); see also J.H. McIlwaine, Theses on Africa, 1963-1975, Accepted by Universities in the United Kingdom and Ireland (London, 1978).

Reproductions and Data Bases

177. CD-ROMS in Print, 1987-: An International Guide. Westport, CT, 1987-.

Of growing use to the historian for online data base searching.

178. Dodson, Suzanne Cates. Microform Research Collections: A Guide. 2nd ed. Westport, CT, 1984.

Listing by title of 375 microform research collections; see also Ann Niles, An Index to Microform Collections (Westport, CT, 1984).

179. Guide to Microforms in Print: Author/Title, 1978-. Westport, CT, 1978-.

Annual listing of archival materials, monographs, journals, newspapers, government publications, etc., available on microform; see also the companion Guide to Microforms in Print: Subject, 1978- (Westport, CT, 1978-).

180. Hall, James Logan. On-line Information Retrieval Sourcebook. London, 1977.

See too his On-line Bibliographic Data Bases: 1979 Directory (London, 1979).

181. Library and Information Science Abstracts, no. 1-, Jan./Feb. 1969-. London, 1969-.

International coverage of information in hard copy, microfilm and computer-readable form.

182. Maxfield, Doris Morris, et al. On-line Database Search Services Directory. 2nd ed. Detroit, MI, 1988.

A guide to more than 1,700 sources providing computerized information retrieval services.

183. Williams, Martha E., et al., eds. Computer-Readable Data Bases: A Directory and Data Sourcebook. 2 vols. Chicago, IL, 1985.

Vol. 2 for the humanities; covers more than 5,000 data bases, both word-oriented and numeric.

2. Reference Works

Biographical Dictionaries, Lists and Directories

184. Bellamy, Joyce M., and Saville, John, eds. Dictionary of Labour Biography. 8 vols. London, 1972-87.

Coverage from about 1790; vol. 8 for indexes; see too the complementary Biographical Dictionary of Modern British Radicals, vol. 1-, 1770-1830, edited by Joseph O. Baylen and Norbert J. Gossman (Hassocks, 1979-).

185. Bidwell, Robin, ed. Bidwell's Guide to Government Ministers. 3 vols. London, 1973-74.

Vol. 1: The Major Powers and Western Europe, 1900-1971; vol. 3: The British Empire and Successor States, 1900-1972; see also Rulers and Governments of the World, 3 vols., edited by Martha Ross (New York, 1977-78).

186. Biography Index: A Cumulative Index to Biographical Material in Books and Magazines. Vol. 1-. New York, 1946-.

Quarterly with annual cumulation; index by name, profession and dates of birth and death.

187. Blaug, Mark, ed. Who's Who in Economics: A Biographical Dictionary of Major Economists, 1700-1986. 2nd ed. Cambridge, MA, 1986.

188. Boylan, Henry. A Dictionary of Irish Biography. 2nd ed. London, 1988.

See also The Dictionary of Welsh Biography Down to 1940 (London, 1959); and Who's Who in Scottish History, compiled by Gordon Donaldson and Robert S. Morpeth (New York, 1974).

189.　British and Irish Biographies, 1840-1940. Edited by David Lewis Jones. Oxford, 1984.

Reproduces on microfiche 272 biographical dictionaries; index of names.

190.　British Imperial Calendar and Civil Service List. London, 1809-1973.

Irregular, with varied titles and contents; usually gives royal households, holders of public office, with official position, honours and salary; superseded by The Civil Service Year Book, 1974- (London, 1974-).

191.　Burke, Sir John Bernard, and Burke, John. Burke's Genealogical and Heraldic History of the Peerage, Baronetage, and Knightage. London, 1826-.

Arranged alphabetically by title; gives full lineage; see also Burke's Genealogical and Heraldic History of the Landed Gentry (London, 1936-); irregular.

192.　Cokayne, George Edward. The Complete Peerage: Or, A History of the House of Lords and All Its Members from the Earliest Times. 13 vols. London, 1910-59.

Vol. 13: Peerage Creations and Promotions from 22 Jan. 1901 to 31 Dec. 1938; the most complete record of the peerage.

193.　Colonial Office List, 1862-1966. London, 1862-1966.

Annual to 1940, not published 1941-45; biennial 1946-66; usually includes extensive historical and statistical material, with maps and biographical section; superseded by A Year Book of the Commonwealth, 1967- (London, 1967-).

194.　Crawford, Anne, et al., eds. The Europa Biographical Dictionary of British Women. London, 1983.

Alphabetical listing of over 1,000 notable women.

195.　Current Biography Yearbook. Vol. 1-. New York, 1940-.

74

Until 1986 Current Biography; monthly, with annual cumulation; international in scope; see also Current Biography: Cumulated Index, 1940-1985 (New York, 1986).

196.   Debrett's Peerage, Baronetage, Knightage and Companionage, with Her Majesty's Royal Warrant Holders. London, 1769-.

Numerous subsequent title changes; biographical data, living children and collateral branches; from 1976, Debrett's Peerage and Baronetage; see also Leslie Gilbert Pine, The New Extinct Peerage, 1884-1971 (London, 1972).

197.   Dictionary of National Biography. Edited by Sir Leslie Stephen and Sir Sidney Lee. 22 vols. London, 1908-09.

With supplements: 1901-11 (1912), 1912-21 (1927), 1922-30 (1937), 1931-40 (1949), 1941-50 (1959), 1951-60 (1971), 1961-70 (1981), 1971-80 (1986), and a new five-year span beginning for 1981-85 (1990), with an index for 1901-1980 in one alphabetical sequence; a basic reference work for English biography; signed articles a source in themselves; for example, Sir Orme Sargent wrote about Sir Nevile Henderson and Sir Eric Phipps; errata notes cumulated in Corrections and Additions to the Dictionary of National Biography, 1923-1963 (Boston, MA, 1966); over 6,000 short abstracts of original entries reproduced in The Concise Dictionary of National Biography, Part 2, 1901-1970 (London, 1982); A Chronological and Occupational Index to the Dictionary of National Biography, compiled by David Bank (London, 1985), groups occupations into 20 categories; the lives of 645 individuals who died between 1915 and 1980 are recorded in Great Britons: Twentieth-Century Lives, edited by Harold Oxbury (London, 1985).

198.   Dod's Parliamentary Companion, 1832-. London, 1832-.

Annual; includes biographies of royal family and members of parliament, details of procedure, ministries and government departments; see also Who's Who of British Members of Parliament, 1832-1979, edited by Michael Stenton and Stephen Lees, 4 vols. (Brighton, 1976-81); vol. 3 for 1919-45; based on Dod's Parliamentary Companion, with additional information on subsequent career and date of death.

199.   Foreign Office List and Diplomatic and Consular Year Book. Edited by the Staff of the Foreign Office. London, 1806-1965.

Vital annual information on organisation of the Foreign Office and statement of service of members; includes foreign embassies, legations and consulates in Great Britain; superseded by The Diplomatic Service List, 1966- (London, 1966-); see also The Air Force List, formerly The Monthly Air Force List (London, 1918-); The Army List (London, 1814-); and The Navy List (London, 1814-).

200. International Bibliography of Biography, 1970-1987. 12 vols. London, 1988.

Based on the holdings of the British Library; vols. 1-5 for subject sequence; vols. 6-12 for author/title index.

201. International Who's Who, 1935-. London, 1935-.

Biographies of internationally prominent individuals.

202. Jeremy, David J., and Shaw, Christine, eds. Dictionary of Business Biography: A Biographical Dictionary of Business Leaders Active in Britain in the Period 1860-1980. 5 vols. London, 1984-86.

Extensive annotated articles; indexes, errata and contributors in Supplement (London, 1986).

203. Jones, Barry Owen, and Dixon, M. V. The Macmillan Dictionary of Biography. 2nd ed. London, 1986.

Biographical entries on about 7,000 figures of historical importance; more in Longman Dictionary of 20th Century Biography, edited by Asa Briggs et al. (London, 1985); and The Blackwell Biographical Dictionary of British Political Life in the Twentieth Century, edited by Keith Robbins (Oxford, 1990).

204. Josephson, Harold, et al., eds. Biographical Dictionary of Modern Peace Leaders. Westport, CT, 1985

See also Biographical Dictionary of Internationalists, edited by Warren F. Kuehl (Westport, CT, 1983).

205. Kelly's Handbook to the Titled, Landed and Official Classes, 1880-. London, 1880-.

Brief sketches of those with hereditary or honourary titles, members of parliament, government officials and public personalities.

206. Obituaries from The Times, 1961-1970: Including an Index to All Obituaries and Tributes Appearing in The Times during the Years, 1961-1970. Edited by Frank C. Roberts. Reading, 1975.

Continued as Obituaries from The Times, 1971-1975 (Reading, 1978); volume for 1951-60 published in 1979; index also includes tributes; greater international coverage in The Annual Obituary, 1980-, edited by Roland Turner et al. (London, 1981-).

207. Pickrill, D.A. Ministers of the Crown. London, 1981.

Lists holders of public offices under the crown from the earliest records to 1981.

208. Thomson, Theodore Radford. A Catalogue of British Family Histories. 3rd ed. London, 1976.

209. Tunney, Christopher. A Biographical Dictionary of World War II. London, 1972.

Over 400 sketches of service personnel, statesmen, etc.; see also David Mason, Who's Who in World War II (London, 1978); War Lords: Military Commanders of the Twentieth Century, edited by Michael Carver (London, 1976); and more generally, John Keegan and Andrew Wheatcroft, Who's Who in Military History (London, 1976).

210. Vacher's Parliamentary Companion, 1831-. London, 1831-.

Subtitled: Lists of the House of Lords and House of Commons with Members Town Addresses and Other Information Indispensable in Parliamentary Business; irregular.

211. Who's Who: An Annual Biographical Dictionary with Which Is Incorporated "Men and Women of the Time." London, 1849-.

Annual; the original who's who reference work; mainly British biographies; fairly detailed information supplied by individuals themselves.

212. Who Was Who, 1897-1915, 1916-1928, 1929-1940, 1941-1950, 1951-1960, 1961-1970, 1971-1980: A Companion to Who's Who:

Containing the Biographies of Those Who Died during the Period. 7 vols. London, 1928-81.

Essentially the original sketches, with corrections, additional information and date of death; see also Who Was Who: A Cumulated Index, 1897-1980 (London, 1981).

Annual Surveys and News Digests and Indexes

213.   Almanach de Gotha: Annuaire généalogique, diplomatique et statistique, 1763-. Gotha, 1763-1959.

Annual, not published 1945-58; a standard work on European genealogy, and worldwide statistical information.

214.   Annual Register of World Events: A Review of the Year, 1758-. London, 1761-.

Prior to 1954 known as Annual Register; includes articles on annual developments, international organisations and assessments of law, the arts, economics, etc.

215.   British Broadcasting Corporation. Monitoring Service: Monitoring Report. Reading, 1940-.

Daily concise summaries of major news items; Digest of World Broadcasts, 1939-1947 available on microfilm.

216.   Europa Year Book: A World Survey. London, 1926-.

Since 1960 in annual two-volume editions; all aspects of international organisation and individual countries; more than 100 pages usually devoted to the United Kingdom.

217.   Facts on File: World News Digest with Index. Vol. 1-, Oct.-Nov. 1940-. New York, 1940-.

Weekly, with annual bound volumes; classified digest of news arranged by subject; five-year index, published 1957-.

218.   International Year Book and Statesman's Who's Who, 1953-. London, 1953-.

Annual; political and statistical data on international organisations and individual countries; biographical section

219. Keesing's Contemporary Archives: Weekly Diary of World Events with Index Continually Kept Up-to-Date. Vol. 1-, 1 July 1931-. London, 1931-.

Including public documents and source references; indexes at intervals cumulated every two years; vol. 1 preceded by a supplement, "Synopsis of Important Events, 1918-1931"; monthly since vol. 29, Jan. 1983-.

220. Milner, Anita Cheek. Newspaper Indexes: A Location and Subject Guide for Researchers. 3 vols. Metuchen, NJ, 1977.

Surveys card files and unpublished indexes; US emphasis.

221. Royal Institute of International Affairs. The Bulletin of International News. 22 vols. London, 1925-45.

A daily digest of international news; see also Royal Institute of International Affairs, Review of the Foreign Press, 1939-1945 (London, 1939-45, repr. Munich, 1980); ten different series, mainly geographical, in 27 vols.

222. ————. Survey of International Affairs, 1920/23-. London, 1925-73.

Prewar series, 1920-38, 17 vols., edited by A.J. Toynbee et al.; wartime series, 1939-46, 11 vols., edited by A.J. Toynbee; increasingly dated, but a useful starting point for informed contemporary analysis; accompanied by Documents on International Affairs, 1928-63, edited by John W. Wheeler-Bennett et al. (London, 1929-73); the 1963 volume in both series the last to be published by Chatham House; see also Consolidated Index to the Survey of International Affairs, 1920-1938, and Documents on International Affairs, 1920-1938, compiled by Edith M.R. Ditmas (London, 1967).

223. Statesman's Year-Book: Statistical and Historical Annual of the States of the World, 1864-. Vol. 1-. London, 1864-.

Compendium of documents, statistics and current information on politics, economics and society worldwide; see also the companion volume, Statesman's Year-Book Historical Companion, edited by John Paxton (London, 1988).

224.   The Times, London. Index to The Times, 1906-1972. London, 1907-73.

Title varies; index gives date, page and column; from 1973 renamed The Times Index (Reading, 1973-); also indexes Sunday Times, Times Educational Supplement, Times Literary Supplement and Times Higher Education Supplement; separate series for Times Literary Supplement Index, vol. 1-, 1902-39 (Reading, 1978-).

225.   Webber, Rosemary. World List of National Newspapers: A Union List of National Newspapers in Libraries in the British Isles. London, 1976.

Title listing with index by country; excluded are titles in the British Library's Newspaper Library at Colindale.

Encyclopaedias and Dictionaries

226.   Abraham, Louis Arnold, and Hawtrey, Stephen Charles. Abraham's and Hawtrey's Parliamentary Dictionary. 3rd ed. London, 1970.

Definitions and some longer articles on British parliamentary practice and procedure; see also Norman W. Wilding and Philip Laundy, An Encyclopaedia of Parliament, 4th ed. (New York, 1971).

227.   Académie Diplomatique Internationale. Dictionnaire diplomatique. Edited by A.-F. Frangulis. 7 vols. Paris, 1933-68.

A standard reference work; vol. 5 for biographical details.

228.   Diplomaticheskii slovar'. Edited by A.A. Gromyko et al. 3 vols. 4th ed. Moscow, 1984-86.

Dictionary of modern diplomacy and international affairs, with Soviet emphasis.

229.   Encyclopaedia Britannica: A New Survey of Universal Knowledge. 14th ed. Chicago, 1929.

This edition contained signed articles, many by prominent diplomatic personalities, on current topics; vol. 1 contained a list of initials, names of contributors and their separate subjects.

230. Haensch, Günther, ed. Dictionary of International Relations and Politics: Systematic and Alphabetical in Four Languages - German, English/American, French, Spanish. 2nd ed. Munich, 1975.

Grouped by subject; detailed table of contents and index.

231. Marwick, Arthur, ed. The Illustrated Dictionary of British History. London, 1980.

2,000 short entries on topics and people; see also Christopher Haigh, The Cambridge Historical Encyclopedia of Great Britain and Ireland (London, 1985); A Dictionary of British History, edited by J.P. Kenyon (London, 1981); and A Dictionary of British History, 1815-1973, edited by Frank E. Hugget: (Oxford, 1974).

232. Palmer, Alan. The Penguin Dictionary of Twentieth-Century History, 1900-1982. 2nd ed. London, 1983.

See also his The Penguin Dictionary of Modern History, 1789-1945, 2nd ed. (London, 1983).

233. Plano, Jack C., and Olton, Roy. The International Relations Dictionary. 4th ed. Santa Barbara, CA, 1988.

"Major concepts" in 12 subject chapters.

234. Seth, Ronald. Encyclopaedia of Espionage. London, 1972.

Emphasis on Anglo-Soviet-American activities; see also Richard Deacon, Spyclopaedia: The Comprehensive Handbook of Espionage (London, 1987); Henry S.A. Becket, The Dictionary of Espionage (New York, 1986); Christopher Dobson and Ronald Payne, The Dictionary of Espionage (London, 1984); and Vincent and Nan Buranelli, Spy-Counterspy: An Encyclopedia of Espionage (New York, 1982).

235. Steinberg, Sigfrid H., and Evans, I.H., eds. Steinberg's Dictionary of British History. 2nd ed. London, 1970.

No biographical entries; still relevant is J.A. Brendon, A Dictionary of British History (London, 1937).

236. Vincent, Jack Ernest. A Handbook of International Relations: A Guide to Terms, Theory and Practice. Woodbury, NJ, 1969.

237.   Weigall, David. Britain and the World, 1815-1986: A Dictionary of International Relations. London, 1987.

Includes historical and biographical entries, definitions of terms and concepts, a chronology and some maps.

238.   Wheal, Elizabeth-Anne, et al. A Dictionary of the Second World War. London, 1989.

See also Bryan Perrett and Ian Hogg, Encyclopedia of the Second World War (London, 1989); Christopher Chant, The Encyclopedia of Codenames of World War II (London, 1986); Velikaia otechestvenaia voina, 1941-1945gg.: Slovar', edited by U.V. Plotnikov (Moscow, 1985); Louis L. Snyder, Historical Guide to World War II (Westport, CT, 1982); The Historical Encyclopedia of World War II, edited by Marcel Baudot et al. (London, 1980); and The Simon and Schuster Encyclopedia of World War II, edited by Thomas Parrish (New York, 1978).

Statistical and Factual

239.   An Almanack, 1869-. Vol. 1-, 1869. London, 1869-.

Also known as Whitaker's Almanack; An Account of the Astronomical and Other Phenomena and a Vast Amount of Information Respecting the Government, Finances, Population, Commerce, and General Statistics of the Various Nations of the World with an Index.

240.   Butler, David, and Butler, Gareth, eds. British Political Facts, 1900-1985. 6th ed. London, 1986.

Detailed information, charts and tables on ministries, party and election statistics, treaties, etc.

241.   Central Statistical Office. Annual Abstract of Statistics. Vol. 1-, 1840/53-. London, 1854-.

Annual; vols. 1-83 issued as Statistical Abstract for the United Kingdom, covering preceding 15 years; vol. 83 for 1924-38, published in 1940; vol. 84 appeared in 1948 and covered 1935-46.

242.   Cook, Chris, and Stevenson, John. The Longman Handbook of Modern British History, 1714-1987: Essential Facts and Figures. 2nd ed. London, 1987.

REFERENCE WORKS

243.   Fryde, E.B., et al. Handbook of British Chronology: Royal
        Historical Society Guides and Handbooks, no.2. 3rd ed. London,
        1986.

        Includes lists of rulers, officers of state and parliamentary tables;
        see also Handbook of Dates for Students of History: Royal
        Historical Society Guides and Handbooks, no. 4, edited by C.R.
        Cheney (London, 1975).

244.   Kendall, Maurice G., ed. Sources and Nature of the Statistics of
        the United Kingdom. 2 vols. London, 1952-57.

245.   League of Nations. Statistical Yearbook of the League of Nations,
        1926-1942/44. Geneva, 1927-45.

        Annual survey of worldwide business and commerce; continued by
        the Statistical Yearbook of the United Nations (1949-).

246.   Liesner, Thelma. Economic Statistics, 1900-1933. London, 1985.

        See also C.H. Feinstein, Statistical Tables of National Income,
        Expenditure and Output of the United Kingdom, 1855-1965
        (London, 1976); and London and Cambridge Economic Service,
        The British Economy: Key Statistics, 1900-1970 (London, 1973).

247.   Mitchell, Brian R. British Historical Statistics. London, 1988.

        Commentaries, tables and sources on economic and social
        statistics to 1980-81; the successor to Abstract of British
        Historical Statistics, edited by Brian R. Mitchell and Phyllis
        Deane (London, 1962), and Second Abstract of British Historical
        Statistics, edited by Brian R. Mitchell and H.G. Jones (London,
        1971).

Atlases and Gazetteers

248.   American Geographical Society of New York. Map Department.
        Index to Maps in Books and Periodicals. 10 vols. Boston, MA,
        1968.

        First Supplement (1971); Second Supplement (1976).

249.   Banks, Arthur. A World Atlas of Military History. 3 vols. New
        York, 1973-84.

        Vol. 3 for 1861-1945 (1978).

250. Bartholomew Gazetteer of Britain. Compiled by Oliver Mason. Edinburgh, 1977.

Statistical section updated to 1971 census; see also The Times Index-Gazetteer of the World (London, 1965).

251. Bickmore, D.P., and Shaw, M.A. The Atlas of Britain and Northern Ireland. London, 1963.

Intended as a national atlas; mainly physical and economic maps of Britain at midcentury.

252. Cook, Chris, and Stevenson, John, comps. Longman Atlas of Modern British History: A Visual Guide to British Society and Politics, 1700-1970. London, 1978.

Divided into economic, social and political history.

253. Darby, H.C., and Fullard, Harold, eds. New Cambridge Modern History Atlas. London, 1970.

288 pages of maps, with subject index; vol. 14 of the New Cambridge Modern History, vol. 1- (London, 1957-).

254. Freeman-Grenville, G.S.P. Atlas of British History. London, 1979.

From prehistoric times to 1978; likewise see Historical Atlas of Britain, edited by Malcolm E. Falkus and John Gillingham (London, 1981).

255. Gilbert, Martin. British History Atlas. London, 1968.

All 118 maps enhanced with additional historical information; among his other atlases see The Macmillan Atlas of the Holocaust (New York, 1982); First World War History Atlas, 2nd ed. (London, 1985); Recent History Atlas: 1870 to the Present Day, 3rd ed. (London, 1977).

256. The Times, London. The Times Atlas of the Second World War. Edited by John Keegan. London, 1989.

See also Charles Messenger, World War Two Chronological Atlas (London, 1989); Richard Natkiel, Atlas of World War II (New York, 1985); Peter Young, Atlas of the Second World War (London, 1973); James F. Horrabin, An Atlas-History of the

Second Great War, 10 vols. (London, 1942-46); and The Oxford War Atlas, 4 vols. (New York, 1941-46).

257.   ———. The Times Atlas of the World: Mid-Century Edition. Edited by John Bartholomew and Times Publication Company. 5 vols. London, 1955-59.

Each volume covers a different section of the world, and each has its own index-gazetteer; see also The Times Atlas of the World: Seventh Comprehensive Edition (London, 1937); and The Times Concise Atlas of World History, edited by Geoffrey Barraclough, rev. ed. (London, 1986).

3. Scholarly Journals

Guides, Lists and Indexes

258.   American Historical Association. Recently Published Articles, vol. 1-, 1976-. Washington, DC, 1976-.

Previously a part of the American Historical Review.

259.   Boehm, Eric H., et al., eds. Historical Periodicals Directory. 5 vols. Santa Barbara, CA, 1981-86.

Arranged by geographic area and country; vol. 2 for western European titles; vol. 5 for subject and title indexes.

260.   Book Review Digest, 1905-, vol. 1-. New York, 1905-.

A monthly index of reviews from 83 periodicals; see also Book Review Digest: Author/Title Index, 1905-1974, edited by Leslie Dunmore-Leiber, 4 vols. (New York, 1976); Book Review Index, 1965-, vol.1- (Detroit, MI, 1965-); cumulated index for 1965-84, 10 vols. (1985); Combined Retrospective Index to Book Reviews in Scholarly Journals, 1886-1974, edited by Evan Ira Farber et al., 15 vols. (Arlington, VA, 1979-82); and Combined Retrospective Index to Book Reviews in Humanities Journals, 1802-1974, edited by Evan Ira Farber et al., 10 vols. (Woodbridge, CT, 1982-84).

261.   British Humanities Index, 1962-. London, 1963-.

Quarterly, with annual cumulation, containing separate subject and author sections; indexes about 400 British periodicals; formerly Subject Index to Periodicals, 1915-1961 (London, 1915-61).

262.   British Union-Catalogue of Periodicals: A Record of the Periodicals of the World, from the Seventeenth Century to the Present Day, in British Libraries. Edited by James Douglas Stewart et al. 4 vols. London, 1955-58.

Supplement to 1960 (London, 1962); lists more than 140,000 titles filed in 441 libraries in the United Kingdom; then as British Union-Catalogue of Periodicals, New Periodical Titles, 1960/68, 1980 (London, 1964-81); annual afterwards; from 1981 Serials in the British Library (London, 1981-).

263.   The Combined Retrospective Index Set to Journals in History, 1838-1974. Edited by Annadel N. Wile. 11 vols. Washington, DC, 1977-78.

Vols. 1-4 for world history; vols. 10-11, author index; more than 1,000 English-language journals.

264.   Fyfe, Janet, comp. History Journals and Serials: An Analytical Guide. New York, 1986.

Detailed commentaries on 671 current English-language titles worldwide.

265.   Harrison, Royden John, et al. The Warwick Guide to British Labour Periodicals, 1790-1970: A Check List. Hassocks, 1977.

Over 4,000 titles with library locations.

266.   Henige, David, comp. Serial Bibliographies and Abstracts in History: An Annotated Guide. Westport, CT, 1986.

A guide to bibliographies in history serials worldwide.

267.   Historical Abstracts 1775-1945: Bibliography of the World's Periodical Literature. Vol. 1-, 1955-. Edited by Eric H. Boehm et al. Santa Barbara, CA, 1955-.

Signed abstract articles on all aspects of history from 1775 to 1945 published by 1964; beginning vol. 17, 1971, published in two parts: Part B for the twentieth century; indexes over 2,000 periodicals including articles in transactions, proceedings and Festschriften;

five-year indexes, beginning vols. 17-20 (1970-74), for Part B; from vol. 31 (1980) includes new books and theses; data base available for online computer search.

268. Index to Book Reviews in Historical Periodicals, 1972-1976. Edited by John W. Brewster and Joseph A. McLeod. 5 vols. Metuchen, NJ, 1975-77.

Annual index to reviews in about 100 English-language periodicals; entry by author, with a title index; each volume includes approximately 5,000 reviews.

269. International Review of Periodical Literature: British History, 1988, vol. 1-. Edited by Michael Bentley. Cambridge, 1989-.

International coverage of 400 articles on British history published in 1988; one section devoted to post-1750 period.

270. Kirby, J.L. A Guide to Historical Periodicals in the English Language. London, 1970.

Historical Association, Helps for Students of History, no. 80; annotated list by period, area and specialisation.

271. Kramm, Heinrich. Bibliographie historischer Zeitschriften, 1939-1951. 3 vols. Marburg, 1952-54.

Vol. 2 for Britain; periodicals subdivided by subject.

272. Marconi, Joseph V. Indexed Periodicals: A Guide to 170 Years of Coverage in 33 Indexing Services. Ann Arbor, MI, 1976.

273. Readers' Guide to Periodical Literature, 1900-. Vol. 1-. New York, 1905-.

Indexes 176 periodicals of general interest.

274. Social Sciences and Humanities Index: Formerly International Index, 1907/15-74. 61 vols. New York, 1916-74.

A cumulative index of scholarly journals from Britain and the United States; superseded by Humanities Index, vol. 1- (New York, 1974-), and Social Sciences Index, vol. 1- (New York, 1974-); both quarterly, with annual cumulation.

275. Social Sciences Citation Index, 1972-. Philadelphia, PA, 1973-.

International index to principal journals in the social sciences; data base for online computer searching.

276. Steiner, Dale R. Historical Journals: A Handbook for Writers and Reviewers. Santa Barbara, CA, 1981.

Information about the editorial policies and publishing requirements of 390 American and Canadian titles.

277. Ulrich's International Periodicals Directory: A Classified Guide to Current Periodicals, Foreign and Domestic. New York, 1932-.

From vol. 27 (1988-89) includes titles previously listed in the companion Irregular Serials and Annuals: An International Directory (New York, 1967-87); updates in Ulrich's Quarterly (New York, 1977-); all Ulrich's publications available for computer search.

278. Walford, Albert John. Walford's Guide to Current British Periodicals in the Humanities and Social Sciences. London, 1985.

Covers over 3,000 journals; entries include titles and former titles, frequency, and comments on contents.

279. Woodworth, David P., and Goodair, Christine M. Current British Journals: A Bibliographical Guide. 5th ed. Boston Spa, 1989.

Information on 7,499 current periodicals, societies and their publications; see also the annual British Library, Current Serials Received (London, 1989).

Select British Titles

280. Bulletin of the John Rylands University Library of Manchester. Manchester, 1903-. Biannual.

Among other British libraries which produce their own journals, with occasional historical articles; see for example The Bodleian Library Record (1914-); and The British Library Journal (1975-).

281. Business History. London, 1958-. Quarterly.

Edited by the Business History Unit of London University.

282. Economic History Review. Cambridge, 1927-. Quarterly.

All aspects of the subject and related disciplines; annual list of publications on British and Irish economic history.

283. English Historical Review. London, 1886-. Quarterly.

Among the leading British scholarly journals; approximately 500 reviews and notices of books per year.

284. Historical Journal. Cambridge, 1958-. Quarterly.

Formerly Cambridge Historical Journal, 1923-1957; limited book reviews; significant articles on foreign policy.

285. Historical Journal of Film, Radio and Television. Oxford, 1981-. Semiannual.

Explores the impact of mass communications on political and social history; includes reports on media collections, etc.

286. Historical Research: The Bulletin of the Institute of Historical Research. London, 1923-. Triannual.

Until 1986 published as The Bulletin of the Institute of Historical Research; articles, "Notes and Documents" and "Historical News"; issues regular theses supplement, and corrections to Dictionary of National Biography.

287. History: The Journal of the Historical Association. London, 1912-. Triannual.

Emphasis on British and European history; review articles, editorial notes and extensive section of book reviews.

288. History Today. London, 1951-. Monthly.

Illustrated and with short articles written by historians.

289. International Affairs. London, 1922-. Quarterly.

Journal of the Royal Institute of International Affairs; many government spokesmen contributed articles during the 1918-45 period.

290. Journal of American Studies. Cambridge, 1967-. Triannual.

For the British Association for American Studies; other such area journals include Journal of African History (1960-); Journal of Latin American Studies (1969-); European History Quarterly (1984-); Journal of Imperial and Commonwealth History (1972-); Middle Eastern Studies (1964-); Modern Asian Studies (1967-); Bulletin of the British Society for Middle Eastern Studies (1974-); Slavonic and East European Review (1922-); and Soviet Studies (1949-).

291.   Journal of Contemporary History. London, 1966-. Quarterly.

Specialises in twentieth-century history, including foreign affairs; occasional thematic issues; vol. 21 contains Cumulative Index, Vols. 1-21, with author-subject index.

292.   Journal of Newspaper and Periodical History. London, 1984-. Triannual.

From the seventeenth to the twentieth century; includes "Sources of Newspaper and Periodical History."

293.   Journal of the Royal United Services Institute for Defence Studies. London, 1857-. Quarterly.

Minor variations in title; articles on international relations and strategic studies; see also The Consolidated Author and Subject Index to the Journal of the Royal United Service Institution, 1857-1963, edited by Robin Higham (Ann Arbor, MI, 1964).

294.   Journal of the Society for Army Historical Research. London, 1921-. Quarterly.

Includes edited documents, such as autobiographies and letters, and lists of doctoral research on the subject.

295.   Oral History: Journal of the Oral History Society. Colchester, 1971-. Semiannual.

Economic, social, political and military aspects, including reports of work in progress, news of conferences, etc.

296.   Past and Present: A Journal of Historical Studies. Oxford, 1952-. Quarterly.

Articles and debates on British and European subjects.

297.   Political Quarterly. London, 1930-. Quarterly.

Emphasis on British domestic and foreign policy; for background see The Political Quarterly in the Thirties, edited by William A. Robson (London, 1971).

298.   Proceedings of the British Academy. London, 1903-. Annual.

Usually publishes one historical lecture by fellows; includes obituary notices of historians who were fellows; see also K. Balasundara Gupta, Cumulative Index to the Proceedings of the British Academy, Vol.1 (1903) to Vol. 54 (1968) (Metuchen, NJ, 1971).

299.   Review of International Studies. Sevenoaks, 1975-. Quarterly.

Formerly British Journal of International Studies; interdisciplinary contributions on foreign policy, including the debate on appeasement.

300.   Round Table: The Commonwealth Journal of International Affairs. London, 1910-. Quarterly.

Founded in 1910 to promote imperial unity; interwar articles reflect informed opinion on foreign and Commonwealth policies.

301.   Times Literary Supplement. London, 1902-. Weekly.

Currently publishes extensive review articles.

302.   Transactions of the Royal Historical Society. Fourth Series, vols. 1-32, London, 1918-50. Fifth Series, vol. 1-, London, 1951-. Annual.

Contains papers read to the society in the previous year; see also A Centenary Guide to the Publications of the Royal Historical Society, 1868-1968, and of the Former Camden Society, 1838-1897, compiled by Alexander Taylor Milne (London, 1968).

303.   Wiener Library Bulletin. London, 1946-. Quarterly.

Reflects research interests of the Wiener Library and the Institute of Contemporary History, including antisemitism and totalitarianism; see also The Wiener Library Bulletin Index 1946/47-1968, compiled by Helen Kehr (Nendeln, 1979).

B. PARLIAMENT AND GOVERNMENT

1. Records, Guides and Indexes

304.   Catalogue of Government Publications, 1922-. London, 1923-.

Annual; continues the Quarterly List . . . of Official Publications (London, 1897-1922); usefully amalgamated in Cumulative Index to the Annual Catalogues of Her Majesty's Stationery Office Publications, 1922-1972, compiled by Ruth Matteson Blackmore, 2 vols. (Washington, DC, 1976).

305.   Comfort, A.F., and Loveless, Christine. Guide to Government Data: A Survey of Unpublished Social Science Material in Libraries of Government Departments in London. London, 1974.

Information on materials produced from 1940.

306.   Craig, F.W.S. British Parliamentary Election Results, 1918-1949. 3rd ed. (London, 1983).

See also his British Electoral Facts, 1832-1987, 5th ed. (London, 1989); Chronology of British Parliamentary By-Elections, 1833-1987 (London, 1987); British General Election Manifestos, 1900-1974 (London, 1975); Minor Parties at British Parliamentary Elections, 1885-1974 (London, 1975); Boundaries of Parliamentary Constituencies, 1885-1972 (Chichester, 1972); and British Parliamentary Election Statistics, 1918-1970, 2nd ed. (London, 1971); and Ivor Crewe and Anthony Fox, British Parliamentary Constituencies: A Statistical Compendium (London, 1987).

307.   Ford, Percy, and Ford, Grace. A Guide to Parliamentary Papers: What They Are; How to Find Them; How to Use Them. 3rd ed. Shannon, 1972.

An introductory guide; with an appendix for lists of indexes, guides and catalogues to sources; see also the same authors' A Breviate of Parliamentary Papers, 1917-1939 (Oxford, 1951); continued in A Breviate of Parliamentary Papers, 1940-1954: War and Reconstruction (Oxford, 1961).

308. Kinnear, Michael. The British Voter: An Atlas and Survey since 1885. London, 1981.

Examines "the social, economic and organisation background of British politics" (Introduction).

309. Ollé, James G. An Introduction to British Government Publications. 2nd ed. London, 1973.

Including parliamentary and nonparliamentary publications; see also Frank Rodgers, A Guide to British Government Publications (New York, 1980); and David Butcher, Official Publications in Britain, 2nd ed. (London, 1990).

310. Parliament. Parliamentary Debates: House of Commons; House of Lords. Fifth Series. vol. 1-. London, 1909-.

Official, complete and verbatim reports of debates and all division lists; sessional indexes.

311. Parliament, House of Commons. General Alphabetical Index to the Bills, Reports, Estimates, Accounts and Papers Printed by Order of the House of Commons and to the Papers Presented by Command, 1801-1948/49. 4 vols. London, 1853-1960.

Vol. 4 for general index, 1900-1949; a useful guide is A Numerical Finding List of British Command Papers Published 1833-1962, compiled by Edward Di Roma and Joseph A. Rosenthal (New York, 1967).

312. ————. General Index to the Bills, Reports and Papers, Printed by Order of the House of Commons and to the Reports and Papers Presented by Command, 1900-1948/49. London, 1960.

Subjet index to documents included in parliamentary papers of House of Commons.

313. Pemberton, John E. British Official Publications. 2nd ed. London, 1973.

Detailed description and explanation of various categories of government publications; useful table of command papers and royal commissions; see also Directory of British Official Publications: A Directory to Sources, compiled by Stephen Richard, 2nd ed. (London, 1984).

314. Richard, Stephen. British Government Publications: An Index to Chairmen and Authors. 4 vols. London, 1982-84.

For committees and commissions of inquiry; vol. 2 for 1900-1940; vol. 3 for 1941-78; supersedes British Government Publications: An Index to Chairmen and Authors, 1941-1966, edited by Annie Mary Morgan (London, 1969).

315. Rodgers, Frank. Serial Publications in the British Parliamentary Papers, 1900-1968: A Bibliography. Chicago, IL, 1971.

About 1,300 serials in the House of Commons Sessional Papers since 1900; arranged by issuing agency.

316. Staveley, Ronald, and Piggott, Mary. Government Information and the Research Worker. 2nd ed. London, 1965.

Information on resources, facilities and services; separate chapter on the Foreign Office.

317. The Times, London. House of Commons, 1910-. London, 1910-.

With polling results, biographies of members, statistics, etc.; not published for the elections of 1922, 1923, 1924.

2. Treaties: Guides and Texts

318. Carnegie Endowment for International Peace. The Treaties of Peace, 1919-1923. 2 vols. New York, 1924.

319. Foreign Office. British and Foreign State Papers, 1812-. Vol. 1-. London, 1841-.

Annual with some delays; confidential papers not included; each volume with country-subject index and chronological list of documents; beginning with vol. 116, 1922, incorporates Hertslet's Commercial Treaties, 31 vols. (London, 1827-1925).

320. ———. Treaty Series, 1892-. London, 1892-.

Issued as command papers, although numbered and indexed to be bound separately; periodic general indexes; for a complete consolidated index see Clive Parry and Charity Hopkins, An Index of British Treaties, 1101-1968, 3 vols. (London, 1970).

321.   Grenville, J.A.S., ed. The Major International Treaties 1914-1945: A History and Guide with Texts. 2nd ed. London, 1988.

Vol. 2, edited with Bernard Wasserstein, for treaties since 1945.

322.   Israel, Fred L., ed. Major Peace Treaties of Modern History, 1648-1967. 5 vols. New York, 1967-80.

323.   League of Nations. Treaty Series: Publication of Treaties and International Engagements Registered with the Secretariat of the League. 205 vols. Geneva, 1920-46.

Index compiled every 500 treaties; for earlier period see The Consolidated Treaty Series, edited by Clive Parry, vol. 1- (New York, 1969-).

324.   Mostecky, Vaclav, ed. Index to Multilateral Treaties: A Chronological List of Multi-Party International Agreements from the Sixteenth Century through 1963, with Citations to Their Text. Cambridge, MA, 1965.

325.   Rohn, Peter H. World Treaty Index. 5 vols. 2nd ed. Santa Barbara, CA, 1983-84.

Index and inventory to some 44,500 treaties; vol. 1 for League of Nations treaty series; vol. 3 includes national treaty collections; vols. 4-5 contain index sections.

326.   Toscano, Mario. The History of Treaties and International Politics, vol. 1, An Introduction to the History of Treaties and International Politics: The Documentary and Memoir Sources. Baltimore, MD, 1966.

Analysis of the variety of diplomatic documents, with a chapter on treaty collections.

327.   United Nations Secretariat. Systematic Survey of Treaties for the Pacific Settlement of International Disputes, 1928-1948. Lake Success, NY, 1949.

3. Official Diplomatic Series and Coloured Books

British

328.   Cabinet Office, Cabinet History Series. <u>Principal War Telegrams and Memoranda, 1940-1943</u>. 7 vols. London, 1976.

Mainly telegrams exchanged between London and commanders in the field; arranged geographically for Middle East, Far East, India, Washington and miscellaneous.

329.   Foreign and Commonwealth Office. <u>Documents on British Policy Overseas</u>. Edited by Rohan Butler et al. London, 1984-.

Series 1, 1945-50, vol. 1-, for the Potsdam conference, July-Aug. 1945.

330.   Foreign Office. <u>Documents Concerning German-Polish Relations and the Outbreak of Hostilities between Great Britain and Germany on September 3, 1939</u>. Cmd. 6106. London, 1939.

Last of the interwar foreign affairs command papers, or "Blue Books," presented to parliaments; a convenient guide to all such material is Robert Vogel, <u>A Breviate of British Diplomatic Blue Books, 1919-1939</u> (Montreal, Québec, 1963); arranged chronologically with subject index.

331.   ———. <u>Documents on British Foreign Policy, 1919-1939</u>. Edited by Sir Llewellyn Woodward, Rohan Butler, W.N. Medlicott, et al. London, 1946-.

In progress; Series 1, 1919-29, vols. 1-27, covers 1919-25, complete (1947-86); Series 1A, 1925-30, vols. 1-7, complete (1966-75); Series 2, 1929-38, vols. 1-21, to cover 1930-38 (1946-84); Series 3, March 1938-3 September 1939, vols. 1-10, complete (1946-61); editors given "access to all papers in the Foreign Office Archives, and freedom in the selection and arrangement of documents" (Preface); chronological presentation of documents with reference given to original Foreign Office file numbers.

Non-British

332.   Australia, Department of Foreign Affairs. <u>Documents on Australian Foreign Policy, 1937-1949</u>. Edited by R.G. Neale et al. Vol. 1-. Canberra, 1975-.

In progress; vols. 1-7 for 1938-44.

333. Belgium, Académie Royale de Belgique. Documents diplomatiques belges, 1920-1940. Edited by Charles de Visscher and Fernand Vanlangenhove. 5 vols. Brussels, 1964-66.

334. Belgium, Ministry of Foreign Affairs. The Official Account of What Happened, 1939-1940. New York, 1940.

Foreign coloured books for the period 1918-45 are numerous and often difficult to locate; others on the immediate origins and early years of the war include France, Ministère des Affaires Etrangères, Le Livre Jaune Français: Documents diplomatiques, 1938-1939, Pièces relatives aux événements et aux négociations qui ont précédé l'ouverture des hostilités entre l'Allemagne d'une part, la Pologne, la Grande-Bretagne et la France d'autre part (Paris, 1939); (Eng. trans., London, 1940); Germany, Auswärtiges Amt, Dokumente zur Vorgeschichte des Krieges, Weissbuch 1940, Nr. 3 (Berlin, 1939); one of several such German publications; Greece, Ministry of Foreign Affairs, The Greek White Book: Diplomatic Documents Relating to Italy's Aggression against Greece (London, 1942); Netherlands, Ministry of Foreign Affairs, Netherlands Orange Book: Summary of the Principal Matters Dealt with . . . in Connection with the State of War . . . . (Leiden, 1940); Poland, Ministry of Foreign Affairs, The Polish White Book: Official Documents Concerning Polish-German and Polish-Soviet Relations, 1933-1939 (London, 1940).

335. Canada, Department of External Affairs. Documents on Canadian External Relations. Vol. 1-. Ottawa, Ontario, 1967-.

Vols. 2-10 cover period 1919-45.

336. France, Ministère des Affaires Etrangères. Documents diplomatiques français, 1932-1939. Paris, 1963-.

Series 1 for July 1932-Dec. 1935; series 2 for Jan. 1936-39.

337. Germany, Auswärtiges Amt. Documents on German Foreign Policy, 1918-1945. Edited by an Anglo-French-American Board of Editors. Five series. Washington and London, 1949-.

English translation for Series C, to cover Jan. 1933-Aug. 1937; Series D, complete in 13 vols., covers Sept. 1937-Dec. 1941; German only, Akten zur deutschen auswärtigen Politik, 1918-1945 (Baden-Baden and Göttingen, 1950-), for Series A, to cover 1918-

Nov. 1925; Series B, covers Dec. 1925-Jan. 1933; Series E, complete in 8 vols., covers Dec. 1941-45.

338.   Hungary, Ministry of Foreign Affairs. Papers and Documents Relating to the Foreign Relations of Hungary. Budapest, 1939-46.

Two vols., covering 1919-Aug. 1921 published; continued in other publications; see for example Institute of History of the Hungarian Academy of Sciences, Diplomáciai iratok Magyarország külpolitikájahoz, 1936-1945, edited by László Zsigmond (Budapest, 1962-); 5 vols. to 1982; the last volume covering 1940-41.

339.   Italy, Ministero degli Affari Esteri, Commissione per la Pubblicazione dei Documenti Diplomatici. I documenti diplomatici italiani, 1861-1943. Nine series. Rome, 1952-.

Series 6, 1918-22; Series 7, 1922-35; Series 8, 1935-39; Series 9, 1939-43.

340.   Netherlands, Departement van Buitenlandse Zaken. Documenten betreffende de buitenlandse politiek van Nederland, 1919-1945. Three series. 's Gravenhage, 1976-.

Series A, 1919-30; Series B, 1931-40; Series C, 1940-45.

341.   New Zealand, Department of Internal Affairs. Documents Relating to New Zealand's Participation in the Second World War, 1939-1945. 3 vols. Wellington, 1949-63.

342.   Portugal, Ministério dos Negócios Estrangeiros. Dez anos de política externa, 1936-1947: A nação portuguesa e a segunda guerra mundial. Lisbon, 1961-.

Vol. 1 for relations with Britain, 1936-39; additional documentation in following volumes.

343.   Reparation Commission. Official Documents. 23 vols. London, 1922-30.

344.   Switzerland, Commission Nationale pour la Publication de Documents Diplomatiques Suisses. Documents diplomatiques suisses, 1848-1945. Bern, 1979-.

In progress; vols. 7-10 for Nov. 1918-Dec. 1933.

345. United States, Department of State. Foreign Relations of the United States: Diplomatic Papers. Washington, DC, 1861-.

Until 1931 entitled Papers Relating to the Foreign Relations of the United States; complete for 1918-45; see too Cumulated Index to the U.S. Department of State Papers Relating to the Foreign Relations of the United States, 1939-1945, 2 vols. (White Plains, NY, 1981).

346. USSR, Ministerstvo Inostrannikh Del SSSR. Dokumenty vneshnei politiki SSSR. Edited by A.A. Gromyko et al. 21 vols. Moscow, 1957-77.

Documents from Soviet archives and foreign sources; covers the period 1917-38.

347. USSR and Czechoslovakia, Academiia Nauk SSSR i Chekhoslovatskaia Academiia Nauk. Dokumenty i materialy po istorii Sovetsko-Chekhoslovatskikh otnoshenii. Moscow, 1973-.

Vols. 1-4 for Nov. 1917-May 1945; vol. 5 to Feb. 1948.

348. USSR and German Democratic Republic, Ministerstvo Inostrannikh Del SSSR i Ministerstvo Inostrannikh Del GDR. Sovetsko-Germanskie otnosheniia ot peregovorov v Brest-Litovske do podpisaniia rapallskogo dogovora. 2 vols. Moscow, 1968-71.

See also USSR and German Democratic Republic, Ministerstvo Inostrannikh Del SSSR i Ministerstvo Inostrannikh Del GDR, Sovestsko-Germanskie otnosheniia, 1922-1925 gg., 2 vols. (Moscow, 1977).

349. USSR and Poland, Academiia Nauk SSSR i Polskaia Academiia Nauk. Dokumenty i materialy po istorii sovetsko-polskikh otnoshenii. Vol. 1-. Moscow, 1963-.

Vols. 1-8 for Feb. 1917-Dec. 1945.

350. Vatican, Secrétairerie d'Etat. Actes et documents du Saint Siège relatifs à la seconde guerre mondiale. Edited by Pierre Blet et al. 11 vols. Rome, 1965-81.

4. Unofficial British Documents

For the intending researcher there are now available some important collections of previously unpublished documents from the Public Record Office. These are in addition to the many collections from Foreign Office files which can be consulted on microform.

351.   Foreign Office. British Documents on Foreign Affairs: Reports and Papers from the Foreign Office Confidential Print. Edited by Kenneth Bourne and D. Cameron Watt. Frederick, MD, 1984-.

         Part 2 subtitled: From the First to the Second World War; eventually to comprise more than 420 volumes; subdivided by 11 geographic and subject series, including the Soviet Union, the Middle East, North America, Latin America, Asia, Europe, the Paris peace conference, and the League of Nations; reprints of the Confidential Print comprising important telegrams and other reports printed originally for limited circulation by the Foreign Office.

352.   ————. Weekly Political Intelligence Summaries, 1939-1947. 16 vols. London, 1983.

         Originally prepared by the Political Intelligence Department (later the Research Department) of the Foreign Office; contains 416 individual summaries.

5. British Official Histories

Historical works, sponsored by the British government and published under its auspices, are known as official histories. For the first world war the British government commissioned mainly military histories. A series of economic and social histories was sponsored and published by the Carnegie Endowment for International Peace. In 1942 the British war cabinet decided that a series of civil histories should be commissioned, covering the economic, administrative and social experience of the war. Initially, these histories were intended for confidential use, their purpose being "to fund experience for Government use." A military series, including studies of foreign policy and intelligence, and a medical series were added after the war. At that time it was decided to release all these volumes to the public. The original publication dates, constrained by the then existing 50-year rule, included references only to publicly available documents. Reprints of many of these volumes, however, are now available with source references to confidential departmental files once again a part of the text.

BRITISH OFFICIAL HISTORIES

Guides and Historiography

353.   Butler, J.R.M. "The British Official Military History of the Second World War." Military Affairs, 22(1958), 149-51.

   See also Sir James E. Edmonds and "Pardon," "The British Official Histories of the Two World Wars," Army Quarterly, 64(1952), 196-205.

354.   Connell, John. "Official History and the Unofficial Historian." Journal of the Royal United Services Institution, 110(1965), 329-34.

355.   Higham, Robin, ed. Official Histories: Essays and Bibliographies from around the World. Manhattan, KS, 1970.

   A survey by country of official histories.

356.   HMSO. Histories of the First and Second World Wars: Government Publications Sectional List, no. 60. London, 1982.

   Complete annotated list of British official histories; notes which are still in print, reprints and prices.

Official Histories

357.   Edmonds, Sir James E. The Occupation of the Rhineland, 1918-1929. London, 1987.

   A facsimile edition from HMSO of the account first published in 1944 and limited to 100 copies.

358.   Foot, M.R.D. SOE in France: An Account of the Work of the British Special Operations Executive in France, 1940-1944. London, 1966.

   An official history, though not part of the series edited by Sir James Butler, based on surviving SOE files held by the Foreign and Commonwealth Office which commissioned the work; see also the companion volumes by Charles Cruickshank, SOE in Scandinavia (London, 1986); and SOE in the Far East (London, 1983).

359.   Hinsley, F.H., et al. British Intelligence in the Second World War: Its Influence on Strategy and Operations. 5 vols. London, 1979-90.

Not published by HMSO, but an official history; vol. 1 from Sept. 1939-June 1941; vol. 2, June 1941-43 (1981); vol. 3, part 1, from mid-1943 to mid-1944; part 2, from D–day planning to the end of the war; with bibliography and appendixes; vol. 4, Security and Counter Intelligence (London, 1990); and vol. 5, Strategic Deception (London, 1990).

360.   History of the Second World War: United Kingdom Civil Series. Edited by Sir Keith Hancock. London, HMSO, 1949-62.

Relevant volumes include C.B.A. Behrens, Merchant Shipping and the Demands of War (London, 1955, repr. 1978); Central Statistical Office, Statistical Digest of the War (London, 1951, repr. 1975); H. Duncan Hall, North American Supply (London, 1956, repr. 1982); H. Duncan Hall et al., Studies of Overseas Supply (London, 1956, repr. 1982); W.K. Hancock and M.M. Gowing, British War Economy (London, 1949, repr. 1975); William N. Medlicott, Economic Blockade, 2 vols. (London, 1952-59, repr. 1978); T.H. O'Brien, Civil Defence (London, 1955, repr. 1982); D.J. Payton-Smith, Oil: A Study in Wartime Policy and Administration (London, 1971); M.M. Postan, British War Production (London, 1952, repr. 1975); M.M. Postan et al., Design and Development of Weapons (London, 1964, repr. 1971); R.S. Sayers, Financial Policy, 1939-1945 (London, 1956, repr. 1982); and J.D. Scott and Richard Hughes, Administration of War Production (London, 1955, repr. 1982); reprints contain source references.

361.   History of the Second World War: United Kingdom Military Histories. Edited by Sir James Butler. London, HMSO, 1952-.

Relevant selected volumes include Basil Collier, The Defence of the United Kingdom (London, 1957); F.S.V. Donnison, Civil Affairs and Military Government: Central Organisation and Planning (London, 1966); his British Military Administration in the Far East, 1943-1946 (London, 1956); and Civil Affairs and Military Government in North-West Europe, 1944-1946 (London, 1961); Major L.F. Ellis et al., Victory in the West, 1944-1945, 2 vols. (London, 1962-69); and his The War in France and Flanders, 1939-1940 (London, 1953); Norman H. Gibbs et al., Grand Strategy, 1933-August 1945, 6 vols. (London, 1956-76, vols. 2, 6, repr. 1974); C.R.S. Harris, Allied Military Administration of Italy, 1943-1945 (London, 1957); Major-General S. Woodburn Kirby et al., The War Against Japan, 5 vols. (London, 1962-69); Major-General I.S.O. Playfair et al., The Mediterranean and the Middle East, 6 vols. (London, 1954-87, vols. 1-5, repr. 1967-84); Captain Stephen W. Roskill, The War at Sea, 1939-1945, 3 vols. (London,

1954-61); and Sir Charles Webster and Noble Frankland, <u>The Strategic Air Offensive against Germany, 1939-1945</u>, 4 vols. (London, 1961); reprints contain source references.

362. Richards, Denis, and Saunders, Hilary St. G. <u>History of the Royal Air Force, 1939-1945</u>. 3 vols. London, 1953-54, repr. 1975.

Part of the HMSO series "Popular Military History."

363. Woodward, Sir Llewellyn. <u>British Foreign Policy in the Second World War</u>. 5 vols. London, 1971-76.

The complete text with footnotes and references; single–volume abridgement, with amendments but without references, published as <u>British Foreign Policy in the Second World War</u> (London, 1962, repr. 1972); both official histories, not part of the series edited by Sir James Butler, written under the auspices of the Cabinet Office.

C. MEMOIRS AND BIOGRAPHIES

Memoirs, diaries and collections of speeches and letters are a valuable source for the British diplomatic historian. Two aspects, however, pose immediate problems. Firstly, this literature is voluminous. Despite a propensity towards reticence and understatement in public life, former British officials seemingly cannot help putting pen to paper in retirement. A second problem relates to the quality of this memorialist output. As in all other branches of literature, it is naturally of uneven quality. But the researcher would be cautioned against treating this material lightly. In many cases, the reticence and understatement, carried into the written material, barely disguises revelations of the utmost value. In other words, British diplomatic memoirs must be read very carefully and between the lines. The rewards are often most gratifying.

The entries for this literature given below are necessarily selective. An attempt has been made to note only material having direct bearing on the foreign policymaking process and its implementation. This is most widely interpreted in the case of British publications. There follows, in addition, a selection of non-British materials. Here the entries have been limited to non-British diplomats and officials posted, at some point, to London.

It should be noted that career annotations are confined mainly to highlights between 1918 and 1945. Entries followed by an asterisk indicate that the writer has been the subject of a biography listed below in the biographical section, pages 161-85.

1. Memoirs, Diaries, Speeches and Letters

British

364.   Addison, Christopher (1st Viscount Addison).* Politics from Within, 1911-1918. 2 vols. London, 1924,

Diary-based memoir of first minister of Health, 1919-21; minister without portfolio, 1921; minister of Agriculture and Fisheries, 1929-31; see also his Four and a Half Years: A Personal Diary from June 1914 to January 1919, 2 vols. (London, 1934).

MEMOIRS

365.   Alexander, 1st Earl, of Tunis (Field-Marshal Sir Harold R.L.G. Alexander).* The Alexander Memoirs, 1940-1945. Edited by John North. London, 1962.

General officer commanding, Burma, 1942; commander-in-chief, Middle East, 1942-43; deputy commander-in-chief, North Africa, 1943; general officer commanding allied forces in Sicily, 1943-44; commander-in-chief, allied armies in Italy, 1944.

366.   Amery, Julian. Approach March: A Venture in Autobiography. London, 1973.

Described as his "pre-political memoirs" (Preface); attaché British legation, Belgrade, 1939-40; with Albanian resistance, 1944; see also his Sons of the Eagle (London, 1948).

367.   Amery, Leopold C.M.S. My Political Life. 3 vols. London, 1953-55.

Memoirs by an independent Conservative; first lord of the Admiralty, 1922-24; secretary of state for the Colonies, 1924-29; and for Dominion Affairs, 1925-29; see also his The German Colonial Claim (London, 1939); and John Barnes and David Nicholson, eds., The Leo Amery Diaries, vol. 1, 1896-1929 (London, 1980); vol. 2, 1929-1945, edited by John Barnes and David Nicholson (London, 1988); includes diaries, and papers.

368.   Angell, Sir Norman.* After All. London, 1951.

From the founder of the Union of Democratic Control; proponent of the League of Nations, briefly an MP, and winner of the Nobel peace prize for 1933; author of more than 40 books including the widely translated The Great Illusion (London, 1910); and Peace with the Dictators? (London, 1938).

369.   Asquith, Herbert Henry (1st Earl of Oxford and Asquith).* Memories and Reflections, 1852-1927. 2 vols. London, 1928.

Wartime prime minister until 1916, and leader of the Liberal party until 1926; vol. 2 for postwar period; background in his Fifty Years of Parliament, 2 vols. (London, 1926); see also Speeches (London, 1927); and H.H. Asquith: Letters to Venetia Stanley, edited by Michael and Eleanor Brock (London, 1982); of related interest is Margot Asquith, Autobiography, 2 vols. (London, 1920-22); More Memories (London, 1933); and Off the Record (London, 1943).

370.   Atholl, Duchess of (Katharine Marjory Stewart-Murray). Working Partnership. London, 1958.

Parliamentary secretary, Board of Education, 1924-29; resigned parliamentary seat in protest against appeasement, 1938.

371.   Attlee, Clement Richard (1st Earl Attlee).* As It Happened. London, 1954.

Member of both pre-world war two Labour governments; leader of the Labour party, 1935-55; lord privy seal, 1940-42; deputy prime minister, 1942-45; prime minister, 1945-51; see also his War Comes to Britain: Speeches of the Rt. Hon. C.R. Attlee, M.P., edited by John Dugdale (London, 1940); and Purpose and Policy: Selected Speeches, May 1945-November 1946 (London, 1947).

372.   Avon, 1st Earl of (Robert Anthony Eden).* The Eden Memoirs. 3 vols. London, 1960-65.

Carefully written memoirs, based on private papers and government archives, of an MP, 1923-57; various positions in area of foreign affairs, 1926-35; secretary of state for Foreign Affairs, 1935-38; for Dominion Affairs, 1939-40; for War, 1940; for Foreign Affairs, 1940-45; later prime minister, 1955-57; memoirs written in reverse order; hence vol. 2, Facing the Dictators, examines the 1930s; vol. 3, The Reckoning, covers wartime affairs; collected speeches and articles include Places in the Sun (London, 1926); with preface by Stanley Baldwin; Foreign Affairs (London, 1939); Freedom and Order: Selected Speeches 1939-1946 (London, 1947); for an understanding of the personality, see his Another World, 1897-1917 (London, 1976).

373.   Bailey, Frederick Marshman. Mission to Tashkent. London, 1946.

Served world war one; political officer in Mesopotamia and Persia, 1917-18; mission in central Asia, 1918-20; political officer, Sikkim, 1921-28; minister to the court of Nepal, 1935-38; see also his No Passport to Tibet (London, 1957).

374.   Baker, Arthur. The House Is Sitting. London, 1958.

Chief of the parliamentary staff of The Times, 1934-55.

375.   Baldwin, 1st Earl, of Bewdley (Stanley Baldwin)*. This Torch of Freedom: Speeches and Addresses. London, 1935.

President of the Board of Trade, 1921-22; chancellor of the Exchequer, 1922-23; prime minister, 1923-24, 1924-29, 1935-37; lord president of the Council, 1931-35; other collections are On England (London, 1926); Our Inheritance (London, 1928); Service of Our Lives (London, 1937); and An Interpreter of England (London, 1939).

376.   Balfour, Arthur James (1st Earl of Balfour).* Opinions and Arguments from Speeches and Addresses of the Earl of Balfour, 1910-1927. London, 1927.

Prime minister, 1902-05; foreign secretary, 1916-19; lord president of the Council, 1919-22, 1925-29; see also his Chapters of Autobiography, edited by Mrs. Edgar [Blanche] Dugdale (London, 1930).

377.   Balfour, Harold (1st Baron Balfour of Inchrye). Wings over Westminster. London, 1973.

MP, 1929-45; parliamentary under-secretary of state for Air, 1938-44; minister resident in west Africa, 1944-45.

378.   Balfour, Sir John. Not Too Correct an Aureole: The Recollections of a Diplomat. Salisbury, 1983.

Served at Budapest, Sofia, Belgrade, Madrid and Washington, 1919-41; minister at Lisbon, 1941-43; and Moscow, 1943-45.

379.   Barclay, Sir Roderick Edward. Ernest Bevin and the Foreign Office, 1932-1969. London, 1975.

A memoir despite the title; entered diplomatic service, 1932; served at embassies in Brussels, Paris, Washington, and in Foreign Office, 1932-46; counsellor in Foreign Office, 1946-49.

380.   Barnes, George Nicoll. From Workshop to War Cabinet. London, 1924.

MP, 1906-22; minister plenipotentiary, Paris peace conference, 1919; minister without portfolio, 1919.

381.   Bartlett, Vernon. I Know What I Liked. London, 1974.

An autobiographical work from a very prolific writer, broadcaster, journalist and MP; London director of the League of Nations secretariat, 1922-32; see too his And Now, Tomorrow (London,

1960); This Is My Life (London, 1937); and Behind the Scenes at the Paris Peace Conference, 1919 (London, 1919).

382.   Bayford, 1st Baron (Sir Robert Sanders). Real Old Tory Politics: The Political Diaries of Sir Robert Sanders, Lord Bayford, 1910-1935. Edited by John Ramsden. London, 1984.

MP, 1910-23, 1924-29; junior lord of the Treasury, 1919; undersecretary for War, 1921-22.

383.   Beadon, Colonel Roger Hammet. Some Memories of the Peace Conference. London, 1933.

With British delegation to Paris peace conference, 1919; employed by Colonial Office in Iraq, 1925-28.

384.   Beatty, David (Admiral of the Fleet 1st Earl Beatty).* The Beatty Papers: Selections from the Private and Official Correspondence of Admiral of the Fleet Earl Beatty, vol. 1-, 1902-1918. Edited by Bryan Ranft. London, 1989-.

Accepted surrender of German fleet, 1918; first sea lord, 1919-27.

385.   Bell, Sir Gawain. Shadows on the Sand: Memoirs. London, 1983.

Sudan political service, 1931; seconded to the government of Palestine, 1938; with Arab Legion, 1942-45.

386.   Bentwich, Norman, and Bentwich, Helen. Mandate Memories, 1918-1948. London, 1964.

Director of High Commission for Refugees from Germany, 1933-35; attorney-general, government of Palestine, 1920-31; among his numerous books see also My Seventy-Seven Years (London, 1962).

387.   Bilainkin, George. Diary of a Diplomatic Correspondent. London, 1942.

Excerpts for 1940; diplomatic correspondent for the Allied newspaper chain; see also his Second Diary of a Diplomatic Correspondent (London, 1947).

388.   Birse, A.H. Memoirs of an Interpreter. London, 1967.

Foreword by Lord Avon; joined intelligence department of War Office, 1940; Russian-language interpreter for Winston Churchill at major wartime conferences.

389.   Boothby, Baron (Robert J.G. Boothby). Recollections of a Rebel. London, 1978.

Often in the public eye, but rarely in office; MP, 1924-58; parliamentary private secretary to Winston Churchill, 1926-29; parliamentary secretary, minister of Food, 1940-41; see also the earlier memoir, I Fight to Live (London, 1947); and the collection of articles, speeches and sketches in My Yesterday, Your Tomorrow (London, 1962).

390.   Brabazon, 1st Baron, of Tara (John T.C. Moore Brabazon). The Brabazon Story. London, 1956.

Parliamentary secretary, ministry of Transport, 1923-24, 1924-27; minister of Transport, 1940-41; minister of Aircraft Production, 1941-42.

391.   Bridgeman, William Clive (1st Viscount Bridgeman of Leigh). The Modernisation of Conservative Politics: The Diaries and Letters of William Bridgeman, 1904-1935. Edited by Philip Williamson. London, 1988.

MP, 1906-29; parliamentary secretary, Board of Trade, 1919-20; secretary of Mines, 1920-22; home secretary, 1922-24; first lord of the Admiralty, 1924-29.

392.   Bridges, Sir Tom. Alarms and Excursions: Reminiscences of a Soldier. London, 1938.

Military member of Balfour mission, 1917; head of British Mission Allied Armies of the Orient, 1918-20.

393.   Brockway, Baron (Archibald Fenner Brockway). Inside the Left: Thirty Years of Platform, Press, Prison and Parliament. London, 1942.

Antiwar activist; prolific writer; and prominent ILP and Labour party member; continued in Outside the Right (London, 1963); see also Towards Tomorrow (London, 1977), and 98 Not Out (London, 1986).

394.   Brownrigg, Lieutenant-General Sir W. Douglas S. Unexpected: A
        Book of Memories. London, 1942.

        At War Office and in China, 1919-31; commander various brigades,
        1931-38; military secretary, secretary of state for War, 1938-39;
        adjutant-general to BEF, 1939-40.

395.   Bruce, Henry James. Silken Dalliance. 1946.

        Secretary-general, British delegation, interallied commission for
        Bulgaria, 1921; British delegate, 1924-26; adviser, National Bank
        of Hungary, 1931; see also his Thirty Dozen Moons (London,
        1949).

396.   Buchan, John (1st Baron Tweedsmuir).* Memory Hold-the-Door.
        London, 1940.

        Subordinate director, ministry of Information, 1917-18; MP, 1927-
        35; governor-general, Canada, 1935-40.

397.   Buchanan, Sir George William. My Mission to Russia and Other
        Diplomatic Memories. 2 vols. London, 1923.

        Ambassador to Russia, 1910-18; Italy, 1919-21.

398.   Bullard, Sir Reader William. The Camels Must Go: An
        Autobiography. London, 1961.

        Consul at Jedda, 1923-25; Athens, 1925-28; Addis Ababa, 1928;
        Moscow, 1930; Leningrad, 1931-34; Rabat, 1934; minister at
        Jedda, 1936-39; and Tehran, 1939-46; see also his Letters from
        Teheran (London, 1990).

399.   Busk, Sir Douglas Laird. The Craft of Diplomacy. London, 1967.

        Joined diplomatic service, 1929; served in Foreign Office and
        Tehran, Budapest, Moscow, Tokyo, Ankara and Baghdad; later
        ambassador to Ethiopia, 1952-56.

400.   Butler, Sir Harold Beresford. Confident Morning. London, 1950.

        Attended Paris peace conference, 1919; deputy-director and later
        director International Labour Office, 1920-38; minister in charge of
        British Information Services, Washington, 1942-46; see also his
        The Lost Peace: A Personal Impression (London, 1941).

MEMOIRS

401. Butler, R.A. "Rab" (1st Baron Butler).* The Art of the Possible. London, 1971.

MP, 1929-65; under-secretary of state for Foreign Affairs, 1938-41; minister of Education, 1941-45; to be read with his The Difficult Art of Autobiography (London, 1968); additional reminiscences, including a sketch of Lord Halifax, in The Art of Memory: Friends in Perspective (London, 1982).

402. Cadogan, Sir Alexander. The Diaries of Sir Alexander Cadogan, O.M., 1938-1945. Edited by David Dilks. London, 1971.

Indispensable diaries of the permanent under-secretary of state for Foreign Affairs, 1938-46.

403. Cameron, Sir Donald. My Tanganyika Service and Some Nigeria. Edited by Robert Heussler. 2nd ed. New York, 1982.

Colonial administrator; governor and commander-in-chief of Tanganyika Territory, 1925-31; of Nigeria, 1931-35.

404. Campbell, Sir Gerald. Of True Experience. London, 1949.

Consul-general various cities in the United States, 1920-38; high commissioner in Canada, 1938-41; director-general, British Information Services, New York, 1941-42; minister at Washington, 1942-45.

405. Carton de Wiart, Sir Adrian. Happy Odyssey. London, 1950.

Served both world wars; head of British military mission in Poland, 1939.

406. Cecil, 1st Viscount, of Chelwood (E.A. Robert Cecil).* A Great Experiment. London, 1941.

Assistant secretary of state for Foreign Affairs, 1918; minister of Blockade, 1916-18; lord privy seal, 1923-24; chancellor of the Duchy of Lancaster, 1924-27; Nobel peace prize, 1937; see also his All the Way (London, 1949).

407. Chamberlain, Sir Austen.* Down the Years. London, 1935.

MP, 1892-1937; chancellor of the Exchequer, 1919-21; lord privy seal, 1921-22; foreign secretary, 1924-29; Nobel peace prize, 1925;

first lord of the Admiralty, 1931; see also his earlier Peace in Our Time: Addresses on Europe and the Empire (London, 1928).

408. Chamberlain, Neville.* In Search of Peace: Speeches, 1937-1938. Edited by Arthur Bryant. London, 1939.

An essential collection by the minister of Health, 1923, 1924-29, 1931; chancellor of the Exchequer, 1923-24, 1931-37; prime minister, 1937-40; lord president of the Council, 1940; see also the expanded version The Struggle for Peace (London, 1939).

409. Chandos, 1st Viscount (Oliver Lyttleton). The Memoirs of Lord Chandos. London, 1962.

MP, 1940-54; president of the Board of Trade, 1940-41; minister of state and member of the war cabinet, 1942-45; for family and personal background, see his From Peace to War: A Study in Contrast, 1857-1918 (London, 1968).

410. Channon, Sir Henry. Chips: The Diaries of Sir Henry Channon. Edited by Robert Rhodes James. London, 1967.

MP, 1935-58; parliamentary private secretary to under-secretary of state for Foreign Affairs, 1938-41.

411. Chatfield, 1st Baron (Admiral of the Fleet Alfred E.M. Chatfield). The Navy and Defence. London, 1942.

Supplemented by It Might Happen Again (London, 1947); first sea lord and chief of naval staff, 1933-38; minister for Co-ordination of Defence, 1939-40.

412. Churchill, Sir Winston Spencer.* Winston S. Churchill: His Complete Speeches, 1897-1963. Edited by Robert Rhodes James. 8 vols. London, 1974.

A nearly definitive collection of speeches by the secretary for War and Air, 1919-21; secretary for Air and Colonies, 1921; Colonial secretary, 1921-22; chancellor of the Exchequer, 1924-29; first lord of the Admiralty, 1939-40; prime minister and minister of Defence, 1940-45; prime minister, 1951-55; condensed version in Churchill Speaks: Winston S. Churchill in Peace and War, Collected Speeches, 1897-1963 (London, 1980); see also The Collected Essays of Sir Winston Churchill, 4 vols. (London, 1976); Churchill's own style of memoir-histories, copiously documented,

MEMOIRS

are The World Crisis, 1914-1918, 4 vols. (London, 1923-27); and The Second World War, 6 vols. (London, 1948-54).

413.   Citrine, Walter M. (1st Baron Citrine). Men and Work: An Autobiography. London, 1964.

Sequel in Two Careers (London, 1967); from the general-secretary of the Trades Union Congress, 1926-46; see also his I Search for Truth in Russia (London, 1938); and My American Diary (London, 1941).

414.   Clayton, Sir Gilbert Falkingham. An Arabian Diary. Edited by Robert O. Collins. Berkeley, CA, 1969.

Adviser to ministry of Interior, Egypt, 1919-22; chief secretary, Palestine, 1922-25; negotiated treaty of Jeddah, 1927.

415.   Cleugh, Eric Arthur. Without Let or Hindrance: Reminiscences of a British Foreign Service Officer. London, 1960.

Consular service, 1919; vice-consul, Paris, 1924-28; consul in New York, 1935-39; and Los Angeles, 1939-45.

416.   Clynes, John Robert. Memoirs: 1869-1937. 2 vols. London, 1937.

Food controller, 1918-19; lord privy seal, 1924; secretary of state for Home Affairs, 1929-31.

417.   Cockburn, Claud. In Time of Trouble: An Autobiography. London, 1956.

Continued in Crossing the Line (London, 1958); and View from the West (London, 1961); controversial reminiscences from the editor of The Week, 1933-46; and diplomatic correspondent of the Daily Worker, 1935-46; selected journalism in Cockburn in Spain, edited by James Pettifer (London, 1986); see also Patricia Cockburn, The Years of "The Week" (London, 1968); and her memoir, Figure of Eight (London, 1985).

418.   Cockerill, Sir George Kynaston. What Fools We Were. London, 1944.

Director of special intelligence, 1915-19; MP, 1918-31.

419.   Collier, Sir Laurence. Flight from Conflict. London, 1944.

Served in Foreign Office, 1913-41; minister to Norway, 1941; ambassador to Norwegian government, 1942-50.

420.   Colville, Sir John. The Fringes of Power: 10 Downing Street Diaries, 1939-1955. London, 1985.

Assistant private secretary to Neville Chamberlain, 1939-40; to Winston Churchill, 1940-41, 1943-45; and to Clement Attlee, 1945; see also the pen portraits of contemporaries in his The Churchillians (London, 1981); and Footprints in Time: Memories (London, 1976).

421.   Cooper, Alfred Duff (1st Viscount Norwich).* Old Men Forget. London, 1953.

With War Office and Treasury, 1928-35; secretary of state for War, 1935-37; first lord of the Admiralty, 1937-38; minister of Information, 1940-41; chancellor of the Duchy of Lancaster, 1941-43; the Munich crisis' most famous resignation; see also some of his collected press writings in The Second World War: First Phase (London, 1939); and of related interest, Lady Diana Cooper, The Light of Common Day (London, 1959); and A Durable Fire: The Letters of Duff and Diana Cooper, 1913-1950, edited by Artemis Cooper (London, 1983).

422.   Craigie, Sir Robert. Behind the Japanese Mask. London, 1946.

Entered Foreign Office, 1907; counsellor, then assistant under-secretary of state, 1928-37; ambassador to Japan, 1937-41.

423.   Crawford, 27th Earl of (David Lindsay). The Crawford Papers, 1892 to 1940. Edited by John Vincent. Manchester, 1984.

Lord privy seal, 1916-19; chancellor of the Duchy of Lancaster, 1919-21; first commissioner of Works and minister of Transport, 1921-22.

424.   Croft, 1st Baron (Henry Page Croft). My Life of Strife. London, 1948.

MP, 1910-40; joint parliamentary under-secretary of state for War, 1940-45; see also his Spain: The Truth at Last (London, 1937).

425.   Crosby, Sir Josiah. Siam: The Crossroads. London, 1945.

Minister in Panama, 1931-34; Siam, 1934-41.

426.   Crozier, Brigadier-General Frank Percy. A Brass Hat in No Man's Land. London, 1930.

Served with the Lithuanian army against Germany, 1919; against Bolsheviks, 1919-20; and on Polish front, 1919-20.

427.   Crozier, William P. Off the Record: Political Interviews, 1933-1943. Edited by A.J.P. Taylor. London, 1973

Transcripts of interviews by the editor of the Manchester Guardian, 1932-44.

428.   Cunningham, 1st Viscount, of Hyndhope (Admiral of the Fleet Andrew Browne Cunningham).* A Sailor's Odyssey. London, 1951.

Deputy chief of naval staff, 1938-39; ccmmander-in-chief, Mediterranean, 1939; chief of naval staff, 1943-46.

429.   D'Abernon, 1st Viscount (Edgar Vincent). An Ambassador of Peace: Pages from the Diary of Viscount D'Abernon. 3 vols. London, 1929-30.

Began diplomatic career in 1880; ambassador at Berlin, 1920-26; see also his Portraits and Appreciations (London, 1931); and Viscountess D'Abernon, Red Cross and Berlin Embassy, 1915-1926 (London, 1946).

430.   Dalton, Hugh (Baron Dalton).* Memoirs. 3 vols. London, 1953-62.

Parliamentary under-secretary, Foreign Office, 1929-31; minister of Economic Warfare, 1940-42; president of Bcard of Trade, 1942-45; vols. 1 and 2 for 1887-1945; see also The Political Diary of Hugh Dalton, 1918-1940, 1945-1960 (London, 1987) and The Second World War Diary of Hugh Dalton, 1940-1945 (London, 1986), both edited by Ben Pimlott; of interest is Hugh Dalton's Hitler's War: Before and After (London, 1940).

431.   Davies, Sir Joseph. The Prime Minister's Secretariat, 1916-1920. Newport, 1951.

Secretary, prime minister's secretariat, 1917-20. MP, 1918-22.

432.   De Chair, Somerset. The Golden Carpet. London, 1944.

MP, 1935-45; parliamentary private secretary (unpaid) to Oliver Lyttelton, 1942-44; prolific novelist and commentator; see his The Impending Storm (London, 1930); and Divided Europe (London, 1931).

433.   De Guingand, Sir Francis. From Brass Hat to Bowler Hat. London, 1979.

Entered army, 1919; military assistant to secretary of state for War, 1939-40; director of military intelligence, Middle East, 1942; chief of staff, 8th army, 1942-44; 21st army group, 1944-45; see also his Operation Victory (London, 1947); and Generals at War (1964).

434.   Delmer, Sefton. An Autobiography. 2 vols. London, 1961-62.

Diplomatic and war correspondent of Daily Express, 1927-40; at Foreign Office, 1941-45; engaged in "black propaganda"; see also his The Counterfeit Spy (London, 1973).

435.   Denham, Henry. Inside the Nazi Ring: A Naval Attaché in Sweden, 1940-1945. London, 1984.

Naval attaché, Denmark, 1940; Stockholm, 1940-47.

436.   Domville, Admiral Sir Barry Edward. By and Large. London, 1936.

Director of naval intelligence division, Admiralty, 1927-30; president, Royal Naval College, Greenwich, 1932-34; active in right-wing organisations; autobiography continued in Look to Your Moat (London, 1937); and From Admiral to Cabin Boy (London, 1947).

437.   Douglas, Baron, of Kirtleside (Marshal of the Royal Air Force William Sholto Douglas). Years of Combat. London, 1963.

Assistant chief of air staff, 1938-40; chief of air staff, 1940; air officer commanding-in-chief, various commands, 1940-45; sequel in Years of Command (London, 1966).

438.   Dreyer, Admiral Sir Frederic Charles. The Sea Heritage. London, 1955.

Assistant chief of naval staff, 1924-27; deputy chief of naval staff, 1930-33; commander-in-chief, China station, 1933-36; temporary chief of naval air services, 1942.

439. Driberg, Tom. A Ruling Passion. London, 1977.

Journalist (Hickey columnist) with Daily Express; MP, 1942-55; see also his Colonnade, 1937-1947 (London, 1949).

440. Dugdale, Blanche. Baffy: The Diaries of Blanche Dugdale, 1936-1947. Edited by Norman Rose. London, 1973.

A.J. Balfour's niece and biographer; active in League of Nations Union.

441. Dukes, Sir Paul. The Unending Quest: Autobiographical Sketches. London, 1950.

Intelligence service in Russia, 1918-20; The Times correspondent, 1921.

442. Eccles, 1st Viscount (David McAdam Eccles). Life and Politics: A Moral Diagnosis. London, 1967.

MP, 1943-62; economic adviser to ambassadors at Madrid and Lisbon, 1940-42; ministry of Production, 1942-43; see also Sybil and David Eccles, By Safe Hand (London, 1982).

443. Ede, James Chuter (Baron Chuter-Ede). Labour and the Wartime Coalition: From the Diary of James Chuter Ede, 1941-1945. Edited by Kevin Jefferys. London, 1987.

MP, 1923, 1929-31, 1935-64; parliamentary secretary to minister of Education, 1940-45.

444. Edmonds, Cecil John. Kurds, Turks and Arabs: Politics, Travel and Research in North-Eastern Iraq, 1919-1925. London, 1957.

Entered consular service, 1910; adviser to the ministry of the Interior, Iraq, 1935-45.

445. Einzig, Paul. In the Centre of Things: An Autobiography. London, 1960.

Correspondent with the Financial News, 1921, 1923, 1939-45; prolific author on finance, economics, appeasement, etc.

446.   Ellis, Charles Howard. The Transcaspian Episode, 1918-1919. London, 1963.

Served European war, 1914-19; Foreign Office and consular posts in Turkey, Berlin, Far East and the United States, 1921-39; colonel on staff of missions in the United States, Egypt and Far East, 1939-45.

447.   Esher, 2nd Viscount (Reginald Baliol Brett).* Journals and Letters of Reginald, Viscount Esher, 1870-1930. Edited by Maurice Brett and Oliver Brett. 4 vols. London, 1934-38.

Member, Committee of Imperial Defence, 1905-18; head of a British mission in Paris, 1914-18.

448.   Foot, Sir Hugh. A Start in Freedom. London, 1964.

Colonial service, 1929-42; British military administration, Cyrenaica, 1943; colonial secretary, Cyprus, 1943-45.

449.   Francis-Williams, Baron (Francis Williams). Nothing So Strange: An Autobiography. London, 1970.

Journalist and author; editor of Daily Herald, 1936-40; controller of news and censorship, ministry of Information, 1941-45.

450.   Fremantle, Admiral Sir Sydney R. My Naval Career, 1880-1928. London, 1949.

Deputy-chief of naval staff, 1918-19; commander-in-chief, Portsmouth station, 1923-25.

451.   Fuller, Major-General John F.C.* Memoirs of an Unconventional Soldier. London, 1936.

Staff duties, War Office directorate, 1918-22; military assistant to chief of the imperial general staff, 1926-27; prolific author on military affairs.

452.   Gallacher, William. Revolt on the Clyde: An Autobiography. London, 1936.

Continued in <u>The Last Memoirs of Willie Gallacher</u> (London, 1966); "socialist agitator" (<u>Who's Who</u>); Communist party MP, 1935-50; see also his <u>The Chosen Few: A Sketch of Men and Events in Parliament</u> (London, 1940); and <u>The Rolling of the Thunder</u> (London, 1947).

453.   Geddes, 1st Baron (Auckland Campbell Geddes).* <u>The Forging of a Family</u>. London, 1952.

Minister of National Service, 1919; minister of Reconstruction, 1919; president of the Board of Trade, 1919-20; ambassador at Washington, 1920-24.

454.   Gibbs, Air Marshal Sir Gerald Ernest. <u>Survivor's Story</u>. London, 1956.

Served with RAF, 1918-41; director of overseas operations, Air ministry, 1942-43; senior air staff officer, 3rd tactical air force headquarters, southeast Asia, 1943-44.

455.   Gladwyn, 1st Baron (H.M. Gladwyn Jebb). <u>Memoirs</u>. London, 1972.

Diplomatic service at home and abroad, 1924-40; appointed to ministry of Economic Warfare, 1940; head of Reconstruction Department, 1942; counsellor in Foreign Office, attending wartime conferences, 1943-45.

456.   Glubb, Sir John Bagot.* <u>The Changing Scenes of Life: An Autobiography</u>. London, 1983.

Chief of general staff, the Arab Legion, Jordan, 1939-56; among many others of his books see also his <u>A Soldier with the Arabs</u> (London, 1957).

457.   Goddard, Air Marshal Sir Victor. <u>Skies to Dunkirk: A Personal Memoir</u>. London, 1982.

Served first world war, 1914-18; deputy director of intelligence, Air ministry, 1938-39; chief of air staff, New Zealand, 1941-43; with air command, southeast Asia, 1943-46.

458.   Godley, General Sir Alexander. <u>Life of an Irish Soldier</u>. London, 1939.

Began military service, 1886; military secretary to the secretary of state for War, 1920-22; commander-in-chief, British army on the Rhine, 1922-24; governor and commander-in-chief, Gibraltar, 1928-33.

459.   Gollancz, Sir Victor.* Reminiscences of Affection. London, 1968.

Publisher and writer; founded the Left Book Club, 1936; see also his My Dear Timothy: An Autobiographical Letter to His Grandson (London, 1952); More for Timothy (London, 1953); Is Mr. Chamberlain Saving the Peace? (London, 1939); and Russia and Ourselves (London, 1941).

460.   Gore-Booth, Baron (Sir Paul Henry Gore-Booth). With Great Truth and Respect. London, 1974.

Served Foreign Office, 1933-36; Vienna, 1936-37; Tokyo, 1938-42; and Washington, 1942-45; attended UNRRA conference, 1943; later first permanent under-secretary of the combined Foreign and Commonwealth Office; editor of the 5th edition of Satow's Guide to Diplomatic Practice (London, 1978).

461.   Grafftey-Smith, Sir Laurence Baton. Bright Levant. London, 1970.

Entered consular service, 1914; served at Cairo, 1925-35; consul-general to Albania, 1939-40; minister to Saudi Arabia, 1945-47.

462.   Graham, Walter Gerald Cloete. China through One Pair of Eyes: Reminiscences of a Consular Officer, 1929-1950. London, 1984.

Entered consular service in China, 1928; served in Peking, Nanking, Shanghai, Mukden and Tientsin; consul, Port Said, 1942-44; Chengtu, 1944-45.

463.   Grant Watson, Herbert Adolphus. An Account of a Mission to the Baltic States in the Year 1919. London, 1957.

Employed on special service in the Baltic provinces, 1919; transferred to Lisbon, 1920; counsellor of embassy, 1925; minister to Central American Republics, 1928-33; Cuba, 1933-35; Finland, 1935-37; and Cuba, 1937-40.

464.   Greene, Sir Hugh Carleton. The Third Floor Front. London, 1969.

Daily Telegraph correspondent, expelled from Berlin, 1939; joined BBC, 1940; later headed BBC from 1960-69.

465.   Gregory, John Duncan. On the Edge of Diplomacy: Rambles and Reflections, 1902-1928. London, 1929.

Assistant secretary, Foreign Office, 1920-25; assistant under-secretary of state, Foreign Office, 1925-28.

466.   Grey, 1st Viscount, of Falloden (Sir Edward Grey).* Twenty-Five Years, 1892-1916. 2 vols. London, 1925.

MP, 1885-1916; foreign secretary, 1905-16; president, League of Nations Union, from 1918; temporary ambassador to the United States, 1919.

467.   Griffith-Boscawan, Sir Arthur S.T. Memories. London, 1925.

Minister of Agriculture and Fisheries, 1921-22; minister of Health, 1922-23.

468.   Grigg, P.J. Prejudice and Judgement. London, 1948.

Principal private secretary to successive chancellors of the Exchequer, 1921-30; with Customs and Revenue, and Inland Revenue, 1930-34; finance member of government of India, 1934-39; permanent under-secretary of state for War, 1939-42; secretary of state for War, 1942-45.

469.   Haig, Field-Marshal Sir Douglas (1st Earl Haig).* The Private Papers of Douglas Haig, 1914-1919. Edited by Robert Blake. London, 1952.

Commander-in-chief, BEF, 1915-18; commander-in-chief, home forces, 1919-21.

470.   Hailsham, Baron, of St. Marylebone (Quinton McGarel Hogg). A Sparrow's Flight: The Memoirs of Lord Hailsham of St. Marylebone. London, 1990.

MP, 1938-50; joint parliamentary under-secretary for Air, 1945; see also his The Door Wherein I Went (London, 1975).

471.   Haldane, 1st Viscount, of Cloan (Richard B. Haldane).* An Autobiography. London, 1929.

Lord chancellor, 1912-15, 1924.

472. Halifax, 1st Earl of (Edward Frederick Lindley Wood, 1st Baron Irwin).* Fulness of Days. London, 1957.

President of the Board of Education, 1922-24, 1932-35; minister of Agriculture, 1924-25; viceroy of India, 1926-31; secretary of state for War, 1935; lord privy seal, 1935-37; secretary of state for Foreign Affairs, 1938-40; ambassador at Washington, 1941-46; speeches in Viscount Halifax: Speeches on Foreign Affairs, edited by H.H.E. Craster (London, 1940); and The American Speeches of the Earl of Halifax (London, 1947).

473. Hamilton, Mary Agnes. Remembering My Good Friends. London, 1944.

Includes diplomats and politicians; by a biographer (of J. Ramsay MacDonald and Arthur Henderson), novelist and civil servant; MP, 1929-31; see also Up-Hill All the Way (London, 1953).

474. Hankey, 1st Baron (Maurice Pascal Alers Hankey).* The Supreme Command, 1914-1918. 2 vols. London, 1961.

Secretary, Committee of Imperial Defence, 1912-18; cabinet, 1919-38; minister without portfolio in war cabinet, 1939-40; chancellor of the Duchy of Lancaster, 1940-41; paymaster-general, 1941-42; a director, Suez Canal Company, 1938-39, 1945-62; British secretary, numerous interwar conferences, 1919-32; continued in The Supreme Control at the Paris Peace Conference, 1919: A Commentary (London, 1963); see also his Diplomacy by Conference: Studies in Public Affairs, 1920-1946 (London, 1946); Politics, Trials and Errors (Oxford, 1950); and Government Control in War (London, 1945).

475. Hardinge, 1st Baron, of Penshurst (Charles Hardinge).* Old Diplomacy: The Reminiscences of Lord Hardinge of Penshurst. London, 1947.

Permanent under-secretary of state for Foreign Affairs, 1916-20; ambassador at Paris, 1920-23.

476. Hardinge, Sir Arthur Henry. A Diplomatist in Europe. London, 1927.

Entered Foreign Office, 1880; ambassador to Spain, 1913-27; see also his A Diplomat in the East (London, 1928).

477.   Harington, General Sir Charles. Tim Harington Looks Back. London, 1940.

Deputy chief, imperial general staff, 1918-20; general officer commanding-in-chief, army of Black Sea, 1920-21; allied forces of occupation in Turkey, 1921-23; governor of Gibraltar, 1933-38.

478.   Harris, Marshal of the Royal Air Force Sir Arthur.* Bomber Offensive. London, 1947.

Joined RAF, 1919; deputy chief of air staff, 1940-41; commander-in-chief, Bomber Command, 1942-45.

479.   Harris, Henry Wilson. Life So Far. London, 1954.

MP, 1945-50; editor of the Spectator, 1932-53; author of numerous books on foreign policy, the League of Nations and disarmament.

480.   Harris, Sir Percy Alfred. Forty Years in and out of Parliament. London, 1947.

MP, 1922-45; chief whip, Liberal parliamentary party, 1935-45.

481.   Harvey, 1st Baron, of Tasburgh (Oliver Charles Harvey). The Diplomatic Diaries of Oliver Harvey, 1937-1940. Edited by John Harvey. London, 1970.

Continued in The War Diaries of Oliver Harvey, 1941-1945 (London, 1978); principal private secretary to secretary of state for Foreign Affairs, 1936-39, 1941-43; minister at Paris, 1940; assistant under-secretary of state, Foreign Office, 1943-46.

482.   Harvie-Watt, Sir George S. Most of My Life. London, 1980.

Assistant government whip, 1938-40; parliamentary private secretary to Winston Churchill, 1941-45.

483.   Hastings, Sir Patrick. The Autobiography of Sir Patrick Hastings. London, 1948.

MP, 1922-26; attorney-general, 1924; playwright.

484.   Hayter, Sir William. A Double Life. London, 1974.

Served Foreign Office, 1930; Vienna, 1931; Moscow, 1934; Foreign Office, 1937; China, 1938; Washington, 1941; Foreign Office, 1944-48; see also his The Diplomacy of the Great Powers (London, 1961).

485.   Headlam-Morley, Sir James.   A Memoir of the Paris Peace Conference, 1919.   Edited by Agnes Headlam-Morley et al. London, 1972.

Assistant director, political intelligence department, Foreign Office, 1918-20; historical adviser, Foreign Office, 1920-29.

486.   Henderson, Sir Nevile Meyrick.   Failure of a Mission: Berlin, 1937-1939.   London, 1940.

Served at St. Petersburg, Tokyo, Rome, Nish, Paris, 1905-21; counsellor, and then acting high commissioner, Constantinople, 1921-24; served at Cairo, 1924-28; Paris, 1928-29; minister at Belgrade, 1925-35; ambassador at Buenos Aires, 1935-37; and at Berlin, 1937-39; additional reminiscences, essential for an understanding of the man, in Water under the Bridges (London, 1945).

487.   Henderson, Sir Nicholas.   The Private Office: A Personal View of Five Foreign Secretaries and of the Government from the Inside. London, 1984.

Assistant private secretary to Anthony Eden, Ernest Bevin, 1944-47; and private secretary to three other foreign ministers, 1963-65.

488.   Hewlett, Sir William Meyrick.   Forty Years in China.   London, 1943.

Acting consul-general at Chengtu, 1916-22; consul at Amoy, 1923-27; consul-general, Nanking, 1927-31; Hankow, 1932-35.

489.   Hodgson, Sir Robert MacLeod.   Spain Resurgent.   London, 1953.

Commercial counsellor in Russia, 1919-21; agent, British commercial mission to Soviet government, 1921-24; chargé d'affaires at Moscow, 1924-27; minister to Albania, 1928-36; British agent in nationalist Spain, 1937-39; chargé d'affaires at Burgos, 1939; diplomatic adviser to the ministry of Information, 1944-45.

MEMOIRS

490.   Hodson, Sir Arnhold Wienholt.   Seven Years in Southern
         Abyssinia. London, 1927.

         Consular service, Abyssinia, 1914-26; governor of Falkland
         Islands, 1926-30; Sierra Leone, 1930-34; Gold Coast, 1934-41; see
         also his Where Lions Reign (London, 1929).

491.   Hohler, Sir Thomas Beaumont.   Diplomatic Petrel. London, 1942.

         Minister at Budapest, 1920-24; Santiago, 1924-27; minister to
         Denmark, 1928-33; special emissary to Colombia, 1938.

492.   Hollis, Sir Leslie Chasemore.   One Marine's Tale. London, 1956.

         Admiralty, plans division, 1932-36; assistant secretary,
         Committee of Imperial Defence, 1936; senior assistant secretary
         in office of war cabinet, 1939-46; another volume in collaboration
         with James Leasor, War at the Top (London, 1959).

493.   Home, 14th Earl of (Alexander Frederick Douglas-Home).* The
         Way the Wind Blows. London, 1976.

         Parliamentary private secretary to Neville Chamberlain, 1937-39;
         joint parliamentary under-secretary, Foreign Office, 1945; prime
         minister, 1963-64; see also his Letters to a Grandson (London,
         1983).

494.   Howard, 1st Baron, of Penrith (Sir Esme William Howard).*
         Theatre of Life, 1863-1936. 2 vols. London, 1935-36.

         Minister to Sweden, 1913-19; ambassador to Spain, 1919-24;
         USA, 1924-30; member, British delegation to Paris peace
         conference, 1919; see also his The Prevention of War by Collective
         Action (London, 1933).

495.   Hunt, Sir David. A Don at War. London, 1966.

         Served world war two, 1940-45; colonel general staff, allied force
         headquarters, 1945-46; continued in On the Spot (London, 1975).

496.   Ironside, 1st Baron (Field-Marshal William Edmund Ironside).
         Archangel, 1918-1919. London, 1953.

         Commander-in-chief British forces in Russia, 1918-19;
         quartermaster-general in India, 1933-36; governor, Gibraltar, 1938-

39; inspector-general of overseas forces, 1939; chief of the imperial general staff, 1939-40; commander-in-chief, home forces, 1940; further diary extracts in High Road to Command, 1920-1922, edited by 2nd Baron Ironside (London, 1972); and The Ironside Diaries, 1937-1940, edited by Roderick Macleod and Denis Kelly (London, 1962).

497.   Ismay, Baron (General Hastings Lionel Ismay).* Memoirs. London, 1960.

Assistant secretary, Committee of Imperial Defence, 1925-30; deputy secretary, 1936-38; secretary, 1938; chief of staff to minister of Defence, 1940-46; deputy secretary, military, to war cabinet, 1940-45.

498.   James, Admiral Sir William Milburne. The Sky Was Always Blue. London, 1951.

Prolific author on naval affairs; deputy chief of naval staff, 1935-38; commander-in-chief, Portsmouth, 1939-42; chief of naval information, 1943-44; MP, 1943-45; see also his Portsmouth Letters (London, 1946).

499.   Jay, Douglas. Change and Fortune. London, 1980.

Journalist with The Times and the Economist, 1930s; assistant secretary, ministry of Supply, 1941-43; principal assistant secretary, Board of Trade, 1943-45.

500.   Johnston, Thomas. Memories. London, 1952.

Parliamentary under-secretary for Scotland, 1929-31; lord privy seal, 1931; secretary of state for Scotland, 1941-45.

501.   Jones, Thomas. A Diary with Letters, 1931-1950. London, 1954.

Deputy secretary, cabinet, 1916-30; first secretary, Pilgrim Trust, 1930-45; to be supplemented by Whitehall Diary, edited by Keith Middlemas, 3 vols. (London, 1969-71).

502.   Kelly, Sir David Victor. The Ruling Few: Or, the Human Background to Diplomacy. London, 1953.

Served at Buenos Aires, Foreign Office, Lisbon, Mexico, Brussels, Stockholm and Cairo, 1919-37; counsellor in Foreign Office, 1938-39; minister at Berne, 1940-42.

126

503.   Kennedy, Major-General Sir John Noble. The Business of War.
         London, 1957.

         Deputy director of military operations, 1938; director of plans,
         1939; director of military operations, War Office, 1940-43;
         assistant chief of imperial general staff, 1943-45.

504.   Keyes, 1st Baron (Roger Keyes).* The Naval Memoirs of
         Admiral of the Fleet Sir Roger Keyes. 2 vols. London, 1934-35.

         Entered navy, 1885; deputy chief of naval staff, 1921-25;
         commander-in-chief, various stations, 1925-31; MP, 1934-43;
         director of combined operations, 1940-41; early career in
         Adventures Ashore and Afloat (London, 1937); private papers in
         The Keyes Papers: Selections from the Private and Official
         Correspondence of Admiral of the Fleet Lord Keyes, edited by
         Paul G. Halpern, 3 vols. (London, 1979-81).

505.   Keynes, Baron (John Maynard Keynes).* The Collected Writings
         of John Maynard Keynes. Edited for the Royal Economic
         Society. 30 vols. London, 1971-89.

         Principal representative of the Treasury, Paris peace conference,
         1919; member, committee on finance and industry, 1929-31;
         returned to Treasury, 1940; attended Bretton Woods conference,
         1944; engaged in negotiations with United States on lend-lease,
         1944-45; vol. 30 for index and guide to location of all Keynes's
         writings in the series; see additionally Essays in Persuasion
         (London, 1931); and Essays in Biography (London, 1933).

506.   Killearn, 1st Baron (Miles Wedderburn Lampson).* The Killearn
         Diaries, 1934-1946. Edited by Trefor Ellis Evans. London, 1972.

         Entered Foreign Office, 1903; minister to China, 1926-33; high
         commissioner for Egypt and the Sudan, 1934-36; ambassador to
         Egypt and high commissioner for the Sudan, 1936-46.

507.   Kilmuir, 1st Viscount (David Patrick Maxwell Fyfe). Political
         Adventure. London, 1964.

         MP, 1935-54; solicitor-general, 1942-45; attorney-general, 1945;
         deputy chief prosecutor, trial of Nazi war criminals, Nuremberg,
         1945-46.

508.   King, Cecil. With Malice toward None: A War Diary. Edited by
         William Armstrong. London, 1970.

Journalist and publisher; with Daily Mirror and Sunday Pictorial, 1929-63; see also his Strictly Personal (London, 1969).

509. King Hall, Sir Stephen. My Naval Life, 1906-1929. London, 1952.

Admiralty naval staff, 1919-20, 1928-29; intelligence officer, Mediterranean fleet, 1925-26; Atlantic fleet, 1927-28; founded K-H Newsletter Service, 1936.

510. Kirkbride, Sir Alec. A Crackle of Thorns: Experiences in the Middle East. London, 1956.

Service in Transjordan and Palestine, 1921-45; British representative to Permanent Mandates Commission, Geneva, 1936, 1938 and 1939; see also his An Awakening: The Arab Campaign, 1917-1918 (London, 1971).

511. Kirkpatrick, Sir Ivone. The Inner Circle. London, 1959.

Foreign Office, 1920-30; 1st secretary, British embassy, Berlin, 1933-38; director of foreign division, ministry of Information, 1940; controller, European services, BBC, 1941-45; assistant, then permanent under-secretary of state, Foreign Office, 1945-50, 1953-57.

512. Knatchbull-Hugessen, Sir Hughe M. Diplomat in Peace and War. London, 1949.

Minister to the Baltic states, 1930-34; minister at Tehran, 1934-36; ambassador to China, 1936-38; Turkey, 1939-44; and Belgium, 1944-47.

513. Lansbury, George.* My Life. London, 1928.

MP, 1922-40; editor of Daily Herald, 1919-23; first commissioner of works, 1929-31; leader of the Labour party, 1931-35, see also My Quest for Peace (London, 1938).

514. Lascelles, Sir Alan. End of an Era: The Letters and Journals of Sir Alan Lascelles, 1887-1920. London, 1986.

Assistant private secretary to Prince of Wales, 1920-29; secretary to governor-general of Canada, 1931-35; assistant private secretary to King George V, 1935, and to King George VI, 1935-43; continued in In Royal Service, 1920-1936 (London, 1989).

515.   Lawford, Valentine. Bound for Diplomacy. London, 1963.

Entered diplomatic service, 1934; transferred to Paris, 1937; assistant private secretary to Lord Halifax, Anthony Eden and Ernest Bevin, 1939-46; on whom see his "Three Ministers," Cornhill Magazine, 169(1957), 73-99.

516.   Lawrence, Thomas Edward [Thomas Edward Shaw].* Seven Pillars of Wisdom: A Triumph. London, 1926.

"Lawrence of Arabia"; British delegation, Paris peace conference, 1919; adviser on Arab affairs, Colonial Office, 1921-22; with RAF, 1922-35; see also Revolt in the Desert (London, 1927); The Letters of T.E. Lawrence, edited by David Garnett (London, 1938); and The Letters of T.E. Lawrence, edited by Malcolm Brown (London, 1988).

517.   Lawson, 1st Baron (John James Lawson). A Man's Life. London, 1932.

MP, 1919-49; financial secretary to War Office, 1924; parliamentary secretary to ministry of Labour, 1929-31; secretary of state for War, 1945-56.

518.   Lee, 1st Viscount, of Fareham (Arthur Hamilton Lee). A 'Good Innings': The Private Papers of Viscount Lee of Fareham. Edited by Alan Clark. London, 1974.

Director-general of food production, 1917-18; minister of Agriculture and Fisheries, 1919-21; first lord of the Admiralty, 1921-22; delegate to Washington conference, 1921-22.

519.   Lee, Air Vice-Marshal Arthur S. Gould. Special Duties: Reminiscences of a Royal Air Force Staff Officer in the Balkans, Turkey and the Middle East. London, 1946.

Chief instructor, Turkish Air Force College, 1937-40; chief of air section, British armistice control commission, Rumania, 1944; chief of British military-air mission to Marshal Tito, 1945.

520.   Lee, Jennie (Baroness Lee of Ashridge). This Great Journey: A Volume of Autobiography, 1904-1945. London, 1963.

MP, 1929-31, 1945-70; married Aneurin Bevan, 1934; see also her My Life with Nye (London, 1980).

521.   Leeper, Sir Reginald Wildig Allen. When Greek Meets Greek.
         London, 1950.

         Foreign Office, 1918-23, 1929-43; 1st secretary, British legation,
         Warsaw, 1923-24, 1927-29; Riga, 1924; Constantinople, 1925;
         ambassador at the court of the king of the Hellenes, 1943-46.

522.   Leith-Ross, Sir Frederick. Money Talks: Fifty Years of
         International Finance. London, 1968.

         British representative on finance board of Reparation Commission,
         1920-25; deputy controller, finance, the Treasury, 1925-32; chief
         economic adviser to the government, 1932-46; director-general,
         ministry of Economic Warfare, 1939-42; deputy director-general,
         European office, UNRRA, 1944-45.

523.   Liddell Hart, Sir Basil Henry.* Memoirs. 2 vols. London, 1965-
         66.

         Military theorist, lecturer and author of over 30 books; military
         correspondent of the Daily Telegraph, 1925-35; of The Times,
         1935-39; personal adviser to Leslie Hore-Belisha, 1937-38.

524.   Lindley, Sir Francis Oswald. A Diplomat off Duty. London, 1928.

         Foreign Office, 1897; high commissioner, Vienna, 1919-20;
         minister, 1920; Athens, 1922-23; Oslo, 1923-29; ambassador to
         Portugal, 1929-31; and Japan, 1931-34.

525.   Lloyd George, David (1st Earl Lloyd-George of Dwyfor).* War
         Memoirs. 6 vols. London, 1933-36.

         MP, 1890-1945; prime minister, 1916-22; see also The Truth about
         Reparations and War-Debts (London, 1932); The Truth about the
         Peace Treaties, 2 vols. (London, 1938); and Lloyd George: Family
         Letters, 1885-1936, edited by Kenneth O. Morgan (London, 1973).

526.   Lockhart, Sir Robert Bruce. The Diaries of Sir Robert Bruce
         Lockhart. Edited by Kenneth Young. 2 vols. London, 1973-81.

         Vol. 1 to 1938; vol. 2 to 1965; commercial secretary, Prague, 1919-
         22; with Evening Standard, 1929-37; political intelligence
         department, Foreign Office, 1939-40; deputy under-secretary of
         state, Foreign Office, 1941-45; author of numerous books,
         including the pen portraits in Giants Cast Long Shadows (London,
         1960); Friends, Foes and Foreigners (London, 1957); Comes the

Reckoning (London, 1947); and Memoirs of a British Agent (London, 1932).

527.   Lomax, Sir John Garnett. The Diplomatic Smuggler. London, 1965.

Consular service, 1920-38; commercial counsellor, Madrid, 1940; Berne, 1941; Angora, 1943; commercial minister, Buenos Aires, 1946-49.

528.   Londonderry, 7th Marquess of (Charles Stewart Henry Vane-Tempest-Stewart). Ourselves and Germany. London, 1938.

Under-secretary for Air, 1920-21; secretary of state for Air, 1931-35; lord privy seal and leader of the House of Lords, 1935; see also his Wings of Destiny (London, 1943); and for background, H. Montgomery Hyde, The Londonderrys: A Family Portrait (London, 1979).

529.   Long, 1st Viscount (Walter Long).* Memories. London, 1923.

Secretary of state for the Colonies, 1916-18; first lord of the Admiralty, 1919-21.

530.   Lothian, 11th Marquess of (Philip Henry Kerr).* Pacifism Is Not Enough: The Collected Lectures and Speeches by the 11th Marquess of Lothian. Edited by John Pinder and Andrea Bosco. London, 1990.

Private secretary to Lloyd George, 1916-21; secretary to Rhodes trustees, 1925-39; chancellor of the Duchy of Lancaster, 1931; under-secretary of state for India, 1931-32; ambassador to the United States, 1939-40; see also The American Speeches of Lord Lothian, July 1939 to December 1940 (London, 1940); and the abridged version, with a memoir by Sir Edward Grigg, Lord Lothian Speaks to America (London, 1941).

531.   Low, Sir David.* Low's Autobiography. London, 1956.

Political cartoonist, the Star, 1919-26, Evening Standard, 1926-49; "derided Hitler and Mussolini" (Concise DNB, 1901-1970); selections published in, among others, Low's Political Parade (London, 1936).

532.   Luke, Sir Harry Charles. Cities and Men. 3 vols. London, 1953-56.

British chief commissioner, Georgia, Armenia and Azerbaijan, 1920; colonial service, Palestine, Sierra Leone, Malta and Fiji, 1920-42.

533. Lytton, 2nd Earl of (Victor Alexander George Robert Bulwer-Lytton). The Web of Life. London, 1938.

Governor of Bengal, 1922-27; chairman of League of Nations mission to Manchuria, 1932; chairman, Council of Aliens, 1939-41.

534. McDonald, Iverach. A Man of the Times. London, 1976.

With Yorkshire Post, and then The Times; diplomatic correspondent, 1937-48.

535. MacDonald, Malcolm John. People and Places: Random Reminiscences. London, 1969.

Son of J. Ramsay MacDonald; MP, 1929-45; parliamentary under-secretary, Dominions Office, 1931-35; secretary of state for Dominion Affairs, 1935-38, 1938-39; secretary of state for Colonies, 1935, 1938-40; minister of Health, 1940-41; high commissioner to Canada, 1941-46; writer on ornithology; see also Titans and Others (London, 1972).

536. McFadyean, Sir Andrew. Recollected in Tranquillity. London, 1964.

Treasury representative, Paris, 1919-20; secretary to British delegation, Reparation Commission, 1920-22; general secretary, Reparation Commission, 1922-24; and Dawes committee, 1924; see also his earlier Reparation Reviewed (London, 1930).

537. Maclean, Sir Fitzroy. Eastern Approaches. London, 1949.

MP, 1941-74; 3rd secretary, Foreign Office, 1933; transferred to Paris, 1934, and to Moscow, 1937; 2nd secretary, 1938; transferred to Foreign Office, 1939; resigned, 1939; brigadier commanding British military mission to Tito, 1943-45; see also his Disputed Barricade (London, 1957).

538. Macmillan, Baron (Hugh Pattison Macmillan). A Man of Law's Tale. London, 1952.

Assistant director of intelligence, ministry of Information, 1918; lord advocate in Labour government, 1924; minister of Information, 1939-40.

539.   Macmillan, Harold (Earl of Stockton).* Memoirs. 6 vols. London, 1966-73.

Vols. 1 and 2 for 1914-45; MP, 1924-29, 1931-64; parliamentary secretary, ministry of Supply, 1940-42; parliamentary under-secretary of state, Colonies, 1942; minister resident at allied headquarters in northwest Africa, 1942-45; secretary for Air, 1945; prime minister, 1957-63; see also his War Diaries: Politics and War in the Mediterranean, January 1943-May 1945 (London, 1984); The Past Masters: Politics and Politicians, 1906-1939 (London, 1975); and The Price of Peace: Notes on the World Crisis (London, 1938, for private circulation).

540.   Macready, Sir Gordon. In the Wake of the Great. London, 1965.

Assistant secretary, Committee of Imperial Defence, 1926-32; assistant chief of the imperial general staff, 1940-42; chief of British army staff, Washington, 1942.

541.   Malcolm, Sir Ian. Vacant Thrones: A Parliamentary Sketchbook, 1895-1931. London, 1931.

MP, 1910-19; private secretary to A.J. Balfour at Paris peace conference, 1919.

542.   Mallaby, Sir George Charles. From My Level. London, 1965.

Served in military secretariat of war cabinet, 1942-45; further recollections in Each in His Office: Studies of Men in Power (London, 1972).

543.   Marshall-Cornwall, General Sir James Handyside. Wars and Rumours of War: A Memoir. London, 1984.

Attended Paris peace conference, 1919; military attaché, Berlin, Stockholm, Oslo, and Copenhagen, 1928-32; chief of British military mission to Egyptian army, 1937-38; general officer commanding-in-chief, western command, 1941-42; see also his Geographic Disarmament (London, 1935).

544.   Martel, Sir Giffard. An Outspoken Soldier. London, 1949.

Deputy director of mechanisation, War Office, 1938-39; head of military mission at Moscow, 1943-44; of interest also are his The Problem of Security (London, 1941); and The Russian Outlook (London, 1947).

545. Martin, Kingsley.* Father Figures: A First Volume of Autobiography, 1897-1931. London, 1966.

With the Manchester Guardian, 1927-31; then editor, New Statesman, 1931-60; prolific author; concluded as Editor: A Second Volume of Autobiography, 1931-1945 (London, 1968).

546. Masterman, Sir John C. On the Chariot Wheel: An Autobiography. London, 1975.

Lieutenant, intelligence corps, 1940; employed with BIA section of MI5, 1941-45.

547. Maugham, 1st Viscount (Frederic Herbert Maugham). At the End of the Day. London, 1954.

Lord chancellor, 1938-39; still important is his The Truth about the Munich Crisis (London, 1944).

548. Meade, James. The Collected Papers of James Meade. 4 vols. Edited by Susan Howson and Donald Moggridge. London, 1988-90.

Member economic section of League of Nations, 1938-40; economic assistant, 1940-45, and director, 1946-47, economic section, Cabinet Offices; vol. 4 for The Cabinet Office Diary, 1944-1946.

549. Meinertzhagen, Colonel Richard.* Middle East Diary, 1917-1956. London, 1959.

Member of Paris peace delegation, 1919; chief political officer in Palestine and Syria, 1919-20; military adviser, Middle East department, Colonial Office, 1921-24; War Office, 1939-40; see also Army Diary, 1899-1926 (London, 1960); and Diary of a Black Sheep (London, 1964); listed recreations as "silence, solitude and space" (Who's Who).

550. Mersey, 2nd Viscount (Charles Clive Bigham). A Picture of Life, 1872-1940. London, 1941.

Entered diplomatic service, 1896; attached to British delegation, Paris peace conference, 1919; deputy speaker, House of Lords, 1933-56; continued in Journal and Memories (London, 1952); other publications include The Chief Ministers of England (London, 1923).

551.   Mitchell, Sir Harold Paton. Into Peace. London, 1945.

Parliamentary private secretary, Department of Overseas Trade, 1931-35; ministry of Labour, 1939-41; ministry of Supply, 1941; liaison officer to Polish forces, 1944; vice-chairman of Conservative party, 1942-45; see also his In My Stride (London, 1951).

552.   Montgomery, Field-Marshal 1st Viscount, of Alamein (Bernard Law Montgomery).* Memoirs. London, 1958.

The last in a series of military memoirs; served both world wars; commander, 8th army from July 1942; commander-in-chief, north France, 1945; commander, 21st army group, 1944-45.

553.   Moran, 1st Baron, of Manton (Charles McMoran Wilson). Winston Churchill: The Struggle for Survival, 1940-1965. London, 1966.

Diaries of personal physician to Winston Churchill.

554.   Morgan, General Sir Frederick Edgeworth. Peace and War: A Soldier's Life. London, 1961.

Began military service, 1913; chief of staff to supreme allied commander, 1943-44; deputy chief of staff to supreme commander, allied expeditionary force, 1944-45; see also his Overture to Overlord (London, 1950).

555.   Morgan, John Hartman. Assize of Arms: Being the Story of the Disarmament of Germany and Her Rearmament, 1919-1939. 2 vols. London, 1945.

Memoir-history; with British military section, Paris peace conference, 1919; member, Inter-Allied Control Commission for the Disarmament of Germany, 1919-23.

556.   Morrison, Baron, of Lambeth (Herbert Stanley Morrison).* An Autobiography. London, 1960.

Minister of Transport, 1929-31; minister of Supply, 1940; home secretary and minister of Home Security, 1940-45; see too his Government and Parliament (London, 1954).

557. Mosley, Sir Oswald Ernald.* My Life. London, 1968.

Married, 1st, Lady Cynthia Curzon; 2nd, Diana Mitford; chancellor of the Duchy of Lancaster, 1929-30; leader of the British Union of Fascists; of related interest is Diana Mosley, A Life of Contrasts (London, 1977); and Loved Ones: Pen Portraits (London, 1985), including Oswald Mosley.

558. Mottistone, 1st Baron (John Edward Bernard Seely). Adventure. London, 1930.

Parliamentary under-secretary and deputy minister, ministry of Munitions, 1918-19; under-secretary of state for Air, 1919; see also his Fear and Be Slain: Adventures by Land, Sea and Air (London, 1931).

559. Mott-Radclyffe, Sir Charles. Foreign Body in the Eye: A Memoir of the Foreign Service. London, 1975.

Honourary attaché, diplomatic service, Athens and Rome, 1936-38; member, military mission to Greece, 1940-41; liaison officer in Syria, 1941; MP, 1942-70; parliamentary private secretary to secretary of state for India, 1944-45; later member of Plowden Commission on Overseas Representation Services, 1963-64.

560. Mountbatten, 1st Earl, of Burma (Admiral of the Fleet Louis Mountbatten).* Personal Diary of Admiral the Lord Louis Mountbatten, Supreme Allied Commander, South-East Asia, 1943-1946. Edited by Philip Ziegler. London, 1988.

Naval career, 1913-42; chief of combined operations, 1942-43; supreme allied commander, southeast Asia, 1943-46.

561. Muggeridge, Malcolm.* Chronicles of Wasted Time. 2 vols. London, 1972-73.

Member, editorial staff, 1930-32, and Moscow correspondent, 1932-33, Manchester Guardian; assistant editor, Calcutta Statesman, 1934-35; served with British intelligence, 1939-45; see also his Like It Was: The Diaries of Malcolm Muggeridge, edited by John Bright-Holmes (London, 1981).

562.   Murray, Gilbert.* Gilbert Murray: An Unfinished Autobiography. Edited by Jean Smith and Arnold Toynbee. London, 1960.

"Classical scholar and internationalist" (Concise DNB, 1901-1970); founder of the League of Nations Union and chairman of its executive council, 1923-38; a fragment of autobiography with seven contributions from friends.

563.   Myers, Brigadier Edmund C.W. Greek Entanglement. London, 1955.

With SOE, Middle East, 1939-44; northwest Europe, 1944-45.

564.   Neame, Sir Philip. Playing with Strife. London, 1946.

Entered army, 1908; deputy chief of the general staff, BEF, France, 1939-40; general officer commanding-in-chief, Cyrenaica, 1941.

565.   Nevinson, Henry Woodd. Changes and Chances. London, 1923.

On staff of the Nation, 1907-23; Manchester Guardian correspondent at various international conferences, 1921-29; autobiography continued in More Changes, More Chances (London, 1925); and Last Changes, Last Chances (London, 1928); abridged as Fire of Life (London, 1935).

566.   Nicolson, Sir Harold.* Harold Nicolson: Diaries and Letters, 1930-1962. Edited by Nigel Nicolson. 3 vcls. London, 1966-68.

Author, critic and MP; entered Foreign Office, 1909; with British delegation to Paris peace conference, 1919; at League of Nations, 1919-20; served at Foreign Office and abroad, 1920-29; parliamentary secretary to ministry of Information, 1940-41.

567.   Oliphant, Sir Lancelot. An Ambassador in Bonds. 2nd ed. London, 1947.

Entered Foreign Office, 1903; counsellor, 1923; assistant under-secretary of state, 1929-36; deputy under-secretary of state for Foreign Affairs, 1936-39; ambassador to Belgium, 1939; captured and interned in Germany, 1940-41; returned to Foreign Office, 1941-44.

568.   O'Malley, Sir Owen St. Clair. The Phantom Caravan. London, 1954.

Counsellor, Foreign Office, 1933-37; minister to Hungary, 1939-41; ambassador to Poland, 1942-45; and Portugal, 1945-47; and of related interest, Ann Bridge, Permission to Resign: Goings-On in the Corridors of Power (London, 1971).

569.   Oppenheimer, Sir Francis. Stranger Within: Autobiographical Pages. London, 1960.

Financial commissioner to Austria, 1919.

570.   Parkinson, Sir Cosmo. The Colonial Office from Within, 1909-1945. London, 1947.

Joined Colonial Office, 1909; permanent under-secretary of state for the Colonies, 1937-40, 1940-42; permanent under-secretary of state for Dominion Affairs, 1940.

571.   Parmoor, 1st Baron (Charles Alfred Cripps). A Retrospect: Looking Back Over a Life of More than Eighty Years. London, 1936.

Lord president of the Council, 1924, 1929-31; British representative at League of Nations Council, 1924; leader of the House of Lords, 1929-31.

572.   Parrott, Sir Cecil. The Tightrope. London, 1975.

Post-1945 memoirs continued in The Serpent and the Nightingale (London, 1977); tutor to King Peter of Yugoslavia, at Belgrade, 1934-39; served with British legation, Oslo, 1939-40; Stockholm, 1940-45; later director of research, librarian and keeper of the papers at the Foreign Office, 1957-60.

573.   Passfield, 1st Baron (Sidney James Webb).* The Letters of Sidney and Beatrice Webb. 3 vols. Edited by Norman MacKenzie. London, 1978.

MP, 1922-29; president of the Board of Trade, 1924; secretary of state for Dominion Affairs, 1929-30; and for Colonies, 1929-31; vol. 3 for 1912-47; see also The Diary of Beatrice Webb, 1873-1943, edited by Norman and Jeanne MacKenzie, 4 vols. (London, 1982-85); entire typescript diaries available on microfiche; and Beatrice Webb, Our Partnership (London, 1948).

574.   Peck, John. Dublin from Downing Street. London, 1978.

Assistant private secretary to first lord of the Admiralty, 1937-39; to minister for Co-ordination of Defence, 1939-40; and to Winston Churchill, 1940-46.

575.   Percy, Eustace (Baron Percy of Newcastle). Some Memories. London, 1958.

Diplomatic service, 1911-19; MP, 1921-37; president, Board of Education, 1924-29; minister without portfolio, 1935-36.

576.   Peterson, Sir Maurice Drummond. Both Sides of the Curtain. London, 1950.

Entered Foreign Office, 1913; served at Washington, Prague, Tokyo, Cairo and Madrid; minister to Bulgaria, 1936-38; ambassador to Iraq, 1938-39; Spain, 1939-43; and Turkey, 1944-46.

577.   Pethick-Lawrence, Baron (Frederick William Pethick-Lawrence).* Fate Has Been Kind. London, 1942.

MP, 1923-31, 1935-45; financial secretary to the Treasury, 1929-31; secretary of state for India and Burma, 1945-47.

578.   Philby, H.A.R. "Kim."* My Silent War. London, 1968.

Intelligence agent of USSR, 1933-63; joined SIS, 1940; in charge of Iberian desk, 1940; head of anti-Soviet section, 1944-49.

579.   Philby, Harry St. John Bridger.* Arabian Days. London, 1948.

His autobiography until the age of 50; numerous other books on the Arab world; entered Indian civil service, 1907; adviser to ministry of the Interior, Mesopotamia, 1920-21; chief British representative, Transjordan, 1921-24; imprisoned under Section 18B, Defence Regulations, 1940; father of Kim Philby.

580.   Piggott, Major-General Francis Stewart Gilderoy. Broken Thread: An Autobiography. London, 1950.

Foreword by Lord Hankey; general staff, War Office, 1920-21; military attaché at Tokyo, 1921-26, 1936-39; deputy military secretary, War Office, 1931-35.

581.   Ponsonby, Sir Charles Edward. Ponsonby Remembers. London, 1965.

MP, 1935-50; parliamentary private secretary to Anthony Eden, 1940-45; see also his The Ponsonby Family, 1929-1970 (Woodstock, 1970).

582.   Pownall, Lieutenant-General Sir Henry. Chief of Staff: The Diaries of Lieutenant-General Sir Henry Pownall. Edited by Brian Bond. 2 vols. London, 1973-74.

Covers period 1933-44; with Committee of Imperial Defence, 1933-36; director of military operations and intelligence, War Office, 1938-39; chief of general staff, BEF, 1939-40; vice-chief of imperial general staff, War Office, 1941; commander-in-chief, Far East, 1941-42; Persia-Iraq, 1943; chief of staff to Admiral Lord Louis Mountbatten, 1943-45.

583.   Preston, Sir Thomas Hildebrand. Before the Curtain. London, 1950.

Consular and diplomatic service in Russia, Italy and Lithuania, 1913-41; counsellor at Cairo, 1941-45.

584.   Price, George Ward. I Know These Dictators. London, 1938.

Journalist and war correspondent, with Daily Mail; see too the same author's Year of Reckoning (London, 1939); and Extra-Special Correspondent (London, 1957).

585.   Pritt, Denis Nowell. The Autobiography of D.N. Pritt. 3 vols. London, 1965-66.

Socialist MP, 1935-50; prolific writer, including Light on Moscow (London, 1939); and U.S.S.R., Our Ally (London, 1941); see also his From Right to Left (London, 1965).

586.   Radcliffe, Baron (Cyril John Radcliffe). Not in Feather Beds. London, 1968.

Director-general, ministry of Information, 1941-45.

587.   Randall, Sir Alec Walter George. Vatican Assignment. London, 1956.

Served British legation, Vatican, 1925-30; Bucharest, 1930-33; Foreign Office, 1933-35; Copenhagen, 1935-38; Foreign Office counsellor, 1938-45; see also his The Pope, the Jews and the Nazis (London, 1964).

588. Redcliffe-Maud, Baron (John Primatt Redcliffe-Maud). Experiences of an Optimist: The Memoirs of John Redcliffe-Maud. London, 1981.

Second secretary, ministry of Food, 1941-44; and office of ministry of Reconstruction, 1944-45; delegate to UNRRA conference, 1943.

589. Rees, Goronwy. A Chapter of Accidents. London, 1972.

Fellow of All Souls, 1931; leader writer, Manchester Guardian, 1932; assistant editor, the Spectator, 1936; see too A Bundle of Sensations (London, 1960).

590. Reith, 1st Baron (John C.W. Reith).* Into the Wind. London, 1949.

Director-general, BBC, 1927-38; minister of Information, 1940; minister of Transport, 1940; minister of Works, 1940-42; with Admiralty, 1943-45; see also his Wearing Spurs (London, 1966); and The Reith Diaries, edited by Charles Stuart (London, 1976).

591. Rendel, Sir George Williams. The Sword and the Olive: Recollections of Diplomacy and the Foreign Service, 1913-1954. London, 1957.

Head of the eastern department, Foreign Office, 1930-38; minister to Bulgaria, 1938-41; ambassador to Yugoslav government in London, 1941-43; British representative on European committee of UNRRA, 1944-47.

592. Rennell, 1st Baron, of Rodd (James Rennell Rodd). Social and Diplomatic Memories: Third Series, 1902-1919. London, 1925.

Ambassador at Rome, 1908-19; British delegate to League of Nations, 1921, 1923; president, court of conciliation between Austria and Switzerland, 1925; MP, 1928-32.

593. Repington, Charles à Court.* After the War: A Diary. London, 1922.

Military correspondent with the <u>Morning Post</u>, <u>The Times</u>, and the <u>Daily Telegraph</u>; see also his <u>The First World War, 1914-1918: Personal Experiences</u>, 2 vols. (London, 1920); and <u>Policy and Arms</u> (London, 1924)

594. Richmond, Admiral Sir Herbert.* <u>Statesmen and Sea Power</u>. London, 1946.

President of Royal Naval College, Greenwich, 1920-23; commander-in-chief, East Indies, 1923-25; commandant, Imperial Defence College, 1926-28; numerous publications on naval strategy.

595. Riddell, 1st Baron (George Allardice Riddell). <u>Lord Riddell's War Diary, 1914-1918</u>. London, 1933.

Newspaper proprietor; chairman, <u>News of the World</u>, 1903-34; represented British press at peace conferences, 1919-22; continued in his <u>Intimate Diary of the Peace Conference and After, 1918-1923</u> (London, 1933); see also <u>The Riddell Diaries, 1908-1923</u>, edited by J.M. McEwen (London, 1986).

596. Robbins, Baron (Lionel Robbins).* <u>Autobiography of an Economist</u>. London, 1971.

Director, economic section of the offices of the war cabinet, 1941-45.

597. Robertson, Field-Marshal Sir William Robert.* <u>Soldiers and Statesmen, 1914-1918</u>. 2 vols. London, 1926.

Chief of imperial general staff, 1915-18; general officer, commander-in-chief, Britain, 1918-19; commander-in-chief, British army on the Rhine, 1919-20; see also his <u>From Private to Field-Marshal</u> (London, 1921); and <u>The Military Correspondence of Field-Marshal Sir William Robertson, December 1915-February 1918</u>, edited by David Woodward (London, 1990).

598. Roll, Sir Eric. <u>Crowded Hours</u>. London, 1985.

Member, then deputy head, British Food Mission, Washington, 1941-46; see also his <u>The Combined Food Board: A Study in Wartime International Planning</u> (Stanford, CA, 1956).

599. Rootham, Jasper St. John. <u>Demi-Paradise</u>. London, 1960.

Private secretary to Neville Chamberlain, 1938-39; Treasury, 1939-40; later with Bank of England; see also his <u>Miss Fire: The Chronicle of a British Mission to Mihailovic, 1943-1944</u> (London, 1946).

600.   Rothermere, 1st Viscount (Harold Sidney Harmsworth). <u>My Campaign for Hungary</u>. London, 1939.

Newspaper proprietor, <u>Daily Mail</u>, <u>Daily Mirror</u>, etc.; controlled Associated Newspapers, 1922-32; see also <u>My Fight to Rearm Britain</u> (London, 1939); and <u>Warnings and Predictions</u> (London, 1939).

601.   Russell, Sir Thomas Wentworth. <u>Egyptian Service, 1902-1946</u>. London, 1949.

Entered Egyptian civil service, 1902; served under 29 different ministers of Interior, 1922-46.

602.   Ryan, Sir Andrew. <u>The Last of the Dragomans</u>. London, 1951.

Entered Levant consular service, 1897; embassy dragoman, Constantinople, 1907-14, 1921-22; member, British delegation, Lausanne conference, 1922-23; consul-general at Rabat, 1924-30; minister at Jedda, 1930-36; and Albania, 1936-39.

603.   Salter, Baron (Sir James Arthur Salter). <u>Memoirs of a Public Servant</u>. London, 1961.

General secretary, Reparation Commission, 1920-22; director, economic and finance section, League of Nations, 1919-20, 1922-31; MP, 1937-50, 1951-53; parliamentary secretary, ministry of Shipping, 1939-41; War Transport, 1941; head of British merchant shipping mission, Washington, 1941-43; senior deputy director-general, UNRRA, 1944; chancellor of the Duchy of Lancaster, 1945; further recollections in <u>Personality in Politics</u> (London, 1947); and <u>Slave of the Lamp: A Public Servant's Notebook</u> (London, 1967).

604.   Samuel, 1st Viscount, of Mount Carmel (Herbert Louis Samuel).* <u>Memoirs</u>. London, 1945.

MP, 1902-18, 1929-35; high commissioner, Palestine, 1920-25; secretary of state for Home Affairs, 1931-32; leader of Liberal parliamentary party, 1931-35.

605.   Schuster, Sir George. Private Work and Public Causes: A Personal Record, 1881-1978. Cowbridge, 1979.

Chief assistant to organiser of international credits, League of Nations, 1921; member, advisory committee to the Treasury, 1921-22; financial secretary, Sudan government, 1922-27; economic and financial adviser, Colonial Office, 1927-28; finance member of executive council of viceroy of India, 1928-34; MP, 1938-45.

606.   Scott, Charles Prestwich.* Political Diaries, 1911-1928. Edited by Trevor Wilson. London, 1970.

Editor of the Manchester Guardian, 1872-1929.

607.   Scott, Sir Harold Richard. Your Obedient Servant. London, 1959.

Entered Home Office, 1911; deputy secretary, later secretary, ministry of Home Security, 1940-43; permanent secretary, ministry of Aircraft Production, 1943-45.

608.   Selby, Sir Walford H.M. Diplomatic Twilight, 1930-1940. London, 1953.

Principal private secretary to secretary of state for Foreign Affairs, 1924-32; minister at Vienna, 1933-37; ambassador at Lisbon, 1937-40.

609.   Selous, Gerald Holgate. Appointment to Fez. London, 1956.

Consul at Casablanca, 1924-28; Basra, 1929-32; commercial counsellor at Cairo, 1933-38; and Brussels, 1938-40; with Department of Overseas Trade, 1940-42.

610.   Shakespeare, Sir Geoffrey Hithersay. Let Candles Be Brought In. London, 1949.

Private secretary to David Lloyd George, 1921-23; parliamentary secretary, ministry of Health, 1932-36; Board of Education, 1936-37; Admiralty, 1937-40; and Department of Overseas Trade, 1940; parliamentary under-secretary of state, Dominions Office, 1940-42.

611.   Shinwell, Baron (Emanuel Shinwell). Conflict without Malice: An Autobiography. London, 1955.

Financial secretary, War Office, 1929-30; parliamentary secretary to Department of Mines, 1924, 1930-31; see also I've Lived Through It All (London, 1973); and Lead with the Left (London, 1981).

612. Sillitoe, Sir Percy.* Cloak without Dagger. London, 1955.

Colonial service, 1920-23; director-general, MI5, 1946-53.

613. Simon, 1st Viscount, of Stackpole Elidor (John Allsebrook Simon). Retrospect. London, 1952.

MP, 1906-18, 1922-40; secretary of state for Foreign Affairs, 1931-35; for Home Affairs, 1935-37; chancellor of the Exchequer, 1937-40; lord chancellor, 1940-45; see also his earlier Comment and Criticisms (London, 1930); and Portrait of My Mother (London, 1937).

614. Skrine, Sir Clarmont Percival. World War in Iran. London, 1962.

Entered Indian civil service, 1912; served as political agent, consul-general various postings, 1921-39; resident for the Punjab states, 1939-41; consul-general at Meshed, 1942-46; see also his Chinese Central Asia (London, 1926).

615. Slessor, Marshal of the Royal Air Force Sir John. The Central Blue. London, 1956.

Air staff, Air ministry, 1928-30; director of plans, Air ministry, 1937-41; assistant chief of air staff, 1942; among other publications on the subject, see his Air Power and Armies (London, 1936).

616. Slim, 1st Viscount (Field-Marshal Sir William Slim).* Defeat into Victory. London, 1956.

Various commands, Sudan, Syria-Persia-Iraq, Burma and India, 1939-45; commander-in-chief, allied land forces, southeast Asia, 1945-46; further recollections in Unofficial History (London, 1959).

617. Snell, Baron (Henry Snell). Men, Movements and Myself. London, 1936.

MP, 1922-31; parliamentary under-secretary of state, India Office, 1931; deputy leader, House of Lords, 1940-44.

618.   Snowden, 1st Viscount (Philip Snowden).* An Autobiography. 2
        vols. London, 1934.

        MP, 1906-18, 1922-31; chancellor of the Exchequer, 1924, 1929-31,
        1931; lord privy seal, 1931-32.

619.   Spears, Major General Sir Edward. Assignment to Catastrophe.
        2 vols. London, 1954.

        Head of British military mission, Paris, 1917-20; MP, 1922-24,
        1931-45; head of British mission to General de Gaulle, 1940;
        headed mission to Syria and Lebanon, 1941; minister to Syria and
        Lebanon, 1942-44; additional memoirs, Two Men Who Saved
        France (London, 1966); The Picnic Basket (London, 1967); and
        Fulfilment of a Mission: Syria and Lebanon, 1941-1944 (London,
        1977); and of related interest, Mary Borden (Lady Spears),
        Journey Down a Blind Alley (London, 1946).

620.   Spender, J.A.* Life, Journalism and Politics. 2 vols. London,
        1927.

        Editor of the Westminster Gazette, 1896-1922; prolific author and
        biographer.

621.   Steed, Henry Wickham. Through Thirty Years, 1892-1922: A
        Personal Narrative. 2 vols. London, 1924.

        Editor of The Times, 1919-22; historian and lecturer.

622.   Stevenson, Frances (Countess Lloyd George of Dwyfor). The
        Years That Are Past. London, 1967.

        Private secretary to Lloyd George, 1912-43; married to him, 1943;
        more in her Lloyd George: A Diary, edited by A.J.P. Taylor
        (London, 1971); and My Darling Pussy: The Letters of Lloyd
        George and Frances Stevenson, 1913-1941, edited by A.J.P.
        Taylor (London, 1975).

623.   Stirling, Walter Francis. Safety Last. London, 1953.

        Chief staff officer to T.E. Lawrence; adviser, Albanian government,
        1923-31; intelligence work, Balkans, 1940; military commander,
        East Syria, 1943.

624.   Storrs, Sir Ronald. Orientations. London, 1937.

Military governor of Jerusalem, 1917-20; governor, Cyprus, 1926-32; and Northern Rhodesia, 1932-34; lecturer and journalist, 1940-43.

625.   Strabolgi, 10th Baron (Joseph M. Kenworthy). Sailors, Statesmen - and Others: An Autobiography. London, 1933.

Entered Royal Navy, 1902; MP, 1919-31; prolific author on naval subjects.

626.   Strang, 1st Baron (William Strang). Home and Abroad. London, 1956.

Entered Foreign Office, 1919; counsellor at Moscow, 1930-32; assistant under-secretary of state in Foreign Office, 1939-43; representative on European Advisory Commission, 1943-45; later permanent under-secretary of state, Foreign Office, 1949-53.

627.   Streat, Sir Raymond. Lancashire and Whitehall: The Diary of Sir Raymond Streat. Edited by Marguerite Dupree. 2 vols. Manchester, 1987.

Vol. 1, 1931-39; vol. 2, 1939-57; director and secretary, Manchester Chamber of Commerce; secretary, Export Council, Board of Trade, 1940; chairman, Cotton Board, 1940-57.

628.   Strong, Major-General Sir Kenneth W.D. Intelligence at the Top: The Recollections of an Intelligence Officer. London, 1968.

Military attaché, Berlin, 1920-43; head of General Eisenhower's intelligence staff, 1943-45; director-general, political intelligence department, Foreign Office, 1945-47; see also Men of Intelligence: A Study of the Roles and Decisions of Chiefs of Intelligence from World War I to the Present Day (London, 1970).

629.   Stuart, 1st Viscount, of Findhorn (James Gray Stuart). Within the Fringe: An Autobiography. London, 1967.

MP, 1923-59; a lord commissioner of the Treasury, 1935-41; joint parliamentary secretary to the Treasury, and government chief whip, 1941-45.

630.   Stuart, Sir Campbell. Opportunity Knocks Once. London, 1952.

Deputy director of propaganda in enemy countries, 1918; representative of The Times at Imperial press conferences, 1920-

30; with ministry of Information, 1939; director of propaganda in enemy countries, 1939-40; director of The Times, 1919-60.

631. Swinton, 1st Earl of (Philip Cunliffe-Lister, Baron Masham).* I Remember. London, 1948.

President of Board of Trade, 1922-23, 1924-29, 1931; secretary of state for Colonies, 1931-35; for Air, 1935-38; minister resident in west Africa, 1942-44; minister for Civil Aviation, 1944-45; further recollections in Sixty Years of Power: Some Memories of the Men Who Wielded It (London, 1966).

632. Swinton, Major-General Sir Ernest. Over My Shoulder. London, 1951.

Assistant secretary, Committee of Imperial Defence and war cabinet, 1913-14, 1915-18; controller of information, Air ministry, 1919-21; visited Hitler, 1936.

633. Sykes, Major-General Sir Frederick. From Many Angles: An Autobiography. London, 1942.

Chief of air staff, 1918-19; MP, 1922-28, 1940-45; governor of Bombay, 1928-33; company director; member of numerous government committees.

634. Sylvester, Albert James. Life with Lloyd George. Edited by Colin Cross. London, 1975.

Diary extracts, 1931-45; private secretary to secretary of war cabinet and cabinet, 1916-21; to successive prime ministers, 1921-23; principal private secretary to Lloyd George, 1923-45.

635. Symes, Sir Stewart. Tour of Duty. London, 1946.

Colonial service in Palestine, Tanganyika and Sudan, 1920-40; representative to Permanent Mandates Commission, Geneva, 1926, 1928, 1933.

636. Tallents, Sir Stephen. Man and Boy. London, 1943.

Chief British delegate for relief and supply of Poland, 1919; commissioner for the Baltic provinces, 1919-20; secretary, Empire Marketing Board, 1926-33; controller, public relations and then overseas service, BBC, 1935-41.

MEMOIRS

637. Tedder, 1st Baron (Marshal of the Royal Air Force Arthur William Tedder). With Prejudice: The War Memoirs. London, 1966.

Director of training, Air ministry, 1934-36; air commander-in-chief, Mediterranean air command, 1943; deputy supreme commander, allied air forces in Europe, 1943-45; see also his Air Power in War (London, 1948).

638. Teichman, Sir Eric. Travels of a Consular Officer in Eastern Tibet. London, 1922.

Chinese consular service, 1907; attached to legation at Peking, 1907-19; Chinese secretary, then counsellor, Peking, 1919-36; see also his Affairs of China: A Survey of the Recent History and Present Circumstances of the Republic of China (London, 1938); Journey to Turkistan (London, 1937); and Travels of a Consular Officer in North-West China (London, 1921).

639. Temperley, Arthur C. The Whispering Gallery of Europe. London, 1938.

Foreword by Anthony Eden; military attaché, The Hague, 1920-24; deputy director, military operations and intelligence, War Office, 1928-33; military representative at the League of Nations, 1925-38.

640. Templewood, 1st Viscount (Sir Samuel John Gurney Hoare).* Nine Troubled Years. London, 1954.

MP, 1910-44; secretary of state for Air, 1922-24, 1924-29; for India, 1931-35; for Foreign Affairs, 1935; first lord of the Admiralty, 1936-37; secretary of state for Home Affairs, 1937-39; lord privy seal, 1939-40; ambassador to Spain on special mission, 1940-44; other publications include The Fourth Seal (London, 1930); Ambassador on Special Mission (London, 1946); and Empire of the Air: The Advent of the Air Age, 1922-1929 (London, 1957).

641. Tennant, Ernest W.D. True Account. London, 1957.

Businessman; frequent visitor to interwar Germany; member of the Anglo-German Fellowship.

642. Thomas, James Henry.* My Story. London, 1937.

Secretary of state for Colonies, 1924, 1931, 1935-36; lord privy seal, 1929-30; secretary of state for the Dominions, 1930-35.

643. Thompson, Sir Geoffrey Harington. Front Line Diplomat. London, 1959.

Entered diplomatic service, 1920; served at home and abroad, including South America, Spain, United States, Iraq and Turkey, 1920-45.

644. Thomson, Rear-Admiral George Pirie. Blue Pencil Admiral. London, 1947.

Chief press censor, ministry of Information, 1941-45.

645. Thurtle, Ernest. Time's Winged Chariot: Memoirs and Comments. London, 1945.

Parliamentary private secretary to the minister of Pensions, 1924; secretary, ministry of Information, 1941-45.

646. Tilley, Sir John Anthony Cecil. London to Tokyo. London, 1942.

Entered Foreign Office, 1893; assistant secretary, 1919-20; ambassador to Brazil, 1921-25; and Tokyo, 1926-31.

647. Tizard, Sir Henry.* A Scientist in and out of the Civil Service. London, 1955.

Permanent secretary, Department of Scientific and Industrial Research, 1927-29; chairman, Aeronautical Research Committee, 1933-43; chairman, Air Defence Committee, 1935-40, responsible for development of radar; adviser, ministry of Aircraft Production, 1940-42.

648. Tree, Ronald. When the Moon Was High: Memoirs of Peace and War, 1897-1942. London, 1975.

MP, 1933-45; parliamentary private secretary to R.S. Hudson, 1936-38; and Sir John Reith, Alfred Duff Cooper, and Brendan Bracken, 1940-43.

649. Trevelyan, Baron (Humphrey Trevelyan). Public and Private. London, 1980.

Indian political service, 1932-47; later deputy under-secretary of state, Foreign Office, 1962; other publications include Worlds Apart (London, 1971); and Diplomatic Channels (London, 1973).

650. Vansittart, Baron (Robert Gilbert Vansittart).* Lessons of My Life: The Autobiography of Lord Vansittart. London, 1943.

Entered Foreign Office, 1903; secretary to Lord Curzon, 1920-24; assistant under-secretary of state for Foreign Affairs, 1928-30; permanent under-secretary of state for Foreign Affairs, 1930-38; chief diplomatic adviser to foreign secretary, 1938-41; further memoirs in The Mist Procession (London, 1958); of related interest are Black Record: Germans Past and Present (London, 1941); and Bones of Contention (London, 1945); and plays and film scripts.

651. Wavell, Archibald Percival (1st Earl Wavell).* Speaking Generally: Broadcasts, Orders and Addresses in Time of War, 1939-1943. London, 1946.

Military career, 1903-41; commander-in-chief, India, 1941; supreme commander, southwest Pacific, 1941-43; viceroy of India, 1943-47; see also his The Viceroy's Journal, edited by Penderel Moon (London, 1973); and Soldiers and Soldiering (London, 1953).

652. Wedgwood, Josiah Clement (1st Baron Wedgwood).* Memoirs of a Fighting Life. London, 1941.

MP, 1906-42; chancellor of the Duchy of Lancaster, 1924.

653. Weir, Sir Cecil McAlpine. Civilian Assignment. London, 1953.

Industrialist and public servant; with ministry of Supply, and Board of Trade, 1940-46.

654. Wellesley, Sir Victor. Diplomacy in Fetters. London, 1944.

Page of honour to Queen Victoria, 1887-92; counsellor, far eastern department, Foreign Office, 1920-24; assistant then deputy under-secretary, 1924-36; see also his Recollections of a Soldier-Diplomat (London, 1947).

655. West, Air Commodore F.M.F. "Freddie." Winged Diplomat. London, 1962.

Air attaché, Helsingfors, Riga, Tallin, Kovno, 1936-1938; Rome, 1940; Berne, 1940.

656.   Wheeler-Bennett, Sir John W. Knaves, Fools and Heroes: In Europe between the Wars. London, 1974.

Diplomatic historian and biographer; assistant director, British Press Service, New York, 1940-41; head of New York office of Political Warfare Mission, 1942-44; with Foreign Office, 1944; assistant to British political adviser to SHAEF, 1944-45; memoirs continued in Special Relationships: America in Peace and War (London, 1975); and Friends, Enemies and Sirens (London, 1978); see too his A Wreath to Clio: Studies in British, American and German Affairs (New York, 1967).

657.   Willert, Sir Arthur. Washington and Other Memories. Boston, 1972.

Journalist with The Times, 1906-20; ministry of Information representative, Washington, 1917-18; joined Foreign Office, 1921; resigned as head of news department, 1935; with ministry of Information, 1939-45; see also his The Road to Safety: A Study in Anglo-American Relations (London, 1952)

658.   Wilson, 1st Baron (Field-Marshal Sir Henry Maitland Wilson). Eight Years Overseas, 1939-1947. London, 1950.

General officer commander-in-chief, Egypt, 1939; Cyrenaica, 1941; Greece, 1941; and Persia-Iraq command, 1942-43; commander-in-chief, Middle East, 1943; supreme allied commander, Mediterranean, 1944; head of British joint staff mission, Washington, 1944-45.

659.   Wilson, Sir Arnold.* Mesopotamia, 1917-1920: A Clash of Loyalties. London, 1931.

Civil commissioner in Persian Gulf, 1918-20; with Anglo-Persian Oil Company, 1921-32; MP, 1933-40; diary extracts in Walks and Talks (London, 1934); Thoughts and Talks (London, 1938); Walks and Talks Abroad (London, 1936); and More Thoughts and Talks (London, 1939).

660.   Wilson, Field-Marshal Sir Henry Hughes.* The Military Correspondence of Field-Marshal Sir Henry Wilson, 1918-1922. Edited by Keith Jeffrey. London, 1985.

Chief of the imperial general staff, 1918-22.

661. Windsor, Edward, Duke of.* A King's Story. London, 1951.

Prince of Wales, 1910-36; succeeded as king and abdicated, 1936; and of related interest the Duchess of Windsor, The Heart Has Its Reasons (London, 1956).

662. Wingate, Sir Ronald Evelyn Leslie. Not in the Limelight. London, 1959.

Indian political service, 1919-39; with joint planning staff, offices of the war cabinet, 1939-45.

663. Winterbotham, Frederick William. The Ultra Spy: An Autobiography. London, 1989.

Air staff and Foreign Office, 1929-45; served that time with the Secret Intelligence Service; see also his The Nazi Connection (London, 1978); and Secret and Personal (London, 1969).

664. Winterton, 6th Earl (Edward Turnour).* Orders of the Day. London, 1953.

MP, 1904-51; parliamentary under-secretary for India, 1922-24, 1924-29; chancellor of the Duchy of Lancaster, 1937-39; member of the cabinet, 1938-39; further random recollections in Fifty Tumultuous Years (London, 1955).

665. Woolf, Leonard Sidney.* Downhill All the Way: An Autobiography of the Years 1919-1939. London, 1967.

Literary editor, The Nation, 1923-30; joint editor, Political Quarterly, 1931-59; continued in The Journey Not the Arrival Matters: An Autobiography of the Years, 1939-1969 (London, 1969); see also his Letters, edited by Frederic Spotts (London, 1990).

666. Woolton, 1st Earl of (Frederick James Marquis). Memoirs. London, 1959.

Minister of Food, 1940-43; minister of Reconstruction, 1943-45; lord president of the Council, 1945, 1951-52.

667. Young, Arthur Primrose. Across the Years. London, 1971.

In contact with anti-Hitler resistance, 1937-39; with ministry of Labour, 1940-41.

668.   Zetland, 2nd Marquess of (Lawrence John Lumley Dundas, Earl of Ronaldshay). 'Essayez': Memoirs. London, 1956.

Secretary of state for India, 1935-40; and Burma, 1937-40.

669.   Zuckerman, Baron (Sir Solly Zuckerman). From Apes to Warlords, 1904-1946. London, 1978.

Scientific advisory posts, RAF, 1939-46; continued in Monkeys, Men and Missiles: An Autobiography (London, 1989).

Non-British in London

670.   Alphand, Hervé. L'étonnement d'être: Journal, 1939-1973. Paris, 1977.

Director, economic affairs, Free French in London, 1941-44.

671.   Azcárate, Pablo de. Mi embajada en Londres durante la guerra civil española. Barcelona, 1976.

Member of League of Nations secretariat, 1922-33; deputy secretary-general, 1933-36; Spanish ambassador at London, 1936-39; see also his League of Nations and National Minorities: An Experiment (London, 1945).

672.   Bastianini, Giuseppe. Uomini, cose, fatti: Memorie di un ambasciatore. Milan, 1959.

Italian ambassador at London, 1939-40.

673.   Beneš, Eduard. Pameti od Mnichova k nové válce a k novému vitežstvi. Prague, 1947. Eng. trans., Memoirs: From Munich to New War and New Victory. London, 1954.

The first, and only, of three projected volumes by the Czech president, 1935-38; and president of the Czech National Committee in London, 1939-45.

674.   Blondel, Jules-François. Ce que mes yeux ont vu de 1900 à 1950: Récit d'un diplomate. 2 vols. Arras, n.d.

Attached to London embassy, 1919-21; director of Comité National Français in London, 1942; see also Au fil de la carrière: Récit d'un diplomate, 1911-1938 (Paris, 1960).

675. Cambon, Pierre Paul. Correspondance, 1870-1924. 3 vols. Paris, 1940-46.

French ambassador at London, 1898-1920.

676. Casey, Baron (Richard Gardiner Casey). Personal Experience, 1939-1946. London, 1962.

Minister of state resident in the Middle East, and member of the British war cabinet, 1942-43; later Australian foreign minister, 1951-60; see also his Friends and Neighbours (Melbourne, 1954).

677. Dawes, Charles Gates. Journal as Ambassador to Great Britain. New York, 1939.

Recollections, based largely on diaries, of US ambassador to London, 1929-32; equally important on the Dawes plan is his A Journal of Reparations (New York, 1939).

678. Dirksen, Herbert von. Moskau, Tokio, London: Erinnerungen und Betrachtungen zu 20 Jahren deutscher Aussenpolitik, 1919-1939. Stuttgart, 1949. Abr. Eng. trans., Moscow, Tokyo, London: Twenty Years of German Foreign Policy. London, 1951.

German ambassador at London, 1938-39.

679. Fitz Randolph, Sigismund-Sizzo. Der Frühstücksattaché aus London. Stuttgart, 1954.

Press attaché at German embassy in London, 1933-39.

680. Franckenstein, Sir George. Facts and Features of My Life. London, 1939.

Austrian minister at London, 1920-38.

681. Gaulle, Général Charles de. Mémoires de guerre. 3 vols. Paris, 1954-59. Eng. trans., War Memoirs, 2 vols. London, 1955-59.

Commander-in-chief, Fighting French Forces, 1940-43; president, French Committee for National Liberation, 1943-44; president, provisional government of the French republic, 1944-46; see also his Lettres, notes, carnets (Paris, 1980-84).

682.   Golikov, Marshal Filip Ivanovich. S Voennoi missiei v Anglii i SSHA. Moscow, 1986. Eng. trans., On a Military Mission to Great Britain and the USA. Moscow, 1987.

Headed Soviet military mission to Britain and the USA, July-August 1941.

683.   Grandi, Dino. Il mio paese: Ricordi autobiographici. Edited by Renzo De Felice. Bologna, 1985.

Italy's ambassador at London, 1932-39; see also his 25 luglio: Quarant'anni dopo (Bologna, 1983); and Dino Grandi racconta l'evitabile "Asse," edited by Gianfranco Bianchi (Milan, 1984).

684.   Gripenberg, Georg Achates. Finland and the Great Powers: Memoirs of a Diplomat. Lincoln, NE, 1965.

Finnish minister at London, 1933-41.

685.   Groussard, Georges A. Service secret, 1940-1945. Paris, 1964.

On secret mission to London, 1941; worked with British intelligence, 1942-45.

686.   Hägglöf, Gunnar. Diplomat: Memoirs of a Swedish Envoy in London, Paris, Berlin, Moscow and Washington. London, 1972.

Attached to Swedish consulate-general in London, 1928-29; minister accredited to Belgian and Netherlands wartime governments in London, 1944.

687.   Harriman, W. Averell. Special Envoy to Churchill and Stalin, 1941-1946. With the assistance of Elie Abel. New York, 1975.

Roosevelt's special representative to London, with rank of minister, 1941; Combined Shipping Adjustment Board representative in London, 1941.

688.   Henle, Günter. Weggenosse des Jahrhunderts. Stuttgart, 1968.

Served at German embassy in London, 1931-36.

689. Hesse, Fritz. Das Spiel um Deutschland. Munich, 1953. Eng. trans., Hitler and the English. London, 1954.

Deutsches Nachrichten Büro representative and press attaché at German embassy, London, 1935-39; see also his Das Vorspiel zum Kriege: Englandberichte und Erlebnisse eines Tatzeugen, 1935-1945 (Leoni am Starnberger See, 1979).

690. Hymans, Paul. Mémoires. 2 vols. Brussels, 1958.

Belgian minister at London, 1915-17; minister of Foreign Affairs, 1918-20, 1924-25, 1927-36; see also his Fragments d'histoire: Impressions et souvenirs (Brussels, 1940).

691. Kharlamov, Admiral Nikolai. Trudnaia missiia. Moscow, 1983. Eng. trans., Difficult Mission. Moscow, 1986.

Head of Soviet military mission, London, 1941-45.

692. Kleffens, Eelco Nicolaas van. The Rape of the Netherlands. London, 1940.

Dutch minister of Foreign Affairs, 1939-46; with government in exile, London, 1940-45.

693. Lee, Raymond E. The London Observer: The Journal of General Raymond E. Lee, 1940-1941. Edited by James R. Leutze. London, 1972.

US military attaché, London, 1935-39, 1940-41.

694. Maisky, Ivan. Vospominaniia sovetskogo posla. 2 vols. Moscow, 1964.

Counsellor, Soviet embassy, London, 1925-27; then Soviet ambassador, 1932-43; translations from the Russian have appeared as Journey into the Past (London, 1962); Who Helped Hitler? (London, 1964); Spanish Notebooks (London, 1966); and Memoirs of a Soviet Ambassador: The War, 1939-1943 (London, 1967); of related interest is his Before the Storm (London, 1944).

695. Massey, Vincent. What's Past is Prologue. London, 1963.

Canadian high commissioner at London, 1935-46.

696.   Massigli, René. *Une comédie des erreurs, 1943-1956.* Paris, 1978.

Commissioner for foreign affairs, Free French, 1943-44; ambassador at London, 1944-55.

697.   Monick, Emmanuel. *Pour mémoire.* Paris, 1970.

French financial attaché, London, 1934-40.

698.   Monnet, Jean. *Mémoires.* Paris, 1976. Eng. trans., *Memoirs.* London, 1978.

French representative on various interallied executive committees, London, 1917-18; chairman, Anglo-French economic coordination committee, 1939; member, British Supply Council, Washington, 1940-43.

699.   Moravec, General Frantisek. *Master of Spies: The Memoirs of General Moravec.* London, 1975.

Head of Czechoslovak military intelligence in Prague, and then with exiled organisation in London, 1937-45.

700.   Palmstierna, Erik. *Atskelliga egenheter.* Stockholm, 1950.

Swedish minister at London, 1920-37.

701.   Passy, Colonel [André Dewavrin]. *Souvenirs.* 3 vols. Monte Carlo, 1947-51.

Head of counterintelligence for Free French in London, 1940-43.

702.   Pearson, Lester B. *Mike: The Memoirs of the Right Honourable Lester B. Pearson.* 3 vols. Toronto, Ontario, 1972-75.

Counsellor to Canadian high commission in London, 1935-41; later Canadian prime minister, 1963-68.

703.   Putlitz, Wolfgang Gans Edler Herr zu. *Unterwegs nach Deutschland: Erinnerungen eines ehemaligen Diplomaten.* Berlin, 1956. Abr. Eng. trans., *The Putlitz Dossier.* London, 1957.

Headed consular division, German embassy, London, 1934-38.

704. Raczynski, Count Edward. W Sojuszniczym Londynie: Dziennik Ambasadora Edwarda Raczynskiego, 1939-1945. London, 1960. Eng. trans., In Allied London. London, 1962.

Polish ambassador at London, 1934-45; acting Polish minister for Foreign Affairs, 1941-43; see also his The British-Polish Alliance: Its Origin and Meaning (London, 1948).

705. Reventlow, Eduard. I dansk tjeneste. Copenhagen, 1956.

Danish minister at London, 1938-47.

706. Ribbentrop, Joachim von. Zwischen London und Moskau: Erinnerungen und letzte Aufzeichnungen Edited by Anneliese von Ribbentrop. Leoni am Starnberger See, 1953. Eng. trans., The Ribbentrop Memoirs. London, 1954.

German ambassador at London, 1936-38.

707. Ritchie, Charles. The Siren Years: A Canadian Diplomat Abroad, 1937-1945. London, 1974.

Second secretary, Canadian high commission, London, 1939; 1st secretary, 1943-45; later high commissioner.

708. Rueff, Jacques. Oeuvres complètes: I, De l'aube au crépuscule; Autobiographie de l'auteur. Paris, 1977.

Financial attaché, French embassy, London, 1930-33; more in his Combats pour l'ordre financier: Mémoires et documents pour servir à l'Histoire du dernier demi-siècle (Paris, 1972).

709. Saint-Aulaire, Comte Auguste de. Confession d'un vieux diplomate. Paris, 1953.

Ambassador at London, 1920-24; see also his Je suis diplomate (Paris, 1954).

710. Schweppenburg, Leo Geyr von. Erinnerungen eines Militärattachés, London, 1933-1937. Stuttgart, 1949. Eng. trans., The Critical Years. London, 1952.

German military attaché in London, 1933-37; foreword by Leslie Hore-Belisha.

711. Shigemitsu, Mamoru. Japan and Her Destiny: My Struggle for Peace. London, 1958.

Japanese ambassador at London, 1938-41.

712. Smuts, Jan Christiaan. Selections from the Smuts Papers. Edited by W.K. Hancock and Jean van der Poel. 7 vols. London, 1966-73.

Vols. 5-6 for 1919-45; South African representative, imperial war cabinet, 1917-18; prime minister, 1919-24; at Paris peace conference, 1919.

713. Soustelle, Jacques. Envers et contre tout. 2 vols. Paris, 1947-50.

Joined Charles de Gaulle in London, 1940; active in Free French information services; vice-chief of cabinet, 1944.

714. Stirling, Alfred. Lord Bruce: The London Years. Melbourne, 1974.

Memoir-history-biography by counsellor in the Australian high commission; mainly dealing with period 1936-45.

715. Thayer, Charles W. Hands across the Caviar. London, 1953.

US foreign service, 1933-53; in London, 1943-44.

716. Velebit, Vladimir. Secanja. Zagreb, 1983.

Head of the Yugoslav partisan mission to the Middle East and London, 1943-45.

717. Vogel, Georg. Diplomat unter Hitler und Adenauer. Düsseldorf, 1969.

Various diplomatic postings, including consular division, London, 1937-39.

718. Wimmer, Lothar. Expériences et tribulations d'un diplomate autrichien entre deux guerres, 1929-1938. Neuchâtel, 1946.

Austrian legation counsellor in London, 1930-34; and later ambassador, 1951-55; continued in Zwischen Ballhausplatz und Downing Street (Vienna, 1958).

719.   Winant, John Gilbert. <u>A Letter from Grosvenor Square: An Account of a Stewardship</u>. London, 1947.

US ambassador at London, 1941-46; only covers events of 1941; see also his <u>Our Greatest Harvest: Selected Speeches</u> (London, 1950).

720.   Yoshida, Shigeru. <u>The Yoshida Memoirs: The Story of Japan in Crisis</u>. London, 1961.

Japanese ambassador at London, 1936-38.

2. British Biographies

721.   Aldington, Richard. <u>Lawrence of Arabia: A Biographical Enquiry</u>. London, 1955.

Subsequent studies include Suleiman Mousa, <u>T.E. Lawrence: An Arab View</u> (London, 1966); Phillip Knightley and Colin Simpson, <u>The Secret Lives of Lawrence of Arabia</u> (London, 1969); John E. Mack, <u>A Prince of Our Disorder</u> (London, 1976); H. Montgomery Hyde, <u>Solitary in the Ranks: Lawrence of Arabia as Airman and Private Soldier</u> (London, 1978); Desmond Stewart, <u>T.E. Lawrence</u> (London, 1977); Malcolm Brown and Julia Cave, <u>A Touch of Genius: The Life of T.E. Lawrence</u> (London, 1988); Jeremy Wilson, <u>Lawrence of Arabia: The Authorised Biography</u> (London, 1989); and <u>T. E. Lawrence: Soldier, Writer, Legend: New Essays</u>, edited by Jeffrey Meyers (London, 1990).

722.   Anderson, Mosa. <u>Noel Buxton: A Life</u>. London, 1952.

MP, 1910-18, 1922-30; minister of Agriculture, 1924, 1929-30.

723.   Aspinall-Oglander, Cecil. <u>Roger Keyes</u>. London, 1951.

See also Roger Keyes, <u>Outrageous Fortune</u> (London, 1990).

724.   Ayerst, David. <u>Garvin of the Observer</u>. London, 1985.

Editor of the <u>Observer</u>, 1908-42; see also Katharine Garvin, <u>J.L. Garvin: A Memoir</u> (London, 1948); and for background, Alfred M. Gollin, <u>The Observer and J.L. Garvin, 1908-1914</u> (London, 1960).

725.   Beesly, Patrick. <u>Very Special Admiral: The Life of Admiral J.H. Godfrey, CB.</u> London, 1980.

Deputy director, plans division, Admiralty, 1933-35; director of naval intelligence, 1939-42.

726.   Birkenhead, Earl of. <u>Halifax: The Life of Lord Halifax</u>. London, 1965.

Based on Lord Halifax's private papers; supersedes previous biographies such as Alan Campbell Johnson, <u>Viscount Halifax</u> (London, 1941); and Stuart Hodgson, <u>Lord Halifax</u> (London, 1941).

727.   ———. <u>The Prof. in Two Worlds</u>. London, 1961.

Official life of Frederick Alexander Lindemann, 1st Baron Cherwell; Churchill's personal scientific adviser in wartime; another study is R.F. Harrod, <u>The Prof.: A Personal Memoir of Lord Cherwell</u> (London, 1959).

728.   ———. <u>Walter Monckton</u>. London, 1969.

1st Viscount Monckton; deputy director-general and then director-general of ministry of Information, 1940-41; solicitor-general, 1945.

729.   Blake, Robert. <u>The Unknown Prime Minister: The Life and Times of Andrew Bonar Law, 1858-1923.</u> London, 1955.

Chancellor of the Exchequer, 1916-18; prime minister, 1922-23.

730.   Blaxland, Gregory. <u>J.H. Thomas: A Life for Unity</u>. London, 1964.

See also Basil Fuller, <u>The Life Story of the Rt. Hon. J.H. Thomas: A Statesman of the People</u> (London, 1943).

731.   Bolitho, Hector. <u>Alfred Mond: First Lord Melchett</u>. London, 1933.

MP, 1906, 1910-23, 1924-28; minister of Health, 1921-22; see also Jean Goodman, <u>The Mond Legacy</u> (London, 1982); based on family papers.

732.   Bonham-Carter, Victor. <u>Soldier True: The Life and Times of Field-Marshal Sir William Robertson, 1860-1933</u>. London, 1963.

733.   Bowle, John. <u>Viscount Samuel: A Biography</u>. London, 1957.

734.   Boyle, Andrew. <u>Montagu Norman: A Biography</u>. London, 1967.

Governor of the Bank of England, 1920-44; equally useful is Sir Henry Clay, Lord Norman (London, 1957).

735. ———. Only the Wind Will Listen: Reith of the B.B.C. London, 1972.

736. ———. Trenchard: Man of Vision. London, 1962.

Authorised biography of 1st Viscount Trenchard; chief of air staff, 1918-29; see also Wing-Commander H.R. Allen, The Legacy of Lord Trenchard (London, 1972).

737. Brittain, Vera. Pethick-Lawrence: A Portrait. London, 1963.

738. Broderick, Alan Houghton. Near to Greatness: A Life of the Sixth Earl Winterton. London, 1965.

739. Brown, Anthony Cave. The Secret Servant: The Life of Sir Stewart Menzies, Head of British Intelligence, 1939-1952. London, 1987.

First assigned to intelligence, 1916; military liaison officer with MI6, 1919-39; "appointed 'C,' head of MI6, 1939; responsible also for supervision of Government Code and Cypher School, which broke the German 'Enigma' code" (Concise DNB, 1901-1970).

740. Brown, Gordon. Maxton. Edinburgh, 1986.

MP, 1922-46; chairman, ILP, 1926-31, 1934-46; see also William Knox, James Maxton (London, 1987); John McNair, James Maxton: The Beloved Rebel (London, 1955); and Gilbert McAllister, James Maxton: The Portrait of a Rebel (London, 1935).

741. Buchan, William. John Buchan: A Memoir. London, 1982.

By his son; see also Janet Adam Smith, John Buchan: A Biography (London, 1965); and Arthur C. Turner, Mr. Buchan, Writer (London, 1949).

742. Bullock, Alan. The Life and Times of Ernest Bevin. 3 vols. London, 1960-83.

Minister of Labour and National Service, 1940-45; secretary of state for Foreign Affairs, 1945-51; see also Mark Stephens,

Ernest Bevin (London, 1981); Francis Williams, Ernest Bevin (London, 1952); and Trevor Evans, Bevin (London, 1946).

743.   Busch, Briton Cooper. Hardinge of Penshurst: A Study in the Old Diplomacy. Hamden, CT, 1980.

744.   Butler, Ewan. Mason-Mac: The Life of Lieutenant-General Sir Noel Mason-MacFarlane. London, 1972.

Military attaché in Europe, including Berlin, 1937-39; commander-in-chief, Gibraltar, 1942-44; chief commissioner, allied control commission for Italy, 1944.

745.   Butler, J.R.M. Lord Lothian (Philip Kerr), 1882-1940. London, 1960.

More in The Larger Idea: Lord Lothian and the Problem of National Sovereignty, edited by John Turner (London, 1988); and Lord Lothian: Una vita per la pace, edited by Giulio Guderzo (Florence, 1986).

746.   Callwell, Sir Charles Edward. Field-Marshal Sir Henry Wilson: His Life and Diaries. 2 vols. London, 1927.

Authorised biography; vol. 2 for 1917-22; see also Bernard Ash, The Lost Dictator: A Biography of Field-Marshal Sir Henry Wilson (London, 1968); and Basil Collier, Brasshat: A Biography of Field-Marshal Sir Henry Wilson, 1864-1922 (London, 1961).

747.   Campbell, John. F.E. Smith: First Earl of Birkenhead. London, 1983.

Attorney-general, 1915-19; lord chancellor, 1920-22; secretary of state for India, 1924-28; still useful are William Camp, The Glittering Prizes (London, 1960); and Earl of Birkenhead, Frederick Edwin, 1st Earl of Birkenhead, 2 vols. (London, 1933-35).

748.   Cecil, David. The Cecils of Hatfield House: An English Ruling Family. London, 1973.

Including 1st Viscount Cecil of Chelwood; see also Kenneth Rose, The Later Cecils (London, 1975).

749.   Chalmers, William Scott. Full Cycle: The Biography of Admiral Sir Bertram Home Ramsay. London, 1959.

On staff of Imperial Defence College, 1931-33; allied naval commander-in-chief, expeditionary force, 1944-45; see also David Woodward, Ramsay at War: The Fighting Life of Admiral Sir Bertram Ramsay (London, 1957).

750.   Charmley, John. Duff Cooper: The Authorised Biography. London, 1986.

Of related interest, see Philip Ziegler, Diana Cooper (London, 1981).

751.   ———. Lord Lloyd and the Decline of the British Empire. London, 1987.

MP, 1918-23, 1924-25; high commissioner for Egypt and the Sudan, 1925-29; chairman of the British Council, 1937-41; secretary of state for the Colonies, 1940-41; based on Lloyd's private papers; see also Colin Forbes Adam, Life of Lord Lloyd (London, 1948); Lord Lloyd, The British Case (London, 1939); and his Egypt since Cromer, 2 vols. (London, 1933-34).

752.   Churchill, Randolph S. Lord Derby, "King of Lancashire": The Official Life of Edward, Seventeenth Earl of Derby, 1865-1948. London, 1959.

Secretary of state for War, 1916-18, 1922-24; ambassador to France, 1918-20.

753.   Churchill, Randolph S., and Gilbert, Martin. Winston S. Churchill. 8 vols. London, 1966-88.

The official biography; only vols. 1-2 by Randolph S. Churchill; vols. 4-7 for 1917-45; Randolph S. Churchill and Martin Gilbert, Winston S. Churchill: Companion Volume (London, 1967-); in several parts, each companion volume publishes material from the Churchill papers and numerous other sources; supersedes all current or the many previous biographies such as William Manchester, The Last Lion: Winston Spencer Churchill, vol. 1, 1874-1932; vol. 2, 1932-1940 (London, 1983-88); and Henry Pelling, Winston Churchill, 2nd. ed. (London, 1989); assessments include Kenneth W. Thompson, Winston Churchill's World View: Statesmanship and Power (London, 1983); Churchill: A Profile, edited by Peter Stansky (New York, 1973); Robert Rhodes James, Churchill: A Study in Failure, 1900-1939 (London, 1970); and A.J.P. Taylor et al., Churchill Revised: A Critical Assessment (London, 1969); and of related interest, Mary Soames, Clementine

Churchill (London, 1979); and Brian Roberts, Randolph: A Study of Churchill's Son (London, 1984).

754. Clark, Ronald W. Tizard. London, 1965.

755. Cline, Catherine Ann. E.D. Morel, 1873-1924: The Strategies of Protest. Belfast, 1980.

Secretary and part founder, Union of Democratic Control; joined ILP, 1918; MP, 1922-24.

756. Cocker, Mark. Richard Meinertzhagen: Soldier, Scientist and Spy. London, 1989.

See also John Lord, Duty, Honour, Empire: The Life and Times of Colonel Richard Meinertzhagen. London, 1970.

757. Cockerill, A.W. Sir Percy Sillitoe. London, 1975.

758. Collier, Basil. Leader of the Few: The Authorised Biography of Air Chief Marshal the Lord Dowding of Bentley Priory. London, 1957.

Director of training, Air ministry, 1926-29; air officer commanding-in-chief, fighter command, 1936-40; on special duty in Washington, 1940-41; see also Robert Wright, Dowding and the Battle of Britain (London, 1969).

759. Colville, John R. Man of Valour: The Life of Field-Marshal the Viscount Gort. London, 1972.

Chief of imperial general staff, 1937-39; commander-in-chief, British field force, 1939-40, commander-in-chief, Gibraltar, 1941-42; Malta, 1942-44; and Palestine, 1944-45.

760. Cooke, Colin. The Life of Richard Stafford Cripps. London, 1957.

Solicitor-general, 1930-31; ambassador to Russia, 1940-42; lord privy seal, 1942; minister of Aircraft Production, 1942-45; see also Eric Estorick, Stafford Cripps: A Biography (London, 1949); and Patricia Strauss, Cripps (London, 1943).

761. Coote, Colin. A Companion of Honour: The Story of Walter Elliot. London, 1965.

Financial secretary to the Treasury, 1931-32; minister of Agriculture and Fisheries, 1932-36; secretary of state for Scotland, 1936-38; minister of Health, 1938-40; director of public relations, War Office, 1941-42.

762. Cross, J.A. Lord Swinton. London, 1982.

763. ———. Sir Samuel Hoare: A Political Biography. London, 1977.

764. Dayer, Roberta Allbert. Finance and Empire: Sir Charles Addis, 1861-1945. London, 1988.

Director, Bank of England, 1918-32; vice-chairman, Bank for International Settlements, 1929-32.

765. Deacon, Richard. "C": A Biography of Sir Maurice Oldfield, Head of MI6. London, 1985.

Intelligence corps, Middle East, 1941-46; deputy and then head of MI6, 1973-78.

766. Dilks, David. Neville Chamberlain, vol. 1, Pioneering and Reform, 1869-1929. London, 1984-.

Also based on Chamberlain's papers and still valuable is Keith Feiling, The Life of Neville Chamberlain (London, 1946); see too H. Montgomery Hyde, Neville Chamberlain (London, 1976); William R. Rock, Neville Chamberlain (New York, 1969); Iain Macleod, Neville Chamberlain (London, 1961); Derek Walker-Smith, Neville Chamberlain (London, 1940); Duncan Keith-Shaw, Prime Minister Neville Chamberlain (London, 1939); Stuart Hodgson, The Man Who Made the Peace: The Story of Neville Chamberlain (London, 1938); and the family biographies by D.H. Elletson, The Chamberlains (London, 1966); and Sir Charles Petrie, The Chamberlain Tradition (London, 1952).

767. Dixon, Piers. Double Diploma: The Life of Sir Pierson Dixon, Don and Diplomat. London, 1968.

Served at British embassies in Madrid, 1932; Ankara, 1936; and Rome, 1938; principal private secretary to the secretary of state for Foreign Affairs, 1943-48.

768. Donaldson, Frances. Edward VIII. London, 1974.

See also Philip Ziegler, King Edward VIII (London, 1990); and Michael Bloch, The Duke of Windsor's War (London, 1983).

769.   Donoghue, Bernard, and Jones, G.W. Herbert Morrison: Portrait of a Politician. London, 1973.

770.   Dutton, David. Austen Chamberlain: Gentleman in Politics. London, 1985.

Of continuing value is Sir Charles Petrie, The Life and Letters of the Rt. Hon. Sir Austen Chamberlain, 2 vols. (London, 1939-40); vol. 2 for 1915-36.

771.   Edwards, Ruth Dudley. Victor Gollancz: A Biography. London, 1987.

772.   Evans, Trefor Ellis. Mission to Egypt, 1934-46: Lord Killearn, High Commissioner and Ambassador. Cardiff, 1971.

Author in consular service, 1937-41; private secretary to Lord Killearn, 1941-45.

773.   Foot, Michael. Aneurin Bevan: A Biography. 2 vols. London, 1962-73.

MP, 1929-60; editor, Tribune, 1942-45; minister of Health and Housing, 1945-51; vol. 1 for 1897-1945; see also John Campbell, Nye Bevan and the Mirage of British Socialism (London, 1987); Vincent Brome, Aneurin Bevan (London, 1953); and Mark M. Krug, Aneurin Bevan: Cautious Rebel (London, 1961).

774.   Fraser, David. Alanbrooke. London, 1982.

Based on war diaries and letters of Field-Marshal Sir Alan Brooke, 1st Viscount Alanbrooke; commander-in-chief, home forces, 1940-41; chief of the imperial general staff, 1941-46; see also Sir Arthur Bryant, The Turn of the Tide, 1939-1943 (London, 1957); and Triumph in the West, 1943-1946 (London, 1959).

775.   Gardner, Brian. Allenby. London, 1965.

1st Viscount, Field-Marshal Sir Edmund Allenby; military career, 1884-1917; commander-in-chief, Egyptian expeditionary force, 1917-19; high commissioner for Egypt, 1919-25; see also Field-Marshal Viscount Wavell, Allenby: A Study in Greatness, 2 vols. (London, 1940-44).

776.   Gilbert, Martin. Plough My Own Furrow: The Story of Lord Allen of Hurtwood as Told through His Writings and Correspondence. London, 1965.

Chairman, ILP, 1922-26; director, Daily Herald, 1925-30; advocate of Anglo-German conciliation in 1930s; visited Hitler twice; see also Arthur Marwick, Clifford Allen: The Open Conspirator (London, 1964); and of related interest, Lady Marjory Allen, Memoirs of an Uneducated Lady (London, 1975).

777.   ———. Sir Horace Rumbold: Portrait of a Diplomat, 1869-1941. London, 1973.

Minister at Berne, 1916-19; and Warsaw, 1919-20; high commissioner, Constantinople, 1920-24; ambassador at Madrid, 1924-28; and Berlin, 1928-33.

778.   Gollin, Alfred M. Proconsul in Politics: A Study of Lord Milner in Opposition and in Power. London, 1964.

Minister without portfolio, 1916-18; secretary of state for War, 1918; secretary of state for Colonies, 1918-21; other studies include Terence O'Brien, Milner (London, 1979); John Marlowe, Milner (London, 1976); Edward Crankshaw, The Forsaken Idea: A Study of Viscount Milner (London, 1952); and John Evelyn Wrench, Alfred, Lord Milner, 1854-1925 (London, 1958).

779.   Graves, Philip. The Life of Sir Percy Cox. London, 1941.

Acting minister, Tehran, 1918-20; high commissioner in Iraq, 1920-23.

780.   Grieves, Keith. Sir Eric Geddes: Business and Government in War and Peace. Manchester, 1990.

First lord of the Admiralty, 1918-19; MP, 1917-22; minister of Transport, 1919-21

781.   Groot, Gerard J. De. Douglas Haig, 1861-1928. London, 1988.

See also James Marshall-Cornwall, Haig as Military Commander (London, 1973); John Terraine, Haig: The Educated Soldier (London, 1963); John Charteris, Field-Marshal Earl Haig (London, 1929); and Alfred Duff Cooper, Haig, 2 vols. (London, 1935-36).

782.   Hamilton, Nigel. Monty. 3 vols. London, 1981-86.

Vol. 1 to 1942; vol. 2, 1942-44; vol. 3, 1944-76; other studies include Monty at Close Quarters: Recollections of the Man, edited by T.E.B. Howarth (London, 1985); Alun Chalfont, Montgomery of Alamein (London, 1976); Ronald Lewin, Montgomery as Military Commander (London, 1971); Ronald W. Clark, Montgomery of Alamein (London, 1960); and Alan Moorehead, Montgomery (London, 1946).

783.   Hammond, John Lawrence.   C.P. Scott of the "Manchester Guardian." London, 1934.

784.   Harington, General Sir Charles. Plumer of Messines. London, 1935.

1st Viscount Plumer; governor of Malta, 1919-24; high commissioner in Palestine, 1925-28.

785.   Harris, Henry Wilson. J.A. Spender. London, 1946.

786.   Harris, Kenneth. Attlee. London, 1982.

The official biography; of equal interest is Trevor Burridge, Clement Attlee: A Political Biography (London, 1986); both supersede previous studies such as Francis Williams, A Prime Minister Remembers (London, 1961); and Roy Jenkins, Mr. Attlee: An Interim Biography (London, 1948).

787.   Hassall, Christopher. Edward Marsh. London, 1959.

Private secretary to Winston Churchill, 1917-22, 1924-29; to J.H. Thomas, 1924, 1929-36; and to Malcolm MacDonald, 1936-37.

788.   Hill, Prudence. To Know the Sky: The Life of Air Chief Marshal Sir Roderic Hill. London, 1962.

Director, technical development, Air ministry, 1938-40; director-general, research and development, ministry of Aircraft Production, 1940-41; air marshal commanding air defence of Britain, 1943-44; fighter command, 1944-45.

789.   Hoggart, Simon, and Leigh, David. Michael Foot: A Portrait. London, 1981.

Assistant editor, Tribune, 1937-38; acting editor, Evening Standard, 1942; later editor, Tribune, and leader of the Labour party, 1980-83.

790.   Hore-Belisha, Leslie (Baron Hore-Belisha). The Private Papers of Hore-Belisha. Edited by R.J. Minney. London, 1960.

MP, 1923-45; parliamentary secretary, Board of Trade, 1931-32; financial secretary to Treasury, 1932-34; minister of Transport, 1934-37; secretary of state for War, 1937-40; minister of National Insurance, 1945.

791.   Horne, Alistair. Macmillan. 2 vols. London, 1988-89.

The official biography; vol. 1 for the period to 1956; see also Nigel Fisher, Harold Macmillan: A Biography (London, 1982); George Hutchinson, The Last Edwardian at No. 10: An Impression of Harold Macmillan (London, 1980); Anthony Sampson, Macmillan: A Study in Ambiguity (London, 1967); and Emrys Hughes, Macmillan: Portrait of a Politician (London, 1962).

792.   Howard, Anthony. RAB: The Life of R.A. Butler. London, 1987.

The authorised biography; see also Patrick Cosgrave, R.A. Butler: An English Life (London, 1981); Francis Boyd, Richard Austen Butler (London, 1956); and Gerald Sparrow, "R.A.B.": Study of a Statesman (London, 1956).

793.   Howarth, Patrick. Intelligence Chief Extraordinary: The Life of the Ninth Duke of Portland. London, 1986.

Entered Diplomatic Service, 1915; served variously Warsaw, Paris, The Hague, Athens, Santiago, 1919-37; transferred to Foreign Office, 1937; chairman, Joint Intelligence Committee, 1939-45.

794.   Hubback, David. No Ordinary Press Baron: A Life of Walter Layton. London, 1985.

Director, economic and finance section, the League of Nations, 1920; editor, The Economist, 1922-38; chairman, News Chronicle, 1930-50; with ministry of Supply, 1940-42; and ministry of Production, 1941-43.

795.   Humble, Richard. Fraser of North Cape: The Life of Admiral of the Fleet Lord Fraser, 1888-1981. London, 1983.

Third sea lord, 1939-42; commander-in-chief, home fleet, 1943-44; eastern fleet, 1944; Pacific fleet, 1945-46.

796.   Hunt, Barry D. Sailor-Scholar: Admiral Sir Herbert Richmond, 1871-1946. Waterloo, Ontario, 1982.

President, Royal Naval War College, Greenwich, 1920-23; commandant of the Imperial Defence College, 1927-28; see also Arthur J. Marder, Portrait of an Admiral: The Life and Papers of Sir Herbert Richmond (London, 1952).

797.   Hunter, Ian. Malcolm Muggeridge: A Life. London, 1980.

798.   Hyde, H. Montgomery. The Quiet Canadian: The Secret Service Story of Sir William Stephenson. London, 1962.

Director of British Security Co-ordination, part of M16, in New York, 1940-46; see also William Stevenson, A Man Called Intrepid: The Secret War (London, 1976).

799.   ———. Strong for Service: The Life of Lord Nathan of Churt. London, 1968.

Lawyer and public servant; legal adviser to Zionist Organisation and Economic Board of Palestine; MP, 1929-35, 1937-40; under-secretary of state, War Office, 1945.

800.   James, Robert Rhodes. Anthony Eden. London, 1986.

Based on Eden's public and private papers; an attempt to understand; as was Sidney Aster, Anthony Eden (London, 1976); previous studies are David Carlton, Anthony Eden (London, 1981); Denis Bardens, Portrait of a Statesman (London, 1955); Lewis Broad, Sir Anthony Eden (London, 1955); Alan Campbell-Johnson, Sir Anthony Eden: A Biography (London, 1955); William Rees-Mogg, Sir Anthony Eden (London, 1956); and Randolph S. Churchill, The Rise and Fall of Sir Anthony Eden (London, 1959); see also Anthony Nutting, "Lord Avon," in The Prime Ministers, edited by Herbert van Thal, vol. 2 (London, 1975); of interest is V.G. Trukhanovskii, Antoni Eden (Moscow, 1983).

801.   ———. Memoirs of a Conservative: J.C.C. Davidson's Memoirs and Papers, 1910-1937. London, 1969.

Chancellor of the Duchy of Lancaster, 1923-24; parliamentary secretary, Admiralty, 1924-27; chancellor of the Duchy of Lancaster, 1931-37.

802. James, Admiral Sir William Milburne. The Eyes of the Navy: A Biographical Study of Admiral Sir Reginald Hall. London, 1955.

Director of intelligence division, Admiralty war staff, 1914-18; MP, 1918-23, 1925-29; organised, with Winston Churchill's approval, a team of codebreakers for naval and diplomatic codes in Room 40 of the Admiralty Old Block.

803. Jones, James Harry. Josiah Stamp: The Life of the First Baron Stamp of Shortlands. London, 1964.

British representative on the Dawes committee, 1924; and the Young committee, 1929; director, Bank of England, 1928-41; member, Economic Advisory Council, 1930-41.

804. Jones, Raymond A. Arthur Ponsonby: The Politics of Life. London, 1989.

MP, 1922-30; under-secretary, Foreign Office, 1924; under-secretary, Dominion Affairs, 1929; parliamentary secretary, ministry of Transport, 1929-31; chancellor, Duchy of Lancaster, 1931; leader, Labour party opposition in House of Lords, 1931-35.

805. Judd, Denis. King George VI, 1895-1952. London, 1982.

See also Sarah Bradford, George VI (London, 1989); and John W. Wheeler-Bennett, King George VI: His Life and Reign (London, 1958).

806. ———. Lord Reading. London, 1982.

Lord chief justice of England, 1913-21; special ambassador to USA, 1918; viceroy of India, 1921-26; secretary of state for Foreign Affairs, 1931; supersedes previous studies by H. Montgomery Hyde, Lord Reading: The Life of Rufus Isaacs, First Marquess of Reading (London, 1967); and 2nd Marquess of Reading, Rufus Isaacs: First Marquess of Reading, 2 vols. (London, 1942-45); vol. 2 for 1914-35; and Stanley Jackson, Rufus Isaacs (London, 1936).

807. Knightley, Phillip. Philby: The Life and Views of the KGB Masterspy. London, 1988.

See also Patrick Seale and Maureen McConville, Philby: The Long Road to Moscow (New York, 1973); Bruce Page et al., Philby: The Spy Who Betrayed a Generation (London, 1968); and E.H. Cookridge [Edward Spiro], The Third Man: The Full Story of Kim Philby (London, 1968).

808. Koss, Stephen. Asquith. London, 1976.

See too Roy Jenkins, Asquith, 2nd ed. (London, 1986); and the earlier J.A. Spender and Cyril Asquith, The Life of Herbert Henry Asquith: Lord Oxford and Asquith, 2 vols. (London, 1932).

809. ———. Lord Haldane: Scapegoat for Liberalism. London, 1969.

See also E.M. Spiers, Haldane: An Army Reformer (London, 1980); Dudley Sommer, Haldane of Cloan: His Life and Times, 1856-1928 (London, 1960); Sir Frederick Maurice, Haldane, 1856-1928: The Life of Viscount Haldane of Cloan, 2 vols. (London, 1937-39); and Sir Charles Harris, Lord Haldane (London, 1928).

810. Laffin, John. Swifter than Eagles: A Biography of Air Chief Marshal Sir John Salmond. London, 1964.

Air officer commanding-in-chief, air defence of Great Britain, 1925-29; chief of the air staff, 1930-33; with ministry of Aircraft Production, 1939-41.

811. Laybourn, Keith. Philip Snowden: A Biography, 1864-1937. London, 1988.

See also Colin Cross, Philip Snowden (London, 1966); and Andreas M. Andreades, Philip Snowden (London, 1930).

812. Lees-Milne, James. The Enigmatic Edwardian: The Life of Reginald, 2nd Viscount Esher. London, 1986.

See also Peter Fraser, Lord Esher: A Political Biography (London, 1973).

813. ———. Harold Nicolson: A Biography. 2 vols. London, 1980-81.

814. Leventhal, F.M. Arthur Henderson. Manchester, 1989.

Secretary of Labour party, 1911-34; home secretary, 1924; secretary of state for Foreign Affairs, 1929-31; Nobel peace prize, 1934; see also Mary Agnes Hamilton, Arthur Henderson: A Biography (London, 1938); and Edwin Jenkins, From Foundry to Foreign Office: The Romantic Life Story of the Rt. Hon. Arthur Henderson, M.P. (London, 1933).

815.   Lewin, Ronald. The Chief: Field-Marshal Lord Wavell, Commander-in-Chief and Viceroy, 1939-1947. London, 1980.

Other studies by John Connell [J.H. Robertson], Wavell, 2 vols. (London, 1964-69); Sir Bernard Fergusson, Wavell: Portrait of a Soldier (London, 1961); Robert Woollcombe, The Campaigns of Wavell, 1939-1943 (London, 1959); Robert J. Collins, Lord Wavell, 1883-1941: A Military Biography (London, 1947); and R.H. Kiernan, Wavell (London, 1945).

816.   ———. Slim the Standardbearer: A Biography of Field-Marshal the Viscount Slim. London, 1976.

See also Sir Geoffrey Evans, Slim as Military Commander (London, 1969).

817.   Lunt, James. Glubb Pasha: A Biography. London, 1984.

818.   Lysaght, Charles Edward. Brendan Bracken. London, 1979.

Official biography of 1st Viscount Bracken; parliamentary private secretary to Winston Churchill, 1940-41; minister of Information, 1941-45; first lord of the Admiralty, 1945; see also My Dear Max: The Letters of Brendan Bracken to Lord Beaverbrook, 1925-1958, edited by Richard Cockett (London, 1990); Andrew Boyle, Poor, Dear Brendan (London, 1974); and Anon., Brendan Bracken, 1901-1958: Portraits and Appreciations (London, 1958).

819.   Mackay, Ruddock F. Balfour: Intellectual Statesman. London, 1985.

Well researched; but see also Max Egremont, Balfour: A Life of Arthur James Balfour (London, 1980); Sydney H. Zebel, Balfour: A Political Biography (London, 1973); Kenneth Young, Arthur James Balfour (London, 1963); Blanche E.C. Dugdale, Arthur James Balfour: First Earl of Balfour, 2 vols. (London, 1936); and Sir Ian Malcolm, Lord Balfour: A Memory (London, 1930).

820. McKercher, B.J.C. Esme Howard: A Diplomatic Biography. London, 1989.

821. Macksey, Kenneth. Armoured Crusader: A Biography of Major-General Sir Percy Hobart. London, 1967.

Inspector, Royal Tank Corps, 1933-36; deputy director of staff duties, War Office, 1937; director of military training, War Office, 1937-38.

822. McLachlan, Donald. In the Chair: Barrington-Ward of "The Times," 1927-1948. London, 1971.

Assistant editor, the Observer, 1919-27; and The Times, 1927-41; editor, The Times, 1941-48.

823. Mallet, Sir Charles. Lord Cave: A Memoir. London, 1931.

Minister, Home Office, 1916-19; lord chancellor, 1922-24, 1924-28.

824. Marlowe, John. Late Victorian: The Life of Sir Arnold Talbot Wilson. London, 1967.

825. Marquand, David. Ramsay MacDonald. London, 1977.

Supersedes previous and subsequent studies such as Austen Morgan, J. Ramsay MacDonald (Manchester, 1987); Benjamin Sacks, J. Ramsay MacDonald in Thought and Action (Albuquerque, NM, 1952); Lord Elton, The Life of James Ramsay MacDonald, 1866-1919 (London, 1939); Lauchlin MacNeill Weir, The Tragedy of Ramsay MacDonald: A Political Biography (London, 1938); H.H. Tiltman, J. Ramsay MacDonald: Labour's Man of Destiny (London, 1929); and Mary Agnes Hamilton, J. Ramsay MacDonald (London, 1929).

826. Marrin, Albert. Sir Norman Angell. Boston, MA, 1979.

827. Masters, Anthony. Nancy Astor: A Life. London, 1981.

First woman MP, 1919-45; wife of 2nd Viscount Astor; hostess for the "Cliveden Set"; other studies include John Grigg, Nancy Astor: Portrait of a Pioneer (London, 1980); Christopher Sykes, Nancy: The Life of Lady Astor (London, 1972); and Maurice Collis, Nancy Astor (London, 1960); of related interest, see David Sinclair, The Astors and Their Times (London, 1984); Lucy Kavaler, The

Astors (London, 1966); and Michael Astor, Tribal Feeling (London, 1963).

828.   Mearsheimer, John J. Liddell Hart and the Weight of History. London, 1988.

A very critical account; see also Brian Bond, Liddell Hart: A Study of His Military Thought (London, 1977).

829.   Middlemas, Keith, and Barnes, John. Baldwin: A Biography. London, 1969.

Most thorough study; further biographies by Roy Jenkins, Baldwin (London, 1987); Kenneth Young, Stanley Baldwin (London, 1976); H. Montgomery Hyde, Baldwin: The Unexpected Prime Minister (London, 1973); Arthur W. Baldwin, My Father: The True Story (London, 1955); D.C. Somervell, Stanley Baldwin (London, 1953); G.M. Young, Stanley Baldwin (London, 1952); Bechhofer Roberts, Stanley Baldwin: Man or Miracle? (London, 1936); and H. Wickham Steed, The Real Stanley Baldwin (London, 1930).

830.   Monroe, Elizabeth. Philby of Arabia. London. 1973.

Based on private and public collections of papers; comprehensive bibliography of Philby's works.

831.   Montgomery, Brian. Shenton of Singapore: Governor and Prisoner of War. London, 1984.

Governor and commander-in-chief, Straits Settlement, 1934; on fall of Singapore interned by Japanese, 1942-45; "tried without success to correct official history of the war in Malaya" (Concise DNB, 1901-1970); the authorised biography.

832.   Morgan, Kenneth O., and Morgan, Jane. Portrait of a Progressive: The Political Career of Christopher, Viscount Addison. London, 1980.

Supersedes R.J. Minney, Viscount Addison: Leader of the House (London, 1958).

833.   Morris, A.J.A. C.P. Trevelyan, 1870-1958: Portrait of a Radical. Belfast, 1977.

MP, 1922-31; president, Board of Education, 1924, 1929-31.

834. Murray, Lady Mildred Octavia. The Making of a Civil Servant: Sir Oswyn Murray, Secretary of the Admiralty, 1917-1936. London, 1940.

Permanent secretary, Admiralty, 1917-36.

835. Newman, Aubrey. The Stanhopes of Chevening. London, 1969.

Includes the 7th Earl Stanhope; parliamentary under-secretary of state for Foreign Affairs, 1934-36; first lord of the Admiralty, 1938-39; lord president of the Council, 1939-40.

836. Nicol, Graham. Uncle George: Field-Marshal Lord Milne of Salonika and Rubislaw. London, 1976.

Entered army, 1885; general officer commanding-in-chief, eastern command, 1923-26; chief of the imperial general staff, 1926-33.

837. Nicolson, Nigel. Alex: The Life of Field-Marshal Earl Alexander of Tunis. London, 1973.

See also Norman Hillson, Alexander of Tunis (London, 1952); and W.G.F. Jackson, Alexander of Tunis (London, 1971).

838. O'Brien, D.P. Lionel Robbins. London, 1988.

839. O'Halpin, Eunan. Head of the Civil Service: A Biography of Sir Warren Fisher. London, 1989.

Permanent secretary to Treasury and head of civil service, 1919-39.

840. Pack, S.W.C. Cunningham: The Commander. London, 1974.

See also Oliver Warner, Cunningham of Hyndhope, Admiral of the Fleet: A Memoir by Oliver Warner (London, 1967).

841. Perham, Margery. Lugard. 2 vols. London, 1960.

1st Baron Lugard; soldier, administrator and author; governor-general of Nigeria, 1914-19; member, Permanent Mandates commission of the League of Nations, 1922-36.

842. Petrie, Sir Charles. Walter Long and His Times. London, 1936.

843.   Pimlott, Ben. <u>Hugh Dalton</u>. London, 1985.

844.   Pope-Hennessy, James. <u>Lord Crewe, 1858-1945: The Likeness of a Liberal</u>. London, 1955.

Robert O.A. Crewe-Milnes; ambassador at Paris, 1922-28; secretary of state for War, 1931.

845.   Postgate, Raymond. <u>The Life of George Lansbury</u>. London, 1951.

846.   Pound, Reginald, and Harmsworth, Geoffrey. <u>Northcliffe</u>. London, 1959.

Alfred Charles William Harmsworth; journalist and newspaper proprietor, founded Amalgamated Press, 1887; founded <u>Daily Mail</u> and <u>Daily Mirror</u>; chief proprietor of <u>The Times</u>, 1908; director of propaganda in enemy countries, 1918; see also Paul Ferris, <u>The House of Northcliffe</u> (London, 1971); Tom Clarke, <u>Northcliffe in History</u> (London, 1950); and Hamilton Fyfe, <u>Northcliffe</u> (London, 1930).

847.   Radice, Lisanne. <u>Beatrice and Sidney Webb: Fabian Socialists</u>. London, 1984.

848.   Read, Anthony, and Fisher, David. <u>Colonel Z: The Life and Times of a Master of Spies</u>. London, 1984.

Lieutenant-Colonel Sir Claude Edward Marjoribanks Dansey, 1876-1947; "in charge of all operations, world-wide, for British intelligence" (Prologue).

849.   Reader, William J. <u>Architect of Air Power: The Life of the First Viscount Weir of Eastwood, 1877-1959</u>. London, 1968.

Government's leading civilian adviser on rearmament; chairman of advisory committee on civil aviation, 1919; adviser, Air ministry, 1935-39; director-general of explosives, ministry of Supply, 1939-41; chairman of Tank Board, 1942.

850.   Reid, P.R. <u>Winged Diplomat: The Life Story of Air Commodore "Freddie" West</u>. London, 1962.

Air attaché, British legations in Helsingfors, Riga, Tallin, Kovno, 1936-38; Rome, 1940; Berne, 1940-45.

851. Reynolds, P.A., and Hughes, E.J. The Historian as Diplomat: Charles Kingsley Webster and the United Nations, 1939-1946. London, 1976.

With British delegation, Paris peace conference, 1918-19; director of British Library of Information, New York, 1941-42; Foreign Office, 1943-46; prolific diplomatic historian.

852. Richards, Denis. Portal of Hungerford: The Life of Marshal of the R.A.F. Viscount Portal of Hungerford. London, 1978.

Director of organisation, Air ministry, 1937-38; member of Air Council, 1939-40; air officer commander-in-chief, bomber command, 1940; chief of the air staff, 1940-45.

853. Robbins, Keith. Sir Edward Grey: A Biography of Lord Grey of Falloden. London, 1971.

See also G.M. Trevelyan, Grey of Falloden: Being the Life of Sir Edward Grey Afterwards Viscount Grey of Falloden (London, 1937).

854. Rolph, C.H. Kingsley: The Life, Letters and Diaries of Kingsley Martin. London, 1973.

855. Ronaldshay, Earl of (2nd Marquess of Zetland). The Life of Lord Curzon. 3 vols. London, 1928.

Official biography of the viceroy of India, 1898-1905; secretary of state for Foreign Affairs, 1919-24; lord privy seal, 1924-25; among subsequent studies see Harold Nicolson, Curzon: The Last Phase, 1919-1925 (London, 1934); Leonard Mosley, Curzon: The End of an Epoch (London, 1960); and Kenneth Rose, Superior Person (London, 1969); of related interest is Marchioness Curzon, Reminiscences (London, 1955).

856. Rose, Kenneth. King George V. London, 1983.

See also Harold Nicolson, King George the Fifth: His Life and Reign (London, 1952); Arthur Bryant, George V (London, 1936); Sir George Arthur, King George V (London, 1929); of interest is James Pope-Hennessy, Queen Mary, 1867-1953 (London, 1959).

857. Rose, Norman. Vansittart: Study of a Diplomat. London, 1978.

More in Ian Colvin, <u>Vansittart in Office: An Historical Survey of the Origins of the Second World War Based on the Papers of Sir Robert Vansittart</u> (London, 1965).

858. Roskill, Stephen W. <u>Admiral of the Fleet Earl Beatty, The Last Naval Hero: An Intimate Biography</u>. London, 1980.

See also Charles Beatty, <u>Our Admiral: A Biography of Admiral of the Fleet Earl Beatty</u> (London, 1980); William Scott Chalmers, <u>The Life and Letters of David, Earl Beatty</u> (London, 1951); and Geoffrey Rawson, <u>Earl Beatty, Admiral of the Fleet</u> (London, 1930).

859. ———. <u>Hankey: Man of Secrets</u>. 3 vols. London, 1970-74.

Of related interest, see John F. Naylor, <u>A Man and an Institution: Sir Maurice Hankey, the Cabinet Secretariat and the Custody of Cabinet Secrecy</u> (London, 1984).

860. Rowland, John, and Cadman, 2nd Baron. <u>Ambassador for Oil: The Life of John Cadman, First Baron Cadman</u>. London, 1960.

Technical adviser, director and later chairman, Anglo-Iranian Oil Company, 1921-41; member Economic Advisory Council, 1930; government adviser on oil, 1939-41.

861. Rowland, Peter. <u>Lloyd George</u>. London, 1975.

The best complete biography; in progress are Bentley B. Gilbert, <u>David Lloyd George, a Political Life</u>, vol. 1, <u>The Architect of Change, 1863-1912</u> (London, 1987-); and John Grigg, <u>Lloyd George</u>, vol. 3, <u>From Peace to War, 1912-1916</u> (London, 1985-); other studies include Martin Pugh, <u>Lloyd George</u> (London, 1988); Lady Olwen Carey Evans, <u>Lloyd George Was My Father</u> (Llandysul, 1985); William Richard Philip George, <u>Lloyd George: Backbencher</u> (Llandysul, 1983) and his earlier <u>The Making of Lloyd George</u> (London, 1976); John Campbell, <u>Lloyd George: The Goat in the Wilderness, 1922-1931</u> (London, 1977); Kenneth O. Morgan, <u>Lloyd George</u> (London, 1974); the same author's <u>David Lloyd George: Welsh Radical as World Statesman</u> (Cardiff, 1963); Donald McCormick, <u>The Mask of Merlin</u> (London, 1963); Richard Lloyd George, <u>Lloyd George</u> (London, 1960); William George, <u>My Brother and I</u> (London, 1958); Frank Owen, <u>Tempestuous Journey: Lloyd George, His Life and Times</u> (London, 1954); Thomas Jones, <u>Lloyd George</u> (London, 1951); Malcolm Thompson, <u>Lloyd George: The Official Biography</u> (London, 1948); A.J. Sylvester, <u>The Real</u>

Lloyd George (London, 1947); and Tom Clarke, My Lloyd George Diary (London, 1939).

862.   Ryan, W. Michael. Lieutenant-Colonel Charles à Court Repington: A Study in the Interaction of Personality, the Press, and Power. New York, 1987.

863.   Sansom, Katherine. Sir George Sansom and Japan. Tallahassee, FL, 1972.

Commercial counsellor, British embassy, Tokyo, 1923-40; minister at Washington, 1942-47.

864.   Saward, Dudley. Bomber Harris: The Story of Marshal of the Royal Air Force Sir Arthur Harris. London, 1984.

The authorised biography, based on the Harris papers; see also Charles Messenger, "Bomber" Harris and the Strategic Bombing Offensive, 1939-1945 (London, 1984).

865.   Seymour-Ure, Colin, and Schoff, Jim. David Low. London, 1985.

866.   Skidelsky, Robert. John Maynard Keynes, vol. 1, Hopes Betrayed, 1883-1920. London, 1983-.

See also Charles H. Hession, John Maynard Keynes (London, 1984); Roy F. Harrod, The Life of John Maynard Keynes (London, 1951); Essays on John Maynard Keynes, edited by Milo Keynes (London, 1980); and Seymour E. Harris, John Maynard Keynes: Economist and Policy Maker (London, 1955).

867.   ———. Oswald Mosley. London, 1975.

See also Nicolas Mosley, Rules of the Game: Sir Oswald and Lady Cynthia Mosley, 1896-1933 (London, 1982); and the continuation in Beyond the Pale (London, 1983).

868.   Stocks, Mary. Eleanor Rathbone: A Biography. London, 1949.

Independent MP, 1929-46; active in League of Nations Union and refugee problems; see also Eleanor Rathbone, War Can be Averted (London, 1938).

869.   ———. Ernest Simon of Manchester. Manchester, 1963.

1st Baron Simon of Wythenshawe; MP, 1923-24, 1929-31; parliamentary secretary, ministry of Health, 1931; member, Economic Advisory Council, 1932-45.

870. Taylor, A.J.P. Beaverbrook. London, 1972.

Authorised life of William Maxwell Aitken, 1st Baron Beaverbrook; minister of Information, 1918; minister for Aircraft Production, 1940-41; minister of Supply, 1941-42; lord privy seal, 1943-45; of interest is Alan Wood, The True History of Lord Beaverbrook (London, 1965); Tom Driberg, Beaverbrook: A Study in Power and Frustration (London, 1956); and David Farrer, G - For God Almighty: A Personal Memoir of Lord Beaverbrook (London, 1969).

871. Taylor, H.A. Jix - Viscount Brentford. London, 1933.

Biography of Sir William Joynson-Hicks; financial secretary to the Treasury, 1923; minister of Health, 1923-24; home secretary, 1924-29.

872. Thomas, Hugh. John Strachey. London, 1973.

MP, 1929-31; parliamentary private secretary to Sir Oswald Mosley; helped found Left Book Club, 1936; under-secretary of state for Air, 1945; see also Michael Newman, John Strachey (Manchester, 1989).

873. Trythall, Anthony John. "Boney" Fuller: The Intellectual General. London, 1977.

See also Brian Holden Reid, J.F.C. Fuller: Military Thinker (London, 1987); an "interpretive study of the military writings" (Preface).

874. Tulloch, Major-General Derek. Wingate in Peace and War. London, 1972.

Major-General Orde Charles Wingate; military career, Sudan, Palestine, Transjordan and Ethiopia, 1928-41; commander of special force (Chindits), India and Burma, 1942-44; see also Peter Mead, Orde Wingate and the Historians (Braunton, 1987); and Christopher Sykes, Orde Wingate (London, 1959).

875. Vernon, Betty D. Ellen Wilkinson, 1891-1947. London, 1982.

MP, 1924-31, 1935-47; parliamentary private secretary to minister of Health, 1929-31; parliamentary secretary, ministry of Home Security, 1940-45.

876.   Warner, Philip. Auchinleck: The Lonely Soldier. London, 1981.

Commander-in-chief, Middle East, 1941-42; India, 1940-41, 1943-47; still valuable is John Connell [J.H. Robertson], Auchinleck: A Biography of Field-Marshal Sir Claude Auchinleck (London, 1959); see also Roger Parkinson, The Auk: Auchinleck, Victor at Alamein (London, 1977).

877.   Waterfield, Gordon. Professional Diplomat: Sir Percy Loraine of Kirkharle Bt., 1880-1961. London, 1973.

At Paris peace conference, 1919; minister to Persia, 1921-26; and Athens, 1926-29; high commissioner for Egypt and the Sudan, 1929-33; ambassador to Turkey, 1933-39; and Rome, 1939-40.

878.   Wedgwood, C.V. The Last of the Radicals: Josiah Wedgwood, MP. London, 1951.

879.   Wemyss, Lady Wester. The Life and Letters of Lord Wester Wemyss. London, 1935.

First sea lord, 1917-19; at Paris peace conference, 1919.

880.   Wheeler-Bennett, John W. John Anderson: Viscount Waverly. London, 1962.

Permanent under-secretary of state, Home Office, 1922-32; governor of Bengal, 1932-37; lord privy seal, 1938-39; home secretary, 1939-40; lord president of the Council, 1940-43; chancellor of the Exchequer, 1943-45.

881.   Whittaker, D.J. Fighter for Peace: Philip Noel-Baker, 1889-1982. York, 1989.

Member, League of Nations secretariat, 1919-22; MP, 1929-31, 1936-70; parliamentary secretary to secretary of state for Foreign Affairs, 1929-31; to ministry of War Transport, 1942-45; Nobel peace prize, 1959.

882.   Williams, Philip Maynard. Hugh Gaitskell: A Political Biography. London, 1979.

Principal private secretary to minister of Economic Warfare, 1940-42; principal assistant secretary, Board of Trade, 1942-45; leader of the Labour party, 1955-63; supersedes Geoffrey McDermott, Leader Lost: A Biography of Hugh Gaitskell (London, 1972); see also the appreciations in Hugh Gaitskell, 1906-1963, edited by W.T. Rodgers (London, 1964); and The Diary of Hugh Gaitskell, 1945-1956, edited by Philip Maynard Williams (London, 1983)

883. Wilson, Duncan. Gilbert Murray, OM, 1866-1957. London, 1987.

See also Francis West, Gilbert Murray: A Life (London, 1984); both based on the Gilbert Murray papers.

884. ———. Leonard Woolf: A Political Biography. London, 1978.

885. Wingate, Sir Ronald. Lord Ismay: A Biography. London, 1970.

886. Wood, Ian S. John Wheatley. Manchester, 1990.

MP, 1922-30; minister of Health, 1924.

887. Wrench, John Evelyn. Geoffrey Dawson and Our Times. London, 1955.

Editor of The Times, 1912-19, 1923-41.

888. Young, Kenneth. Sir Alec Douglas-Home. London, 1970.

See also John Dickie, The Uncommon Commoner: Sir Alec Douglas-Home (London, 1964); and Emrys Hughes, Sir Alec Douglas-Home (London, 1964).

889. Ziegler, Philip. Mountbatten: The Official Biography. London, 1985.

See also Richard Hough, Mountbatten: Hero of Our Time (London, 1980); Charles Smith, Fifty Years with Mountbatten (London, 1980); John Terraine, The Life and Times of Lord Mountbatten (London, 1968); and of related interest, Richard Hough, Edwina, Countess Mountbatten of Burma (London, 1983).

1. Histories of Britain, 1918-1945

890.   Havighurst, Alfred F. Britain in Transition: The Twentieth
        Century. 4th ed. London, 1985.

        A comprehensive survey with good coverage of foreign policy;
        similar surveys include T.O. Lloyd, Empire to Welfare State:
        English History, 1906-1985, 3rd ed. (London, 1986); Robert
        Blake, The Decline of Power, 1915-1964 (London, 1985); Max
        Beloff, Wars and Welfare: Britain, 1914-1945 (London, 1983);
        Keith Robbins, Eclipse of a Great Power: Modern Britain, 1870-
        1975 (London, 1983); Anthony Wood, Great Britain, 1900-1965
        (London, 1978); Arthur Marwick, Britain in the Century of Total
        War, 1900-1967 (London, 1968); and L.C.B. Seaman, Post-
        Victorian Britain, 1900-1951 (London, 1966).

891.   James, Robert Rhodes. The British Revolution: British Politics,
        1880-1939. 2 vols. London, 1976-77.

        Vol. 2 is subtitled: From Asquith to Chamberlain, 1914-1939; see
        also Martin Pugh, The Making of Modern British Politics, 1867-
        1939 (London, 1982).

892.   McElwee, William. Britain's Locust Years, 1918-1940. London,
        1962.

        Argumentative on the interwar years; should be supplemented by
        the very detailed C.L. Mowat, Britain between the Wars, 1918-
        1940 (London, 1955); and Ronald Blythe, The Age of Illusion:
        England in the Twenties and Thirties, 1919-1940 (London, 1963).

893.   Medlicott, W.N. Contemporary England, 1914-1964, with
        Epilogue, 1964-1974. London, 1976.

Extensive coverage of foreign policy from a diplomatic historian; similarly see Roy Douglas, World Crisis and British Decline, 1929-1956 (London, 1986).

894.   Pelling, Henry. Modern Britain, 1885-1955. London, 1960.

A brief survey of all aspects, including foreign policy; in the same category can be included Peter Teed, The Move to Europe: Britain 1880-1972 (London, 1976); Arthur Marwick, The Explosion of British Society, 1914-1970 (London, 1971); Bentley B. Gilbert, Britain since 1918 (London, 1967); E.E. Reynolds and N.H. Brasher, Britain in the Twentieth Century, 1900-1964 (London, 1966); and David Thomson, England in the Twentieth Century, 1914-1963 (London, 1965).

895.   Taylor, A.J.P. English History, 1914-1945. London, 1965.

Vol. 14 of the "Oxford History of England"; stimulating in its frequent analysis of foreign policy; extensive, annotated bibliography.

2. Foreign Policy Surveys

896.   Altrincham, 1st Baron (Sir Edward Grigg). British Foreign Policy. London, 1944.

Parliamentary secretary to ministry of Information, 1939-40; financial secretary, War Office, 1940; joint parliamentary under-secretary of state for War, 1940-42; minister resident in the Middle East, 1944-45; see also his Britain Looks at Germany (London, 1938); and The Faith of an Englishman (London, 1936).

897.   Barnett, Correlli. The Collapse of British Power. London, 1972.

An examination of "how the long-rotting and cumulatively over-strained structure of British power swiftly collapsed under the shock of the Second World War" (Preface); further detailed analysis in The Audit of War (London, 1986).

898.   Bartlett, C.J. British Foreign Policy in the Twentieth Century. London, 1989.

A brief interpretation based on the "high politics" approach (Introduction).

899.   Beloff, Max. Imperial Sunset. 2 vols. London, 1969-89.

        Vol. 1 for 1897-1921; vol. 2, 1921-42.

900.   Carr, E.H. Britain: A Study of Foreign Policy from the Versailles
        Treaty to the Outbreak of War. London, 1939.

        Preface by Lord Halifax; for the wider European context see Carr's
        The Twenty Years' Crisis, 1919-1939 (London, 1946); and
        International Relations between the Two World Wars, 1919-1939
        (London, 1947); also interesting is his Great Britain as a
        Mediterranean Power (Nottingham, 1937).

901.   Dilks, David, ed. Retreat from Power: Studies in Britain's
        Foreign Policy of the Twentieth Century. 2 vols. London, 1981.

        A collection of 14 essays, some previously published; topics
        include the Foreign Office and the Dominions, the Hoare-Laval
        pact, appeasement and intelligence, Chamberlain and Churchill in
        1940, and Operation Bracelet.

902.   Foot, M.R.D. British Foreign Policy since 1898. London, 1956.

        Other early studies include D.C. Somervell, Between the Wars
        (London, 1948); Sir Charles Petrie, Twenty Years' Armistice - and
        After: British Foreign Policy since 1918 (London, 1940); Michael
        Foot, Armistice, 1918-1939 (London, 1940); Maurice Bruce,
        British Foreign Policy (London, 1938); Ian Campbell Hannah, A
        History of British Foreign Policy (London, 1938); and G.P. Gooch,
        British Foreign Policy since the War (London, 1935).

903.   Haig, Anthony. Congress of Vienna to Common Market: An
        Outline of British Foreign Policy, 1815-1972. London, 1973.

904.   Hayes, Paul. The Twentieth Century, 1880-1939. London, 1978.

        The last in a "Modern British Foreign Policy" series; very critical.

905.   Keith, Arthur B., ed. Speeches and Documents on International
        Affairs, 1918-1937. 2 vols. London, 1938.

        A standard collection of documentary material.

906.   Kennedy, Aubrey Leo. Old Diplomacy and New, 1876-1922: From
        Salisbury to Lloyd George. London, 1922.

Journalist and later assistant foreign editor of The Times, 1910-41; with European service of the BBC, 1941-45.

907.   Kennedy, Paul. The Realities Behind Diplomacy: Background Influences on British External Policy, 1865-1980. London, 1980.

An interesting synthesis, including the results of recent research; and more generally his The Rise and Fall of the Great Powers (London, 1988).

908.   Lowe, C.J., and Dockrill, M.L. The Mirage of Power: British Foreign Policy, 1902-1922. 3 vols. London, 1972.

Vol. 2 for 1914-22; vol. 3 contains documents.

909.   McDermott, Geoffrey. The Eden Legacy and the Decline of British Diplomacy. London, 1969.

A survey with too much emphasis on one individual.

910.   Medlicott, W.N. British Foreign Policy since Versailles, 1919-1963. 2nd ed. London, 1968.

911.   Murray, Arthur Cecil (3rd Viscount Elibank). Reflections on Some Aspects of British Foreign Policy between the Two World Wars. London, 1946.

Assistant military attaché, Washington, 1917-18; see also his Master and Brother (London, 1945); and At Close Quarters (London, 1946); both based on his wartime experiences.

912.   Northedge, F.S. The Troubled Giant: Britain among the Great Powers, 1916-1939. London, 1966.

His Descent from Power: British Foreign Policy, 1945-1973 (London, 1974) is equally perceptive.

913.   Porter, Bernard. Britain, Europe and the World, 1850-1986: Delusions of Grandeur. 2nd ed. London, 1987.

Argues that Britain's decline was "inevitable" (Preface); see also Anthony Clayton, The British Empire as a Superpower, 1919-1939 (London, 1986); no footnotes, but extensive bibliography.

914.   Reynolds, P.A. British Foreign Policy in the Inter-War Years.
         London, 1954.

         Still useful as an introductory approach.

915.   Rothstein, Andrew. British Foreign Policy and Its Critics, 1830-
         1950. London, 1969.

         By a former member of the Information department, Soviet trade
         delegation in London.

916.   Seton-Watson, R.W. Britain and the Dictators: A Survey of Post-
         War British Policy. London, 1938.

         Concludes with the Anschluss; continued in From Munich to
         Danzig (London, 1939); revised and enlarged edition of Munich
         and the Dictators (London, 1939).

917.   Strang, Lord. Britain in World Affairs: A Survey of the
         Fluctuations in British Power and Influence, Henry VIII to
         Elizabeth II. London, 1961.

918.   Taylor, A.J.P. The Trouble Makers: Dissent over Foreign Policy,
         1792-1939. London, 1957.

         Significantly concludes in 1939.

919.   Trukhanovskii, V.G. Vneshniaia politika anglii na pervom etape
         obshchego krizisa kapitalizma, 1918-1939 gg. Moscow, 1961.

920.   Wiener, Joel H., ed. Great Britain: Foreign Policy and the Span of
         Empire: A Documentary History, 1689-1971. 4 vols. New
         York, 1972.

3. Dimensions of Foreign Policy

For many years the study of British foreign policy was limited to an analysis of multilateral relations. More recently, historians have widened their search. The "missing dimensions" of foreign policy are currently being examined in great detail and are yielding interesting results. It is now possible to understand and demonstrate the choices and limits facing the politicians, diplomats and the military in the interwar years. For resistance and refugee and intelligence dimensions see pages 315-32.

The Military Dimension

921.   Barclay, Cyril N. On Their Shoulders: British Generalship in the Lean Years, 1939-1942. London, 1964.

Served both world wars; writer on military subjects.

922.   Barker, Rachel. Conscience, Government and War: Conscientious Objection in Great Britain, 1939-1945. London, 1982.

Well-documented and detailed account of pacifism and civil-military relations; other studies include R.J.Q. Adams and Philip P. Poirer, The Conscription Controversy in Great Britain, 1900-1918 (London, 1987); Thomas C. Kennedy, "Public Opinion and the Conscientious Objector, 1915-1919," Journal of British Studies, 12(1973), 105-19; John Rae, Conscience and Politics: The British Government and the Conscientious Objector to Military Service, 1916-1919 (London, 1970); Denis Hayes, Challenge of Conscience: The Story of the Conscientious Objectors of 1939-1949 (London, 1949); and his Conscription Conflict: The Conflict of Ideas in the Struggle for and against Military Conscription in Britain between 1901 and 1939 (London, 1949).

923.   Barnett, Correlli. Britain and Her Army, 1509-1970: A Military, Political and Social Survey. London, 1970.

Similarly see Field-Marshal Lord Carver, The Seven Ages of the British Army (London, 1984); Jock Haswell, The British Army: A Concise History (London, 1981); and more specifically, David Fraser, And We Shall Shock Them: The British Army in the Second World War (London, 1983).

924.   Baylis, John. Anglo-American Defence Relations, 1939-1984: The Special Relationship. 2nd ed. London, 1984.

See too Maritime Strategy and the Balance of Power: Britain and America in the Twentieth Century, edited by John B. Hattendorf and Robert S. Jordan (Oxford, 1989).

925.   Bialer, Uri. The Shadow of the Bomber: The Fear of Air Attack and British Politics, 1932-1939. London, 1980.

Argues that policy was determined less by "a consistent set of strategic objectives, but according to idiosyncratic conceptions of national security" (Introduction); see also his "Elite Opinion and Defence Policy: Air Power Advocacy and British Rearmament during the 1930s," British Journal of International Studies, 6(1980), 32-51; "The British Chiefs of Staff and the 'Limited Liability' Formula of 1938: A Note," Military Affairs, 42(1978), 98-99; " 'Humanization' of Air Warfare in British Foreign Policy on the Eve of the Second World War," Journal of Contemporary History, 13(1978), 79-96; "The Danger of Bombardment from the Air and the Making of British Air Disarmament Policy, 1932-1934," in War and Society: A Yearbook of Military History, vol. 1, edited by Brian Bond and Ian Roy (London, 1975); and for background Neville Jones, The Beginnings of Strategic Air Power: A History of the British Bomber Force, 1923-1939 (London, 1987).

926.   Blair, P.E. "Air Power and Appeasement," in Essays Presented to Michael Roberts. Edited by John Bossy and Peter Jupp. Belfast, 1976.

927.   Bond, Brian. British Military Policy between the Two World Wars. London, 1980.

On the military constraints affecting foreign policy and vice versa; useful appendix with biographical notes; see also Brian Bond and Williamson Murray, "The British Armed Forces, 1918-1939," in Military Effectiveness, vol. 2, The Interwar Period, edited by Allan R. Millet and Williamson Murray (London, 1988); the continuation by Williamson Murray, "British Military Effectiveness in the Second World War," in vol. 3, The Second World War (London, 1988); and Barry R. Posen, The Sources of Military Doctrine: France, Britain and Germany between the World Wars (London, 1984).

928.   Brice, Martin H. The Royal Navy and the Sino-Japanese Incident, 1937-1941. London, 1973.

929.   Brundu Olla, Paola. L'equilibrio difficile: Gran Bretagna, Italia e Francia nel Mediterraneo, 1930-1937. Milan, 1980.

Includes British and Italian archival materials; see also Mariano Gabriele, "Mediterraneo 1935-1936: La situazione militare marittima nella visione britannica," Rivista marittima, 119(1986), 21-36.

930.   Coghlan, Francis A. "Armaments, Economic Policy and Appeasement: Background to British Foreign Policy, 1931-1937." History, 57(1972), 205-16.

See also Mark Thomas, "Rearmament and Economic Recovery in the Late 1930s," Economic History Review, 36(1983), 552-73.

931. Collier, Basil. The Lion and the Eagle: British and Anglo-American Strategy, 1900-1950. London, 1972.

932. Dean, Sir Maurice. The Royal Air Force and Two World Wars. London, 1979.

Assistant principal, then assistant under-secretary of state, Air ministry, 1929-46.

933. Dennis, Peter. Decision by Default: Peacetime Conscription and British Defence, 1919-1939. Durham, NC, 1972.

A well-documented study; see also his The Territorial Army, 1907-1940 (London, 1987); and "The Reconstitution of the Territorial Force, 1918-1920," in Swords and Covenants, edited by Adrian Preston and Peter Dennis (London, 1976).

934. Dilks, David. " 'The Unnecessary War'? Military Advice and Foreign Policy in Great Britain, 1931-1939," in General Staffs and Diplomacy Before the Second World War. Edited by Adrian Preston. London, 1978.

935. Dunbabin, John. "British Rearmament in the 1930s: A Chronology and Review." Historical Journal, 18(1975), 581-609.

936. Ehrman, John. Cabinet Government and War, 1890-1940. London, 1958.

The Lees Knowles lectures for 1957.

937. Ferris, John Robert. Men, Money, and Diplomacy: The Evolution of British Strategic Policy, 1919-1926. London, 1989.

A well-documented analysis of the interrelationship between "the diplomatic, financial and military elements" of British strategic policy (Introduction); see also his "Treasury Control, the Ten Year Rule, and British Service Policies, 1919-1924," Historical Journal, 30(1987), 859-83; "The Theory of a 'French Air Menace': Anglo-French Relations and the British Home Defence Air Force Programmes of 1921-1925," Journal of Strategic Studies, 10(1987), 62-83; and "A British 'Unofficial' Aviation Mission and Japanese Naval Developments, 1919-1929," Journal of Strategic Studies, 5(1982), 416-39.

938.   Fridenson, Patrick, and Lecuir, Jean. La France et la Grande-
         Bretagne face aux problèmes aériens, 1935-mai 1940. Paris,
         1976.

         On French efforts to tighten cooperation in air defence matters;
         see also their "L'organisation de la coopération aérienne franco-
         britannique, 1935-mai 1940," Revue d'histoire de la deuxième
         guerre mondiale, 19(1969), 43-74.

939.   Gibbs, Norman H. "British Strategic Doctrine, 1918-1939," in The
         Theory and Practice of War: Essays Presented to Captain B.H.
         Liddell Hart on His Seventieth Birthday. Edited by Michael
         Howard. London, 1965.

         See also his "The Naval Conferences of the Interwar Years: A
         Study in Anglo-American Relations," Naval War College Review,
         30(1977), 50-63; "Das britische Aufrüstungsprogramm 1933 bis
         1939 und das Ausmass seiner Abhängigkeit von der Entwicklung
         in Deutschland," in Wirtschaft und Rüstung am Vorabend des
         Zweiten Weltkrieges, edited by Friedrich Forstmeier and Hans-
         Erich Volkmann (Düsseldorf, 1975); and The Origins of Imperial
         Defence (London, 1955).

940.   Gordon, G.A.H. British Seapower and Procurement between the
         Wars: A Reappraisal of Rearmament. London, 1988.

         See also B.B. Schofield, British Sea Power: Naval Policy in the
         Twentieth Century (London, 1967).

941.   Gowing, Margaret M. Britain and Atomic Energy, 1939-1945.
         London, 1965.

         Commissioned by the British Atomic Energy Authority; continued
         in Independence and Deterrence: Britain and Atomic Energy,
         1945-1952, 2 vols. (London, 1974).

942.   Hall, Christopher. Britain, America and Arms Control, 1921-1937.
         New York, 1987.

         On the "Washington naval system" and the end of British
         maritime supremacy; based on British and American archives.

943.   Hall, Hines H. "British Air Defense and Anglo-French Relations,
         1921-1924." Journal of Strategic Studies, 4(1981), 271-84.

944.   Harris, J.P. "The 'Sandys Storm': The Politics of British Air Defence in 1938." <u>Historical Research: The Bulletin of the Institute of Historical Research</u>, 62(1989), 3:8-36.

See also his "Two War Ministers: A Reassessment of Duff Cooper and Hore-Belisha," <u>War and Society</u>, 6(1988), 65-78; "British Armour and Rearmament in the 1930s," <u>Journal of Strategic Studies</u>, 11(1988), 220-44; and "The British General Staff and the Coming of War, 1933-1939," <u>Bulletin of the Institute of Historical Research</u>, 59(1986), 196-211.

945.   Higham, Robin. <u>Armed Forces in Peacetime: Britain, 1918-1940, a Case Study</u>. London, 1962.

All aspects of the subject including disarmament, rearmament, and "politicians and defence"; annotated bibliography; see also his <u>The Military Intellectuals in Britain, 1918-1939</u> (New Brunswick, NJ, 1966).

946.   Hoffmann, Bruce. <u>The Failure of British Military Strategy within Palestine, 1939-1947</u>. Bar-Ilan, 1983.

With 25 documents on the subject from the Public Record Office, and related commentary in English and Hebrew.

947.   Howard, Michael. <u>The Continental Commitment: The Dilemma of British Defence Policy in the Era of Two World Wars</u>. London, 1972.

The Ford lectures of 1971; "a starting point for further study of an inexhaustible subject" (Preface); see also his <u>Studies in War and Peace</u> (London, 1970); <u>War and the Liberal Conscience</u> (London, 1978); and <u>The Causes of Wars and Other Essays</u> (London, 1983).

948.   Hyde, H. Montgomery. <u>British Air Policy between the Wars, 1918-1939</u>. London, 1976.

949.   James, Peter V. "Britain and Airpower at Versailles, 1919-1920." <u>International History Review</u>, 5(1983), 39-58.

950.   Jeffrey, Keith. <u>The British Army and the Crisis of Empire, 1918-1922</u>. Manchester, 1984.

Focuses on Ireland, India and the Middle East; see also his "Sir Henry Wilson and the Defence of the British Empire, 1918-1922," Journal of Imperial and Commonwealth History, 5(1977), 270-93.

951.   Johnson, Franklyn Arthur. Defence by Committee: The British Committee of Imperial Defence, 1885-1959. London, 1960.

Useful bibliography; foreword by Lord Ismay; see too Lord Hankey, "The Origin and Development of the Committee of Imperial Defence," Army Quarterly, 14(1927), 254-73; and Major-General H.L. Ismay, "The Machinery of the Committee of Imperial Defence," Journal of the Royal United Service Institution, 84(1939), 241-57.

952.   Joubert de la Ferté, Sir Philip. The Third Service: The Story behind the Royal Air Force. London, 1955.

Air officer commanding-in-chief, various assignments, 1934-39, 1941-43; assistant chief of air staff, 1941-43; deputy chief of staff, South East Asia Command, 1943-45; see also his Fun and Games (London, 1964).

953.   Kemp, Peter. The Fleet Air Arm. London, 1954.

Editorial staff, The Times, 1936-39, 1945-50; naval intelligence division, 1939-45; see also his Victory at Sea, 1939-1945 (London, 1957); and for "the impact of air power on the Royal Navy" (Preface), Geoffrey Till, Air Power and the Royal Navy, 1914-1945 (London, 1979).

954.   Kennedy, Paul. The Rise and Fall of British Naval Mastery. London, 1976.

See also his "Strategy versus Finance in Twentieth-Century Great Britain," International History Review, 3(1981), 44-61; The Contradiction between British Strategic Planning and Economic Requirements in the Era of Two World Wars (Washington, DC, 1980), from the International Security Studies Program: The Wilson Center, Working Papers no. 11; " 'Splendid Isolation' gegen 'Continental Commitment': Das Dilemma der britischen Deutschlandstrategie in der Zwischenkriegszeit, 1919-1939," in Tradition und Neubeginn: Internationale Forschungen zur deutschen Geschichte im 20. Jahrhundert, edited by Joachim Hütter et al. (Cologne, 1975); and Strategy and Diplomacy, 1870-1945: Eight Studies (London, 1983); six of which focus on Britain and Anglo-German affairs.

955.   Kyba, Patrick. Covenants without the Sword: Public Opinion and British Defence Policy, 1931-1935. Waterloo, Ontario, 1983.

Based on a selection of cabinet papers and an extensive study of newspapers and periodicals.

956.   Leutze, James R. Bargaining for Supremacy: Anglo-American Naval Collaboration, 1937-1941. Chapel Hill, NC, 1977.

Draws on a very wide array of British and American archives, private papers and interviews; see also his "Technology and Bargaining in Anglo-American Naval Relations, 1938-1946," U.S. Naval Institute Proceedings, 103(1977), 51-61; and Malcolm Murfett, Fool-Proof Relations: The Search for Anglo-American Naval Cooperation during the Chamberlain Years, 1937-1940 (Singapore, 1984).

957.   Liddell Hart, Basil H. The British Way in Warfare. London, 1932.

See also the same author's When Britain Goes to War (London, 1935); Europe in Arms (London, 1937); The Defence of Britain (London, 1939); Thoughts on War (London, 1944); and more generally Ronald Lewin, "Sir Basil Liddell Hart: The Captain Who Taught Generals," International Affairs 47(1971), 79-86; and Sir Frederick Pile, "Liddell Hart and the British Army, 1919-1939," in The Theory and Practice of War: Essays Presented to Captain B.H. Liddell Hart, edited by Michael Howard (London, 1965).

958.   Louis, William Roger. British Strategy in the Far East, 1919-1939. London, 1971.

959.   Luvaas, Jay. The Education of an Army: British Military Thought, 1815-1940. Chicago, IL, 1964.

960.   Marder, Arthur J. From the Dreadnought to Scapa Flow: The Royal Navy in the Fisher Era, 1904-1919. 5 vols. London, 1961-70.

Vol. 5 for 1918-19; see also his "The Influence of History on Sea Power: The Royal Navy and the Lessons of 1914-1918," Pacific Historical Review, 41(1972), 413-43; From the Dardanelles to Oran: Studies of the Royal Navy in War and Peace, 1915-1940 (London, 1974); Operation "Menace": The Dakar Expedition and the Dudley North Affair (London, 1976); and his last work, with Japanese sources, Old Friends, New Enemies: The Royal Navy and the Japanese Navy, Strategic Illusions 1936-1941 (London, 1981).

961.   Meyers, Reinhard. Britische Sicherheitspolitik, 1934-1938. Düsseldorf, 1976.

Based on a limited selection of cabinet material; see also his "Industrie, Handel und Finanz in der britischen Aufrüstung der dreissiger Jahre," Neue Politische Literatur, 26(1981), 191-212.

962.   Murray, Williamson. The Change in the European Balance of Power, 1938-1939: The Path to Ruin. Princeton, NJ, 1984.

See too his "The Role of Italy in British Strategy, 1938-1939," Journal of the Royal United Services Institute for Defence Studies, 124(1979), 43-49.

963.   Parker, R.A.C. "Economics, Rearmament and Foreign Policy: The United Kingdom before 1939 - A Preliminary Study." Journal of Contemporary History, 10(1975), 637-47.

See also his "Ökonomie, Aufrüstung und Aussenpolitik Grossbritanniens vor 1939," in Wirtschaft und Rüstung am Vorabend des Zweiten Weltkrieges, edited by Friedrich Forstmeier and Hans-Erich Volkmann (Düsseldorf, 1975); and "British Rearmament, 1936-39: Treasury, Trade Unions and Skilled Labour," English Historical Review, 96(1981), 306-43.

964.   Peden, G.C. British Rearmament and the Treasury, 1932-1939. Edinburgh, 1979.

Based mainly on cabinet and Treasury files, and some personal interviews; see also his "Arms, Government and Businessmen, 1935-1945," in Businessmen and Politics: Studies of Business Activity in British Politics, 1900-1945, edited by John Turner (London, 1984); "The Burden of Imperial Defence and the Continental Commitment Reconsidered," Historical Journal, 27(1984), 405-23; and "Sir Warren Fisher and British Rearmament against Germany," English Historical Review, 94(1979), 29-47.

965.   Powers, Barry D. Strategy without Slide-Rule: British Air Strategy, 1914-1939. London, 1976.

Besides the military aspects, includes public opinion, the press and political thought; thorough bibliography.

966. Pratt, Lawrence R. East of Malta, West of Suez: Britain's Mediterranean Crisis, 1936-1939. London, 1975.

See also the same author's "The Anglo-American Naval Conversations on the Far East of January 1938," International Affairs, 47(1971), 745-63.

967. Pritchard, R. John. Far Eastern Influences upon British Strategy towards the Great Powers, 1937-1939. London, 1987.

See also his "The Far East as an Influence on the Chamberlain Government's Pre-War European Policies," Millennium, 2(1973), 7-23.

968. Rader, Ronald R. "Anglo-French Estimates of the Red Army, 1936-1937." Soviet Armed Forces Review Annual, 3(1979), 265-80.

See too Peter Deli, "The Manchester Guardian and the Soviet Purges, 1936-1938," Survey, 28(1984), 119-65.

969. Ranft, Bryan, ed. Ironclad to Trident: 100 Years of Defence Commentary, Brassey's 1886-1986. London, 1986.

An anthology with 14 brief articles on the 1920-45 period.

970. Reussner, André. Les conversations franco-britanniques d'état-major, 1935-1939. Vincennes, 1969.

971. Richardson, Dick. The Evolution of British Disarmament Policy in the 1920s. London, 1989.

Which the author describes as "one of procrastination verging on duplicity" (Preface).

972. Roskill, Stephen W. Naval Policy between the Wars, 1919-1939. 2 vols. London, 1968-76.

Very detailed analysis; vol. 1 to 1929; see also Sir Peter Gretton, "Naval Policy between the Wars," Journal of the Royal United Service Institution, 113(1968), 151-52.

973. Salewski, Michael. Entwaffnung und Militärkontrolle in Deutschland, 1919-1927. Munich, 1966.

The most thorough study of the subject; see also Jürgen Heideking, "Vom Versailler vertrag zur Genfer Abrüstungskonferenz: Das Scheitern der alliierten Militärkontrollpolitik gegenüber Deutschland nach dem Ersten Weltkrieg," Militärgeschichtliche Mitteilungen, 28(1980), 45-68; and John P. Fox, "Britain and the Inter-Allied Military Commission of Control," Journal of Contemporary History, 4(1969), 143-64.

974. Shay, Robert Paul. British Rearmament in the Thirties: Politics and Profits. Princeton, NJ, 1977.

Argues that "appeasement was evolved in the belief that it might compensate for Britain's military weakness" (Introduction); includes Treasury papers and archives of business associations and private individuals.

975. Silverman, Peter. "The Ten Year Rule." Journal of the Royal United Services Institute for Defence Studies, 116(1971), 42-45.

And the responses by K. Booth, "The Ten Year Rule: An Unfinished Debate," ibid., 58-63; and Stephen W. Roskill, "The Ten Year Rule: The Historical Facts," ibid., 117(1972), 69-71.

976. Smith, Malcolm. British Air Strategy between the Wars. London, 1984.

Thorough and informative; see also his "The Treasury and Appeasement," Trivium, 15(1980), 91-99; "The Royal Air Force, Air Power and British Foreign Policy, 1932-1937," Journal of Contemporary History, 12(1977), 153-74; and "The RAF and Counter-Force Strategy before World War II," Journal of the Royal United Services Institute for Defence Studies, 121(1976), 68-73.

977. Stanbridge, G.T. "The Chiefs of Staff Committee: 50 Years of Joint Direction." Journal of the Royal United Services Institute for Defence Studies, 118(1973), 25-32.

978. Terraine, John. The Right of the Line: The Royal Air Force in the European War, 1939-1945. London, 1985.

979. Trotter, Ann. "The Dominions and Imperial Defence: Hankey's Tour in 1934." Journal of Imperial and Commonwealth History, 2(1974), 318-32.

980. Watt, D.C. Too Serious a Business: European Armed Forces and the Approach to the Second World War. London, 1975.

The origins of the second world war interpreted as "a civil war" (Chapter 1); useful bibliography; see also his "Anglo-German Naval Negotiations on the Eve of the Second World War," Journal of the Royal United Service Institution, 103(1958), 201-07, 384-91.

981.   Winton, Harold R. To Change an Army: General Sir John Burnett-Stuart and British Armoured Doctrine, 1927-1938. Lawrence, KS, 1988.

Director of military operations and intelligence, War Office, 1922-26; general officer commanding-in-chief, southern command, 1934-38; see also Lucio Ceva, "I 'Tank Advocates' e la strategia britannica, 1918-1940," Storia contemporanea, 17(1986), 87-92; and Robert H. Larson, The British Army and the Theory of Armored Warfare, 1918-1940 (Newark, NJ, 1984).

982.   Wrench, David J. "The Influence of Neville Chamberlain on Foreign and Defence Policy, 1932-1935." Journal of the Royal United Services Institute for Defence Studies, 125(1980), 49-57.

Foreign Economic Policy

983.   Andeopoulos, George J. "The International Financial Commission and Anglo-Greek Relations, 1928-1933." Historical Journal, 31(1988), 341-64.

See also Mark Mazower, "Economic Diplomacy between Great Britain and Greece in the 1930s," Journal of European Economic History, 17(1988), 603-19.

984.   Becker, Josef, and Hildebrand, Klaus. Internationale Beziehungen in der Weltwirtschaftskrise, 1929-1933. Munich, 1980.

Proceedings of a conference at Augsburg in 1979.

985.   Boyce, Robert. British Capitalism at the Crossroads, 1919-1932: A Study in Politics, Economics and International Relations. London, 1987.

An interesting and well-documented study.

986.   Bunselmeyer, Robert E. The Cost of the War, 1914-1919: British Economic War Aims and the Origins of Reparation. Hamden, CT, 1975.

Based on Public Record Office material and private papers.

987.   Clarke, Sir Richard. Anglo-American Economic Collaboration in War and Peace, 1942-1949. Edited by Sir Alec Cairncross. London, 1982.

        Four essays; author with the ministries of Information, Economic Warfare, Supply and Production, 1939-45.

988.   Costigliola, Frank. "Anglo-American Financial Rivalry in the 1920's." Journal of Economic History, 37(1977), 911-34.

        The background is in his Awkward Dominion: American Political, Economic, and Cultural Relations with Europe, 1919-1933 (London, 1984).

989.   Davenport-Hines, R.P.T. "Vickers' Balkan Conscience: Aspects of Anglo-Romanian Armaments, 1918-1939." Business History, 25(1983), 287-319.

        See also his "Vickers and Schneider: A Comparison of New British and French Multinational Strategies, 1916-1926," in Historical Studies in International Corporate Business, edited by Alice Teichova et al. (London, 1989); and "The British Marketing of Armaments, 1885-1935," in Markets and Bagmen, edited by R.P.T. Davenport-Hines (London, 1986).

990.   Davenport-Hines, R.P.T., and Jones, Geoffrey, eds. British Business in Asia since 1860. London, 1989.

        With chapters on Iran, Russia, Asia, India, Thailand, Malaysia, China and Japan.

991.   Dayer, Roberta Allbert. Bankers and Diplomats in China, 1917-1925: The Anglo-American Relationship. London, 1981.

        See also her "The British War Debts to the United States and the Anglo-Japanese Alliance, 1920-1923," Pacific Historical Review, 45(1976), 569-95.

992.   Dohrmann, Bernd. Die englische Europapolitik in der Wirtschaftskrise, 1921-1923: Zur Interdependenz von Wirtschaftsinteressen und Aussenpolitik. Munich, 1980.

        Based on a wide selection of British archives, including the Board of Trade and the Treasury.

993.   Drummond, Ian M. British Economic Policy and the Empire, 1919-1939. London, 1972.

Long introductory essay, with 36 related documents; see also his Imperial Economic Policy, 1917-1949: Studies in Expansion and Protection (London, 1974); and with Norman Hillmer, Negotiating Freer Trade: The United Kingdom, the United States, Canada, and the Trade Agreements of 1938 (Waterloo, Ontario, 1989).

994.   Eckes, Alfred E. A Search for Solvency: Bretton Woods and the International Monetary System, 1941-1971. Austin, TX, 1975.

995.   Fung, Edmund S.K. "Britain, Japan and Chinese Tariff Autonomy, 1927-1928." Proceedings of the British Association for Japanese Studies, 6(1981), 21-36.

See also his "The Sino-British Rapprochement, 1927-1931," Modern Asian Studies, 17(1983), 79-105.

996.   Garamvölgyi, Judit. Aus den Anfärgen sowjetischer Aussenpolitik: Das britisch-sowjetrussische Handelsab-kommen von 1921. Köln, 1967.

See too M.W. Glenny, "The Anglo-Soviet Trade Agreement, March 1921," Journal of Contemporary History, 5(1970), 63-82.

997.   Hilton, Stanley E. Brazil and the Great Powers, 1930-1939: The Politics of Trade Rivalry. Austin, TX, 1975.

Specifically the United States, Germany and Great Britain; with the use of Brazilian archives.

998.   Hinkkanen-Lievonen, Merja-Liisa. British Trade and Enterprise in the Baltic States, 1919-1925. Helsinki, 1984.

999.   Hogan, Michael J. Informal Entente: The Private Structure of Cooperation in Anglo-American Economic Diplomacy, 1918-1928. Columbia, MO, 1977.

See also his "Informal Entente: Public Policy and Private Management in Anglo-American Petroleum Affairs, 1918-1924," Business History Review, 48(1974), 187-205.

1000.   Jones, Geoffrey. The History of the British Bank of the Middle East. 2 vols. London, 1986.

Vol. 1, for the period 1889-1952, subtitled: Banking and Empire in Iran; vol. 2: Banking and Oil; see too Geoffrey Jones and Clive Trebilcock, "Russian Industry and British Business, 1910-1930: Oil and Armaments," Journal of European Economic History, 11(1982), 61-103.

1001.   Kaiser, David E. Economic Diplomacy and the Origins of the Second World War: Germany, Britain, France and Eastern Europe, 1930-1939. Princeton, NJ, 1981.

A useful study of prewar economic diplomacy; see also György Ránki, Economy and Foreign Policy: The Struggle of the Great Powers for Hegemony in the Danube Valley, 1919-1939 (New York, 1983); with Hungarian, British, French and German documentation.

1002.   Kottman, Richard H. Reciprocity and the North Atlantic Triangle, 1932-1938. Ithaca, NY, 1968.

An attempt to analyse the "neglected dimension" of the 1930s; based on American and Canadian sources; see also Arthur W. Schatz, "The Anglo-American Trade Agreement and Cordell Hull's Search for Peace, 1936-1938," Journal of American History, 57(1970), 85-103; Carl Kreider, The Anglo-American Trade Agreement: A Study of British and American Commercial Policies, 1934-1939 (Princeton, NJ, 1943); Henry J. Tasca, World Trading Systems: A Study of American and British Commercial Policies (Paris, 1939); and Percy W. Bidwell, Our Trade with Britain: Bases for a Reciprocal Tariff Agreement (New York, 1938).

1003.   Loveday, Alexander. Britain and World Trade and Other Essays. London, 1931.

War Office, 1915-1919; joined League of Nations secretariat, 1919; director of its financial section and economic intelligence service, 1931-39; and of the economic, financial and transit department, 1939-46.

1004.   McBeth, B.S. British Oil Policy, 1919-1939. London, 1985.

Includes British, American and Venezuelan sources; more on oil diplomacy in William Stivers, Supremacy and Oil: Iraq, Turkey and the Anglo-American World Order, 1918-1930 (London, 1982); Gareth G. Jones, "The British Government and the Oil Companies, 1912-1924: The Search for an Oil Policy," Historical Journal,

20(1977), 647-72; Helmut Mejcher, Imperial Quest for Oil: Iraq, 1910-1928 (London, 1976); and his "Oil and British Policy towards Mesopotamia, 1914-1918," Middle Eastern Studies, 8(1972), 377-91; Stephen G. Rabe, "Anglo-American Rivalry for Venezuelan Oil, 1919-1929," Mid-America, 58(1976), 97-109; Marian Kent, Oil and Empire: British Policy and Mesopotamian Oil, 1900-1920 (London, 1976); Peter J. Beck, "The Anglo-Persian Oil Dispute, 1932-1933," Journal of Contemporary History, 9(1974), 123-51; his " 'A Tedious and Perilous Controversy': Britain and the Settlement of the Mosul Dispute, 1918-1926," Middle Eastern Studies, 17(1981), 256-76; and E.H. Davenport and Sidney R. Cooke, The Oil Trusts and Anglo-American Relations (London, 1923).

1005. Maisel, Ephraim. "The Formation of the Department of Overseas Trade, 1919-1926." Journal of Contemporary History, 24(1989), 169-90.

1006. Meredith, David. "The British Government and Colonial Economic Policy, 1919-1939." Economic History Review, 28(1975), 484-99.

1007. Murgescu, C. "Nicolae Titulescu, the Negotiator of the Financial Agreement with England in 1925." Revue roumaine d'études internationales, 2(1969), 161-97.

1008. Nicholas, S.J. "British Multinational Investment before 1939." Journal of European Economic History, 11(1982), 605-30.

For the wider background, see British Multinationals: Origins, Management and Performance, edited by Geoffrey Jones (London, 1986).

1009. Offner, Arnold A. "Appeasement Revisited: The United States, Great Britain, and Germany, 1933-1940." Journal of American History, 64(1977), 373-93.

Mainly on economic appeasement.

1010. Osterhammel, Jürgen. Britischer Imperialismus im Fernen Osten: Strukturen der Durchdringung und einheimischer Widerstand auf dem chinesischen Markt, 1932-1937. Bochum, 1982.

See too his "Imperialism in Transition: British Big Business and the Chinese Authorities, 1931-1937," China Quarterly, 98(1984), 260-86.

1011. Parker, R.A.C. "The Pound Sterling, the American Treasury, and British Preparations for War, 1938-1939." English Historical Review, 98(1983), 261-79.

1012. Peden, G.C. "A Matter of Timing: The Economic Background to British Foreign Policy, 1937-1939." History, 69(1984), 15-28.

1013. Platt, D.C.M., ed. Business Imperialism 1840-1930: An Inquiry based on British Experience in Latin America. London, 1977.

       See also J. Fred Rippy, British Investments in Latin America, 1822-1949 (Minneapolis, MN, 1959).

1014. Pugach, Noel H. "Anglo-American Aircraft Competition and the China Arms Embargo, 1919-1921." Diplomatic History, 2(1978), 351-71.

1015. Richardson, J. Henry. British Economic Foreign Policy. London, 1936.

1016. Rooth, T.J.T. "Limits of Leverage: The Anglo-Danish Trade Agreement of 1933." Economic History Review, 37(1984), 211-28.

       For the wider background see Birgit Nüchel Thomsen and Brinley Thomas, Anglo-Danish Trade, 1661-1963: An Historical Survey (Aarhus, 1966).

1017. Rowland, Benjamin M. Commercial Conflict and Foreign Policy: A Study in Anglo-American Relations, 1932-1938. New York, 1987.

       See also his "Preparing the American Ascendancy: The Transfer of Economic Power from Britain to the United States, 1933-1944," in Balance of Power or Hegemony: The Interwar Monetary System, edited by Benjamin M. Rowland (New York, 1976); and in the same collection, Robert Skidelsky, "The Retreat from Leadership: The Evolution of British Foreign Economic Policy, 1870-1939."

1018. Schlote, Werner. British Overseas Trade from 1700 to the 1930s. London, 1952.

1019. Schmidt, Gustav, ed. Konstellationen internationaler Politik, 1924-1932: Politische und wirtschaftliche Faktoren in den

Beziehungen zwischen Westeuropa und den Vereinigten Staaten. Bochum, 1983.

Proceedings of a conference in Dortmund, September 1981; with several contributions on specific British aspects of the subject; see also Gilbert Ziebura, Weltwirtschaft und Weltpolitik, 1922/24-1931 (Frankfurt/M., 1984).

1020.   Shimizu, Hiroshi. Anglo-Japanese Trade Rivalry in the Middle East in the Inter-War Period. London, 1986.

Specifically on the cotton piece-goods trade; based on British, French and Japanese archives.

1021.   Silverman, Dan P. Reconstructing Europe after the Great War. London, 1982.

On Anglo-French-American financial diplomacy, 1918-23; see also Kenneth A. Oye, "The Sterling-Dollar-Franc Triangle: Monetary Diplomacy, 1929-1937," World Politics, 38(1985), 173-99.

1022.   Trotter, Ann. "The Currency Weapon: Japan, Britain, and the United States in China, 1938-1941." Proceedings of the British Association for Japanese Studies, 5(1980), 57-67.

1023.   Wendt, Bernd-Jürgen. Economic Appeasement: Handel und Finanz in der britischen Deutschland-Politik, 1933-1939. Düsseldorf, 1971.

See also his Appeasement 1938: Wirtschaftliche Rezession und Mitteleuropa (Frankfurt/M., 1966); "England und der deutsche 'Drang nach Südosten': Kapitalbeziehungen und Warenverkehr in Südosteuropa zwischen den Weltkriegen," in Deutschland in der Weltpolitik des 19. und 20. Jahrhunderts: Festschrift für Fritz Fischer, edited by Imanuel Geiss and Bernd-Jürgen Wendt (Düsseldorf, 1973); and "Strukturbedingungen der britischen Südosteuropapolitik am Vorabend des Zweiten Weltkrieges," in Wirtschaft und Rüstung am Vorabend des Zweiten Weltkrieges, edited by Friedrich Forstmeier and Hans-Erich Volkmann (Düsseldorf, 1975); Neil Forbes, "London Banks, the German Standstill Agreements and 'Economic Appeasement' in the 1930s," Economic History Review, 40(1987), 571-87; Hans-Jürgen Schröder, "Economic Appeasement: Zur britischen und amerikanischen Deutschlandpolitik vor dem Zweiten Weltkrieg," Vierteljahrshefte für Zeitgeschichte, 30(1982), 82-97; Alice Teichova, "Die deutsch-britischen Wirtschaftsinteressen in

Mittel- und Südosteuropa am Vorabend des Zweiten Weltkriegs,"
in Wirtschaft und Rüstung am Vorabend des Zweiten
Weltkrieges, edited by Friedrich Forstmeier and Hans-Erich
Volkmann (Düsseldorf, 1975); and Ludmila Zhivkova, "British
Economic Policy in the Balkans on the Eve of World War II,"
Studia Balcanica, 4(1971), 169-85.

1024.   Wurm, Clemens A. Industrielle Interessenpolitik und Staat:
        Internationale Kartelle in der britischen Aussen- und
        Wirtschaftspolitik während der Zwischenkriegszeit. Berlin,
        1987.

        See also Harm G. Schroeder, Aussenpolitik und Wirtschafts-
        interesse: Skandinavien im aussenwirtschaftlichen Kalk l
        Deutschlands und Grossbritanniens, 1918-1939 (Frankfurt/M.,
        1983).

Labour Foreign Policy

1025.   Attlee, C.R. War Comes to Britain. London, 1940.

        See also C.R. Attlee et al., Labour's Aims in War and Peace
        (London, 1940).

1026.   Brand, C.F. The British Labour Party: A Short History. Stanford,
        CA, 1964.

        Other histories of the Labour party which have material on foreign
        policy include G.D.H. Cole, A History of the Labour Party from
        1914 (London, 1948); Henry Pelling, A Short History of the Labour
        Party (London, 1961); Emanuel Shinwell, The Labour Story:
        Being a History of the Labour Party (London, 1963); and Francis
        Williams, Fifty Years' March: The Rise of the Labour Party
        (London, 1949).

1027.   Burridge, T.D. British Labour and Hitler's War. London, 1976.

        See also the same author's "Barnacles and Trouble Makers:
        Labour's Left Wing and British Foreign Policy, 1939-1940,"
        Canadian Journal of History, 16(1981), 1-25; and "Great Britain
        and the Dismemberment of Germany at the End of the Second
        World War," International History Review, 3(1981), 565-79.

1028.   Carlton, David. MacDonald Versus Henderson: The Foreign
        Policy of the Second Labour Government. London, 1970.

From the first Hague conference of 1929 to the fall of the government in 1931.

1029.   Cline, Catherine Ann. Recruits to Labour: The British Labour Party, 1914-1931. Syracuse, NY, 1963.

See also her "E.D. Morel and the Crusade against the Foreign Office," Journal of Modern History, 39(1967), 126-37.

1030.   Cowden, Morton H. Russian Bolshevism and British Labour, 1917-1921. New York, 1984.

See too F.M. Leventhal, "Seeing the Future: British Left-Wing Travellers to the Soviet Union, 1919-1932," in The Political Culture of Modern Britain: Studies in Memory of Stephen Koss, edited by J.M.W. Bean (London, 1987); and Stephen Richards Graubard British Labour and the Russian Revolution, 1917-1924 (Cambridge, MA, 1956).

1031.   Cowling, Maurice. The Impact of Labour, 1920-1924. London, 1974.

1032.   Dowse, Robert E. Left in the Centre: The Independent Labour Party, 1893-1940. London, 1966.

See also his "The Independent Labour Party and Foreign Politics, 1918-23," International Review of Social History, 7(1962), 33-46; and Arthur Marwick, "The Independent Labour Party in the Nineteen-Twenties," Bulletin of the Institute of Historical Research, 35(1962), 62-74.

1033.   Fleay, C., and Sanders, M.L. "The Labour Spain Committee: Labour Party Policy and the Spanish Civil War." Historical Journal, 28(1985), 187-97.

1034.   Glasgow, George. MacDonald as Diplomatist: The Foreign Policy of the First Labour Government in Great Britain. London, 1924.

1035.   Gordon, Michael R. Conflict and Consensus in Labour's Foreign Policy, 1914-1965. Stanford, CA, 1969.

1036.   Gorny, Joseph. The British Labour Movement and Zionism, 1917-1948. London, 1983.

An analysis based on Hebrew and English language sources.

1037. Grantham, John T. "Hugh Dalton and the International Post-War Settlement: Labour Foreign Policy Formulation, 1943-1944." Journal of Contemporary History, 14(1979), 713-27.

1038. Gupta, Partha Sarathi. Imperialism and the British Labour Movement, 1914-1964. London, 1975.

1039. Henderson, Arthur. Labour and Foreign Affairs. London, 1922.

1040. Jones, Bill. The Russia Complex: The British Labour Party and the Soviet Union. Manchester, 1977.

Based on interviews, the press, and Labour party sources.

1041. Keserich, Charles. "The British Labour Press and Italian Fascism, 1922-1925." Journal of Contemporary History, 10(1975), 579-90.

1042. Krieger, Wolfgang. Labour Party und Weimarer Republik: Ein Beitrag zur Aussenpolitik der britischen Arbeiterbewegung zwischen Programmatik und Parteitaktik, 1918-1924. Bonn, 1978.

Based on a very wide array of British official archives, Labour party and TUC material, and private papers.

1043. Maddox, William P. Foreign Relations in British Labour Politics, 1900-1924. Cambridge, MA, 1934.

1044. Malmsten, Neal R. "The British Labour Party and the West Indies, 1918-1939." Journal of Imperial and Commonwealth History, 5(1977), 172-205.

1045. Meehan, Eugene J. The British Left Wing and Foreign Policy: A Study of the Influence of Ideology. New Brunswick, NJ, 1960.

1046. Miller, Kenneth E. Socialism and Foreign Policy: Theory and Practice in Britain to 1931. The Hague, 1967.

A thorough discussion, both of theory and practice, of the British "socialist alternative in international relations" (Chapter 1); see also Henry R. Winkler, "The Emergence of a Labour Foreign Policy in Great Britain, 1918-1929," Journal of Modern History, 28(1956), 247-58.

1047. Naylor, John F. Labour's International Policy: The Labour Party in the 1930s. London, 1969.

1048. Newman, Michael. "British Socialists and the Question of European Unity, 1939-1945." European Studies Review, 10(1980), 75-100.

1049. Robbins, Keith. "Labour Foreign Policy and International Socialism: MacDonald and the League of Nations." Annali dell'Instituto Giangiacomo Feltrinelli, 26(1983), 105-33.

See also M.S. Venkataramani, "Ramsay MacDonald and Britain's Domestic Politics and Foreign Relations, 1919-1931: A Study Based on MacDonald's Letters to an American Friend," Political Studies, 8(1960), 231-49; and James Ramsay MacDonald, The Foreign Policy of the Labour Party (London, 1923).

1050. Skop, Arthur L. "The British Labour Party and the German Revolution, November 1918-January 1919.' European Studies Review, 5(1975), 277-97.

1051. Tucker, William Rayburn. The Attitude of the British Labour Party towards European and Collective Security Problems, 1920-1939. Geneva, 1950.

See also his "British Labour and Revision of the Peace Settlement, 1920-1925," Southwestern Social Science Quarterly, 41(1960), 136-49.

1052. Williams, Andrew J. Labour and Russia: The Attitude of the Labour Party to the USSR, 1924-1934. Manchester, 1989.

1053. Windrich, Elaine. British Labour's Foreign Policy. Stanford, CA, 1952.

Public Opinion, Propaganda and the Media

1054. Adamthwaite, Anthony. "The British Government and the Media, 1937-1938." Journal of Contemporary History, 18(1983), 281-97.

See also K.R.M. Short, "A Note on BBC Television News and the Munich Crisis, 1938," Historical Journal of Film, Radio and Television, 9(1989), 165-79; and Nicholas Pronay and Philip M. Taylor, " 'An Improper Use of Broadcasting': The British Government and Clandestine Radio Propaganda Operations against Germany during the Munich Crisis and After," Journal of Contemporary History, 19(1984), 357-84.

1055.   Addison, Paul. "Patriotism under Pressure: Lord Rothermere and British Foreign Policy," in The Politics of Reappraisal, 1918-1939. Edited by Gillian Peele and Chris Cook. London, 1975.

1056.   Aigner, Dietrich. Das Ringen um England: Das deutsch-britische Verhältnis, die öffentliche Meinung, 1933-1939, Tragödie zweier Völker. Munich, 1964.

1057.   Aldgate, Anthony. Cinema and History: British Newsreels and the Spanish Civil War. London, 1979.

With a useful bibliography; critical of what amounted to news management in favour of the government's policy of non-intervention; see also his "British Newsreels and the Spanish Civil War," History, 58(1973), 160-63.

1058.   Balfour, Michael. Propaganda in War, 1939-1945: Organisations, Policies and Publics in Britain and Germany. London, 1979.

Author was with ministry of Information from March 1939 to March 1942; assistant director of intelligence in the Political Warfare Executive; and thereafter in the Psychological Warfare Division of SHAEF from April 1942 until 1945; see also his "A War-Time Exercise in Empathy," in Studien zur Geschichte Englands und der deutsch-britischen Beziehungen: Festschrift für Paul Kluke, edited by Lothar Kettenacker et al. (Munich, 1981); and Ellic Howe, The Black Game (London, 1982).

1059.   Barnes, James J., and Barnes, Patience P. Hitler's "Mein Kampf" in Britain and America: A Publishing History, 1930-1939. London, 1980.

See also James J. Barnes, "Mein Kampf in Britain," Wiener Library Bulletin, 27(1974), 2-10.

1060.   Berselli, Aldo. L'opinione pubblica inglese et l'avvento del fascismo, 1919-1925. Milan, 1971.

See also Richard Bosworth, "The British Press, the Conservatives and Mussolini, 1920-1934," Journal of Contemporary History, 5(1970), 163-82; and Elena Fasano Guarini, "Il 'Times' di fronte al fascismo, 1919-1932," Rivista storica del socialismo, 8(1965), 155-85.

1061. Bishku, Michael B. "The British Press and the Future of Egypt, 1919-1922." International History Review, 8(1986), 604-12.

1062. Black, J.B. Organising the Propaganda Instrument: The British Experience. The Hague, 1975.

1063. Briggs, Asa. The History of Broadcasting in the United Kingdom. 3 vols. London, 1961-70.

See also Gerard Mansell, Let the Truth Be Told: Fifty Years of BBC External Broadcasting (London, 1982).

1064. Camrose, 1st Viscount (William Ewart Berry). British Newspapers and Their Controllers. London, 1947.

Founder of Allied Newspapers, 1924; and adviser to the ministry of Information, 1939-45; see also Carl J. Hambro, Newspaper Lords in British Politics (London, 1958); mainly on Lord Beaverbrook.

1065. Cantril, Hadley, and Strunk, Mildred, eds. Public Opinion, 1935-1946. Princeton, NJ, 1951.

Opinion-poll results from 16 countries; including the British Institute of Public Opinion; results edited by subject; see also The Gallup International Public Opinion Polls: Great Britain, 1937-1975, edited by George H. Gallup, 2 vols. (New York, 1976).

1066. Ceadel, Martin. Pacifism in Britain, 1914-1945: The Defining of a Faith. London, 1980.

Based on an extensive use of archives of peace societies and the literature of the peace movement; see also the same author's Thinking about Peace and War (London, 1987); and "The 'King and Country' Debate, 1933: Student Politics, Pacifism and the Dictators," Historical Journal, 22(1979), 397-422; James Hinton, Protests and Visions: Peace Politics in Britain, 1900-1987 (London, 1988); Campaigns for Peace: British Peace Movements in the Twentieth Century, edited by Richard Taylor and Nigel Young (Manchester, 1989); Michael Pugh, "Pacifism and Politics in Britain, 1931-1935," Historical Journal, 23(1980), 641-56; Keith Robbins, The Abolition of War: The 'Peace Movement' in Britain, 1914-1919 (Cardiff, 1976); David C. Lukowitz, "British Pacifists and Appeasement: The Peace Pledge Union," Journal of Contemporary History, 9(1974), 115-27; and Donald Birn, "A

Peace Movement Divided: Pacifism and Internationalism in Interwar Britain," Peace and Change, 1(1973), 20-24.

1067. Cockett, Richard. Twilight of Truth: Chamberlain, Appeasement and the Manipulation of the Press. London, 1989.

See too his "The Foreign Office News Department and the Struggle against Appeasement," Historical Research: The Bulletin of the Institute of Historical Research, 63(1990), 73-85; "Ball, Chamberlain and Truth," Historical Journal, 33(1990), 131-142; and " 'In Wartime Every Objective Reporter Should Be Shot': The Experience of British Press Correspondents in Moscow, 1941-1945," Journal of Contemporary History, 23(1988), 515-30.

1068. Cole, Robert. Britain and the War of Words in Neutral Europe, 1939-1945. Manchester, 1989.

See too his "The Other 'Phoney War': British Propaganda in Neutral Europe, September-December 1939," Journal of Contemporary History, 22(1987), 455-79; and "The Conflict Within: Sir Stephen Tallents and Planning Propaganda Overseas before the Second World War," Albion, 14(1982), 50-71.

1069. Foster, Alan. " 'The Times' and Appeasement: The Second Phase." Journal of Contemporary History, 16(1981), 441-65.

1070. Gannon, Franklin Reid. The British Press and Germany, 1936-1939. London, 1971.

The "psychology of appeasement" as illustrated in ten major British newspapers, and the archives of The Times and the Manchester Guardian; see also Brigitte Granzow, A Mirror of Nazism: British Opinion and the Emergence of Hitler, 1929-1933 (London, 1964); and G. Kloss, "The Image of Britain and the British in the German National Socialist Press," Wiener Library Bulletin, 24(1970), 21-29.

1071. Goldman, Aaron. "The Link and the Anglo-German Review." South Atlantic Quarterly, 71(1972), 424-33.

1072. Grainger, J.H. Patriotisms: Britain, 1900-1939. London, 1986.

On the "articulations of English/British patriotism, mainly by politicians and publicists" (Preface).

1073. Griffiths, Richard. Fellow Travellers of the Right: British Enthusiasts for Nazi Germany, 1933-1939. London, 1980.

Well-documented analysis; see also Richard Thurlow, Fascism in Britain: A History, 1918-1985 (London, 1987); David S. Lewis, Illusions of Grandeur: Mosley, Fascism and British Society, 1931-1981 (Manchester, 1987); G.C. Webber, The Ideology of the British Right, 1918-1939 (London, 1986); Britain, Fascism and the Popular Front, edited by Jim Fyrth (London, 1985); British Fascism: Essays on the Radical Right in Inter-War Britain, edited by Kenneth Lunn and Richard Thurlow (London, 1980); Robert Benewick, The Fascist Movement in Britain (London, 1972); and David Caute, The Fellow Travellers (London, 1973).

1074. Haworth, Bryan. "The British Broadcasting Corporation, Nazi Germany and the Foreign Office, 1933-1936." Historical Journal of Film, Radio and Television, 1(1981), 47-55.

1075. Heller, Richard. "East Fulham Revisited." Journal of Contemporary History, 6(1971), 172-96.

On this rearmament issue see also Tom Stannage, "The East Fulham By-Election, 25 October 1933," Historical Journal, 14(1971), 165-200; and Martin Ceadel, "Interpreting East Fulham," in By-Elections in British Politics, edited by Chris Cook and John Ramsden (London, 1973).

1076. History of The Times, vol. 4, The 150th Anniversary and Beyond, 1912-1948. 2 parts. London, 1952.

Actually concludes in 1939; continued in Iverach McDonald, The History of The Times, vol. 5, Struggles in War and Peace, 1939-1966 (London, 1984); useful summary in Oliver Woods and James Bishop, The Story of The Times (London, 1983); among other press histories see Duff Hart-Davis, The House the Berrys Built (London, 1990); David Kynaston, The Financial Times: A Centenary History (London, 1988); Douglas Hill, Tribune 40: The First Forty Years of a Socialist Newspaper (London, 1977); David Ayerst, The Manchester Guardian: Biography of a Newspaper (London, 1971); Maurice Edelman, The Mirror: A Political History (London, 1966); Edward Hyams, The New Statesman: The History of the First Fifty Years, 1913-1963 (London, 1963); H.R.G. Whates, The Birmingham Post, 1857-1957 (Birmingham, 1957); Mildred Gibb and Frank Beckwith, The Yorkshire Post: Two Centuries (Leeds, 1954); William Rust, The Story of the Daily Worker (London, 1949); The Economist, 1843-

1943: A Centenary Volume (London, 1943); and Wilfrid H. Hindle, The Morning Post, 1772-1937: Portrait of a Newspaper (London, 1937).

1077.   Kieser, Rolf. Englands Appeasement-Politik und der Aufstieg des Dritten Reiches im Spiegel der britischen Presse, 1933-1939: Ein Beitrag zur Vorgeschichte des Zweiten Weltkrieges. Winterthur, 1964.

Based on a study of ten daily and two Sunday newspapers.

1078.   Koss, Stephen. The Rise and Fall of the Political Press in Britain, vol. 2, The Twentieth Century. London, 1984.

Massively researched in primary sources and very thorough.

1079.   Lewis, John. The Left Book Club: An Historical Record. London, 1970.

See also Gordon Barrick Neavill, "Victor Gollancz and the Left Book Club," The Library Quarterly, 41(1971), 197-214; Stuart Samuels, "The Left Book Club," Journal of Contemporary History, 1(1966), 65-86; and Sheila Hodges, Gollancz: The Story of a Publishing House, 1928-1978 (London, 1978).

1080.   Livingstone, Dame Adelaide. The Peace Ballot. London, 1935.

Organised by the League of Nations Union; the background with detailed results; see also Martin Ceadel, "The First British Referendum: The Peace Ballot, 1934-1935," English Historical Review, 95(1980), 810-39; and J.A. Thompson, "The 'Peace Ballot' and the 'Rainbow' Controversy," Journal of British Studies, 20(1981), 150-70.

1081.   McCallum, R.B. Public Opinion and the Last Peace. London, 1944.

1082.   MacDonald, Callum A. "Radio Bari: Italian Wireless Propaganda in the Middle East and British Countermeasures, 1934-1938." Middle Eastern Studies, 13(1977), 195-207.

1083.   MacKenzie, John M. Propaganda and Empire: The Manipulation of British Public Opinion, 1880-1960. Manchester, 1984.

1084.   McLaine, Ian. Ministry of Morale: Home Front Morale and the Ministry of Information in World War II. London, 1979.

The wartime ministry responsible for "the release of official news; security censorship of the press, films and the BBC; the maintenance of morale; the conduct of publicity campaigns for other departments; and the dissemination of propaganda to enemy, neutral, allied and empire countries" (Introduction).

1085. Madge, Charles, and Harrisson, Tom. Britain by Mass-Observation. London, 1939.

See also the Mass-Observation studies, War Begins at Home (London, 1940); and Home Propaganda (London, 1941).

1086. Margach, James. The Abuse of Power: The War between Downing Street and the Media from Lloyd George to Callaghan. London, 1978.

1087. Meyers, Reinhard. "Das Dritte Reich in britischer Sicht: Grundzüge und Determinanten britischer Deutschlandbilder in den dreissiger Jahren," in Das britische Deutschlandbild im Wandel des 19. und 20. Jahrhundert. Edited by Bernd-Jürgen Wendt. Bochum, 1984.

And in the same collection, Lothar Kettenacker, "Preussen-Deutschland als britisches Feindbild im Zweiten Weltkrieg."

1088. Morris, A.J.A. "The 'Birmingham Post' and Anglo-German Relations, 1933-1935." University of Birmingham Historical Journal, 2(1968), 191-201.

1089. Partner, Peter. Arab Voices: The BBC Arabic Service, 1938-1988. London, 1988.

1090. Postgate, Raymond, and Vallance, Aylmer. England Goes to Press: The English People's Opinion on Foreign Affairs as Reflected in Their Newspapers since Waterloo, 1815-1937. London, 1937.

1091. Pronay, Nicholas. "British Newsreels in the 1930s, Part I: Audience and Producers." History, 56(1971), 411-18.

Continued in "British Newsreels in the 1930s, II: Their Policies and Impact," History, 57(1972), 63-72.

1092. Schadlich, Karlheinz. " 'Appeaser' in Aktion: Hitlers britische Freunde in der Anglo-German Fellowship." Jahrbuch für Geschichte, 3(1969), 197-225.

1093.   Sharf, Andrew. The British Press and Jews under Nazi Rule. London, 1964.

        Based on the Podro collection of press cuttings drawn from 150 British newspapers and periodicals.

1094.   Short, K.R.M., ed. Film and Radio Propaganda in World War II. London, 1983.

        See also Britain and the Cinema in the Second World War, edited by Philip M. Taylor (London, 1988); Anthony Aldgate and Jeffrey Richards, Britain Can Take It: The British Cinema in the Second World War (London, 1986); and Nicholas Pronay and F. Thorpe, British Official Films in the Second World War (Santa Barbara, CA, 1980).

1095.   Stannage, Tom. Baldwin Thwarts the Opposition: The British General Election of 1935. London, 1980.

        Including public opinion as a factor in rearmament; see also James C. Robertson, "The British General Election of 1935," Journal of Contemporary History, 9(1974), 149-64; and Reginald Bassett, "Telling the Truth to the People: The Myth of the Baldwin 'Confession,' " Cambridge Journal, 2(1948), 84-95.

1096.   Steed, H. Wickham. The Press. London, 1938.

1097.   Stubbs, John. "Appearance and Reality: A Case Study of 'The Observer' and J.L. Garvin, 1914-1942," in Newspaper History: From the Seventeenth Century to the Present. Edited by George Boyce et al. London, 1978.

1098.   Tallents, Sir Stephen. The Projection of England. London, 1932.

1099.   Taylor, Philip M. The Projection of Britain Overseas: British Overseas Publicity and Propaganda, 1919-1939. London, 1981.

        A well-documented study, shedding valuable light on the news department of the Foreign Office; see also the same author's "Cultural Diplomacy and the British Council, 1934-1939," British Journal of International Studies, 4(1978), 244-65; " 'If War Should Come': Preparing the Fifth Arm for Total War, 1935-1939," Journal of Contemporary History, 16(1981), 27-51; and more generally Francis Donaldson, The British Council: The First Fifty Years (London, 1984); and Film, Politics and Propaganda, 1918-1945, edited by D.W. Spring and Nicholas Pronay (London, 1981).

1100. West, W.J. Truth Betrayed. London, 1987.

On the relationship, mainly pre-1939, between "radio and politics"; extensive use of the BBC archives.

1101. Willcox, Temple. "Towards a Ministry of Information." History, 69(1984), 398-414.

See too his "Projection or Publicity? Rival Concepts in the Pre-War Planning of the British Ministry of Information," Journal of Contemporary History, 18(1983), 97-116; and Michael Stenton, "British Propaganda and Raison d'Etat, 1935-1940," European Studies Review, 10(1980), 47-74.

1102. Willert, Arthur. "British News Abroad." Round Table, 27 (1937), 533-46, 712-22.

Among his numerous articles, see "Publicity and Propaganda in International Affairs," International Affairs, 17(1938), 809-26; and "British News Controls," Foreign Affairs, 17(1939), 712-22.

1103. Woolf, Stuart. "British Attitudes towards Fascism, 1922-1940," in Inghilterra e Italia nel '900: Atti del convegno di Lucca, Ottobre 1972. Florence, 1973.

Includes seven other essays on aspects of public opinion as a factor in Anglo-Italian relations from 1914-46

The Foreign Office

1104. Anon. [R.L. Buell]. The British Foreign Office. New York, 1929.

For the United States Foreign Policy Association; a survey of organisation and contemporary problems.

1105. Anon. "Changes in the Organisation of the Foreign and Diplomatic Service, 1921." The British Year Book of International Law, 1(1920-21), 97-108.

1106. Ashton-Gwatkin, Frank T.A. The British Foreign Service. Syracuse, NY, 1950.

An insightful survey by a former diplomat and Foreign Office official, 1913-37, and novelist with pen name of John Paris; see also his "Thoughts on the Foreign Office, 1918-1939," Contemporary Review, 188(1955), 374-78.

1107. Beloff, Max. "The Whitehall Factor: The Role of the Higher Civil Service, 1919-1939," in The Politics of Reappraisal, 1918-1939. Edited by Gillian Peele and Chris Cook. London, 1975.

Includes the Foreign Office and the Treasury.

1108. Bishop, Donald G. The Administration of British Foreign Relations. Syracuse, NY, 1961.

A thorough analysis of all aspects, including organisation, administration and overseas operations.

1109. Boadle, Donald G. "The Formation of the Foreign Office Economic Relations Section, 1930-1937." Historical Journal, 20(1977), 919-36.

1110. Boardman, Robert, and Groom, A.J.R., eds. The Management of Britain's External Relations. London, 1973.

A collection of 14 essays, mainly on the post-1945 period, ranging from the organisation of the Foreign Office to the news media and foreign affairs; useful bibliography.

1111. Boyle, Peter G. "The British Foreign Office View of Soviet-American Relations, 1945-1946." Diplomatic History, 3(1979), 307-20.

1112. Bullen, Roger, ed. The Foreign Office, 1782-1982. Frederick, MD, 1984.

Seven papers first presented at a conference to mark the bicentenary of the Foreign and Commonwealth Office; subjects include Lord Curzon, the Foreign Office between the wars, and foreign secretaries as diplomats.

1113. Cecil, Algernon. "The Foreign Office," in The Cambridge History of British Foreign Policy, 1783-1919. Vol. 3. Edited by Sir A. Ward and G.P. Gooch. London, 1923.

1114. Coates, Patrick Devereux. The China Consuls: British Consular Officers, 1843-1943. London, 1988.

Served consular service at Peking, Canton and Kunming, 1937-41; attached to Chinese forces in Burma and India, 1941-44; and to British embassy in China, 1944-46.

1115. Collier, Sir Laurence. "The Old Foreign Office." Blackwood's Magazine, 312(1972), 256-61.

1116. Connell, John. [J.H. Robertson]. The "Office": A Study of British Foreign Policy and Its Makers, 1919-1951. London, 1958.

By a former journalist, soldier, and chief military press censor, India, 1944.

1117. Craig, Gordon A. "The British Foreign Office from Grey to Austen Chamberlain," in The Diplomats, 1919-1939. Edited by Gordon A. Craig and Felix Gilbert. Princeton, NJ, 1953.

Also includes relevant studies of Arthur Henderson, Lord Perth and Nevile Henderson.

1118. Cromwell, Valerie. "The Foreign and Commonwealth Office," in The Times Survey of Foreign Ministries of the World. Edited by Zara Steiner. London, 1982.

1119. Dilks, David. "The British Foreign Office between the Wars," in Shadow and Substance in British Foreign Policy, 1895-1939. Edited by B.J.C. McKercher and D.J. Moss. Edmonton, Alberta, 1984.

In this same collection see also B.J.C. McKercher, "The British Diplomatic Service in the United States and the Chamberlain Foreign Office's Perceptions of Domestic America, 1924-1927: Images, Reality and Diplomacy."

1120. Edwards, Peter G. "The Foreign Office and Fascism, 1924-1929." Journal of Contemporary History, 5(1970), 153-61.

1121. Glenny, W.J. "The Trade Commissioner and Commercial Diplomatic Services." Journal of Public Administration, 2(1924), 276-87.

1122. Goldstein, Erik. "The Foreign Office and Political Intelligence, 1918-1920." Review of International Studies, 14(1988), 275-88.

1123. Hanak, Harry. "The Government, the Foreign Office, and Austria-Hungary, 1914-1918." Slavonic and East European Review, 47(1969) 161-97.

1124. Kennedy, Aubrey Leo. "Reorganisation of the Foreign Service." Quarterly Review, 283(1945), 397-412.

1125.   Lammers, Donald N. "From Whitehall after Munich: The Foreign Office and the Future Course of British Policy." Historical Journal, 16(1973), 831-56.

        See too his "Fascism, Communism and the Foreign Office, 1937-1939," Journal of Contemporary History, 6(1971), 66-86.

1126.   Langford, R. Victor. British Foreign Policy: Its Formulation in Recent Years. Washington, DC, 1942.

1127.   Larner, Christina. "The Amalgamation of the Diplomatic Service with the Foreign Office." Journal of Contemporary History, 7(1972), 107-26.

1128.   Manne, Robert. "The Foreign Office and the Failure of Anglo-Soviet Rapprochement." Journal of Contemporary History, 16 (1981), 725-55.

        On events from 1934 to 1936.

1129.   Nicolson, Sir Harold. Diplomacy. London, 1939.

        Still stimulating despite its age; see also his The Evolution of Diplomatic Method (London, 1954); and "The Foreign Service," in The British Civil Servant, edited by William A. Robson (London, 1937).

1130.   Nightingale, Robert T. The Personnel of the British Foreign Office and Diplomatic Service, 1851-1929. London, 1930.

        Fabian Tract no. 232; argues that the diplomatic staff was too much drawn from the establishment.

1131.   Norton, Henry Kittredge. "Foreign Office Organization." Annals of the American Academy of Political and Social Science, 143(1929), 1-83.

        A comparative study of organisations in Britain, France, Germany, Italy and the United States.

1132.   O'Hara, Valentine J. "The Foreign Office and Lithuania." Contemporary Review, 125(1924), 745-52.

        Member, political mission for the Baltic states, 1919.

1133. Platt, D.C.M. The Cinderella Service: British Consuls since 1825. London, 1971.

1134. Rooke, M.J. "The British Foreign Office and Anti-Semitism in Rumania, 1936-1939." Wiener Library Bulletin, Special Issue: Fifty Years of the Wiener Library (London, 1983), 46-51.

1135. Ross, Graham. "Foreign Office Attitudes to the Soviet Union, 1941-1945." Journal of Contemporary History, 16 (1981), 521-40.

1136. Sallet, Richard. Der diplomatische Dienst: Seine Geschichte und Organisation in Frankreich, Grossbritannien und den Vereinigten Staaten. Stuttgart, 1953.

1137. Selby, Sir Walford. "The Foreign Office." Nineteenth Century and After, 137(1945), 3-12.

1138. Sharp, Alan. "The Foreign Office in Eclipse, 1919-1922." History, 61(1976), 198-218.

1139. Steiner, Zara, and Dockrill, M.L. "The Foreign Office Reforms, 1919-1921." Historical Journal, 17(1974), 131-56.

See also the same authors' "The Foreign Office at the Paris Peace Conference in 1919," International History Review, 2(1980), 55-86; and M.L. Dockrill, "The Foreign Office and the Proposed Institute of International Affairs," International Journal, 50(1980), 665-72.

1140. Strang, Lord. The Foreign Office. London, 1955.

Part of the New Whitehall Series by a Foreign Office career official; see also his "The Formulation and Control of Foreign Policy," Durham University Journal, 49(1957), 98-108; and The Diplomatic Career (London, 1962).

1141. Tilley, Sir John A.C., and Gaselee, Stephen. The Foreign Office. London, 1933.

Written by the Chief Clerk (1913-1918) and Librarian respectively of the Foreign Office; introduction by Sir John Simon; part of the original Whitehall Series published between 1925 and 1935.

1142. Vansittart, Lord. "The Decline of Diplomacy." Foreign Affairs, 28(1950), 177-89.

1143.   Warman, Roberta M. The Foreign Office, 1916-1918: A Study of
          Its Role and Functions. London, 1986.

          See also her "The Erosion of Foreign Office Influence in the
          Making of Foreign Policy, 1916-1918," Historical Journal,
          15(1972), 133-59.

1144.   Watt, D.C. Personalities and Policies: Studies in the Formulation
          of British Foreign Policy in the Twentieth Century. London,
          1965.

          A far-ranging collection of 13 essays; including a useful
          bibliographical essay on research materials for the study of the
          British foreign policymaking élite.

1145.   Willert, Sir Arthur. Aspects of British Foreign Policy. London,
          1928.

          See also the same author's "The Foreign Office from Within,"
          Strand Magazine, 45(1936), 398-405; and The Frontiers of
          England (London, 1935).

1146.   Young, John Wilson. "The Foreign Office and the Departure of
          General de Gaulle, June 1945-January 1946." Historical Journal,
          25(1982), 209-16.

Britain and the League of Nations

British membership in the League of Nations spans the entire life of the
organisation from 1919 to 1945. Considerable research has been done on
specific aspects of Britain's involvement with League-related problems.
However, our view of the entire relationship remains unclear. Between
1919 and 1945 Britain's involvement with the League of Nations alternated
between two distinctive areas. On the one hand, several foreign policy-
related problems, such as the application of sanctions during the Italo-
Ethiopian war, preoccupied policymakers in London in 1935 and 1936. On
the other hand, for almost 26 years Britain participated in the constructive,
less publicised, aspects of League activity. This encompassed such
matters as economic and financial reconstruction in Europe, intellectual
cooperation, control of traffic in drugs and humans, mandates, refugee
resettlement and disarmament. It is these latter areas which are mainly
detailed in the following entries.

1147.   Arnold-Forster, William. The Disarmament Conference. London,
          1931.

By a well-informed commentator; also useful is his "British Policy at the Disarmament Conference," Political Quarterly, 3(1932), 365-80.

1148.   Bachofen, Maja. Lord Cecil und der Völkerbund. Zürich, 1959.

See also Peter Raffo, "The League of Nations Philosophy of Lord Robert Cecil," Australian Journal of Politics and History, 20(1974), 186-96; J.A. Thompson, "Lord Cecil and the Pacifists in the League of Nations Union," Historical Journal, 20(1977), 949-59; David Carlton, "Disarmament with Guarantees: Lord Cecil, 1922-1927," Disarmament and Arms Control, 3(1965), 143-64.

1149.   Barros, James. Office without Power: Secretary-General Sir Eric Drummond, 1919-1933. London, 1979.

16th Earl of Perth; private secretary to the foreign secretary, 1915-19; later ambassador to Italy, 1933-39; see also his The Aland Islands Question: Its Settlement by the League of Nations (London, 1968); and The League of Nations and the Great Powers: The Greek-Bulgarian Incident (London, 1970).

1150.   Beck, Peter. "From the Geneva Protocol to the Greco-Bulgarian Dispute: The Development of the Baldwin Government's Policy towards the Peacekeeping Role of the League of Nations, 1924-1925." British Journal of International Studies, 6(1980), 52-68.

1151.   Bentwich, Norman. England in Palestine. London, 1932.

See also his The Mandates System (London, 1930); other early accounts include A.M. Hyamson, Palestine under the Mandate, 1920-1948 (London, 1950); Royal Institute of International Affairs, Great Britain and Palestine, 1915-1945 (London, 1946); Paul L. Hanna, British Policy in Palestine (Washington, DC, 1942); and Paul Sidebotham, Great Britain and Palestine (London, 1937).

1152.   Bethell, Nicholas. The Palestine Triangle: The Struggle for the Holy Land, 1935-1948. London, 1979.

An analysis of relations between Britain and the Zionists; archival research strongly supplemented by numerous personal interviews; in the same vein see also Evyatar Friesel, The British, Zionism and Palestine: Perceptions and Policies during the Mandate Period (London, 1989); and Joseph Heller, "Anglo-Zionist Relations, 1939-1947," Wiener Library Bulletin, 31(1978), 63-73.

1153.   Birn, Donald. The League of Nations Union, 1918-1945. London, 1981.

See also his "The League of Nations Union and Collective Security," Journal of Contemporary History, 9(1974), 131-59; J.A. Thompson, "The League of Nations Union and Promotion of the League Idea in Great Britain," Australian Journal of Politics and History, 18(1972), 52-61; and Ernest Bramstead, "Apostles of Collective Security: The League of Nations Union and Its Functions," Australian Journal of Politics and History, 13(1967), 347-64.

1154.   Carlton, David. "The Anglo-French Compromise on Arms Limitation, 1928." Journal of British Studies, 8(1969), 141-62.

See also his "Great Britain and the League Council Crisis of 1926," Historical Journal, 11(1968), 354-64; and "The Problem of Civil Aviation in British Disarmament Policy, 1919-1934," Journal of the Royal United Services Institute, 111(1966), 307-16.

1155.   Carter, Gwendolen M. The British Commonwealth and International Security: The Role of the Dominions, 1919-1939. Toronto, Ontario, 1947.

Largely on policies and attitudes toward the League; see also C.A.W. Manning, The Policies of the British Dominions in the League of Nations (London, 1932); and H. Duncan Hall, "The British Commonwealth and the Founding of the League Mandate System," in Studies in International History: Essays Presented to W. Norton Medlicott, edited by K. Bourne and D.C. Watt (London, 1967).

1156.   Cataluccio, F. "La questione arabo dopo la prima guerra mondiale: I mandati britannici in Iraq e Palestine." Archivio storico italiano, 125 (1967), 291-351.

1157.   Cecil, Hugh. "Lord Robert Cecil and the League of Nations during the First World War," in Home Fires and Foreign Fields: British Social and Military Experience in the First World War. Edited by Peter Liddle. London, 1985.

1158.   Chamberlain, Sir Austen. The League. London, 1926.

League of Nations Union, Pamphlet, no. 203.

1159.   Chaput, Rolland A. Disarmament in British Foreign Policy. London, 1935.

1160.   Charvet, Félix. L'influence britannique dans la S.D.N.; Des origines de la S.D.N. jusqu'à nos jours. Paris, 1938.

See also Jean Schwoebel, L'Angleterre et la sécurité collective (Paris, 1938).

1161.   Cohen, Gavriel. Churchill and the Question of Palestine, 1939-1942. Jerusalem, 1976.

Hebrew commentary with British documents in English; see also his The British Cabinet and the Question of Palestine, April-July, 1943 (Tel Aviv, 1976); and Nathaniel Katzburg, From Partition to White Paper: British Policy in Palestine, 1936-1940 (Jerusalem, 1974); with a selection of relevant British documents.

1162.   Cohen, Michael J. Palestine: Retreat from the Mandate: The Making of British Policy, 1936-1945. London, 1978.

Based on British and Zionist archives; see also his Churchill and the Jews (London, 1985); for the context from 1905 to 1948, "American Influence on British Policy in the Middle East during World War II: First Attempts at Coordinating Allied Policy on Palestine," American Jewish Historical Quarterly, 67(1977), 50-70; "Direction of Policy in Palestine, 1936-1945," Middle Eastern Studies, 11(1975), 237-61; "British Strategy and the Palestine Question, 1936-1939," Journal of Contemporary History, 7(1972), 157-83; and "Appeasement in the Middle East: The British White Paper on Palestine, May 1939," Historical Journal, 16(1973), 571-96; continued in "The Testing of a Policy, 1942-1945," Historical Journal, 19(1976), 727-58.

1163.   Crozier, Andrew J. "The Establishment of the Mandates System, 1919-1925: Some Problems Created by the Paris Peace Conference." Journal of Contemporary History, 14(1979), 483-513.

1164.   Cushendun, Lord. "Disarmament." Journal of the Royal Institute of International Affairs, 7(1928), 77-93.

1st Baron Cushendun (Ronald John McNeill); parliamentary under-secretary of state for Foreign Affairs, 1922-24, 1924-25; financial secretary to the Treasury, 1925-27; chancellor of the Duchy of Lancaster, 1927-29.

1165.   Djourovitch, Djoura. Le Protocole de Genève devant l'opinion anglaise. Paris, 1928.

See also David Hunter Miller, The Geneva Protocol (London, 1925); and Arthur Henderson, Labour and the Geneva Protocol (London, 1925).

1166.   Egerton, George W. Great Britain and the Creation of the League of Nations: Strategy, Politics and International Organization, 1914-1919. Chapel Hill, NC, 1978.

See also his "Great Britain and the League of Nations: Collective Security as Myth and History," in The United Nations Library, The League of Nations in Retrospect: Proceedings of the Symposium (New York, 1983); "The Lloyd George Government and the Creation of the League of Nations," American Historical Review, 79(1974), 419-44; more generally, his "Collective Security as Political Myth: Liberal Internationalism and the League of Nations in Politics and History," International History Review, 4(1983), 496-524; and Peter Yearwood, " 'On Safe and Right Lines': The Lloyd George Government and the Origins of the League of Nations, 1916-1918," Historical Journal, 23(1989), 131-55; Peter Raffo, "The Anglo-American Negotiations for a League of Nations," Journal of Contemporary History, 9(1974), 153-76; and Roland N. Stromberg, "Uncertainties and Obscurities about the League of Nations," Journal of the History of Ideas, 32(1972), 139-54.

1167.   Ekoko, A. Edho. "The British Attitude towards Germany's Colonial Irredentism in Africa in the Inter-War Years." Journal of Contemporary History, 14(1979), 287-307.

1168.   Gifford, Prosser, and Louis, William Roger, eds. France and Britain in Africa: Imperial Rivalry and Colonial Rule. New Haven, CT, 1971.

Includes essays on British mandates, 1919-39; see also by the same editors, Imperial Rivalry and Colonial Rule: Britain and Germany in Africa (New Haven, CT, 1967).

1169.   Hailey, 1st Baron (Malcolm Hailey). Britain and Her Dependencies. London, 1943.

Governor, Punjab, 1924-28; United Provinces, 1928-34; member, Permanent Mandates Commission, League of Nations, 1935-39.

1170. Henderson, Arthur. Conference for the Reduction and Limitation of Armaments: Preliminary Report on the Work of the Conference. Geneva, 1936.

Report from the conference president, 1932-34.

1171. Hill, C.J. "Great Britain and the Saar Plebiscite of 13 January 1935." Journal of Contemporary History, 9(1974), 121-42.

See also Margaret Lambert, The Saar (London, 1934); Royal Institute of International Affairs, Information Department Paper, no. 11, The Saar Problem (London, 1934); Sarah Wambaugh, The Saar Plebiscite (London, 1940); and her Plebiscites Since the World War, with a Collection of Official Documents, 2 vols. (Washington, DC, 1933).

1172. Jenks, Clarence Wilfred. Britain and the ILO. London, 1969.

David Davies Memorial Lecture; by the legal adviser to the ILO, 1931-48; later director-general; see also Antony Alcock, The History of the International Labour Organisation (London, 1971); George Alexander Johnston, The International Labour Organisation: Its Work for Social and Economic Progress (London, 1970); by the assistant director of the ILO, 1945-48; and the official history by Margaret Stewart, Britain and the ILO: The Story of Fifty Years (London, 1969).

1173. Klieman, Aaron S. "The Divisiveness of Palestine: Foreign Office Versus Colonial Office on the Issue of Partition, 1937." Historical Journal, 22(1979), 423-41.

1174. Louis, William Roger. Great Britain and Germany's Lost Colonies, 1914-1919. London, 1967.

See also his "The United Kingdom and the Beginning of the Mandates System, 1919-1922," International Organization, 23(1969), 73-96; which analyses the origins of the mandates in light of British archives; "Colonial Appeasement, 1936-1938," Revue belge de philologie et d'histoire, 4(1971), 1175-91; and Kenneth Robinson, The Dilemmas of Trusteeship: Aspects of British Colonial Policy between the Wars (London, 1965).

1175. Mossek, Moshe. Palestine Immigration Policy under Sir Herbert Samuel: British, Zionist and Arab Attitudes. London, 1978.

See too Elie Kedourie, "Sir Herbert Samuel and the Government of Palestine," Middle Eastern Studies, 5(1969), 44-68.

1176. Most, Eckhard. Grossbritannien und der Völkerbund: Studien zur Politik der Friedenssicherung 1925 bis 1934. Frankfurt/M., 1981.

Based on British and German but not League archives.

1177. Murray, Gilbert. "The British People and the League of Nations," in Les origines et l'oeuvre de la Société des Nations. Edited by Pierre Munch. Vol. 1. Copenhagen, 1923.

See also his The League of Nations Movement: Some Recollections of the Early Days (London, 1955).

1178. Noel-Baker, Philip J. (Baron Noel-Baker). The First World Disarmament Conference, 1932-1933, and Why It Failed. London, 1979.

See too his "The League of Nations," in The Baldwin Age, edited by John Ramsden (London, 1960); Disarmament (London, 1926); The League of Nations at Work (London, 1926); The Geneva Protocol for the Pacific Settlement of International Disputes (London, 1925); and "The Making of the Covenant from the British Point of View," in Les origines et l'oeuvre de la Société des Nations, edited by Pierre Munch, vol. 2 (Copenhagen, 1924).

1179. Ovendale, Ritchie. Britain, the United States and the End of the Palestine Mandate, 1942-1948. Woodbridge, 1989.

With British and American documentation; see also Ronald W. Zweig, Britain and Palestine during the Second World War (London, 1986); based on British, Australian and Israeli archives.

1180. Rose, Norman. Gentile Zionists: A Study in Anglo-Zionist Diplomacy, 1929-1939. London, 1973.

Further details in his "The Debate on Partition, 1937-1938: The Anglo-Zionist Aspect, Part I, The Proposal," Middle Eastern Studies, 6(1970), 297-318; continued in "The Withdrawal," Middle Eastern Studies, 7(1971), 3-24; as well as "Palestine's Role in Britain's Imperial Defence: An Aspect of Zionist Diplomacy, 1938-1939," Wiener Library Bulletin, 22(1968), 32-35.

1181. Sharma, Shiva Kumar. Der Völkerbund und die Grossmächte: Ein Beitrag zur Geschichte der Völkerbundspolitik Grossbritanniens, Frankreichs und Deutschlands, 1929-1933. Frankfurt/M., 1978.

A thorough study with a useful bibliography.

1182. Sheffer, Gabriel. "Appeasement and the Problem of Palestine." International Journal of Middle Eastern Studies, 11(1980), 377-99.

See also his "British Colonial Policy-Making towards Palestine, 1929-1939," Middle Eastern Studies, 14(1978), 307-22; and "Intentions and Results of British Policy in Palestine: Passfield's White Paper," Middle Eastern Studies, 9(1973), 43-60.

1183. Sluglett, Peter. Britain in Iraq, 1914-1932. London, 1976.

Largely based on British archival materials; see too Daniel Silverfarb, Britain's Informal Empire in the Middle East: A Case Study of Iraq, 1929-1941 (London, 1986); and his "Great Britain, Iraq and Saudi Arabia: The Revolt of the Ikwan, 1927-1930," International History Review, 4(1982), 222-43.

1184. Upthegrove, Campbell L. Empire by Mandate: A History of the Relations of Great Britain with the Permanent Mandates Commission of the League of Nations. New York, 1954.

And for the general background, Quincy Wright, Mandates under the League of Nations (Chicago, IL, 1930).

1185. Walters, Francis Paul. A History of the League of Nations. 2 vols. London, 1952.

Joined secretariat of League of Nations, 1919; deputy director-general, 1939-40; more recent analyses are Gary B. Ostrower, The League of Nations: The First Decade (Garden City Park, NY, 1991); F.S. Northedge, The League of Nations: Its Life and Times, 1920-1946 (London, 1986); less successful studies include R.M. Iliukhina, Liga Natsii, 1919-1934 (Moscow, 1982); Alfred Pfeil, Der Völkerbund (Darmstadt, 1976); James Avery Joyce, Broken Star: The Story of the League of Nations, 1919-1939 (Swansea, 1978); Elmer Bendiner, A Time for Angels: The Tragicomic History of the League of Nations (New York, 1975); Peter Raffo, The League of Nations (London, 1974); George Scott, The Rise and Fall of the League of Nations (London, 1973); a collection of various documents with commentary in Ruth B. Henig, The League of Nations (Edinburgh, 1973); Byron Dexter, The Years of Opportunity: The League of Nations, 1920-1926 (New York, 1967); and P.A. Reynolds, "The League of Nations," in The New Cambridge Modern History, vol. 12, rev. ed. (London, 1968).

1186.   Wasserstein, Bernard. The British in Palestine: The Mandatory Government and the Arab-Jewish Conflict, 1917-1929. London, 1978.

See also John J. McTague, British Policy in Palestine, 1917-1922 (London, 1983).

1187.   Wheeler-Bennett, John W. Disarmament and Security since Locarno, 1925-1931: Being the Political and Technical Background of the General Disarmament Conference, 1932. London, 1932.

See too his The Disarmament Deadlock (London, 1934).

1188.   Williams, Sir John Fischer. Some Aspects of the Covenant of the League of Nations. London, 1934.

British member, Permanent Court of Arbitration, The Hague, 1936-47; assistant legal adviser, Home Office, 1918-20; British legal representative, Reparation Commission, 1920-30; among his numerous articles and books see "Great Britain and the League," International Affairs, 17(1938), 187-210; and The Geneva Protocol of 1924 (London, 1925).

1189.   Winkler, Henry R. The League of Nations Movement in Great Britain, 1914-1919. New Brunswick, NJ, 1952.

See also the author's "The Development of the League of Nations Idea in Great Britain, 1914-1919," Journal of Modern History, 20(1948), 95-112.

1190.   Yearwood, P.J. " 'Consistently with Honour': Great Britain, the League of Nations and the Corfu Crisis of 1923." Journal of Contemporary History, 21(1986), 559-79.

See too the same author's " 'On the Safe and Right Lines': The Lloyd George Government and the Origins of the League of Nations, 1916-1918," Historical Journal, 32(1989), 131-55.

1191.   Zimmern, Alfred. The League of Nations and the Rule of Law, 1918-1935. London, 1936.

Political intelligence department, Foreign Office, 1918-19; deputy director, League of Nations Institute of Intellectual Co-operation, Paris, 1926-30; deputy director, research department, Foreign Office, 1943-45; see also D.J. Markwell, "Sir Alfred Zimmern Revisited: Fifty Years On," Review of International Studies, 12(1986), 279-92.

4. Bilateral and Area Studies

North and South Atlantic

1192.   Allen, H.C. Conflict and Concord: The Anglo-American Relationship since 1783. New York, 1960

Among such surveys see also Arthur Campbell Turner, The Unique Partnership: Britain and the United States (New York, 1971); Herbert George Nicholas, The United States and Britain (Chicago, IL, 1975); Bruce M. Russett, Community and Contention: Britain and America in the Twentieth Century (Cambridge, MA, 1963); Britain and the United States, edited by Henry L. Roberts and Paul A. Wilson (London, 1953); and Clarence Crane Brinton, The United States and Britain (London, 1945).

1193.   Beloff, Max. "The Special Relationship: An Anglo-American Myth," in A Century of Conflict, 1850-1950: Essays for A.J.P. Taylor. Edited by Martin Gilbert. London, 1966.

See also A.E. Campbell, "The United States and Great Britain: Uneasy Allies," in Twentieth Century American Foreign Policy, edited by John Braeman (Columbus, OH, 1971).

1194.   Clark, William. Less Than Kin: A Study of Anglo-American Relations. London, 1957.

Press attaché, Chicago, 1940-45; later public relations adviser to Anthony Eden; see also his From Three Worlds (London, 1986).

1195.   Fry, Michael G. Illusions of Security: North Atlantic Diplomacy, 1918-1922. Toronto, Ontario, 1972.

On the efforts of the "Atlanticists" to foster permanent Anglo-American cooperation after the first world war; for the general historical background see John Bartlett Brebner, The North Atlantic Triangle: The Interplay of Canada, the United States and Great Britain (London, 1945).

1196.　McMahon, Deirdre. Republicans and Imperialists: Anglo-Irish Relations in the 1930s. London, 1984.

See also Paul Canning, British Policy towards Ireland, 1921-1941 (London, 1985); his "Yet Another Failure for Appeasement? The Case of the Irish Treaty Ports," International History Review, 4(1982), 371-92; G. Boyce, "From War to Neutrality: Anglo-Irish Relations, 1921-1950," British Journal of International Studies, 5(1978), 15-36; D.W. Harkness, "Mr. de Valera's Dominion: Irish Relations with Britain and the Commonwealth, 1932-1938," Journal of Commonwealth Political Studies, 8(1970), 206-28; Hugh Shearman, Anglo-Irish Relations (London, 1948); and for background, Stephen Hartley, The Irish Question as a Problem in British Foreign Policy, 1914-1918 (London, 1987); and Hubert Sturm, Hakenkreuz und Kleeblatt: Ireland, die Alliierten und das "Dritte Reich," 1933-1945, 2 vols. (Frankfurt/M., 1984).

1197.　Reynolds, David. The Creation of the Anglo-American Alliance, 1937-1941: A Study in Competitive Co-operation. London, 1981.

A multifaceted approach to the complex Anglo-American relationship; concentrates on the post-Munich period; useful bibliography; see also his "Lord Lothian and Anglo-American Relations, 1939-1940," Transactions of the American Philosophical Society, 73(1983), 1-65.

1198.　Tella, Guido di, and Watt, D. Cameron, eds. Argentina between the Great Powers, 1939-1946. London, 1989.

Ten essays on various aspects of the Anglo-US-South American triangle; see also Roger Gravil, The Anglo-Argentine Connection, 1900-1939 (Boulder, CO, 1985); and Carlos Escudé, Gran Bretaña, Estados Unidos, y la Declinació Argentina, 1942-1949 (Buenos Aires, 1983).

1199.　Watt, D. Cameron. Succeeding John Bull: America in Britain's Place, 1900-1975. London, 1984.

An analysis of "role perceptions" among British and American foreign policymakers (Preface).

1200. Wigley, Philip G. Canada and the Transition to Commonwealth: British-Canadian Relations, 1917-1926. London, 1977.

1201. Willson, Beckles. America's Ambassadors to England, 1785-1929: A Narrative of Anglo-American Diplomatic Relations. New York, 1929.

Western Europe

1202. Adamthwaite, Anthony. Britain and France, 1914-1945. London, 1982.

See also Britain and France: Ten Centuries, edited by Douglas Johnson et al. (London, 1980); S.M. Osgood, "Le mythe de 'la perfide Albion' en France, 1919-1940," Cahiers d'histoire, 20(1975), 5-20; John C. Cairns, "A Nation of Shopkeepers in Search of a Suitable France: 1919-1940," American Historical Review, 79(1974), 710-43; René Albrecht-Carrié, Britain and France: Adaptations to a Changing Context of Power (New York, 1970); Jean Albert-Sorel, Histoire de France et d'Angleterre: La rivalité, l'entente, l'alliance (Paris, 1950); R.B. McCallum, England and France, 1939-1943 (London, 1944); Catherine Gavin, Britain and France, the Entente Cordiale: A Study of Twentieth Century Relations (London, 1941).

1203. Centre National de la Recherche Scientifique. Les relations franco-britanniques de 1935 à 1939. Paris, 1975.

Twenty-three papers on all aspects of the subject; presented at conferences in London, 1971, and Paris, 1972.

1204. Furnia, Arthur H. The Diplomacy of Appeasement: Anglo-French Relations and the Prelude to World War II, 1931-1938. Washington, DC, 1960.

1205. Gardiner, Rolf, and Rocholl, Heinz. Britain and Germany. London, 1928.

Proceedings of a symposium; British contributors included G.P. Gooch and Kingsley Martin.

1206. Gilbert, Martin. Britain and Germany between the Wars. London, 1964.

A valuable collection of documents with commentary.

1207.   Hachey, Thomas E., ed. Anglo-Vatican Relations, 1914-1939:
        Confidential Annual Reports of the British Ministers to the Holy
        See. Boston, MA, 1972.

        From Public Record Office files FO371.

1208.   Joll, James, ed. Britain and Europe: Pitt to Churchill, 1793-1940.
        London, 1961.

        Includes 19 documents on the 1918-40 period; see also R.C. Birch,
        Britain and Europe, 1871-1939 (London, 1966); G.P. Gooch,
        "England and Europe: A Retrospect," Hungarian Quarterly,
        4(1938), 577-85; and Hugh Dalton, "England and Europe,"
        Contemporary Review, 148(1935), 129-37.

1209.   Jordan, William M. Great Britain, France and the German
        Problem, 1918-1939. London, 1943.

        See also Arnold Wolfers, Britain and France between Two Wars:
        Conflicting Strategies of Peace since Versailles (New York,
        1940).

1210.   Kaarsted, Tage. Great Britain and Denmark, 1914-1920. Odense,
        1979.

        See too Susan Seymour, Anglo-Danish Relations and Germany,
        1933-1945 (Odense, 1982).

1211.   Kettenacker, Lothar, et al., eds. Studien zur Geschichte Englands
        und der deutsch-britischen Beziehungen, Festschrift für Paul
        Kluke. Munich, 1981.

        Subjects include Harold Nicolson, the Rhineland crisis of 1936,
        British propaganda in the 1930s, and war aims.

1212.   Koliopoulos, John S. Greece and the British Connection, 1935-
        1941. London, 1977.

        Based on British and Greek archives; see also his "Anglo-Greek
        Relations during the Abyssinian Crisis of 1935-1936," Balkan
        Studies, 15(1974), 99-106; Marion Einhorn, "Grundzüge und
        Ergebnisse britischer Griechenlandpolitik während des zweiten
        Weltkrieges," Jahrbuch für Geschichte, 34(1987), 339-84; and
        Dimitri Kitsikis, "La Grèce entre l'Angleterre et l'Allemagne de
        1936 à 1941," Revue historique, 238(1967), 85-116; written with
        access to some Greek archives.

1213. Lefèvre, Joseph. L'Angleterre et la Belgique à travers les cinq derniers siècles. Brussels, 1946.

Also useful is The History of Anglo-Belgian Relations, edited by H.W. Howes (London, 1943); see as well Peter Klefisch, Das Dritte Reich und Belgien, 1933-1939 (Frankfurt/M., 1988); and Daniel H. Thomas, The Guarantee of Belgian Independence and Neutrality in European Diplomacy, 1830's -1930's (Kingston, RI, 1983).

1214. Mander, John. Our German Cousins: Anglo-German Relations in the 19th and 20th Centuries. London, 1974.

A cultural and historical analysis; see also Paul Kennedy, "Idealists and Realists: British Views of Germany, 1864-1939," Transactions of the Royal Historical Society, 25(1975), 137-56.

1215. Quartararo, Rosaria. Roma tra Londra e Berlino: La politica estera fascista dal 1930 al 1940. Rome, 1980.

A well-documented study, using both British and Italian archives, and the papers of Dino Grandi; no bibliography but with 200 pages of footnotes; see also the earlier Virginio Gayda, Italia e Inghilterra (Rome, 1941); and Amadeo Giannini, I rapporti italo-inglese (Milan, 1940).

1216. Rostow, Nicholas. Anglo-French Relations, 1934-1936. London, 1984.

Based on available British and French documentation.

1217. Stone, Glyn A. "The Official British Attitude to the Anglo-Portuguese Alliance, 1910-1945." Journal of Contemporary History, 10(1975), 729-46.

1218. Waites, Neville, ed. Troubled Neighbours: Franco-British Relations in the Twentieth Century. London, 1971.

A collection of essays; including Locarno, the Rhineland crisis, Munich and wartime diplomacy.

Eastern Europe and the USSR

1219. Carmi, Ozer. La Grande-Bretagne et la Petite Entente. Geneva, 1972.

From Versailles to its disintegration in 1937; based on a wide variety of sources; see also Günter Reichert, Das Scheitern der kleinen Entente: Internationale Beziehungen im Donauraum von 1933 bis 1938 (Munich, 1971).

1220.   Coates, William P., and Coates, Zelda K. A History of Anglo-Soviet Relations. 2 vols. London, 1943-58.

See too the same authors' Armed Intervention in Russia 1918-1922 (London, 1935).

1221.   Crankshaw, Edward. Britain and Russia. London, 1944.

Similar early studies include B.H. Sumner, Anglo-Soviet Relations (Leeds, 1948); K.W.B. Middleton, Britain and Russia: An Historical Essay (London, 1947); J.A.R. Marriott, Anglo-Russian Relations, 1689-1943 (London, 1944); and F.D. Klingender, Russia - Britain's Ally, 1812-1942 (London, 1942).

1222.   Franke, Reiner. "Die Tschechoslowakei in der politischen Meinung Englands, 1918-1938," in Die demokratisch-parlamentarische Struktur der ersten Tschechoslowakischen Republik. Edited by Karl Bosl. Munich, 1975.

See also Harry Hanak, "Great Britain and Czechoslovakia, 1918-1948: An Outline of Their Relations," in Czechoslovakia Past and Present, edited by Miloslav Rechcigl (The Hague, 1968); and J.V. Polisensky, Britain and Czechoslovakia: A Study in Contacts (Prague, 1966).

1223.   Gorodetsky, Gabriel. The Precarious Truce: Anglo-Soviet Relations, 1924-1927. London, 1977.

Based on British archives and Soviet published sources.

1224.   Karski, Jan. The Great Powers and Poland, 1919-1945: From Versailles to Yalta. New York, 1985.

With multilanguage documentation.

1225.   Keeble, Sir Curtis. Britain and the Soviet Union, 1917-1989. London, 1990.

By a former ambassador at Moscow, 1978-82.

1226.   Kettle, Michael. Russia and the Allies, 1917-1920. London, 1981-.

In progress; vol. 1 for 1917-18; vol. 2, March-November 1918; mainly on Anglo-Soviet relations; among much on the subject see Benjamin D. Rhodes, The Anglo-American Winter War with Russia, 1918-1919: A Diplomatic and Military Tragicomedy (London, 1988); John Silverlight, The Victors' Dilemma: Allied Intervention in the Russian Civil War (London, 1970); John Bradley, Allied Intervention in Russia, 1917-1920 (New York, 1968); and John Swettenham, Allied Intervention in Russia, 1918-1919 and the Part Played by Canada (London, 1967).

1227. Luciuk, Lubomyr L., and Kordan, Bohdan S., eds. Anglo-American Perspectives on the Ukrainian Question, 1938-1951: A Documentary Collection. Kingston, Ontario, 1987.

See too The Foreign Office and the Famine: British Documents on Ukraine and the Great Famine of 1932-1933, edited by Marco Carynnyk et al. (Kingston, Ontario, 1987).

1228. Niedhart, Gottfried. Grossbritannien und die Sowjetunion 1934-1939: Studien zur britischen Politik der Friedenssicherung zwischen den beiden Weltkriegen. Munich, 1972.

See also his "Zwischen Feindbild und Wunschbild: Die Sowjetunion in der britischen Urteilsbildung, 1917-1945," in Der Westen und die Sowjetunion: Einstellungen und Politik gegenüber der UdSSR in Europa und in den USA seit 1917, edited by Gottfried Niedhart (Paderborn, 1983); and "Der Bündniswert der Sowjetunion im Urteil Grossbritanniens, 1936-1939," Militärgeschichtliche Mitteilungen, 5(1971), 55-67.

1229. Northedge, F.S., and Wells, Audrey. Britain and Soviet Communism: The Impact of a Revolution. London, 1982.

A comprehensive account of Anglo-Soviet relations.

1230. Piszczkowski, Tadeusz. Anglia a Polska, 1914-1939: W swietle dokumentow brytyjskich. London, 1975.

Based on Polish secondary sources and Foreign Office materials; see also Marek Baumgart, Wielka Brytania a odrodzona Polska, 1918-1933 (Szczecin, 1985); Mieczyslaw Nurek, Polska w polityce Wielkiej Brytanii w latach 1936-1941 (Warsaw, 1983); Maria Nowak-Kielbikowa, "Anthony Eden w Warszawie, 2-3 Kwietnia 1935r.," Dzieje Najnowsze, 15(1984), 81-96; her "British Policy towards Poland in the 1930's," Acta Poloniae Historica,

40(1979), 97-122; and Polska-Wielka Brytania w latach 1918-1923 (Warsaw, 1975).

1231. Recker, Marie-Luise. England und der Donauraum, 1919-1929: Problem einer europäischen Nachkriegsordnung. Stuttgart, 1976.

Based on British archives, including Treasury and Board of Trade files; see also Marie Sz-Ormos, "Sur les causes de l'échec du pacte danubien, 1934-1935," Acta Historica, 14(1968), 21-81; and for the wider background, György Ránki, Economy and Foreign Policy: The Struggle of the Great Powers for Hegemony in the Danube Valley, 1919-1939 (Boulder, CO, 1983); and Thomas L. Sakmyster, Hungary, the Great Powers and the Danubian Crisis, 1936-1939 (Athens, GA, 1980).

1232. Senn, Alfred E. The Great Powers, Lithuania and the Vilna Question, 1920-1928. Leiden, 1966.

1233. Ullman, Richard H. Anglo-Soviet Relations, 1917-1921. 3 vols. Princeton, NJ, 1961-72.

1234. Vago, Bela. The Shadow of the Swastika: The Rise of Fascism and Anti-Semitism in the Danube Basin, 1936-1939. Farnborough, 1975.

From the point of view of the Foreign Office; includes an appendix of 164 Foreign Office documents on the subject.

1235. Volkov, Fyodor D. Secrets from Whitehall and Downing Street. Moscow, 1986.

See also his SSSR-Angliia, 1929-1945gg. (Moscow, 1964); and Anglo-Sovietskie otnosheniia, 1929-1945gg. (Moscow, 1958); V. Ryzhikov, SSSR-Velikobritanniia, 1924-1986gg. (Moscow, 1987); Aleksei N. Krasilnikov, SSSR i Angliia: Sovetsko-Angliiskie otnosheniia v 1917-1967gg. (Moscow, 1967); his Politika anglii v otnoshenii SSSR, 1929-1932gg. (Moscow, 1959); Viktor Ivanovich Popov, Diplomaticheskie otnosheniia mezhdu SSSR i Angliei, 1929-1939gg. (Moscow, 1965); his Anglo-Sovetskie otnosheniia, 1927-1929gg. (Moscow, 1958); and Svetlana Nikonova, Antisovietskaia vneshnaia politika angliiskikh konservatorov, 1924-1927gg. (Moscow, 1963).

1236. White, Stephen. Britain and the Bolshevik Revolution: A Study in the Politics of Diplomacy, 1920-1924. London, 1979.

Researched in Britain, Dutch, Soviet and American archives.

Middle East

1237. Bullard, Sir Reader William. Britain and the Middle East from Earliest Times to 1963. London, 1964.

Other surveys include Matthew A. Fitzsimons, Empire by Treaty: Britain and the Middle East in the Twentieth Century (London, 1965); John Bagot Glubb, Britain and the Arabs: A Study of Fifty Years, 1908-1958 (London, 1959); and M.V. Seton-Williams, Britain and the Arab States: A Survey of Anglo-Arab Relations, 1920-1948 (London, 1948).

1238. Busch, Briton Cooper. Britain, India and the Arabs, 1914-1921. Berkeley, CA, 1971.

1239. Dann, Uriel, ed. The Great Powers in the Middle East, 1919-1939. New York, 1988.

Proceedings of a 1982 international conference in Tel Aviv; with almost half the contributions on British policy; and see too David Fromkin, A Peace to End All Peace: Creating the Modern Middle East, 1914-1922 (London, 1989).

1240. Darwin, John. Britain, Egypt and the Middle East: Imperial Policy in the Aftermath of War, 1918-1922. London, 1981.

Concentrates on coalition government policy in Egypt, Turkey, Persia and Iraq; see also Elie Kedourie, England and the Middle East: The Destruction of the Ottoman Empire, 1914-1921 (London, 1956); his In the Anglo-Arab Labyrinth: The McMahon-Husayn Correspondence and Its Interpretations, 1914-1939 (London, 1976); both with Arabic-language sources; and Jukka Nevakivi, Britain, France and the Arab Middle East, 1914-1920 (London, 1969).

1241. Friedman, Isaiah. The Question of Palestine, 1914-1918: British-Jewish-Arab Relations. London, 1973.

See also Abdul Latif Tibawi, Anglo-Arab Relations and the Question of Palestine, 1914-1921 (London, 1977); based on British archives and Arabic sources; Neil Caplan, "Britain, Zionism and the Arabs, 1917-1925," Wiener Library Bulletin, 31(1978), 4-17; and more generally his Futile Diplomacy, 2 vols. (London, 1983-86).

1242. Fry, Michael G., and Rabinovich, Itamar. Despatches from Damascus: Gilbert MacKereth and British Policy in the Levant, 1933-1939. Tel Aviv, 1985.

Entered consular service, 1919; consul at Damascus, 1933; consul-general, Addis Ababa, 1940; Foreign Office, 1940-44.

1243. Hale, William, and Bagis, Ali Ihsan. Four Centuries of Turco-British Relations: Studies in Diplomatic, Economic and Cultural Affairs. Beverley, 1984.

Proceedings of a seminar held in 1983 at Ankara; see also Marian Kent, "Great Britain and the End of the Ottoman Empire, 1900-1923," in The Great Powers and the End of the Ottoman Empire, edited by Marian Kent (London, 1984); Stephen F. Evans, The Slow Rapprochement: Britain and Turkey in the Age of Kemal Atatürk, 1919-1938 (Beverley, 1982); Ludmila Zhivkova, Anglo-Turkish Relations, 1933-1939 (London, 1976); with material from Bulgarian archives; the same author's "Anglo-Turkish Relations, 1934-1935," Etudes balkaniques, 7(1971), 82-98; and Philip Graves, Briton and Turk (London, 1941).

1244. Hopwood, Derek. Tales of the British Empire: The British in the Middle East, 1880-1952. London, 1989.

Drawn from the documents in the Middle East Centre, St. Antony's College, Oxford.

1245. Leatherdale, Clive. Britain and Saudi Arabia, 1925-1939: The Imperial Oasis. London, 1983.

Well researched in English-language sources; see also John Baldry, "Anglo-Italian Rivalry in Yemen and Asir, 1900-1934," Die Welt des Islams, 17(1976), 155-93.

1246. McHenry, James A. The Uneasy Partnership on Cyprus, 1919-1939: The Political and Diplomatic Interaction between Great Britain, Turkey and the Turkish Cypriot Community. New York, 1988.

1247. MacMichael, Sir Harold. The Anglo-Egyptian Sudan. London, 1934.

Entered Sudan political service, 1905; governor of Tanganyika, 1933-37; high-commissioner and commander-in-chief, Palestine, 1938-44; see also his The Sudan (London, 1954).

1248.   Monroe, Elizabeth. Britain's Moment in the Middle East, 1914-1971. 2nd ed. Baltimore, MD, 1981.

On staff of the Royal Institute of International Affairs, 1933; director, Middle East division, ministry of Information, 1940-44; see also her The Mediterranean in Politics (London, 1938).

1249.   Morsy, Laila. "The Effect of Italy's Expansion Policies on Anglo-Egyptian Relations in 1935." Middle Eastern Studies, 20(1984), 206-31.

See too her "The Military Clauses of the Anglo-Egyptian Treaty of Friendship and Alliance, 1936," International Journal of Middle East Studies, 16(1984), 67-97.

1250.   Williams, Ann. Britain and France in the Middle East and North Africa, 1914-1967. London, 1968.

See also Henry H. Cumming, Franco-British Rivalry in the Post-War Near East: The Decline of French Influence (London, 1938).

1251.   Wilson, Keith M. Imperialism and Nationalism in the Middle East: The Anglo-Egyptian Experience, 1882-1982. London, 1983.

With more in Robert O. Collins and Francis M. Deng, The British in the Sudan, 1898-1956: The Sweetness and the Sorrow (London, 1984); Robert O. Collins, Shadows in the Grass: Britain in the Southern Sudan, 1918-1956 (New Haven, CT, 1983); Peter Mansfield, The British in Egypt (New York, 1972); John Marlowe, Anglo-Egyptian Relations, 1800-1956, 2nd ed. (London, 1965); L.A. Fabunmi, The Sudan in Anglo-Egyptian Relations: A Case Study in Power Politics, 1800-1956 (London, 1960); and Royal Institute of International Affairs, Great Britain and Egypt, 1914-1951 (London, 1952).

1252.   Wilson, Mary C. King Abdullah, Britain and the Making of Jordan. London, 1987.

1253.   Wright, Sir Denis. The English amongst the Persians during the Qajar Period, 1787-1921. London, 1977.

Based on British and Persian sources; useful bibliography; author was vice-consul at Constantza, 1939-41; Trebizond, 1941-43; acting consul, Mersin, 1943-45; ambassador to Iran, 1963-71; see also his The Persians amongst the English: Episodes in Anglo-Persian History (London, 1985).

1254.   Zürrer, Werner. Persien zwischen England und Russland, 1918-1925: Grossmachteinflüsse und nationaler Wiederaufstieg am Beispiel des Iran. Bern, 1978.

Extensive archival material; see also Houshang Sabahi, British Policy in Persia, 1918-1925 (London, 1990); William J. Olson, Anglo-Iranian Relations during World War I (London, 1984); Ishtiaq Ahmad, Anglo-Iranian Relations, 1905-1919 (Bombay, 1974); and N.S. Fatemi, Diplomatic History of Persia, 1917-1923: Anglo-Russian Power Politics in Iran (New York, 1952).

Asia and the Far East

See also below, "From Manchuria to the Pacific War, 1931-1941," pages 280-84.

1255.   Adamec, Ludwig. Afghanistan's Foreign Affairs to the Mid-Twentieth Century: Relations with the USSR, Germany and Britain. Tucson, AZ, 1974.

1256.   Clifford, Nicholas R. Retreat from China: British Policy in the Far East, 1937-1941. Seattle, WA, 1967.

Relies essentially on American archives; see also his "Britain, America and the Far East, 1937-1940: A Failure in Cooperation," Journal of British Studies, 3(1963), 137-54; and "Sir Frederick Maze and the Chinese Maritime Customs, 1937-1941," Journal of Modern History, 37(1965), 18-34.

1257.   Endicott, Stephen Lyon. Diplomacy and Enterprise: British China Policy, 1933-1937. Vancouver, BC, 1975.

Based on British public and private archives.

1258.   Fitzhardinge, L.F. "Australia, Japan and Great Britain, 1914-1918: A Study in Triangular Diplomacy." Historical Studies, 14(1970), 250-59.

See also D.K. Dignan, "Australia and British Relations with Japan, 1914-1921," Australian Outlook, 21(1967), 135-50.

1259.   Hassnain, F.M. British Policy towards Kashmir, 1846-1921: Kashmir in Anglo-Russian Politics. New Delhi, 1974.

1260. Kennedy, Malcolm D. The Estrangement of Great Britain and Japan, 1917-1935. Manchester, 1969.

See too John Ferris, "From Broadway House to Bletchley Park: The Diary of Captain Malcolm Kennedy, 1934-1946," Intelligence and National Security, 4(1989), 421-50.

1261. Kiernan, E. Victor Gordon. British Diplomacy in China, 1885-1970. London, 1970.

1262. Lowe, Peter. Britain in the Far East: A Survey from 1918 to the Present. London, 1981.

Concentrates largely on China; earlier accounts in Guy Wint, The British in Asia (New York, 1954); Gilbert E. Hubbard, British Far Eastern Policy (New York, 1943); Chin-lin Hsia, British Far Eastern Policy, 1937-1940 (Chungking, 1940); Irving S. Friedman, British Relations with China, 1931-1939 (New York, 1940); and Royal Institute of International Affairs, British Far Eastern Policy (London, 1939).

1263. Nish, Ian. Alliance in Decline: A Study in Anglo-Japanese Relations, 1908-1923. London, 1972.

See too Chung-fu Chang, The Anglo-Japanese Alliance (London, 1931).

1264. Nish, Ian, ed. Anglo-Japanese Alienation, 1919-1952: Papers of the Anglo-Japanese Conference on the History of the Second World War. London, 1982.

Paired chapters, one by a British scholar, one by a Japanese, are used to illustrate differing perspectives; see too Sato Kyozo, Japan and Britain at the Crossroads, 1939-1945: A Study in the Dilemmas of Japanese Diplomacy (Tokyo, 1986).

1265. Pratt, Sir John T. China and Britain. London, 1944.

Chinese consular service, 1909-25; with Foreign Office, 1925-38; head of far eastern section, ministry of Information, 1939-41; see also his War and Politics in China (London, 1943); and "America, Britain and China," Contemporary Review, 158(1940), 47-55.

1266. Rose, Saul. Britain and South-East Asia. Baltimore, MD, 1962.

1267.   Samra, Chattar Singh. India and Anglo-Soviet Relations, 1917-1947. New York, 1959.

1268.   Singh, Amar Kaur Jasbir. Himalayan Triangle: A Historical Survey of British India's Relations with Tibet, Sikkim and Bhutan, 1765-1950. London, 1988.

With multinational documentation; see also Parshotam Mehra, The McMahon Line and After: A Study of the Triangular Contest on India's North-Eastern Frontier between Britain, China and Tibet, 1904-1947 (Delhi, 1974); and Dorothy Woodman, Himalayan Frontiers: A Political Review of British, Chinese, Indian and Russian Rivalries (London, 1969).

1269.   Stremski, Richard. The Shaping of British Policy during the Nationalist Revolution in China. Taipei, 1979.

A publication of Soochow University; based on British and American archives; see too his "Britain and Warlordism in China: Relations with Feng Yu-hsiang, 1921-1928," Journal of Oriental Studies, 11(1973), 91-106; and Chan Lau Kit-Ching, "The Lincheng Incident: A Case Study of British Policy in China between the Washington Conference (1921-1922) and the First Nationalist Revolution (1925-1928)," Journal of Oriental Studies, 10(1972), 172-86.

1270.   Wesley-Smith, Peter. Unequal Treaty, 1898-1997: China, Great Britain and Hong Kong's New Territories. London, 1980.

Both the legal and historical relationship.

5. Appeasement: The Debate

1271.   Beloff, Max. "The Imperial Factor in Appeasement," in Culture, science et développement, Contributions à une histoire de l'homme: Mélanges en l'honneur de Charles Morazé. Toulouse, 1979.

See also his "Appeasement: For and Against," Government and Opposition, 7(1972), 112-19.

1272.   Carlton, David. "Against the Grain: In Defense of Appeasement." Policy Review, 4(1980), 134-50.

1273.   "Cato." [Michael Foot, Frank Owen and Peter Howard]. Guilty
        Men. London, 1940.

        From the Left Book Club; the original and very dramatic statement
        of the "guilty men" thesis; on the origin of this book, see Michael
        Foot, Debts of Honour (London, 1980).

1274.   Cline, Catherine. "Ecumenism and Appeasement: The Bishops of
        the Church of England and the Treaty of Versailles." Journal of
        Modern History, 61(1989), 683-703.

        See too her "British Historians and the Treaty of Versailles,"
        Albion, 20(1988), 43-58.

1275.   Dent, Philip. "The D'Abernon Papers: Origins of 'Appeasement.' "
        British Museum Quarterly, 37(1973), 103-7.

1276.   Dilks, David. "Appeasement Revisited." University of Leeds
        Review, 15(1972), 28-56.

        An inaugural lecture, with material from the Neville Chamberlain
        papers.

1277.   Einzig, Paul. Appeasement before, during and after the War.
        London, 1941.

1278.   Gilbert, Martin. The Roots of Appeasement. London, 1966.

        A pioneering study of appeasement and its historical antecedents.

1279.   Gilbert, Martin, and Gott, Richard. The Appeasers. London, 1963.

        The aims and methods of the "appeasers"; based on considerable
        private information.

1280.   Grenville, J.A.S. "Contemporary Trends in the Study of the British
        'Appeasement' Policies of the 1930s." Internationales Jahrbuch
        für Geschichts- und Geographie-Unterricht, 17(1976), 236-47.

1281.   Gruner, W.D.   " 'British Interest' in der Zwischenkriegszeit:
        Aspekte britischer Europa-Politik 1918-1933," in Gleichgewicht,
        Revision, Restauration: Die Aussenpolitik der Ersten
        Tschechoslowakischen Republik im Europasystem der Pariser
        Vorverträge. Edited by Karl Bosl. Munich, 1976.

An attempt to examine the various structural determinants of external policy, as well as the domestic context; for his further contributions to this debate see also " 'British Interest' und Friedenssicherung: Zur Interaktion von britischer Innen- und Aussenpolitik im frühen 19. Jahrhundert," Historische Zeitschrift, 224(1977), 92-104; and "The British Political, Social and Economic System and the Decision for Peace and War: Reflections on Anglo-German Relations, 1800-1939," British Journal of International Studies, 6(1980), 189-218.

1282. Haigh, R.H., and Turner, P.W. British Politics and Society, 1918-1939: The Effect on Appeasement. Manhattan, KS, 1980.

Based on secondary sources; see also the same authors' Defense Policy between the Wars, 1918-1938, Culminating in the Munich Agreement of September 1938 (Manhattan, KS, 1979).

1283. Herz, John H. "Sinn und Sinnlosigkeit der Beschwichtigungspolitik: Zur Problematik des Appeasement-Begriffes." Politische Vierteljahresschrift, 5(1964), 370-89.

1284. Herzfeld, Hans. "Zur Problematik der Appeasement-Politik," in Geschichte und Gegenwartsbewusstsein, historische Betrachtungen und Untersuchungen: Festschrift für Hans Rothfels zum 70. Geburtstag. Edited by Waldemar Besson and Friedrich von Gaertringen. Göttingen, 1963.

1285. Jones, R.J. Barry. "The Study of 'Appeasement' and the Study of International Relations." British Journal of International Studies, 1(1975), 68-76.

1286. Kennedy, Paul. "The Tradition of Appeasement in British Foreign Policy, 1865-1939." British Journal of International Studies, 2(1976), 195-215.

Analyses appeasement's roots in moral, economic, strategic and domestic motives; see also his " 'Appeasement' and British Defence Policy in the Inter-War Years," British Journal of International Studies, 4(1978), 161-77; and "The Study of Appeasement: Methodological Crossroads or Meeting-Place?" British Journal of International Studies, 6(1980), 181-88.

1287. Lanyi, George A. "The Problem of Appeasement." World Politics, 15(1963), 316-28.

1288.   Lentin, Anthony. Lloyd George, Woodrow Wilson and the Guilt of Versailles: An Essay in the Prehistory of Appeasement. Leicester, 1984.

Well-researched study of the "psychological pre-history of Appeasement" (Introduction).

1289.   Lundgreen, Peter. Die englische Appeasement-Politik bis zum Münchener Abkommen: Voraussetzungen, Konzeption, Durchführung. Berlin, 1969.

Based on a thorough study of politics, opinion and pressure groups in the 1930s.

1290.   MacDonald, C.A.   "Economic Appeasement and the German 'Moderates.' " Past and Present, 56(1972), 105-35.

1291.   Meyers, Reinhard. "International Paradigms, Concepts of Peace, and the Policy of Appeasement." War and Society, 1(1983), 43-66.

1292.   Mommsen, W.J., and Kettenacker, L., eds. The Fascist Challenge and the Policy of Appeasement. London, 1983.

Proceedings of a conference in May 1980, at the German Historical Institute, London; 28 essays, all important, designed "to throw new light on the 1930s" (Foreword).

1293.   Niedhart, Gottfried. "Appeasement: Die britische Antwort auf die Krise des Weltreichs und des internationalen Systems vor dem Zweiten Weltkrieg." Historische Zeitschrift, 226(1978), 67-88.

A useful analysis of the literature; among his other contributions to the discussion see also "Multipolares Gleichgewicht und weltwirtschaftliche Verflechtung: Deutschland in der britischen Appeasement-Politik, 1919-1933," in Die Weimarer Republik: Belagerte Civitas, edited by Michael Stürmer (Königstein/Ts, 1980); "Weltherrschaft versus World Appeasement," Neue Politische Literatur, 23(1978), 281-91; "Britische Deutschlandpolitik vor dem Zweiten Weltkrieg: Friedensbedürfnis und gescheiterte Friedenssicherung," in Aus Politik und Zeitgeschichte, supplement to Das Parlament, 13(1977), 26-39; "Europa in der britischen Weltpolitik vor dem Zweiten Weltkrieg," Francia, 5(1977), 789-97; "Friede als nationales Interesse: Grossbritannien in der Vorgeschichte des Zweiten Weltkriegs," Neue Politische Literatur, 17(1972), 451-70;

and "Weltmacht-Anspruch und Wirklichkeit: Zur britischen Aussenpolitik im 20. Jahrhundert," Neue Politische Literatur, 13(1968), 233-41.

1294. Presseisen, Ernst L. Amiens and Munich: Comparisons in Appeasement. The Hague, 1978.

An attempt at a comparative model of appeasement.

1295. Richardson, J.L. "New Perspectives on Appeasement: Some Implications for International Relations." World Politics, 40(1988), 289-316.

1296. Rock, William R. British Appeasement in the 1930s. London, 1977.

On the origin, motives and proponents of appeasement; good bibliographical essay; see also his "British Appeasement (1930's): A Need for Revision?" South Atlantic Quarterly, 78(1979), 290-301; and for another general introduction, Keith Robbins, Appeasement (London, 1989).

1297. Rowse, A.L. All Souls and Appeasement: A Contribution to Contemporary History. London, 1961.

Of interest is his less known The End of an Epoch: Reflections on Contemporary History (London, 1948); see also Portraits and Views (London, 1979); Memories of Men and Women (London, 1980); Glimpses of the Great (London, 1985); the latter two combined in Memories and Glimpses (London, 1986); and Friends and Contemporaries (London, 1989).

1298. Schlenke, Manfred. "Die Westmächte und das national-sozialistische Deutschland: Motive, Ziele und Illusionen der Appeasement-Politik." Mitteilungen der Gesellschaft der Freunde der Wirtschaftshochschule Mannheim, 16(1967), 35-43.

1299. Schmidt, Gustav. England in der Krise: Grundzüge und Grundlagen der britischen Appeasement-Politik, 1930-1937. Opladen, 1981.

A thematic study based on a wide range of primary and secondary material; condensed English version in The Politics and Economics of Appeasement: British Foreign Policy in the 1930s (Leamington Spa, 1986); see also his "Politisches System und Appeasement-Politik, 1930-1937: Zur Scharnierfunktion der Rüstungspolitik für die britische Innen- und Aussenpolitik," <u>Militärgeschichtliche Mitteilungen</u>, 13(1979), 37-53; "Strategie und Aussenpolitik des 'Troubled Giant,' " <u>Militärgeschichtliche Mitteilungen</u>, 7(1973), 208-18; and "Britische Strategie und Aussenpolitik: Wahlchancen und Determinanten britischer Sicherheitspolitik im Zeitalter der neuen Weltmächte, 1897-1929," <u>Militärgeschichtliche Mitteilungen</u>, 5(1971), 197-218.

1300.   Schroeder, Paul W. "Munich and the British Tradition." <u>Historical Journal</u>, 19(1976), 223-43.

Argues that appeasement was directed towards the traditional policy of maintaining the European balance of power.

1301.   Seeland, Rolf. <u>Appeasement: Eine Methode zur Lösung internationaler Konflikte</u>. Hamburg, 1968.

1302.   Skidelsky, Robert. "Going to War with Germany: Between Revisionism and Orthodoxy." <u>Encounter</u>, 39(1972), 56-65.

1303.   Walker, Stephen G. "Solving the Appeasement Puzzle: Contending Historical Interpretations of British Diplomacy during the 1930s." <u>British Journal of International Studies</u>, 6(1980), 219-46.

1304.   Watt, D.C. "Appeasement: The Rise of a Revisionist School?" <u>Political Quarterly</u>, 36(1965), 191-213.

An early summary of the "orthodox view" and the "new criticism"; see also his "Appeasement Reconsidered: Some Neglected Factors," <u>Round Table</u>, 53(1963), 358-71; "Christian Essay in Appeasement: Lord Lothian and His Quaker Friends," <u>Wiener Library Bulletin</u>, 14(1960), 30-31; and "The Historiography of Appeasement," in <u>Crisis and Controversy: Essays in Honour of A.J.P. Taylor</u>, edited by Alan Sked and Chris Cook (London, 1976).

1305.   Wendt, Bernd-Jürgen. "Die englische Politik des Appeasement in den dreissiger Jahren und ihre Beurteilung in der Geschichtswissenschaft," in <u>Die Grosse Krise der dreissiger Jahre: Vom Niedergang der Weltwirtschaft zum Zweiten Weltkrieg</u>. Edited by Gerhard Schulz. Gottingen, 1985.

See also the same author's "Grossbritannien - Demokratie auf dem Prüfstand: Appeasement als Strategie des Status Quo," in <u>Innen- und Aussenpolitik unter nationalsozialistischer Bedrohung:</u>

Determinanten internationaler Beziehungen in historischen Fallstudien, edited by Erhard Forndran et al. (Opladen, 1977); and "Aspekte der deutschen Appeasement-Forschung," _Internationales Jahrbuch für Geschichts- und Geographie-Unterricht,_ 17(1976), 248-75.

E. PEACEMAKING AND DETENTE, 1918-1933

1. 1920s General

1306. Artaud, Denise. <u>La question des dettes interalliées et la reconstruction de l'Europe, 1917-1929.</u> 2 vols. Paris, 1978.

See too her "La question des dettes interalliées et la reconstruction de l'Europe," <u>Revue historique,</u> 261(1979), 363-82; and <u>La reconstruction de l'Europe, 1919-1929</u> (Paris, 1973).

1307. Bergmann, Carl. <u>Der Weg der Reparationen: Von Versailles über den Dawesplan zum Ziel.</u> Frankfurt/M. 1926.

By a German expert, closely in contact with the British.

1308. Carsten, F.L. <u>Britain and the Weimar Republic: The British Documents.</u> London, 1984.

Based on the files of the Foreign Office and the War Office; another similar study is his <u>The First Austrian Republic, 1918-1938</u> (London, 1986).

1309. Frasure, Carl. <u>British Policy on War Debts and Reparations.</u> Philadelphia, PA, 1940.

1310. Heideking, Jürgen. <u>Areopag der Diplomaten: Die Pariser Botschafterkonferenz der alliierten Hauptmächte und die Probleme der europäischen Politik, 1920-1931.</u> Husum, 1979.

See also his "Oberster Rat, Botschaftskonferenz, Völkerbund," <u>Historische Zeitschrift,</u> 231(1980, 589-630; and Gerhard P. Pink, <u>The Conference of Ambassadors: Paris, 1920-1931</u> (Geneva, 1942).

1311. Kent, Bruce. <u>The Spoils of War: The Politics, Economics and Diplomacy of Reparations, 1918-1932.</u> London, 1989.

Thoroughly researched in American, British, French and German archives and the papers of the Reparation Commission.

1312. Kölling, Mirjam. "Aspekte britischer Aussenpolitik in den zwanziger Jahren." Zeitschrift für Geschichtswissenschaft, 21(1973), 1423-42.

1313. Leffler, Melvyn P. The Elusive Quest: America's Pursuit of European Stability and French Security, 1919-1933. Chapel Hill, NC, 1979.

Based on American archives and numerous collections of private papers; useful bibliography.

1314. Maier, Charles S. Recasting Bourgeois Europe: Stabilization in France, Germany, and Italy in the Decade after World War I. Princeton, NJ, 1975.

A well-documented study of economics, politics and society.

1315. Marks, Sally. The Illusion of Peace: International Relations 1918-1933. New York, 1976.

See also the same author's "Reparations Reconsidered: A Reminder," Central European History, 2(1969), 356-65; David Felix, "Reparations Reconsidered with a Vengeance," Central European History, 4(1971), 171-79; and Sally Marks, "Reparations Reconsidered: A Rejoinder," Central European History, 5(1972), 358-61.

1316. Orde, Anne. British Policy and European Reconstruction after the First World War. London, 1990.

See too her Great Britain and International Security, 1920-1926 (London, 1977); and "Gross-britannien und die Selbstandigkeit Österreichs, 1918-1938," Vierteljahrshefte für Zeitgeschichte, 28(1980), 224-47.

1317. Toynbee, Arnold J. The Conduct of British Empire Foreign Relations since the Peace Settlement. London, 1928.

See also Oswald Hauser, "Das britische Commonwealth zwischen nationaler Souveränität und imperialer Integration, 1917-1931," Vierteljahrshefte für Zeitgeschichte, 16(1968), 230-46.

1318.   Trachtenberg, Marc.   Reparation in World Politics: France and European Economic Diplomacy, 1916-1923. New York, 1980.

A revisionist analysis portraying hardline Englishmen against moderate Frenchmen; see also his "Reparation at the Paris Peace Conference," Journal of Modern History, 5(1979), 24-55; and "Versailles after Sixty Years," Journal of Contemporary History, 17(1982), 487-506.

1319.   Weill-Raynal, Etienne.   Les réparations allemandes et la France. 3 vols. Paris, 1947-49.

By a member of the Reparation Commission.

1320.   Wheeler-Bennett, John W., and Langermann, F.E.   Information on the Problem of Security, 1917-1926. London, 1927.

1321.   Williams, Roland E.L. Vaughan, ed.   The Hungarian Question in the British Parliament, 1919-1930. London, 1933.

Extracts from speeches, questions and answers.

1322.   Williamson, David Graham.   The British in Germany, 1918-1930. London, 1990.

Including British involvement in the Rhineland, Danzig, Upper Silesia and the Inter-Allied Control Commission.

2. Armistice and Peacemaking, 1918-1919

1323.   Anderson, Edgar.   "British Policy toward the Baltic States, 1918-1920." Journal of Central European Affairs, 19(1959), 276-89.

See also the same author's "An Undeclared Naval War: The British-Soviet Naval Struggle in the Baltic, 1918-1920," Journal of Central European Affairs, 22(1962), 43-78; John Bradley, "L'Intervention alliée dans les états baltes, 1919," Revue d'histoire moderne et contemporaine, 23(1976), 236-57; Wilhelm Lenz, "Zur britischen Politik gegenüber den baltischen Deutschen, 1918-1919," in Das Vergangene und die Geschichte: Festschrift für Reinhard Wittram, edited by Rudolf von Thadden et al. (Göttingen, 1973); Edward William Polson Newman, Britain and the Baltic (London, 1930); and the more general study based on German and American archives by Hugh I. Rodgers, Search for

Security: A Study in Baltic Diplomacy, 1920-1934 (Hamden, CT, 1975).

1324.   Arslanian, Artin H. "British Wartime Pledges, 1917-1918: The Armenian Case." Journal of Contemporary History, 13(1978), 517-30.

See also his "Britain and the Question of Mountainous Karabagh," Middle Eastern Studies, 16(1980), 92-104.

1325.   Barraclough, Geoffrey. "Das Britische Reich und der Frieden," in Ideologie und Machtpolitik, 1919: Plan und Werk der Pariser Friedenskonferenzen, 1919. Edited by Hellmuth Rössler. Göttingen, 1966.

1326.   Boothe, Leon E. "A Fettered Envoy: Lord Grey's Mission to the United States, 1919-1920." Review of Politics, 33(1971), 78-94.

See also his "Lord Grey, the United States and the Political Effort for a League of Nations, 1919-1920," Maryland Historical Magazine, 65(1970), 36-54; and Douglas L. Smith, "Viscount Grey's 'Special Mission' and Postwar Anglo-American Relations," Southern Quarterly, 11(1973), 257-74.

1327.   Bosworth, Richard. "Sir Rennell Rodd e l'Italia." Nuova rivista storica, 54(1970), 420-36.

1328.   Burnett, Philip Mason, ed. Reparation at the Paris Peace Conference: From the Standpoint of the American Delegation. 2 vols. New York, 1940.

More than 500 documents, many dealing with Britain.

1329.   Calder, Kenneth J. Britain and the Origins of the New Europe, 1914-1918. London, 1976.

On the wartime problem of national self-determination as dictated by strategic necessities; well documented.

1330.   Callcott, W.R. "The Last War Aim: British Opinion and the Decision for Czechoslovak Independence, 1914-1919." Historical Journal, 27(1984), 979-89.

1331.   Czernin, Ferdinand, ed. Versailles, 1919: The Forces, Events and Personalities that Shaped the Treaty. New York, 1964.

A collection of documents concentrating on five main clauses of the treaty; other general accounts include Charles L. Mee, <u>The End of Order: Versailles, 1919</u> (New York, 1930); George Goldberg, <u>The Peace to End Peace: The Paris Peace Conference of 1919</u> (London, 1969); Pierre Renouvin, <u>Le traité de Versailles</u> (Paris, 1969); and Paul Birdsall, <u>Versailles: Twenty Years After</u> (London, 1941).

1332. Debo, Richard K. "Prelude to Negotiations: The Problem of British Prisoners in Soviet Russia, November 1918-July 1919." <u>Slavonic and East European Review</u>, 58(1980), 58-75.

See also his "Mésentente Glaciale: Great Britain, France, and the Question of Intervention in the Baltic, 1918," <u>Canadian Journal of History</u>, 12(1977), 65-86.

1333. Dimitrov, Theodore D., ed. <u>Harold Nicolson and the Balkans: Confidential Documents</u>. Geneva, 1979.

Prepared for "International Documentation on Macedonia"; deals with 1919; see too John D. Fair, "The Peacemaking Exploits of Harold Temperley in the Balkans, 1918-1921," <u>Slavonic and East European Review</u>, 67(1989), 69-93.

1334. Dockrill, Michael L., and Goold, J. Douglas. <u>Peace without Promise: Britain and the Peace Conferences, 1919-1923</u>. London, 1981.

Based on Foreign Office and cabinet documents, and private papers; see also Michael L. Dockrill, "Britain, the United States, France and the German Settlement, 1918-1920," in <u>Shadow and Substance in British Foreign Policy, 1895-1939</u>, edited by B.J.C. McKercher and D.J. Moss (Edmonton, Alberta, 1984).

1335. Egerton, George W. "Britain and the 'Great Betrayal': Anglo-American Relations and the Struggle for United States Ratification of the Treaty of Versailles, 1919-1920." <u>Historical Journal</u>, 2(1978), 885-911.

See too his "Diplomacy, Scandal and Military Intelligence: The Craufurd-Stuart Affair and Anglo-American Relations, 1918-1920," <u>Intelligence and National Security</u>, 2(1987), 110-34.

1336. Elcock, Howard. <u>Portrait of a Decision: The Council of Four and the Treaty of Versailles</u>. London, 1972.

Mainly based on British sources; see also his "Britain and the Russo-Polish Frontier, 1919-1921," Historical Journal, 12(1969), 137-54.

1337. Fest, W.B. Peace or Partition: The Habsburg Monarchy and British Policy, 1914-1918. London, 1978.

See also Harry Hanak, Great Britain and Austria-Hungary during the First World War: A Study in the Formation of Public Opinion (London, 1962).

1338. Fowler, Wilton B. British-American Relations, 1917-1918: The Role of Sir William Wiseman. Princeton, NJ, 1969.

Chief adviser on American affairs to British delegation, Paris, 1918-19; well-documented with annotated bibliography.

1339. Fry, Michael G. Lloyd George and Foreign Policy, vol. 1, The Education of a Statesman, 1890-1916. Montreal, Québec, 1977-.

See also his "Britain, the Allies, and the Problem of Russia, 1918-1919," Canadian Journal of History, 2(1967), 62-84.

1340. Goldstein, Erik. "Great Britain and Greater Greece, 1917-1920." Historical Journal, 32(1989), 339-56.

For background see M. Llewellyn Smith, Ionian Vision: Greece in Asia Minor, 1919-1922 (London, 1973);

1341. Gruner, W.D. "Friedenssicherung und politisch-soziales System: Grossbritannien auf den Pariser Friedenskonferenzen, 1919," in L'Europe de Versailles, 1918-1923: Bilan, perspectives et controverses. Geneva, 1979.

1342. Guinn, Paul. British Strategy and Politics, 1914-1918. London, 1965.

On the relation between military considerations and domestic politics.

1343. Haupts, Leo. "Zur deutschen und britischen Friedenspolitik in der Krise der Pariser Friedenskonferenz: Britisch-deutsche Separatverhandlungen im April-Mai 1919?" Historische Zeitschrift, 217(1973), 54-98.

On the Anglo-German negotiations at The Hague, which, it is argued, neither power took seriously.

1344. Hoffman, Robert. "The British Military Representative in Vienna, 1919." Slavonic and East European Review, 52(1974), 252-71.

1345. House, Edward Mandell, and Seymour, Charles, eds. What Really Happened at Paris: The Story of the Peace Conference, 1918-1919, by American Delegates. New York, 1921.

1346. Jaffe, Lorna S. The Decision to Disarm Germany: British Policy towards Postwar German Disarmament, 1914-1919. London, 1985.

Based on extensive research at the Public Record Office; see also Gerda Richards Crosby, Disarmament and Peace in British Politics, 1914-1919 (Cambridge, MA, 1957).

1347. Keynes, John Maynard. The Economic Consequences of the Peace. London, 1919.

Continued in A Revision of the Treaty (London, 1922); see also Helmut Lippelt, "J.M. Keynes und das finanzpolitische Ordnungsproblem auf der Pariser Friedenskonferenz," in Das Vergangene und die Geschichte: Festschrift für Reinhard Wittram, edited by Rudolf von Thadden et al. (Göttingen, 1973).

1348. Knudsen, Erik Lance. Great Britain, Constantinople and the Turkish Peace Treaty, 1919-1922. New York, 1988.

See also Paul Helmreich, From Paris to Sèvres: The Partition of the Ottoman Empire at the Peace Conference of 1919-1920 (Columbus, OH, 1974); an analysis of allied diplomacy, based on wide research; and A.E. Montgomery, "The Making of the Treaty of Sèvres of 10 August 1920," Historical Journal, 15(1972), 775-87.

1349. Louis, William Roger. "Great Britain and the African Peace Settlement of 1919." American Historical Review, 71(1966), 874-92.

1350. Mantoux, Etienne. The Carthaginian Peace, or the Economic Consequences of Mr. Keynes. London, 1946.

1351. Mantoux, Paul. Les délibérations du conseil des quatre, 24 mars-28 juin 1919. 2 vols. Paris, 1955.

Interpreter for the supreme war council, 1919; director of the political section, League of Nations, 1920-27; the English translation, Paris Peace Conference, 1919: Proceedings of the Council of Four, March 24-April 18 (Geneva, 1964), is incomplete.

1352.   Marks, Sally. Innocent Abroad: Belgium at the Paris Peace Conference of 1919. Chapel Hill, NC, 1981.

Other full-scale studies for relevant powers include Kay Lundgreen-Nielson, The Polish Problem at the Paris Peace Conference: A Study of the Policies of the Great Powers and the Poles, 1918-1919 (Odense, 1979); N. Petsalis-Diomidis, Greece at the Paris Peace Conference (1919) (Thessaloniki, 1978); Inga Floto, Colonel House in Paris: A Study of American Policy at the Paris Peace Conference, 1919 (Aarhus, 1973); John M. Thompson, Russia, Bolshevism and the Versailles Peace (Princeton, NJ, 1966); Ivo J. Lederer, Yugoslavia at the Paris Peace Conference: A Study in Frontiermaking (London, 1963); Sherman David Spector, Rumania at the Paris Peace Conference (New York, 1962); B.E. Stein, Die "Russische Frage" auf der pariser Friedenskonferenz, 1919-1920 (Leipzig, 1953); Francis Deák, Hungary at the Paris Peace Conference (New York, 1942); Alma Luckau, The German Delegation at the Paris Peace Conference (New York, 1941); and René Albrecht-Carrié, Italy at the Paris Peace Conference (New York, 1938).

1353.   Marston, F.S. The Peace Conference of 1919: Organization and Procedure. London, 1944.

On the mechanics of peacemaking; useful bibliography.

1354.   Martin, Laurence W. Peace without Victory: Woodrow Wilson and the British Liberals. New Haven, CT, 1958.

1355.   Maurice, Sir Frederick. The Armistices of 1918-1943. London, 1943.

Entered army, 1892; director of military operations, imperial general staff, 1915-18.

1356.   Mayer, Arno J. Politics and Diplomacy of Peacemaking: Containment and Counterrevolution at Versailles, 1918-1919. New York, 1967.

1357. Mejcher, Helmut. "British Middle East Policy, 1917-21: The Inter-Departmental Level." Journal of Contemporary History, 8(1973), 81-101.

1358. Mitrokhin, Leonid. Failure of Three Missions. Moscow, 1987.

On Anglo-Soviet relations, 1917-21, in Central Asia.

1359. Nelson, Harold I. Land and Power: British and Allied Policy on Germany's Frontiers, 1916-1919. London, 1963.

1360. Nicolson, Harold. Peacemaking, 1919. London, 1933.

With extensive extracts from the author's 1919 diary; see also his "Peacemaking at Paris: Success, Failure, or Farce?" Foreign Affairs, 25(1947), 190-203.

1361. Northedge, F.S. "1917-1919: The Implications for Britain." Journal of Contemporary History, 3(1968), 191-209.

1362. Paasdivirta, Juhani. The Victors in World War I and Finland: Finland's Relations with the British, French and the United States Governments in 1918-1919. Helsinki, 1965.

1363. Petricioli, Marta. L'occupazione italiana del Caucaso: "Un ingrato servizio" da rendere a Londra. Milan, 1972.

With a brief documentary appendix.

1364. Renouvin, Pierre. L'armistice de Rethcndes: 11 november 1918. Paris, 1968.

Useful bibliography; see also John Terraine, To Win a War: 1918, The Year of Victory (London, 1978); Cyril N. Barclay, Armistice, 1918 (London, 1968); and Harry R. Rudin, Armistice, 1918 (New Haven, CT, 1944).

1365. Riddell, Lord, et al. The Treaty of Versailles and After. London, 1935.

1366. Rothwell, Victor. British War Aims and Peace Diplomacy, 1914-1918. London, 1971.

See also his "Mesopotamia in British War Aims, 1914-1918," Historical Journal, 13(1970), 273-94.

1367.   Sakmyster, Thomas L. "Great Britain and the Making of the Treaty of Trianon," in Essays on World War I: Total War and Peacemaking, A Case Study on Trianon. Edited by Béla K. Király et al. New York, 1982.

And in the same collection, Hugh Seton-Watson, "R.W. Seton-Watson and the Trianon Settlement."

1368.   Schmid, Alex P. Churchills privater Krieg: Intervention und Konterrevolution im russischen Bürgerkrieg, November 1918-März 1920. Zurich, 1974.

Based on British sources; useful bibliography; see also Paul Kluke, "Winston Churchill und die alliierte Intervention im revolutionären Russland," in Innen- und Aussenpolitik: Primat oder Interdependenz? Festschrift zum 60. Geburtstag von Walther Hofer, edited by Urs Altermatt and Judit Garamvölgyi (Stuttgart, 1980).

1369.   Schmidt, Gustav. "Effizienz und Flexibilität politisch-sozialer Systeme: Die deutsche und englische Politik, 1918-1919." Vierteljahrshefte für Zeitgeschichte, 25(1977), 137-87.

See too his "Politische Tradition und wirtschaftliche Faktoren in der britischen Friedensstrategie, 1918-1919," Vierteljahrshefte für Zeitgeschichte, 29(1981), 131-88.

1370.   Schuster, Peter. Henry Wickham Steed und die Hapsburger-monarchie. Vienna, 1970.

With a brief discussion of Wickham Steed and Versailles.

1371.   Stevenson, David. The First World War and International Politics. London, 1988.

Essentially "a work of synthesis" (Preface).

1372.   Temperley, Harold W.V., ed. A History of the Peace Conference of Paris. 6 vols. London, 1920-24.

Issued under the auspices of the Institute (later Royal Institute) of International Affairs; still useful.

1373.   Tillman, Seth P. Anglo-American Relations at the Paris Peace Conference of 1919. Princeton, NJ, 1961.

1374.   Turner, Abraham. "Austen Chamberlain, <u>The Times</u> and the Question of Revision of the Treaty of Versailles - 1933." <u>European History Quarterly</u>, 18(1988), 51-70.

1375.   Vincent, C. Paul. <u>The Politics of Hunger: The Allied Blockade of Germany, 1915-1919</u>. London, 1985.

See also James A. Huston, "The Allied Blockade of Germany, 1918-1919," <u>Journal of Central European Affairs</u>, 10(1950), 145-66.

1376.   Zsuppan, Ferenc Tibor. "The Hungarian Soviet Republic and British Military Representatives, April-June 1919." <u>Slavonic and East European Review</u>, 47(1969), 198-218.

3. The Search for Security, 1920-1924

1377.   Bardoux, Jacques. <u>Lloyd George et la France</u>. Paris, 1923.

See also the same author's <u>Le socialisme au pouvoir, l'expérience de 1924: Le dialogue J. Ramsay MacDonald-Edouard Herriot</u> (Paris, 1930); and <u>L'île et l'Europe</u> (Paris, 1933).

1378.   Beaverbrook, Lord. <u>The Decline and Fall of Lloyd George</u>. London, 1963.

On the 1921-23 period; with documentary appendices.

1379.   Behrendt, Herbert. "L'Angleterre et la France face à Hitler et son putsch en novembre 1923." <u>Francia</u>, 12(1984), 457-72.

1380.   Bertram-Libal, Gisela. <u>Aspekte der britischen Deutschlandpolitik, 1919-1922</u>. Göppingen, 1972.

Argues that Lloyd George pursued a logical policy aimed at the economic rehabilitation of Europe; see also the same author's "Die britische Politik in der Oberschlesienfrage 1919-1922," in <u>Vierteljahrshefte für Zeitgeschichte</u>, 20(1972), 105-32; Joseph F. Harrington, "The League of Nations and the Upper Silesian Boundary Dispute, 1921-1922," <u>Polish Review</u>, 23(1978), 86-101; and F. Gregory Campbell, "The Struggle for Upper Silesia, 1919-1922," in <u>Journal of Modern History</u>, 42(1970), 361-85.

1381.   Boadle, Donald Graeme. <u>Winston Churchill and the German Question in British Foreign Policy, 1918-1922</u>. The Hague, 1973.

Based on published sources and some cabinet archives.

1382.   Busch, Briton Cooper. <u>Mudros to Lausanne: Britain's Frontier in West Asia, 1918-1923</u>. Albany, NY, 1976.

See also A.L. Macfie, "The Straits Question: The Conference of Lausanne, November 1922-July 1923," <u>Middle Eastern Studies</u>, 15(1979), 211-38; and his "The British Decision Regarding the Future of Constantinople, November 1918-January 1920," <u>Historical Journal</u>, 18(1975), 391-400.

1383.   Cassels, Alan. "Repairing the <u>Entente Cordiale</u> and the New Diplomacy." <u>Historical Journal</u>, 23(1980), 133-53.

1384.   Chester, Lewis, et al. <u>The Zinoviev Letter</u>. London, 1967.

On the subject see also E.H. Carr, "The Zinoviev Letter," <u>Historical Journal</u>, 22(1979), 209-10; Christopher Andrew, "More on the Zinoviev Letter," <u>Historical Journal</u>, 22(1979), 211-14; Sibyl Crowe, "The Zinoviev Letter," <u>Journal of Contemporary History</u>, 10(1975), 407-32; Natalie Grant, "The 'Zinoviev Letter' Case," <u>Soviet Studies</u>, 19(1967), 264-77; and Robert D. Warth, "The Mystery of the Zinoviev Letter," <u>South Atlantic Quarterly</u>, 49(1950), 441-53.

1385.   Cienciala, Anna M. "The Secret Anglo-French Agreement on Danzig and the Saar, and Its Consequences, 1919-1926." <u>Zeitschrift für Ostforschung</u>, 27(1978), 434-55.

See also her "German Propaganda for the Revision of the Polish-German Frontier in Danzig and the Corridor: Its Effects on British Opinion and the British Policy-Making Elite in the Years 1919-1933," <u>Antemurale</u>, 20(1976), 77-129.

1386.   Conte, Francis. "Lloyd George et le traité de Rapallo." <u>Revue d'histoire moderne et contemporaine</u>, 23(1976), 44-67.

1387.   Davies, Norman. "Lloyd George and Poland, 1919-1920." <u>Journal of Contemporary History</u>, 6(1971), 132-54.

See also his "Sir Maurice Hankey and the Inter-Allied Mission to Poland, July-August 1920," <u>Historical Journal</u>, 15(1972), 553-61.

1388.   Debo, Richard K. "Lloyd George and the Copenhagen Conference of 1919-1920: The Initiation of Anglo-Soviet Negotiations." Historical Journal, 24(1981), 429-41.

See too Jean Haton, "Une phase décisive de l'histoire des relations anglo-soviétiques après la première guerre mondiale: Les négociations de Copenhague, novembre 1919-février 1920," Revue d'histoire diplomatique, 73(1959), 67-81.

1389.   Dixon, Joe C. Defeat and Disarmament: Allied Diplomacy and the Politics of Military Affairs in Austria, 1918-1922. London, 1986.

1390.   Fink, Carole. The Genoa Conference: European Diplomacy, 1921-1922. London, 1984.

With multinational documentation; see also Stephen White, The Origins of Detente: The Genoa Conference and Soviet Western Relations, 1921-1922 (London, 1985); and John S. Mills, The Genoa Conference (London, 1922).

1391.   Gajda, Patricia A. Postscript to Victory: British Policy and the German-Polish Borderland, 1919-1925. Washington, DC, 1982.

Argues that British policy on the question turned from orthodoxy to revisionism.

1392.   Gardner, Lloyd C. Safe for Democracy: The Anglo-American Response to Revolution, 1913-1923. London, 1984.

On reaction to events in Mexico, China, Germany and Russia.

1393.   Goold, J. Douglas. "Lord Hardinge as Ambassador to France, and the Anglo-French Dilemma over Germany and the Near East, 1920-1922." Historical Journal, 21(1978), 913-37.

1394.   Hall, Hines H. "Lloyd George, Briand, and the Failure of the Anglo-French Entente." Journal of Modern History, 50(1978), Supplement.

1395.   Hooker, James R. "Lord Curzon and the 'Curzon Line.' " Journal of Modern History, 30(1958), 137-38.

1396.   Klieman, Aaron S. Foundations of British Policy in the Arab World: The Cairo Conference of 1921. London, 1970.

1397. Larew, Karl G. "Great Britain and the Greco-Turkish War, 1921-1922." Historian, 35(1973), 256-70.

1398. Loyrette, J.E.L. The Foreign Policy of Poincaré: France and Great Britain in Relation to the German Problem, 1918-1923. London, 1956.

1399. McDougall, Walter A. France's Rhineland Diplomacy, 1914-1924: The Last Bid for a Balance of Power in Europe. Princeton, NJ, 1978.

Based on French, German, Belgian and British archives and private papers; useful bibliography.

1400. Macfarlane, L.J. " 'Hands Off Russia': British Labour and the Russo-Polish War, 1920." Past and Present, 38(1967), 126-52.

See also Siegfried Bunger, "Die 'Hands off Russia' Bewegung in England," Zeitschrift für Geschichtswissenschaft, 6(1958), 1249-83.

1401. Manning, A.F. "Reports of the British Embassy in Rome on the Rise of Fascism." Risorgimento, 1(1980), 33-45.

1402. Marcovitch, Lazare. "Lord Curzon and Pashitch: Light on Jugoslavia, Turkey and Greece in 1922." Journal of Central European Affairs, 13(1953), 329-37.

1403. Marks, Sally. "Ménage à Trois: The Negotiations for an Anglo-French-Belgian Alliance in 1922." International History Review, 4(1982), 524-52.

1404. Martin, Thomas S. "The Urquhart Concession and Anglo-Soviet Relations, 1921-1922." Jahrbücher für Geschichte Osteuropas, 20(1972), 551-70.

1405. Nassibian, Akaby. Britain and the Armenian Question, 1915-1923. London, 1984.

A thorough analysis, with Armenian sources; see also Aneurin Williams, "Armenia, British Pledges and the Near East," Contemporary Review, 121(1922), 418-25.

1406. Nelson, Keith L. Victors Divided: America and the Allies in Germany, 1918-1923. Berkeley, CA, 1975.

Based on American, German, French and British archives.

1407. Nish, Ian. "Britain and the Ending of the Anglo-Japanese Alliance." Bulletin of the Japan Society of London, 53(1967), 2-5.

On this subject see also the same author's "Japan and the Ending of the Anglo-Japanese Alliance," in Studies in International History: Essays Presented to W. Norton Medlicott, edited by K. Bourne and D.C. Watt (London, 1967); Dennis Smith, "The Royal Navy and Japan: In the Aftermath of the Washington Conference, 1922-1926," Proceedings of the British Association for Japanese Studies, 3(1978), 69-86; Ira Klein, "Whitehall, Washington and the Anglo-Japanese Alliance, 1919-1921," Pacific Historical Review, 41(1972), 460-83; Michael G. Fry, "The North Atlantic Triangle and the Abrogation of the Anglo-Japanese Alliance," Journal of Modern History, 39(1967), 46-64; Merze Tate and Fidele Foy, "More Light on the Abrogation of the Anglo-Japanese Alliance," Political Science Quarterly, 74(1959), 532-54; John Chalmers Vinson, "The Drafting of the Four Power Treaty of the Washington Conference," Journal of Modern History, 25(1953), 40-47; the same author's "The Imperial Conference of 1921 and the Anglo-Japanese Alliance," Pacific Historical Review, 21(1962), 257-67; Robert H. Van Meter, "The Washington Conference of 1921-1922: A New Look," Pacific Historical Review, 46(1977), 603-24; Donald Birn, "Open Diplomacy at the Washington Conference of 1921-1922: The British and French Experience," Comparative Studies in Society and History, 12(1970), 297-319; Sadao Asada, "Japan's 'Special Interests' and the Washington Conference, 1921-1922," American Historical Review, 66(1962), 62-70; Burton F. Beers, Vain Endeavor: Robert Lansing's Attempts to End the Anglo-Japanese Rivalry (Durham, NC, 1962); Thomas Buckley, The United States and the Washington Conference, 1921-1922 (Knoxville, TN, 1970); and for background, Roger Dingman, Power in the Pacific: The Origins of Naval Arms Limitation, 1914-1922 (London, 1976).

1408. Ogden, Dennis. "Britain and Soviet Georgia, 1921-1922." Journal of Contemporary History, 23(1988), 245-58.

1409. Olsen, Robert. "Second Time Around: British Policy towards the Kurds, 1921-1922." Welt des Islams, 27(1987), 91-102.

1410. Rupieper, Hermann J. "Die britische Rheinlandpolitik im spannungsfeld der anglo-französischen Beziehungen, 1919-1924," in Problèmes de la Rhénanie, 1919-1930 (Metz, 1975).

1411. Saunders, David. "Britain and the Ukrainian Question, 1912-1920." English Historical Review, 103(1988), 40-68.

1412. Schuker, Stephen A. The End of French Predominance in Europe: The Financial Crisis of 1924 and the Adoption of the Dawes Plan. Chapel Hill, NC, 1976.

Very well-documented; thorough bibliography.

1413. Schwabe, Klaus. "Grossbritannien und die Ruhrkrise," in Die Ruhrkrise 1923. Edited by Klaus Schwabe. Paderborn, 1984.

See also Stephen E. Fritz, "La Politique de la Ruhr and Lloyd Georgian Conference Diplomacy: The Tragedy of Anglo-French Relations, 1919-1923," Proceedings of the Annual Meeting of the Western Society for French History, 3(1975), 566-82; and David G. Williamson, "Great Britain and the Ruhr Crisis, 1923-1924," British Journal of International Studies, 3(1977), 70-91.

1414. Selsam, J. Paul. The Attempts to Form an Anglo-French Alliance, 1919-1924. Philadelphia, PA, 1936.

1415. Seton-Watson, Hugh, and Seton-Watson, Christopher. The Making of a New Europe: R.W. Seton-Watson and the Last Years of Austria-Hungary. London, 1981.

And of related interest, R.W. Seton-Watson i Jugoslaveni: Korespondencija, 1906-1941, edited by Hugh Seton-Watson and Christopher Seton-Watson, 2 vols. (Zagreb, 1976).

1416. Soutou, Georges. "Die deutschen Reparationen und das Seydoux-Projekt, 1920-1921." Vierteljahrshefte für Zeitgeschichte, 23(1975), 237-70.

1417. Stamm, Christoph. Lloyd George zwischen Innen- und Aussenpolitik: Die britische Deutschlandpolitik, 1921-1922. Köln, 1977.

Useful bibliography for German sources on the subject; see also his "Grossbritannien und die Sanktionen gegen Deutschland vom März 1921," Francia, 7(1979), 340-64.

1418. Walder, David. The Chanak Affair. London, 1969.

Based on British archives, interviews and numerous military sources; no footnotes; see also J.G. Darwin, "The Chanak Crisis and the British Cabinet," History, 65(1980), 32-48; and A.E. Montgomery, "Lloyd George and the Greek Question, 1918-1922," in Lloyd George: Twelve Essays, edited by A.J.P. Taylor (London, 1971).

1419. Weidenfeld, Werner. Die Englandpolitik Gustav Stresemanns: Theoretische und praktische Aspekte der Aussenpolitik. Mainz, 1972.

Based on German archives and private papers; useful bibliography.

1420. Zwehl, Konrad von. Die Deutschlandpolitik Englands von 1922 bis 1924 unter besonderer Berücksichtigung der Reparationen und Sanktionen. Augsburg, 1974.

Mainly based on British archives.

4. Detente and Disintegration, 1925-1933

1421. Bennett, Edward W. German Rearmament and the West, 1932-1933. Princeton, NJ, 1979.

By a former member of the Central Intelligence Agency; an extensively documented study, with much of interest on British policy; see also his Germany and the Diplomacy of the Financial Crisis, 1931 (Cambridge, MA, 1962).

1422. Bickert, Hans G. "Die Vermittlerrolle Grossbritanniens während der Reparationskonferenz von Lausanne 1932." Aus Politik und Zeitgeschichte, supplement to Das Parlament, 23(1973), 13-22.

1423. Carlton, David. "Great Britain and the Coolidge Naval Disarmament Conference of 1927." Political Science Quarterly, 83(1968), 573-98.

See also Robert W. Dubay, "The Geneva Naval Conference of 1927: A Study of Battleship Diplomacy," Southern Quarterly, 8(1970), 177-99.

1424. Edwards, Peter G. "The Austen Chamberlain-Mussolini Meetings." Historical Journal, 14(1972), 153-64.

Five meetings, 1924-29; see also his "Britain, Mussolini and the 'Locarno-Geneva System,' " European Studies Review, 10(1980), 1-16.

1425.   Ferrell, Robert H.   Peace in Their Time: The Origins of the Kellogg-Briand Pact. New Haven, CT, 1952.

1426.   Flory, Harriette.   "The Arcos Raid and the Rupture of Anglo-Soviet Relations, 1927." Journal of Contemporary History, 12(1977), 707-23.

See also Roger Schinness, "The Conservative Party and Anglo-Soviet Relations, 1925-1927," European Studies Review, 7(1977), 393-407; Harvey L. Dyck, "German-Soviet Relations and the Anglo-Soviet Break, 1927," Slavic Review, 25(1966), 67-83; and Robert D. Warth, "The Arcos Raid and the Anglo-Soviet Cold War of the 1920s," World Affairs Quarterly, 29(1958), 115-51.

1427.   Glasgow, George.   From Dawes to Locarno: Being a Critical Record of an Important Achievement in European Diplomacy, 1924-1925. London, 1926.

Foreword by J. Ramsay MacDonald.

1428.   Jacobson, Jon. Locarno Diplomacy: Germany and the West, 1925-1929. Princeton, NJ, 1972.

A thorough analysis based mainly on German archives; see also his "The Conduct of Locarno Diplomacy," Review of Politics, 34(1972), 67-81.

1429.   Jaitner, Klaus.   "Deutschland, Brüning und die Formulierung der britischen Aussenpolitik, Mai 1930 bis Juni 1932." Vierteljahrshefte für Zeitgeschichte, 28(1980), 440-86.

1430.   Jarausch, Konrad Hugo.   The Four Power Pact, 1933. Madison, WI, 1965.

See also Zbigniew Mazur, Pakt Czterech (Poznan, 1979); Giancarlo Giordano, Il Patto a Quattro nella politica estera di Mussolini (Bologna, 1976); Jaroslaw Jurkiewicz, Pakt Wschodni (Warsaw, 1963); and Lothar Krecker, "Die diplomatischen Verhandlungen über den Viererpakt vom 15. Juli 1933," Welt als Geschichte, 21(1961), 227-37.

1431.   Karoly, Laszlo. Velikobritaniia i Lokarno. Moscow, 1961.

1432. Lammers, Donald N. "The Engineers' Trial (Moscow, 1933) and Anglo-Soviet Relations." South Atlantic Quarterly, 62(1963), 256-67.

See also his "Britain, Russia and the Revival of Entente Diplomacy, 1934," Journal of British Studies, 6(1967), 99-123; and "The Second Labour Government and the Restoration of Relations with Soviet Russia (1929)," Bulletin of the Institute of Historical Research, 37(1964), 60-72.

1433. MacDonald, J. Ramsay. "The London Naval Conference, 1930." Journal of the Royal Institute of International Affairs, 9(1930), 429-51.

On the same subject see also Raymond G. O'Connor, Perilous Equilibrium: The United States and the London Naval Conference of 1930 (Lawrence, KS, 1962); J.L. Godfrey, "Anglo-American Naval Conversations Preliminary to the London Naval Conference of 1930," South Atlantic Quarterly, 49(1950), 303-16; Conyers Read, "More Light on the London Naval Treaty of 1930," Proceedings of the American Philosophical Society, 93(1949), 290-308; Raymond Bouy, Le désarmement naval: La conférence de Londres (Paris, 1931); and Laura P. Morgan, The Background of the London Naval Conference (Washington, DC, 1931); subsequent events are analysed in Stephen E. Pelz, Race to Pearl Harbor: The Failure of the Second London Naval Conference and the Onset of World War II (Cambridge, MA, 1974); particularly valuable for its use of Japanese foreign ministry archives and private papers.

1434. McKercher, B.J.C. The Second Baldwin Government and the United States, 1924-1929: Attitudes and Diplomacy. London, 1984.

See also his "Wealth, Power and the New International Order: Britain and the American Challenge in the 1920's," Diplomatic History, 12(1988), 411-41; " 'A Dose of Fascismo': Esme Howard in Spain, 1919-1924," International History Review, 9(1987), 555-85; "Belligerent Rights in 1927-1929: Foreign Policy versus Naval Policy in the Second Baldwin Government," Historical Journal, 29(1986), 963-74; "Austen Chamberlain's Control of British Foreign Policy, 1924-1929," International History Review, 6(1984), 570-91; and "A British View of American Foreign Policy: The Settlement of Blockade Claims, 1924-1927," International History Review, 3(1981), 358-84.

1435.   Ministerium für Auswärtige Angelegenheiten der DDR. Locarno-Konferenz 1925: Eine Dokumentensammlung. East Berlin, 1962.

1436.   Newman, Michael. "Britain and the German-Austrian Customs Union Proposal of 1931." European Studies Review, 6(1976), 449-72.

        See too F.G. Stambrook, "A British Proposal for the Danubian States: The Customs Union Project of 1932," Slavonic and East European Review, 42(1963), 64-88.

1437.   Owen, G.L. "The Metro-Vickers Crisis: Anglo-Soviet Relations between Trade Agreements, 1932-1934." Slavonic and East European Review, 49(1971), 92-112.

1438.   Rass, Hans Heinrich. Britische Aussenpolitik, 1929-1931: Ebenen und Faktoren der Entscheidung. Frankfurt/M., 1975.

1439.   Rolo, P.J.V. Britain and the Briand Plan: The Common Market That Never Was. Keele, 1972.

        An inaugural lecture at the University of Keele; see also Emilia Vigliar, L'Unione europea all'epoca del progetto Briand (Milan, 1983); Robert Boyce, "Britain's First 'No' to Europe: Britain and the Briand Plan, 1929-1930," European Studies Review, 10(1980), 17-46; his "British Capitalism and the Idea of European Unity between the Wars," in European Unity in Context: The Interwar Period, edited by Peter M.R. Stirk (London, 1989); Karl Dietrich Erdmann, "Der Europa-Plan Briands im Lichte der englischen Akten," Geschichte in Wissenschaft und Unterricht, 1(1950), 16-32; and Walter Lipgens, "Europäische Einigungsidee 1923-1930 und Briands Europa-Plan im Urteil der deutschen Akten," Historische Zeitschrift, 203(1966), 46-89, 316-63.

1440.   Rössler, Hellmuth, ed. Locarno und die Weltpolitik, 1924-1932. Göttingen, 1969.

        Seven essays; with one on the Commonwealth, 1917-31.

1441.   Schmidt, Gustav, ed. Konstellationen internationaler Politik, 1924-1932: Politische und wirtschaftliche Faktoren in den Beziehungen zwischen Westeuropa und den Vereinigten Staaten. Bochum, 1983.

Proceedings of a conference in Dortmund, 1981; several contributions on British aspects.

1442.   Stambrook, F.G. "The Foreign Secretary and Foreign Policy: The Experiences of Austen Chamberlain in 1925 and 1927." International Review of History and Political Science, 6(1969), 109-27.

See too Margaret Morris, " 'Et l'honneur?' Politics and Principles: A Case Study of Austen Chamberlain," in Warfare, Diplomacy and Politics: Essays in Honour of A.J.P. Taylor, edited by Chris Wrigley (London, 1986).

1443.   Trommer, Aage. "MacDonald in Geneva in March 1933: A Study in Britain's European Policy." Scandinavian Journal of History, 1(1976), 293-312.

For background see Timur F. Dmitrichev, Zhenevskaia konferentsiia po razoruzheniu (Moscow, 1986).

1444.   Urbanitsch, Peter. Grossbritannien und die Verträge von Locarno. Vienna, 1968.

Based on German archives and the papers of Sir Austen Chamberlain, Lord Cecil and Lord D'Abernon; see also Angela Kaiser, "Lord D'Abernon und die Entstehungsgeschichte der Locarno-Verträge," Vierteljahrshefte für Zeitgeschichte, 34(1986), 85-104; F. Bosshard, "Der Vertrag von Locarno 1925: Beginneiner neuen Epoche in Europa," Geschichte, 44(1982), 24-31; Sibyl Crowe, "Sir Eyre Crowe and the Locarno Pact," English Historical Review, 87(1972), 49-74; Jean-Baptiste Duroselle, "The Spirit of Locarno: Illusions of Pactomania," Foreign Affairs, 50(1972) 752-64; F.G. Stambrook, " 'Das Kind': Lord D'Abernon and the Origins of the Locarno Pact," Central European History, 1(1968), 233-63; Douglas Johnson, "Austen Chamberlain and the Locarno Agreements," University of Birmingham Historical Journal, 8(1961), 60-91; Christine Daneva-Mihova, "La politique de Locarno de l'Angleterre et de la France dans les Balkans en 1925 et 1926," Etudes Historiques, 1(1960), 433-64; and George A. Grün, "Locarno: Idea and Reality," International Affairs, 31(1955), 477-85.

1445.   USSR, Ministerstvo Inostrannikh Del. Lokarnskaia Konferentsiia 1925g. Edited by A.F. Dobrov. Moscow, 1959.

1446.   Wheeler-Bennett, John W., and Latimer, Hugh. Information on the Reparation Settlement: Being the Background and History of the Young Plan and the Hague Agreements, 1929-1930. London, 1930.

F. DIPLOMACY IN CRISIS

1. 1930s General

1447.   Bell, P.M.H. "Great Britain and the Rise of Germany, 1932-1934." International Relations, 12(1964), 609-18.

1448.   Bisceglia, Louis. Norman Angell and Liberal Internationalism in Britain, 1931-1935. London, 1982.

See also J.D.B. Miller, Norman Angell and the Futility of War: Peace and the Public Mind (London, 1986); and Cornelia Navari, "The Great Illusion Revisited: The International Theory of Norman Angell," Review of International Studies, 15(1989), 341-58.

1449.   Bright, Charles. "Class Interest and State Policy in the British Response to Hitler," in German Nationalism and the European Response, 1890-1945. Edited by Carole Fink et al. Norman, OK, 1985.

1450.   Conwell-Evans, T.P. None So Blind: A Study of the Crisis Years, 1930-1939, Based on the Papers of M.G. Christie. London, 1947.

Group Captain Malcolm Grahame Christie, air attaché at Berlin, 1927-30, thereafter, part of Sir Robert Vansittart's intelligence network; only 100 copies were printed.

1451.   Cowling, Maurice. The Impact of Hitler: British Politics and British Policy, 1933-1940. London, 1975.

On the relation between foreign and domestic policy.

1452.   Crozier, Andrew J. Appeasement and Germany's Last Bid for Colonies. London, 1988.

On the 1933-38 period; see also his "Imperial Decline and the Colonial Question in Anglo-German Relations, 1919-1939," European Studies Review, 11(1981), 207-42; and "Prelude to Munich: British Foreign Policy and Germany, 1935-1938," European Studies Review, 6(1976), 357-81.

1453.   DeLuca, Anthony R. Great Power Rivalry at the Turkish Straits: The Montreux Conference and Convention of 1936. New York, 1981.

A thorough analysis with background and developments to 1946; based on the documents of leading participants.

1454.   Dilks, David. "Baldwin and Chamberlain," in The Conservatives: A History from Their Origins to 1965. Edited by Lord Butler. London, 1977.

1455.   Duroselle, Jean-Baptiste. La décadence, 1932-1939. Paris, 1979.

Continued in his L'abîme, 1939-1945 (Paris, 1982); principally on France but with material relevant to Britain; likewise see Robert J. Young, In Command of France: French Foreign Policy and Military Planning, 1933-1940 (Cambridge, MA, 1978); Anthony P. Adamthwaite, France and the Coming of the Second World War (London, 1977); and Jacques Néré, The Foreign Policy of France from 1914 to 1945 (London, 1975).

1456.   George, Margaret. The Warped Vision: British Foreign Policy, 1933-1939. Pittsburgh, PA, 1965.

Argues that appeasement was the foreign policy of decadent British conservatism.

1457.   Goldman, Aaron. "Sir Robert Vansittart's Search for Italian Co-operation against Hitler, 1933-1936." Journal of Contemporary History, 9(1974), 93-130.

See also his "Two Views of Germany: Nevile Henderson vs. Vansittart and the Foreign Office, 1937-1939," British Journal of International Studies, 6(1980), 247-77; and Giuliano Cora, "Lord Vansittart e la diplomazia di ieri," Nuova antologia, 484(1962), 19-24.

1458.   Hanak, Harry. "The Visit of Czechoslovak Foreign Minister Dr. Eduard Beneš to Moscow in 1935 as Seen by the British

Minister in Prague, Sir Joseph Addison." Slavonic and East European Review, 54(1976), 586-92.

1459. Harrison, Richard A. "Testing the Water: A Secret Probe towards Anglo-American Military Co-operation in 1936." International History Review, 7(1985), 214-34.

See also his "The Runciman Visit to Washington in January 1937," Canadian Journal of History, 9(1984), 217-39; and "A Presidential Démarche: Franklin D. Roosevelt's Personal Diplomacy and Great Britain, 1936-1937," Diplomatic History, 5(1981), 245-72.

1460. Hauser, Oswald. England und das Dritte Reich: Eine dokumentierte Geschichte der englisch-deutschen Beziehungen von 1933 bis 1939 auf Grund unveröffentlicher Akten aus dem britischen Staatsarchiv. 2 vols. Stuttgart, 1972-82.

Vol. 2 ends in August 1938; an extensive analysis with reprinted documents, many from the Public Record Office; see also his "England und Hitler, 1936-1939," in Am Wendepunkt der europäischen Geschichte, edited by Otmar Franz (Göttingen, 1981); and "England und Hitler," in Was weiter wirkt: Beiträge zur Geschichte des 20. Jahrhunderts, edited by Otmar Franz (Stuttgart, 1971).

1461. Henke, Josef. England in Hitlers politischem Kalkül, 1935-1939. Boppard/R., 1973.

See also Gerhard L. Weinberg, "Hitler and England, 1933-1945: Pretense and Reality," German Studies Review, 8(1985), 299-310; Bernd-Jürgen Wendt, Grossdeutschland (Munich, 1987); Andreas Hillgruber, "England in Hitlers aussenpolitischer Konzeption," Historische Zeitschrift, 218(1974), 65-84; also published as "England's Place in Hitler's Plans for World Dominion," Journal of Contemporary History, 9(1974), 5-22; Axel Kuhn, Hitlers aussenpolitisches Programm: Entstehung und Entwicklung, 1919-1939 (Stuttgart, 1970), which includes an examination of Britain's place in Hitler's foreign policy programme after 1933; and A.V.N. van Woerden, "Hitler Faces England: Theories, Images and Policies," Acta Historiae Neerlandica, 3(1968), 141-59.

1462. Holland, R.F. Britain and the Commonwealth Alliance, 1918-1939. London, 1981.

Based on Public Record Office materials.

1463.   Hughes, Jeffrey L. "The Origins of World War II in Europe: British
         Deterrence Failure and German Expansionism." Journal of
         Interdisciplinary History, 18(1988), 851-91.

1464.   Kennedy, Aubrey Leo. Britain Faces Germany. London, 1937.

1465.   Kennedy, Thomas C. " 'Peace in Our Time': The Personal
         Diplomacy of Lord Allen of Hurtwood, 1933-1938," in Doves and
         Diplomats: Foreign Offices and Peace Movements in Europe
         and America in the Twentieth Century. Edited by Solomon
         Wank. Westport, CT, 1978.

1466.   Kettenacker, Lothar. "Die englische Illusionspolitik vor dem 2.
         Weltkrieg, 1932-1937." Wehrwissenschaftliche Rundschau,
         15(1965), 100-11.

1467.   Ludlow, Peter. "Britain and the Third Reich," in The Challenge of
         the Third Reich. Edited by Hedley Bull. London, 1986.

1468.   Medlicott, W.N. Britain and Germany: The Search for
         Agreement, 1930-1937. London, 1969.

         See too his "Neville Chamberlain," in British Prime Ministers: A
         Portrait Gallery (London, 1953).

1469.   Meyers, Reinhard. "Die Dominions und die britische
         Europapolitik der dreissiger Jahre," in Tradition und Neubeginn:
         Internationale Forschungen zur deutschen Geschichte im 20.
         Jahrhundert. Edited by Joachim Hütter et al. Köln, 1975.

         See also his "Britain, Europe and the Dominions in the 1930s:
         Some Aspects of British, European and Commonwealth Policies,"
         Australian Journal of Politics and History, 22(1976), 36-50; Rudolf
         von Albertini, "England als Weltmacht und der Strukturwandel
         des Commonwealth," Historische Zeitschrift, 208(1969), 52-80;
         and Nicholas Mansergh, Survey of British Commonwealth Affairs:
         Problems of External Policy, 1931-1939 (London, 1952).

1470.   Nish, Ian. "Yoshida as a Diplomat." Proceedings of the British
         Association for Japanese Studies, 3(1978), 87-96.

         Japanese ambassador at London, 1936-38.

1471.   Peters, A.R. Anthony Eden at the Foreign Office, 1931-1938.
         Aldershot, 1986.

On Eden's "particular contribution to the making of foreign policy" (Preface).

1472.   Pozdeeva, Lidiia V. Angliia i remilitarizatsiia Germanii, 1933-1936gg. Moscow, 1956.

See too Max Lüthi, Das britische Parlament und Hitlers Bruch mit dem Versailler System: Ein Beitrag zur parlamentarischen Diskussion über die deutsche Wiederaufrüstung in den Jahren 1933-1935 (Zurich, 1972).

1473.   Rhodes, Benjamin D. "Sir Ronald Lindsay and the British View from Washington, 1930-1939," in Essays in Twentieth-Century American Diplomatic History: Dedicated to Professor Daniel M. Smith. Edited by Clifford L. Egan and Alexander W. Knott. Lanham, MD, 1982.

And in the same collection, Michael Holcomb, "Sir John Simon's War with Henry L. Stimson: A Footnote to Anglo-American Relations in the 1930's."

1474.   Robertson, Esmonde M. Hitler's Pre-War Policy and Military Plans, 1933-1939. London, 1963.

Further thoughts in his "Hitler's Planning for War and the Response of the Great Powers (1938-Early 1939)," in Aspects of the Third Reich, edited by H.W. Koch (London, 1985).

1475.   Rohe, Karl, ed. Die Westmächte und das Dritte Reich, 1933-1939: Klassische Grossmachtrivalität oder Kampf zwischen Demokratie und Diktatur? Paderborn, 1982.

With contributions on British foreign policy, economic appeasement, and Anglo-American relations; useful bibliographical essay.

1476.   Spier, Eugen. Focus: A Footnote to the History of the Thirties. London, 1963.

On the role Spier played in the inception and financing of Churchill's "Focus in Defence of Freedom and Peace"; see also his The Protecting Power (London, 1951).

1477.   Tamchina, Rainer. "In Search of Common Causes: The Imperial Conference of 1937." Journal of Imperial and Commonwealth History, 1(1972), 79-105.

1478. Thompson, Neville. The Anti-Appeasers: Conservative Opposition to Appeasement in the 1930s. London, 1971.

See also his "The Failure of Conservative Opposition to Appeasement in the 1930s," Canadian Journal of History, 3(1968), 27-52.

1479. Waterlow, Sir Sydney P. "The Decline and Fall of Greek Democracy, 1933-1936." Political Quarterly, 18(1947), 95-106, 205-19.

British minister at Bangkok, 1926-28; Addis Ababa, 1928-29; and Athens, 1933-39.

1480. Weinberg, Gerhard L. The Foreign Policy of Hitler's Germany, 1933-1939. 2 vols. Chicago, IL, 1970-80.

Vol. 1 to 1936; broadly researched in primary and secondary sources; very useful bibliography; see also Hans-Adolf Jacobsen, Nationalsozialistische Aussenpolitik, 1933-1938 (Frankfurt/M., 1968); on the nature of Hitler's objectives in foreign policy, including Anglo-German relations, see Klaus Hildebrand, Deutsche Aussenpolitik, 1933-1945: Kalkül oder Dogma? (Stuttgart, 1976); the essays by various scholars on foreign policy methods and relations in Hitler, Deutschland und die Mächte: Materialien zur Aussenpolitik des Dritten Reiches, edited by Manfred Funke (Düsseldorf, 1977); and Nationalsozialistische Diktatur, 1933-1945: Eine Bilanz, edited by Karl Dietrich Bracher et al. (Düsseldorf, 1983); reprinted essays, mostly on the 1930s, in Nationalsozialistische Aussenpolitik, edited by Wolfgang Michalka (Darmstadt, 1978); and Wolfgang Michalka, Ribbentrop und die deutsche Weltpolitik, 1933-1940 (Munich, 1980).

2. From Manchuria to the Pacific War, 1931-1941

1481. Acland, Sir Francis Dyke. Japan Must Be Stopped. London, 1937.

Under-secretary of state for Foreign Affairs, 1911-15.

1482. Agbi, S. Olu. "The Foreign Office and Yoshida's Bid for Rapprochement with Britain in 1936-1937: A Critical Reconsideration of the Anglo-Japanese Conversations." Historical Journal, 21(1978), 173-79.

See also his "The Pacific War Controversy in Britain: Sir Robert Craigie Versus the Foreign Office," Modern Asian Studies, 17(1983), 489-517; and "Britain's Loans Policy in China, 1937-1940," Journal of Oriental Studies, 18(1980), 100-25.

1483. Andrews, E.M. The Writing on the Wall: The British Commonwealth and Aggression in the East, 1931-1935. London, 1987.

Based on archival research in London, Canberra, Melbourne, Wellington and Ottawa; very critical of British policy.

1484. Bassett, Reginald. Democracy and Foreign Policy: A Case History, the Sino-Japanese Dispute, 1931-1933. London, 1952.

On the evolution of public opinion during the crisis.

1485. Borg, Dorothy. The United States and the Far Eastern Crisis of 1933-1938. Cambridge, MA, 1964.

Revelations on British policy by American observers; see also the 26 essays in Pearl Harbour as History: Japanese-American Relations, 1931-1941, edited by Dorothy Borg and Shumpei Okamoto (New York, 1973); on further major power involvement see Gary B. Ostrower, Collective Insecurity: The United States and the League of Nations during the Early Thirties (Cranbury, NJ, 1979); George A. Lensen, The Damned Inheritance: The Soviet Union and the Manchurian Crises, 1924-1935 (Tallahassee, FL, 1974); and John P. Fox, Germany and the Far Eastern Crisis, 1931-1938: A Study in Diplomacy and Ideology (London, 1982).

1486. Casella, Alessandro. Le conflit sino-japonais de 1937 et la Société des Nations. Paris, 1968.

See also the earlier study by Westel W. Willoughby, The Sino-Japanese Controversy and the League of Nations (Baltimore, MD, 1935).

1487. Clive, Sir Robert. Reshaping the Far East. London, 1943.

Lecture to the Royal Central Asian Society by the British ambassador to Japan, 1934-37; and Belgium, 1937-39.

1488. Haggie, Paul. Britannia at Bay: The Defence of the British Empire against Japan, 1931-1941. London, 1981.

Explores the "third dimension" of the threat to Britain (Preface); based on a wide array of Public Record Office documents and various private papers; see also his "Admiral Sir Howard Kelly and the Shanghai Crisis, 1932," Naval Review, 64(1976), 195-202.

1489.   Hecht, Robert A. "Great Britain and the Stimson Note of January 7, 1932." Pacific Historical Review, 38(1969), 177-91.

1490.   League of Nations. Appeal of the Chinese Government: Report of the Commission of Enquiry (Lytton Report). Geneva, 1932.

See also Lord Lytton's analysis in his "The Problem of Manchuria," International Affairs, 11(1932), 737-56; and The League, the Far East and Ourselves (London, 1934); League of Nations Union, Pamphlet, no. 369.

1491.   Lee, Bradford A. Britain and the Sino-Japanese War, 1937-1939: A Study in the Dilemmas of British Decline. Stanford, CA, 1973.

"Appeasement in an East Asian context" (Preface); based on British archival sources; useful bibliographical essay.

1492.   Lowe, Peter. Great Britain and the Origins of the Pacific War: A Study of British Policy in East Asia, 1937-1941. London, 1977.

Principally based on British archives and relevant private papers; see also his "Great Britain and the Coming of the Pacific War, 1939-1941," Transactions of the Royal Historical Society, 14(1974), 43-62; "Great Britain and the Outbreak of War with Japan, 1941," in War and Society: Essays in Honour and Memory of J.R. Western, 1928-1971, edited by M.R.D. Foot (London, 1973); and "The Dilemmas of an Ambassador: Sir Robert Craigie in Tokyo, 1937-1941," Proceedings of the British Association for Japanese Studies, 2(1977), 34-56.

1493.   Megaw, M. Ruth. "The Scramble for the Pacific: Anglo-United States Rivalry in the 1930s." Historical Studies, 17(1977), 458-73.

1494.   Neidpath, James. The Singapore Naval Base and the Defence of Britain's Eastern Empire, 1919-1941. London, 1981.

Origins, development and collapse of the "Singapore strategy"; based on Public Record Office archives, and private papers; of the numerous studies on this subject, see also Ian Hamill, The Strategic Illusion: The Singapore Strategy and the Defence of

Australia and New Zealand, 1919-1942 (Singapore, 1981);
W. David McIntyre, The Rise and Fall of the Singapore Naval
Base, 1919-1942 (London, 1979); Louis Allen, Singapore, 1941-
1942 (London, 1977); Raymond Callahan, The Worst Disaster:
The Fall of Singapore (London, 1977); his "The Illusion of
Security: Singapore, 1919-1942," Journal of Contemporary History,
9(1974), 69-92; and Noel Barber, Sinister Twilight: The Fall of
Singapore (London, 1971).

1495. Rothwell, Victor. "The Mission of Sir Frederick Leith-Ross to the
Far East, 1935-1936." Historical Journal, 18(1975), 147-69.

1496. Shai, Aron. Origins of the War in the East: Britain, China and
Japan, 1937-1939. London, 1976.

A thoroughly documented study; see also the same author's "The
Examines "the Asian context" of appeasement (Preface); based
essentially on British archives; see also his "Was There a Far
Eastern Munich?" Journal of Contemporary History, 9(1974), 161-
69; and "Le conflit anglo-japonais de Tientsin, 1939," Revue
d'histoire moderne et contemporaine, 22(1975), 293-302.

1497. Taboulet, Georges. "La France et l'Angleterre face au conflit sino-
japonais, 1937-1939." Revue d'histoire diplomatique, 88(1974),
112-44.

1498. Thorne, Christopher. The Limits of Foreign Policy: The West, the
League and the Far Eastern Crisis of 1931-1933. London, 1972.

A thoroughly documented study; see also the same author's "The
Shanghai Crisis of 1932: The Basis of British Policy," American
Historical Review, 75(1970), 1616-39; and his collected essays,
many on the Far East in the 1930s and early 1940s, in Border
Crossings: Studies in International History (London, 1988).

1499. Trotter, Ann. Britain and East Asia, 1933-1937. London, 1975.

Based on a variety of British archival materials and private papers
and Japanese-language sources; see also the same author's
"Tentative Steps for an Anglo-Japanese Rapprochement in 1934,"
Modern Asian Studies, 8(1974), 59-83; and "Backstage
Diplomacy: Britain and Japan in the 1930s," Journal of Oriental
Studies, 15(1977), 37-45.

1500. Wheeler, Gerald E. "Isolated Japan: Anglo-American Diplomatic
Cooperation, 1927-1936." Pacific Historical Review, 30(1961),
165-78.

1501. Whyte, Sir Alexander Frederick. The Future of East and West. London, 1932.

MP, 1910-18; political adviser to national government of China, 1929-32; head of American division, ministry of Information, 1939-40; see also his "China, Japan and Manchuria," Nineteenth Century, 111(1932), 281-92; and China and Foreign Powers: An Historical Review of Their Relations, 2nd ed. (London, 1928).

1502. Woodhead, Henry George Wandesforde. A Journalist in China. London, 1934.

One of several books on the Far Eastern crisis by the editor of the Peking and Tientsin Times, 1914-30; with ministry of Information, 1942-45.

3. The Italo-Ethiopian War, 1935-1936

1503. Asante, S.K.B. Pan-African Protest: West Africa and the Italo-Ethiopian Crisis, 1934-1941. London, 1977.

Based on British and west African sources; see also his "The Catholic Missions, British West African Nationalists, and the Italian Invasion of Ethiopia, 1935-1936," African Affairs, 73(1974), 204-16; and Robert G. Weisbord, "British West Indian Reaction to the Italian-Ethiopian War: An Episode in Pan-Africanism," Caribbean Studies, 10(1970), 34-41.

1504. Baer, George W. The Coming of the Italian-Ethiopian War. Cambridge, MA, 1967.

From the Wal Wal incident to the start of the war; see also his "Haile Selassie's Protectorate Appeal to King Edward VIII," Cahiers d'études africaines, 9(1969), 306-12; and Test Case: Italy, Ethiopia and the League of Nations (Stanford, CA, 1976).

1505. Barker, A.J. The Civilizing Mission: The Italo-Ethiopian War, 1935-1936. London, 1968.

For another essentially military account, see Angelo Del Boca, The Ethiopian War, 1935-1941 (Chicago, IL, 1969).

1506. Barros, James. Britain, Greece and the Politics of Sanctions: Ethiopia, 1935-1936. London, 1982.

1507. Brundu Olla, Paola. "Il tentativo di 'detente' italo-britannica dell'autunno 1935." Il politico, 43(1978), 422-46.

1508. Carlton, David. "The Dominions and British Foreign Policy in the Abyssinian Crisis." Journal of Imperial and Commonwealth History, 1(1972), 59-77.

1509. Chukumba, Stephen U. The Big Powers against Ethiopia: Anglo-French-American Maneuvers during the Italo-Ethiopian Dispute, 1934-1938. Washington, DC, 1977.

An attempt at a comparative study; based solely on published accounts and the press; major power involvement is also analysed extensively in Franklin D. Laurens, France and the Italo-Ethiopian Crisis, 1935-1936 (The Hague, 1967); and Brice Harris, The United States and the Italo-Ethiopian Crisis (Stanford, CA, 1964).

1510. Friedlander, Robert A. "New Light on the Anglo-American Reaction to the Ethiopian War, 1935-1936." Mid-America, 45(1963), 115-25.

1511. Goglia, Luigi. "La propaganda italiana a sostegno della guerra contro l'Etiopia svolta in Gran Bretagna nel 1935-1936." Storia contemporanea, 15(1984), 845-906.

1512. Hardie, Frank M. The Abyssinian Crisis London, 1974.

Argues that the crisis was "the first great act of appeasement" (Introduction); based mainly on British sources; for the wider background see Anthony Mockler, Haile Selassie's War (London, 1984).

1513. Kent, Peter C. "Between Rome and London: Pius XI, the Catholic Church and the Abyssinian Crisis of 1935-1936." International History Review, 11(1989), 252-71.

1514. Marder, Arthur J. "The Royal Navy and the Ethiopian Crisis of 1935-1936." American Historical Review, 75(1970), 1327-56.

Further assessed in Rosaria Quartararo, "Imperial Defence in the Mediterranean on the Eve of the Ethiopian Crisis," Historical Journal, 20(1977), 185-220; based on both British and Italian archives; and the same author's "La crisi mediterranea del 1935-1936," Storia contemporanea, 6(1975), 801-46.

1515. Mori, Renato. Mussolini e la conquista dell'Etiopia. Florence, 1978.

A thoroughly documented study; other major studies of relevance include Esmonde M. Robertson, Mussolini as Empire-Builder: Europe and Africa, 1932-1936 (London, 1977); Denis Mack Smith, Mussolini's Roman Empire (London, 1976); Manfred Funke, Sanktionen und Kanonen: Hitler, Mussolini und der internationale Abessinienkonflikt, 1934-1936 (Düsseldorf, 1970); and an earlier work which used some foreign ministry archives, Luigi Villari, Storia diplomatica del conflitto italo-etiopico (Bologna, 1943).

1516. Parker, R.A.C. "Great Britain, France and the Ethiopian Crisis, 1935-1936." English Historical Review, 89(1974), 293-332.

With some extracts from the Royal Archives.

1517. Post, Gaines. "The Machinery of British Policy in the Ethiopian Crisis." International History Review, 1(1979), 522-41.

With more in his "Mad Dogs and Englishmen: British Rearmament, Deterrence and Appeasement, 1934-1935," Armed Forces and Society, 14(1988), 329-57.

1518. Pugh, Martin. "Peace with Italy: BUF Reactions to the Abyssinian War, 1935-1936." Wiener Library Bulletin, 27(1974), 11-18.

1519. Quartararo, Rosaria. "Le origini del piano Hoare-Laval." Storia contemporanea, 8(1977), 749-90.

Other analyses of this incident include James C. Robertson, "The Hoare-Laval Plan," Journal of Contemporary History, 10(1975), 433-64; Marguerite Potter, "What Sealed Baldwin's Lips?" Historian, 27(1964), 21-36; Henderson B. Braddick, "The Hoare-Laval Plan: A Study in International Politics," Review of Politics, 24(1962), 342-64; and Ernst L. Presseisen, "Foreign Policy and British Public Opinion: The Hoare-Laval Pact of 1935," World Affairs Quarterly, 29(1958), 256-77.

1520. Robertson, James C. "The Origins of British Opposition to Mussolini over Ethiopia." Journal of British Studies, 9(1969), 122-42.

For background see his "British Policy in East Africa, March 1891 to May 1935," English Historical Review, 93(1978), 835-44; P.G.

Edwards, "Britain, Fascist Italy and Ethiopia, 1925-1928," European Studies Review, 4(1974), 359-74; Giuseppe Vedovato, "Gli accordi italo-etiopico dell'agosto 1923," Rivista di studi politici internnazionali, 22(1955), 560-634; and Giovanni Buccianti, L'egemonia sull'Etiopia, 1918-1923: Lo scontro diplomatico tra Italia, Francia e Inghilterra (Milan, 1977).

1521. Toscano, Mario. "Eden's Mission to Rome on the Eve of the Italo-Ethiopian Conflict," in Studies in Diplomatic History and Historiography in Honour of G.P. Gooch. Edited by A.O. Sarkissan. London, 1961.

1522. "Vigilantes" [Konni Zilliacus]. Abyssinia: The Essential Facts in the Dispute and an Answer to the Question "Ought We to Support Sanctions?" London, 1935.

A New Statesman and Nation publication; other contemporary studies include Alfred Zimmern, "The League's Handling of the Italo-Abyssinian Dispute," International Affairs, 14(1935), 751-68; his "The Testing of the League," Foreign Affairs, 14(1936), 373-86; Lord Davies, Nearing the Abyss: The Lesson of Ethiopia (London, 1936); Henry Rowan-Robinson, England, Italy, Abyssinia (London, 1935); and Royal Institute of International Affairs, Abyssinia and Italy (London, 1935).

1523. Waley, Daniel Philip. British Public Opinion and the Abyssinian War, 1935-1936. London, 1976.

See also Paul Vaucher and Paul-Henri Siriex, L'Opinion britannique, la Société des Nations, et la guerre italo-éthiopienne (Paris, 1936).

1524. Wilson, Hugh R., Jr. For Want of a Nail: The Failure of the League of Nations in Ethiopia. New York, 1959.

Based on the papers of his father, U.S. minister to Switzerland, 1927-37; see also Armand Cohen, La Société des Nations devant le conflit italo-éthiopien, Décembre 1934-Octobre 1935 (Geneva, 1960).

4. The Anglo-German Naval Agreement, 1935

1525. Best, Richard A. "The Anglo-German Naval Agreement of 1935: An Aspect of Appeasement." Naval War College Review, 34(1981), 68-85.

1526. Bloch, Charles. "La Grande-Bretagne face au réarmement allemand et l'accord naval de 1935." Revue d'histoire de la deuxième guerre mondiale, 16(1966), 41-68.

1527. Brundu Olla, Paola. Le origini diplomatiche dell'accordo navale anglo-tedesco del giugno 1935. Milan, 1974.

Based essentially on British sources; with an appendix of 26 relevant documents; no bibliography.

1528. Dülffer, Jost. "Das deutsch-englische Flottenabkommen vom 18. Juni 1935." Marine-Rundschau, 69(1972), 641-59.

For the wider historical context, see his Weimar, Hitler und die Marine: Reichspolitik und Flottenbau, 1920-1939 (Düsseldorf, 1973); and Rolf Bensel, Die deutsche Flottenpolitik von 1933-1939: Eine Studie über die Rolle des Flottenbaus in Hitlers Aussenpolitik (Frankfurt/M., 1958).

1529. Hall, Hines H. "The Foreign Policy-Making Process in Britain, 1934-1935, and the Origins of the Anglo-German Naval Agreement." Historical Journal, 19(1976), 477-99.

1530. Haraszti, Eva. Treaty-Breakers or "Realpolitiker"? The Anglo-German Naval Agreement of June 1935. Boppard/R., 1974.

Based on an array of European-language sources; with an appendix of 14 documents, most from the Public Record Office.

1531. Ingrim, Robert. Hitlers glücklichster Tag: London, am 18. Juni 1935. Stuttgart, 1962.

1532. Malanowski, Wolfgang. "Das deutsch-englische Flotten-abkommen vom 18. Juni 1935 als Ausgangspunkt für Hitlers doktrinäre Bündnispolitik." Wehrwissenschaftliche Rundschau, 5(1955), 408-20.

1533. Watt, D.C. "The Anglo-German Naval Agreement of 1935: An Interim Judgement." Journal of Modern History, 28(1956), 155-75.

5. The Reoccupation of the Rhineland, 1936

1534. Bolen, C. Waldron. "Hitler Remilitarizes the Rhineland," in Power, Public Opinion, and Diplomacy: Essays in Honor of Eber

Malcolm Carroll. Edited by Lillian Parker Wallace and William C. Askew. Durham, NC, 1959.

1535. Braubach, Max. Der Einmarsch deutscher Truppen in die entmilitarisierte Zone am Rhein im März 1936: Ein Beitrag zur Vorgeschichte des zweiten Weltkrieges. Cologne, 1956.

1536. Brown, Stephen W. "Great Britain and the Rhineland Crisis of 1936." North Dakota Quarterly, 44(1976), 31-43.

1537. Emmerson, James Thomas. The Rhineland Crisis, 7 March 1936: A Study in Multilateral Diplomacy. Ames, IA, 1977.

The most thorough study; based on British and German archives; similarly see also Eva Haraszti, The Invaders: Hitler Occupies the Rhineland (Budapest, 1983); with over 100 pages of documents, mainly British.

1538. Fiedler, R. "Hitlers 'aufregendste' Stunden: Vor 25 Jahren, Einmarsch in die entmilitarisierte Zone." Politische Studien, 12(1961), 168-74.

1539. Funke, Manfred. "7. März 1936: Fallstudie zum aussen-politischen Führungsstil Hitlers.' Aus Politik und Zeitgeschichte, supplement to Das Parlament, 6(1970), 3-34.

1540. Knapp, W.F. "The Rhineland Crisis of March 1936," in The Decline of the Third Republic. St. Antony's Papers, No. 5. Edited by James Joll. London, 1959.

1541. Meyers, Reinhard. "Das Ende des Systems von Locarno: Die Remilitarisierung des Rheinlandes in britischer Sicht," in Centre National de la Recherche Scientifique, Les relations franco-allemandes, 1933-1939. Paris, 1976.

See also his "Sicherheit und Gleichgewicht: Das britische Kabinett und die Remilitarisierung des Rheinlandes 1936," Rheinische Vierteljahrsblätter, 38(1974), 406-49.

1542. Miller, Rod. "Britain and the Rhineland Crisis, 7 March 1936: Retreat from Responsibility or Accepting the Inevitable?" Australian Journal of Politics and History, 33(1987), 60-77.

1543. Robertson, Esmonde M. "Zur Wiederbesetzung des Rheinlandes, 1936." Vierteljahrshefte für Zeitgeschichte, 10(1962), 178-205.

See also his "Hitler and Sanctions: Mussolini and the Rhineland," European Studies Review, 7(1977), 409-35.

1544.   Royal Institute of International Affairs. Germany and the Rhineland: A Record of the Proceedings of Three Meetings Held at Chatham House on March 18, 25 and April 2, 1936. London, 1936.

        Special supplement to International Affairs, April, 1936; contributors included Harold Nicolson, Norman Angell, and Lord Lothian.

1545.   Ruby, Edmond. "Hitler réoccupe la Rhénanie, 7 mars 1936." Ecrits de Paris, 249(1966), 29-43.

1546.   Schuker, Stephen A. "France and the Remilitarization of the Rhineland." French Historical Studies, 14(1986), 299-338.

        See too George Sakwa, "The Franco-Polish Alliance and the Remilitarization of the Rhineland," Historical Journal, 16(1973), 125-46; Charles Keserich, "The Popular Front and the Rhineland Crisis of March 1936," International Review of History and Political Science, 7(1970), 87-102; R. Debicki, "The Remilitarization of the Rhineland and Its Impact on the Franco-Polish Alliance," Polish Review, 14(1969), 45-55; Larry V. Bishop, "England, France and the Rhineland Crisis of 1936," Research Studies, 34(1966), 219-29; R.A.C. Parker, "The First Capitulation: France and the Rhineland Crisis of 1936," World Politics, 8(1955), 355-73; and for the consequences, David Owen Kieft, Belgium's Return to Neutrality: An Essay in the Frustrations of Small Power Diplomacy (London, 1972).

1547.   Watt, D.C. "German Plans for the Reoccupation of the Rhineland: A Note." Journal of Contemporary History, 1(1966), 193-99.

        See also his "The Reoccupation of the Rhineland," History Today, 6(1956), 244-51.

1548.   Yeuell, Donovan P. "The German Occupation of the Rhineland." U.S. Naval Institute Proceedings, 81(1955), 1205-15.

6. The Spanish Civil War, 1936-1939

1549.   Alexander, Bill. British Volunteers for Liberty: Spain, 1936-1939. London, 1982.

An "official history" of the British battalion in the International Brigade; supersedes the earlier, William Rust, Britons in Spain (London, 1939); see also Jim Fyrth, The Signal Was Spain: The Spanish Aid Movement in Britain, 1936-1939 (London, 1986); Hywel Francis, Miners against Fascism: Wales and the Spanish Civil War (London, 1984); and more generally R. Dan Richardson, Comintern Army: The International Brigades and the Spanish Civil War (Lexington, KY, 1982); and Vincent Brome, The International Brigades: Spain, 1936-1939 (London, 1965).

1550.   Alpert, Michael. "Humanitarianism and Politics in the British Response to the Spanish Civil War, 1936-1939." European History Quarterly, 14(1984), 423-40.

1551.   Atholl, Duchess of. Searchlight on Spain. London, 1938.

1552.   Beevor, Anthony. The Spanish Civil War. London, 1982.

A revisionist view of the roles of Britain and the USSR.

1553.   Blythe, Henry. Spain over Britain: A Study of the Strategical Effects of Italian Intervention on the Defense of the British Empire. London, 1937.

1554.   Cable, James. The Royal Navy and the Siege of Bilbao. London, 1979.

On British naval diplomacy in the spring of 1937.

1555.   Edwards, Jill. The British Government and the Spanish Civil War, 1936-1939. London, 1979.

A thorough study based on a wide variety of British and some Spanish sources; supersedes William Kleine-Ahlbrandt, The Policy of Simmering: A Study of British Policy during the Spanish Civil War, 1936-1939 (The Hague, 1962).

1556.   Foreman, John. "L'Attitude de la Grande Bretagne envers l'Italie et l'Espagne, 1936-1938." Relations internationales, 2(1974), 147-63.

1557.   Frank, Willard C. "The Spanish Civil War and the Coming of the Second World War." International History Review, 9(1987), 368-409.

1558.   Gretton, Sir Peter. "The Nyon Conference - the Naval Aspect."
         English Historical Review, 90(1975), 103-12.

         See also James W. Cortada, "Ships, Diplomacy and the Spanish
         Civil War: Nyon Conference, September 1937," Il politico,
         37(1972), 673-89.

1559.   Little, Douglas. Malevolent Neutrality: The United States, Great
         Britain, and the Origins of the Spanish Civil War. Ithaca, NY,
         1985.

         Including the course of the civil war; with new evidence; see also
         his "Red Scare, 1936: Anti-Bolshevism and the Origins of British
         Non-Intervention in the Spanish Civil War," Journal of
         Contemporary History, 23(1988), 291-311.

1560.   Madariaga, Isabel de. "Salvador de Madariaga et le Foreign
         Office: Un episode d'histoire diplomatique, Juillet-décembre
         1936." Revista de Estudios Internacionales, 4(1983), 229-55.

1561.   Schieder, Wolfgang, and Dipper, Christof, eds. Der spanische
         Bürgerkrieg in der internationalen Politik, 1936-1939. Munich,
         1976.

         The international implications are also examined in Robert A.
         Friedlander, "Great Power Politics and Spain's Civil War: The
         First Phase," Historian, 28(1965), 72-95; Dante A. Puzzo, Spain
         and the Great Powers, 1936-1941 (New York, 1962); Patricia van
         der Esch, Prelude to War: The International Repercussions of the
         Spanish Civil War, 1936-1939 (The Hague, 1951); with
         subsequent developments in Marion Einhorn, Wer half Franco?
         Spanien in der Politik Grossbritanniens und der USA, 1939-1953
         (Berlin, 1983).

1562.   Stone, Glyn A. "Britain, Non-Intervention and the Spanish Civil
         War." European Studies Review, 9(1979), 129-49.

         See also I. Pakhomov, Sovetskii Souz i problema
         "nevmeshatelstva" v dela Ispanii, 1936-1939 (Moscow, 1990);
         Giuseppe Vedovato, "Il non intervento in Spagna, 31 luglio 1936-
         19 aprile 1937," Rivisti di studi politici internazionali, 49(1982),
         529-54; David Carlton, "Eden, Blum and the Origins of Non-
         Intervention," Journal of Contemporary History, 6(1971), 40-55;
         M.D. Gallagher, "Léon Blum and the Spanish Civil War," Journal
         of Contemporary History, 6 (1971), 56-64; and Geoffrey Warner,

"France and Non-Intervention in Spain, July-August, 1936," International Affairs, 38(1962), 203-20.

1563. Thomas, Hugh. The Spanish Civil War. 2nd ed. London, 1977.

A very comprehensive military, diplomatic and political analysis; see also Raymond Carr, The Spanish Tragedy: The Civil War in Perspective (London, 1977); Gabriel Jackson, The Spanish Republic and the Civil War, 1931-1939 (Princeton, NJ, 1965); and Hellmuth Günther Dahms, Der spanische Bürgerkrieg, 1936-1939 (Tübingen, 1962).

1564. Watkins, K.W. Britain Divided: The Effect of the Spanish Civil War on British Public Opinion. London, 1963.

Opinion as reflected in newspapers, weeklies and journals; more narrowly, see The Guardian Book of the Spanish Civil War, edited by Robert Haigh et al. (Aldershot, 1986); the civil war as "living history" (Introduction); from the pages of the Manchester Guardian.

1565. Whealey, Robert H. Hitler and Spain: The Nazi Role in the Spanish Civil War, 1936-1939. London, 1989.

See also his "Economic Influence of the Great Powers in the Spanish Civil War: From the Popular Front to the Second World War," International History Review, 2(1983), 229-54; and "Foreign Intervention in the Spanish Civil War," in The Republic and the Civil War in Spain, edited by Raymond Carr (London, 1971); other studies of major power involvement in the civil war include John F. Coverdale, Italian Intervention in the Spanish Civil War (Princeton, NJ, 1975); Hans-Henning Abendroth, Hitler in der spanischen Arena: Die deutsch-spanischen Beziehungen im Spannungsfeld der europäischen Interessenpolitik vom Ausbruch des Bürgerkrieges bis zum Ausbruch des Weltkrieges, 1936-1939 (Paderborn, 1973); Manfred Merkes, Die deutsche Politik gegenüber dem spanischen Bürgerkrieg, 1936-1939 (Bonn, 1969); Richard P. Traina, American Diplomacy and the Spanish Civil War (Bloomington, IN, 1968); and David Cattell, Soviet Diplomacy and the Spanish Civil War (Berkeley, CA, 1957).

G. THE APPROACH TO WAR, 1937-1939

1. General

1566.   Aster, Sidney.   "Ivan Maisky and Parliamentary Anti-appeasement, 1938-1939," in <u>Lloyd George: Twelve Essays</u>. Edited by A.J.P. Taylor. London, 1971.

1567.   Bédarida, François.   "La 'gouvernante anglaise,' " in <u>Edouard Daladier, Chef de Gouvernement, Avril 1938-Septembre 1939</u>. Edited by René Rémond and Janine Bourdin. Paris, 1977.

1568.   Bedts, Ralph F. de.   <u>Ambassador Joseph Kennedy, 1938-1940: An Anatomy of Appeasement.</u> New York, 1985.

American ambassador at London, 1938-40; and on the same subject, Jane Karoline Vieth, "Joseph P. Kennedy and British Appeasement: The Diplomacy of a Boston Irishman," in <u>U.S. Diplomats in Europe, 1919-1941</u>, edited by Kenneth Paul Jones (Santa Barbara, CA, 1981).

1569.   Charmley, John.   <u>Chamberlain and the Lost Peace</u>. London, 1989.

Concludes that "Chamberlain's reputation stands better now than it has ever done" (Epilogue).

1570.   Colvin, Ian.   <u>The Chamberlain Cabinet: How the Meetings in 10 Downing Street, 1937-1939, Led to the Second World War</u>. London, 1971.

1571.   Dilks, David.   " 'We Must Hope for the Best and Prepare for the Worst': The Prime Minister, the Cabinet and Hitler's Germany, 1937-1939." <u>Proceedings of the British Academy</u>, 73(1987), 309-52.

1572.   Fuchser, Larry William.   <u>Neville Chamberlain and Appeasement: A Study in the Politics of History</u>. New York, 1982.

Extensive use of Neville Chamberlain's letters to his family, although without direct quotation.

1573. Gilbert, Martin. "Horace Wilson: Man of Munich." History Today, 32(1982), 3-9.

Includes interview records; see also Rodney Lowe and Richard Roberts, "Sir Horace Wilson, 1900-1935: The Making of a Mandarin," Historical Journal, 30(1987), 641-62.

1574. Höbelt, Lothar. Die britische Appeasementpolitik: Entspannung und Nachrüstung, 1937-1939. Vienna, 1983.

See also his "Die britische Appeasementpolitik am Vorabend des Zweiten Weltkrieges," Österreichische militärische Zeitschrift, 20(1982), 389-404.

1575. Hoggan, David L. Der erzwungene Krieg: Die Ursachen und Urheber des 2. Weltkriegs. Tübingen, 1966.

A revisionist view, never published in English; similarly see Annelies von Ribbentrop, Die Kriegsschuld des Widerstandes: Aus Britischen Geheimdokumenten, 1938-1939 (Leoni am Starnberger See, 1974); her Deutsch-Englische Geheimverbindungen: Britische Dokumente der Jahre 1938 und 1939 im Lichte der Kriegsschuldfrage (Tübingen, 1967); Otto Werner, England's Kriegspolitik gegen Deutschland (Munich, 1971); and Peter H. Nicoll, Englands Krieg gegen Deutschland: Die Ursachen, Methoden und Folgen des Zweiten Weltkriegs (Tübingen, 1963).

1576. Lamb, Richard. The Drift to War. London, 1989.

For the wider background, see his The Ghosts of Peace, 1935-1945 (London, 1987); including the "missed opportunities of preventing the war" (Introduction).

1577. Lukowitz, David C. "George Lansbury's Peace Missions to Hitler and Mussolini in 1937." Canadian Journal of History, 15(1980), 67-82.

1578. MacDonald, C.A. The United States, Britain and Appeasement, 1936-1939. London, 1981.

On "the American impact on British foreign relations in the classic era of appeasement" (Introduction).

1579. Middlemas, Keith. Diplomacy of Illusion: The British Government and Germany, 1937-1939. London, 1972.

1580. Namier, Lewis B. Diplomatic Prelude, 1938-1939. London, 1948.

With Foreign Office, 1915-20; and Jewish Agency for Palestine, 1929-31, 1940-45; see also his Europe in Decay: A Study in Disintegration (London, 1952); and In the Nazi Era (London, 1952); his material contains documents obtained from Czech and Polish diplomats; see too John Coutouvidis, "Lewis Namier and the Polish Government-in-Exile, 1939-1940," Slavonic and East European Review, 62(1984), 421-28.

1581. Orvik, Nils. "From Collective Security to Neutrality: The Nordic Powers, the League of Nations, Britain and the Approach of War, 1935-1939," in Studies in International History: Essays Presented to W. Norton Medlicott. Edited by K. Bourne and D.C. Watt. London, 1967.

1582. Ovendale, Ritchie. Appeasement and the English Speaking World: Britain, the United States, the Dominions and the Policy of 'Appeasement,' 1937-1939. Cardiff, 1975.

Based on British, American and Dominion sources.

1583. Parker, R.A.C. "Grossbritannien und Deutschland, 1936-1937," in Weltpolitik, 1933-1939. Edited by Oswald Hauser. Göttingen, 1973.

1584. Powers, Richard Howard. "Winston Churchill's Parliamentary Commentary on British Foreign Policy, 1935-1938." Journal of Modern History, 26(1954), 179-82.

1585. Rock, William R. Chamberlain and Roosevelt: British Foreign Policy and the United States, 1937-1940. Columbus, OH, 1988.

See also his Appeasement on Trial: British Foreign Policy and Its Critics, 1938-1939 (Hamden, CT, 1966).

1586. Rose, Norman. "The Resignation of Anthony Eden." Historical Journal, 25(1982), 911-31.

1587. Stadelmann, Rudolf. "Deutschland und England am Vorabend des Zweiten Weltkriegs," in Festschrift für Gerhard Ritter zu seinem 60. Geburtstag. Edited by Richard Nürnberger. Tübingen, 1950.

1588. Strauch, Rudi. <u>Sir Nevile Henderson, britischer Botschafter in Berlin von 1937 bis 1939: Ein Beitrag zur diplomatischen Vorgeschichte des Zweiten Weltkrieges</u>. Bonn, 1959.

See too Vaughan B. Baker, "Nevile Henderson in Berlin: A Reevaluation," <u>Red River Valley Historical Journal of World History</u>, 2(1977), 341-57; and John D. Marble, "The Henderson-Weizsäcker Relationship Prior to the Munich Conference," <u>ibid.</u>, 134-40.

1589. Thorne, Christopher. <u>The Approach of War, 1938-1939</u>. London, 1967.

1590. Watt, D.C. "Misinformation, Misconception, Mistrust: Episodes in British Policy and the Approach of War, 1938-1939," in <u>High and Low Politics in Modern Britain: Ten Studies</u>. Edited by Michael Bentley and John Stevenson. London, 1983.

See also his "Roosevelt and Neville Chamberlain: Two Appeasers," <u>International Journal</u>, 28(1973), 185-204; and "South African Attempts to Mediate between Britain and Germany, 1935-1938," in <u>Studies in International History: Essays Presented to W. Norton Medlicott</u>, edited by K. Bourne and D.C. Watt (London, 1967).

1591. Wright, Jonathan, and Stafford, Paul. "Hitler, Britain and the Hossbach Memorandum." <u>Militärgeschichtliche Mitteilungen</u>, 42(1987), 77-123.

2. Anschluss and Munich, 1938

1592. Ashton-Gwatkin, Frank T.A. "The Personal Story of the Runciman Mission." <u>Listener</u>, 40(1948), 595-97.

By a Foreign Office member of the mission; part of an anniversary series published between 21 October and 9 December 1948; other contributors were Robert Bruce Lockhart, Lord Vansittart, Harold Nicolson, Lewis B. Namier, Cyril Falls and Lord Templewood.

1593. Aulach, Harindar. "Britain and the Sudeten Issue, 1938: The Evolution of a Policy." <u>Journal of Contemporary History</u>, 18(1983), 233-59.

See too Keith Robbins, "Konrad Henlein, the Sudeten Question and British Foreign Policy," <u>Historical Journal</u>, 12 (1969), 674-97.

1594.   Black, Naomi. "Decision-Making and the Munich Crisis." British Journal of International Studies, 6(1980), 278-309.

1595.   Bolech Cecchi, Donatella. L'accordo di due imperi: L'accordo italo-inglese del 16 aprile 1938. Milan, 1977.

See also the same author's "I rapporti italo-britannici durante la crisi dei Sudeti e la conferenza di Monaco," Il politico, 41(1976), 277-314; " 'L'accordo di due imperi,' L'accordo italo-inglese del 16 aprile 1938: Le relazioni italo-inglesi dal luglio 1937 alle dimissioni di Anthony Eden," Il politico, 38(1973), 737-69; "L'entrata in vigore dell'accordo anglo-italiano del 16 aprile 1938," Il politico, 41(1976), 449-91; and the continuation in Non bruciare i ponti con Roma: Le relazioni fra l'Italia, la Gran Bretagna e la Francia dall'accordo di Monaco allo scoppio della seconda guerra mondiale (Milan, 1986).

1596.   Braddick, Henderson B. Germany, Czechoslovakia and the "Grand Alliance" in the May Crisis, 1938. Denver, CO, 1969.

Includes some private correspondence with participants in the events; see too William V. Wallace, "The Making of the May Crisis of 1938," Slavonic and East European Review, 41(1963), 368-90; D.C. Watt, "The May Crisis of 1938: A Rejoinder to Mr. Wallace," Slavonic and East European Review, 44(1966), 475-80; William V. Wallace, "A Reply to Mr. Watt," Slavonic and East European Review, 44(1966), 480-86; Gerhard L. Weinberg, "The May Crisis, 1938," Journal of Modern History, 29(1957), 213-25; D.C. Watt, "Hitler's Visit to Rome and the May Weekend Crisis: A Study in Hitler's Response to External Stimuli," Journal of Contemporary History, 9(1974), 23-32; Heinz Königer, Der Weg nach München: Über die Mai- und Septemberkrise im Jahre 1938 und ihre Vorgeschichte (Berlin, 1958); and the same author's "Über die Maikrise von 1938 und ihre Behandlung in der westdeutschen Geschichtsschreibung," Zeitschrift für Geschichtswissenschaft, 7(1959), 60-79.

1597.   Brügel, Johann W. Tschechen und Deutsche, 1918-1938. Munich, 1967.

Czechoslovakia before Munich: The German Minority Problem and British Appeasement Policy (London, 1973) is his adaptation with new British archival material; see also the same author's "Der Runciman Bericht," Vierteljahrshefte für Zeitgeschichte, 26(1978), 652-59.

1598.   Butler, R.A.   "The Issues in British Foreign Policy."   International Affairs, 17(1938), 386-94.

1599.   Calvet, Henri.   "Aux origines de Munich: Le rôle du 'Times.' " Revue d'histoire de la deuxième guerre mondiale, 3(1953), 25-32.

        See also R.J. Mokken, "The Times and Munich," Gazette, 4(1958), 145-63.

1600.   Douglas, Roy.   In the Year of Munich.   London, 1977.

        Written on the basis of Public Record Office material and some private papers; continued in The Advent of War, 1939-1940 (London, 1978); and New Alliances, 1940-1941 (London, 1982); see also his "Chamberlain and Eden, 1937-1938," Journal of Contemporary History, 13(1978), 97-116.

1601.   Dreifort, John.   "France, Britain and Munich: An Interim Assessment."   Proceedings of the Annual Meeting of the Western Society for French History, 1(1973), 356-75.

        See also Gilbert Fergusson, "Munich: The French and British Roles," International Affairs, 44(1968), 649-65.

1602.   Eatwell, Roger.   "Munich, Public Opinion and Popular Front." Journal of Contemporary History, 6(1971), 122-39.

1603.   Fair, John D.   "The Chamberlain-Temperley Connection: Munich's Historical Dimension."   Historian, 48(1985), 1-23.

1604.   Gedye, G.E.R.   Fallen Bastions.   London, 1939.

        Well-informed study by author expelled from Austria by Gestapo, 1938; previously on staff of Inter-allied Rhineland High Commission, Cologne, 1919-22; journalist with The Times, Daily Express, and New York Times, 1922-41; special military duties in Middle East, 1941-45.

1605.   Hadley, William Waite.   Munich: Before and After.   London, 1944.

        By the editor of the Sunday Times, 1932-50; for another informed contemporary account, see Hubert Ripka, Munich: Before and After (London, 1939).

1606.   Haigh, R.H., et al., eds. The Guardian Book of Munich. Aldershot, 1988.

From the pages of the Manchester Guardian.

1607.   Hauner, Milan. "Czechoslovakia as a Military Factor in British Considerations of 1938." Journal of Strategic Studies, 1(1978), 194-222.

See also Jonathan Zorach, "Czechoslovakia's Fortifications: Their Development and Role in the 1938 Munich Crisis," Militärgeschichtliche Mitteilungen, 20(1976), 81-94; and his "The British View of the Czechs in the Era before the Munich Crisis," Slavonic and East European Review, 57(1979), 56-70.

1608.   Hauser, Oswald. "Lord Halifax und Hitler, November 1937," in Staat und Gesellschaft im politischen Wandel: Beiträge zur Geschichte der modernen Welt. Edited by Werner Pöls. Stuttgart, 1979.

See also Lois G. Schwoerer, "Lord Halifax's Visit to Germany, November 1937," Historian, 32(1970), 353-75.

1609.   Hill, Leonidas. "Three Crises, 1938-1939." Journal of Contemporary History, 3(1968), 113-44.

Based on the Weizsäcker papers; analyses the Munich, Prague and Polish crises.

1610.   Institut d'Etudes Slaves. Munich, 1938: Mythes et réalités. Paris, 1979.

A collection of essays; vol. 52 of Revue des études slaves.

1611.   Kennedy, Aubrey Leo. "Munich: The Disintegration of British Statesmanship." Quarterly Review, 286(1948), 425- 44.

1612.   Kenny, Marion L. "The Role of the House of Commons in British Foreign Policy during the 1937-1938 Session," in Essays in Honour of Conyers Read. Edited by Norton Downs. Chicago, IL, 1953.

1613.   Lammers, Donald N. Explaining Munich: The Search for Motive in British Policy. Stanford, CA, 1966.

With emphasis on policy and attitudes towards the USSR; takes into consideration Soviet published sources.

1614. Lee, Dwight Erwin, ed. Munich: Blunder, Plot or Tragic Necessity? Lexington, MA, 1970.

For another selection of contemporary documents and subsequent historical assessments, see also Peace or Appeasement? Hitler, Chamberlain, and the Munich Crisis, edited by Francis L. Loewenheim (Boston, MA, 1965).

1615. Low, Alfred D. The Anschluss Movement, 1931-1938, and the Great Powers. New York, 1985.

On this subject see also Anschluss 1938, edited by Rudolf Neck and Adam Wandruszka (Munich, 1981); Norbert Schausberger, Der Griff nach Österreich; der Anschluss (Vienna, 1978); Jürgen Gehl, Austria, Germany and the Anschluss, 1931-1938 (London, 1963); Lajos Kerekes, Anschluss 1938 (Budapest, 1963); Gordon Brook-Shepherd, Anschluss: The Rape cf Austria (London, 1963); and for background, Rheinhold Wagnleitner, "Die britische Österreichpolitik 1936 oder 'The Doctrine of Putting off the Evil Day,' " in Das Juliabkommen von 1936, edited by Ludwig Jedlicka and Rudolf Neck (Munich, 1977); Ulrich Eichstädt, Von Dollfuss zu Hitler: Geschichte des Anschlusses Österreichs, 1933-1938 (Wiesbaden, 1955).

1616. McMahon, Deirdre. "Ireland, the Dominions and the Munich Crisis." Irish Studies in International Relations, 1(1979), 30-37.

1617. Murray, Williamson. "German Air Power and the Munich Crisis," in War and Society: A Yearbook of Military History. Vol. 2. Edited by Brian Bond and Ian Roy. London, 1977.

See too his "Munich 1938: The Military Confrontation," Journal of Strategic Studies, 2(1979), 282-302; and John Terraine, "The Munich Surrender: An Attempt at a Military Equation," Journal of the Royal United Services Institute for Defence Studies, 127(1982), 56-61.

1618. Newman, Michael. "The Origins of Munich: British Policy in Danubian Europe, 1933-1937." Historical Journal, 21(1978), 371-86.

1619. Parker, R.A.C. "Anglo-French Conversations, April and September 1938," in Centre National de la Recherche

Scientifique, Les relations franco-allemandes, 1933-1939. Paris, 1976.

1620. Pyper, C.B. Chamberlain and His Critics: A Statesman Vindicated. London, 1962.

1621. Quartararo, Rosaria. "Inghilterra e Italia: Dal patto di Pasqua a Monaco, Con un'appendice sul 'canale segreto' italo-inglese." Storia contemporanea, 7(1976), 607-716.

1622. Raschhofer, Hermann. Völkerbund und Münchener Abkommen: Die Staatengesellschaft von 1938. Munich, 1976.

1623. Reed, Douglas. Insanity Fair. London, 1938.

Anti-appeasement sentiment from the Berlin and central European correspondent of The Times, 1929-38; special correspondent, the News Chronicle, 1938-39; among his numerous other works, see the sequel From Smoke to Smother, 1938-1948 (London, 1948); Disgrace Abounding (1939); and A Prophet at Home (London, 1941).

1624. Scott, William. "Neville Chamberlain and Munich: Two Aspects of Power," in The Responsibility of Power: Historical Essays in Honor of Hajo Holborn. Edited by Leonard Krieger and Fritz Stern. New York, 1967.

1625. Smith, Adrian. "Macmillan and Munich: The Open Conspirator." Dalhousie Review, 68(1989), 235-47.

1626. Stronge, Brigadier H.C.T. "The Czechoslovak Army and the Munich Crisis: A Personal Memorandum," in War and Society: A Yearbook of Military History. Vol. 1. Edited by Brian Bond and Ian Roy. London, 1975.

British military attaché, Belgrade and Prague, 1936-39.

1627. Taylor, Telford. Munich: The Price of Peace. New York, 1979.

Over 1,000 pages; massively documented with both published and archival sources; similarly well-documented studies include Boris Celovsky, Das Münchener Abkommen, 1938 (Stuttgart, 1958); and Helmut K.G. Rönnefarth, Die Sudetenkrise in der internationalen Politik: Entstehung, Verlauf, Auswirkung, 2 vols. (Wiesbaden, 1961); fiftieth anniversary analyses are by Tony Gilbert, Treachery at Munich (London, 1989); Robert Kee, Munich:

The Eleventh Hour (London, 1988); Robert Shepherd, A Class Divided: Appeasement and the Road to Munich, 1938 (London, 1988); Robert Rothschild, Les chemins de Munich: Une nuit de sept ans, 1932-1939 (Paris, 1988); François Paulhac, Les accords de Munich et les origines de la Guerre de 1939 (Paris, 1988); and Pierre Le Goyet, Munich, "un traquenard"? (Paris, 1988); other studies are by Stanislav Biman and Roman Cilek, Der Fall Grün und das Münchener Abkommen (Berlin, 1983); Roger Massip and Jean Descola, Il y a 40 ans: Munich (Paris, 1978); Keith Robbins, Munich, 1938 (London, 1968); Laurence Thompson, The Greatest Treason: The Untold Story of Munich (London, 1968); Keith Eubank, Munich (Norman, OK, 1963); John W. Wheeler-Bennett, Munich: Prologue to Tragedy (London, 1948); Henri Noguères, Munich ou la drôle de paix (Paris, 1963); and Geneviève Vallette and Jacques Bouillon, Munich, 1938 (Paris, 1964); for a Soviet-oriented view, see Andrew Rothstein, The Munich Conspiracy (London, 1958).

1628. Teichova, Alice. An Economic Background to Munich: International Business and Czechoslovakia, 1918-1938. London, 1974.

With much on British economic interests in central Europe.

1629. Vital, David. "Czechoslovakia and the Powers, September 1938." Journal of Contemporary History, 1(1966), 37-67.

1630. Volkov, V.K., ed. Munkhen: Preddverie voiny. Moscow, 1988.

Ten essays on various aspects of the subject; see also the same author's Munkhenskii sgovor i Balkanskie strany (Moscow, 1978); and V.G. Poliakov, Angliia i Munkhenskii sgovor, mart-sentiabr 1938g. (Moscow, 1960).

1631. Wallace, William V. "Roosevelt and British Appeasement, 1938." Bulletin of the British Association of American Studies, 5(1962), 4-30.

1632. Watt, D.C. "Der Einfluss der Dominions auf die britische Aussenpolitik vor München 1938." Vierteljahrshefte für Zeitgeschichte, 8(1960), 64-74.

1633. Webster, Charles. "Munich Reconsidered: A Survey of British Policy." International Affairs, 37(1961), 137-53.

1634. Weinberg, Gerhard L. "Munich after 50 Years." Foreign Affairs, 67(1988), 165-78.

With more in Gerhard Weinberg, William R. Rock and Anna M. Cienciala, "Essay and Reflection: The Munich Crisis Revisited," International History Review, 11(1989), 668-88; and Robert J. Beck, "Munich's Lessons Reconsidered," International Security, 14(1989), 161-91.

3. From Munich to Danzig, 1938-1939

1635. Alexandroff, Alan, and Rosecrance, Richard. "Deterrence in 1939." World Politics, 29(1977), 404-24.

See also Robert Jervis, "Deterrence and Perception," International Security, 7(1983), 3-30.

1636. Aster, Sidney. 1939: The Making of the Second World War. London, 1973.

An analysis from the post-Munich period to the outbreak of war; based on an extensive array of private papers, interviews, and Public Record Office materials.

1637. Batowski, Henryk. "The Polish-British and Polish-French Treaties of 1939." Polish Western Affairs, 14(1973), 78-98.

See also his "August 31st, 1939 in Berlin," Polish Western Affairs, 4(1963), 20-50; and Kryzys Dyplomatyczny w Europie: Jesien 1938-Wiosna 1939 (Warsaw, 1962).

1638. Bezymenskii, L.A. "Novye materialy o peregovorakh Vilsona-Voltata, leto 1939g." Novaia i noveishaia istoriia, 23(1979), 83-105.

More in Marcello Dell-Omodarme, "La missione Wohlthat," Rivista di studi politici internazionali, 26(1959), 235-42; and Helmut Metzmacher, "Deutsch-englische Ausgleichs-bemühungen im Sommer 1939," Vierteljahrshefte für Zeitgeschichte, 14(1966), 369-412.

1639. Broszat, Martin. "Die Reaktion der Mächte auf den 15. März 1939." Bohemia: Jahrbuch des Collegium Carolinum, 8 (1967), 253-80.

1640. Cienciala, Anna M. Poland and the Western Powers, 1938-1939:
A Study in the Interdependence of Eastern and Western Europe.
London, 1968.

A well-documented study, including Polish-language materials;
see also her "Poland in British and French Policy in 1939:
Determination to Fight - Or Avoid War," Polish Review,
34(1989), 199-226; and "O Polityce Angielskiej w 1939r," Bellona,
3(1959), 297-301.

1641. Crowe, David M. "Great Britain and the Baltic States, 1938-
1939," in The Baltic States in Peace and War, 1917-1945.
Edited by V. Stanley Vardys and Romuald J. Misiunas. London,
1978.

See also Georg Vigrabs, "Die Stellungnahme der Westmächte und
Deutschlands zu den baltischen Staaten im Frühling und Sommer
1939," Vierteljahrshefte für Zeitgeschichte, 7(1959), 261-79; and
August Rei, "The Baltic Question at the Moscow Negotiations in
1939," East and West, 4 (1955), 20-29.

1642. Doherty, Julian Campbell. Das Ende des Appeasement: Die
britische Aussenpolitik, die Achsenmächte, und Osteuropa nach
dem Münchener Abkommen. Berlin, 1973.

From Munich to the outbreak of war; based on a variety of British
and German archives, private papers and interviews; see also his
"Die Dominions und die britische Aussenpolitik von München bis
zum Kriegsausbruch 1939," Vierteljahrshefte für Zeitgeschichte,
20(1972), 209-34.

1643. Douglas, Roy, ed. 1939: A Retrospect Forty Years After.
London, 1983.

Proceedings of a conference at Surrey University; analysis of the
German, British, French, Polish and Soviet views.

1644. Douglas-Hamilton, James. "Ribbentrop and War." Journal of
Contemporary History, 5(1970), 45-63.

On unofficial Anglo-German contacts in the summer of 1939.

1645. Haining, Peter. The Day War Broke Out: 3 September 1939.
London, 1989.

Similarly, see Sheila Gordon, 3rd of September 1939 (London, 1988); Adrian Ball, The Last Day of the Old World: 3rd September, 1939 (London, 1963); and Ronald Seth, The Day War Broke Out: The Story of the 3rd September, 1939 (London, 1963).

1646. Haraszti, Eva. "Three Documents Concerning Great Britain's Policy in East-Central Europe in the Period after the Munich Agreement." Acta Historica, 22(1976), 139-75.

1647. Henke, Josef. "Hitler und England Mitte August 1939: Ein Dokument zur Rolle Fritz Hesses in den deutsch-britischen Beziehungen am Vorabend des Zweiten Weltkrieges." Vierteljahrshefte für Zeitgeschichte, 21(1973), 231-42.

1648. Hill, Christopher. "1939." Review of International Studies, 15(1989), 319-28.

1649. Kettenacker, Lothar. "Die Diplomatie der Ohnmacht: Die gescheiterte Friedensstrategie der britischen Regierung vor Ausbruch des Zweiten Weltkrieges," in Sommer 1939: Die Grossmächte und der Europäische Krieg. Edited by Wolfgang Benz and Hermann Graml. Stuttgart, 1979.

1650. Kulski, Wladyslaw W. "The Anglo-Polish Agreement of August 25th, 1939: Highlight of My Diplomatic Career." Polish Review, 21(1976), 23-40.

1651. Le Goyet, Pierre. 15 mars 1939: Le premier "coup de Prague." Paris, 1989.

An account based primarily on French archives and sources.

1652. Lenz, Wilhelm, and Kettenacker, Lothar. "Lord Kemsleys Gespräch mit Hitler Ende Juli 1939." Vierteljahrshefte für Zeitgeschichte, 19(1971), 305-21.

1653. Levine, H.S. "The Mediator: Carl J. Burckhardt's Efforts to Avert a Second World War." Journal of Modern History, 45(1973), 439-55.

1654. Lungu, Dov. "The European Crisis of March-April 1939: The Romanian Dimension." International History Review, 7(1985), 390-414.

And for the wider background, his Romania and the European Great Powers, 1933-1940 (Durham, NC, 1989); see also Svetozar Conkov, "The British Policy of Guarantees and Greece (March-

April 1939)," Studia Balcanica, 4(1971), 187-202; A. Chanady and J. Jensen, "Germany, Rumania and the the British Guarantees of March-April, 1939," Australian Journal of Politics and History, 16(1970), 201-17; and David B. Funderburk, "Nadir of Appeasement: British Policy and the Demise of Albania, April 7, 1939," Balkan Studies, 11(1970), 299-304.

1655. MacDonald, C.A. "Britain, France and the April Crisis of 1939." European Studies Review, 2(1972), 151-69.

1656. Manne, Robert. "Some British Light on the Nazi-Soviet Pact." European Studies Review, 11(1981), 83-102.

See also his "The British Decision for Alliance with Russia, May 1939," Journal of Contemporary History, 9(1974), 3-26; and the background in "The Free Hand in the East: British Policy towards East-Central Europe between 'Rhineland' and the Anschluss," Australian Journal of Politics and History, 32(1986), 245-62.

1657. Mosley, Leonard. On Borrowed Time: How World War Two Began. London, 1969.

A popular account, but solidly based on archival material and numerous interviews.

1658. Newman, Simon. The British Guarantee to Poland: A Study in the Continuity of British Foreign Policy. London, 1976.

See also Oswald Hauser, "Die englische Polengarantie 1939: Startschuss zum Kriege?" in Vom Sinn der Geschichte, edited by Otmar Franz (Stuttgart, 1976); Gottfried Niedhart, "Die britisch-französische Garantieerklärung für Polen vom 31. März 1939: Aussen-politischer Kurswechsel der Westmächte?" Francia, 2(1974), 597-618; William R. Rock, "The British Guarantee to Poland, March 1939: A Problem in Diplomatic Decision Making," South Atlantic Quarterly, 65(1966), 229-40; Keith Eubank, "The British Pledge to Poland: Prelude to War," Southwestern Social Science Quarterly, 45(1965), 340-48; Karel Lapter, "Angielskie Gwarancje dla Polski w 1939r," Sprawy Miedzynarodowe, 6(1959), 3-31; and T. Desmond Williams, 'Negotiations Leading to the Anglo-Polish Agreement of 31 March 1939," Irish Historical Studies, 10(1957), 59-93, 156-92.

1659.   Pankrashova, M., and Sipols, V.I. Why War Was Not Prevented:
         A Documentary Review of the Soviet-British-French Talks in
         Moscow, 1939. Moscow, 1970.

         With numerous extracts from Soviet archives; see also Jack R.
         Dukes, "The Soviet Union and Britain: The Alliance Negotiations
         of March-August, 1939," East European Quarterly, 19(1985), 305-
         20; O.A. Rzheshevskii, "Moskovskie peregovory 1939g.," in
         Prichiny vozniknoveniia vtoroi mirovoi voiny, edited by E.M.
         Zhukov (Moscow, 1982); G. Deborine, "Les négotiations anglo-
         franco-soviétiques de 1939 et le traité de non-agression germano-
         soviétique," Recherches internationales à la lumière du marxisme,
         5(1961), 139-66; Ernst Deuerlein, "Die gescheiterte Anti-Hitler-
         Koalition: Die politischen und militärischen Verhandlungen
         zwischen Grossbritannien, Frankreich und der Sowjetunion im
         Frühjahr und Sommer 1939," Wehrwissenschaftliche Rundschau,
         9(1959), 634-50; Horst Schützler, "Die politischen Verhandlungen
         der Sowjetunion mit Grossbritannien und Frankreich im Frühjahr
         und Sommer 1939," Zeitschrift für Geschichtswissenschaft,
         7(1959), 1716-42; and Werner Basler, "Die britisch-französisch-
         sowjetischen Militärbesprechungen im August 1939," Zeitschrift
         für Geschichtswissenschaft, 5(1957), 18-56.

1660.   Parker, R.A.C. "The British Government and the Coming of War
         with Germany, 1939," in War and Society: Historical Essays in
         Honour and Memory of J.R. Western, 1928-1971. Edited by
         M.R.D. Foot. London, 1973.

1661.   Prazmowska, Anita. Britain, Poland and the Eastern Front, 1939.
         London, 1987.

         With British and Polish archives; see also her "War over Danzig?
         The Dilemma of Anglo-Polish Relations in the Months Preceding
         the Outbreak of the Second World War," Historical Journal,
         26(1983), 177-83; and "The Eastern Front and the British
         Guarantee to Poland of March 1939," European Historical
         Quarterly, 14(1984), 183-209.

1662.   Rhodes, Benjamin D. "The British Royal Visit of 1939 and the
         'Psychological Approach' to the United States." Diplomatic
         History, 2(1978), 197-211.

         See also David Reynolds, "FDR's Foreign Policy and the British
         Royal Visit to the U.S.A., 1939," Historian, 45(1983), 461-72.

1663.   Rock, William R. "Grand Alliance or Daisy Chain: British Opinion
         and Policy toward Russia, April-August, 1939," in Power, Public

Opinion, and Diplomacy: Essays in Honor of Eber Malcolm Carroll. Edited by L.P. Wallace and W.C. Askew. Durham, NC, 1959.

1664. Rzheshevsky, Oleg. Europe 1939: Was War Inevitable? Moscow, 1989.

An analysis with documents; see also A.D. Chikvaidze, Angliiskii kabinet nakanune vtoroi mirovoi voiny (Tbilisi, 1976); A.D. Nikonov, The Origins of World War II and the Prewar European Political Crisis of 1939 (Moscow, 1955); and A.M. Nekrich, Politika angliiskogo imperialisma v Evrope, oktiabr 1938-sentiabr 1939 (Moscow, 1955).

1665. Salter, Sir Arthur. Security: Can We Retrieve It? London, 1939.

1666. Shamir, Haim. "Die Kristallnacht, die Notlage der deutschen Juden und die Haltung Englands?" Jahrbuch des Instituts für deutsche Geschichte, 1(1972), 171-214.

For the wider background, see Anthony Read and David Fisher, Kristallnacht (London, 1990); Rita Thalmann and Emmanuel Feinermann, Crystal Night, 9-10 November 1938 (London, 1974); Lionel Kochan, Pogrom: 10 November 1938 (London, 1957); and Hermann Graml, Der 9. November 1938: "Reichskristallnacht," 3rd ed. (Bonn, 1955).

1667. Smith, Gene. The Dark Summer: An Intimate History of the Events That Led to World War II. London, 1987.

In the same vein, see also Stephen Howarth, August '39: The Last Four Weeks of Peace in Europe (London, 1989); Angela Lambert, 1939: The Last Season of Peace (London, 1989); Robert Kee, The World We Left Behind: A Chronicle of the Year 1939 (London, 1984); Nicholas Fleming, August 1939: The Last Days of Peace (London, 1979); and Walther Hofer, War Premeditated (London, 1959).

1668. Stafford, Paul. "Political Autobiography and the Art of the Plausible: R.A. Butler at the Foreign Office, 1938-1939." Historical Journal, 28(1985), 901-22.

See also his "The Chamberlain-Halifax Visit to Rome: A Reappraisal," English Historical Review, 98(1983), 61-100.

1669. Strang, Lord. The Moscow Negotiations. Leeds, 1968.

Analysis from a British participant; other relevant reminiscences are by Admiral Sir Reginald Plunkett-Ernle-Erle-Drax, "Mission to Moscow," Naval Review, 40-41(1952-53), 339-413, 51-63; N.G. Kuznetsov, Pered voina (Moscow, 1968); and André Beaufre, Le Drame de 1940 (Paris, 1965).

1670.   Teichova, Alice. "Die geheimen britisch-deutschen Ausgleichsversuche am Vorabend des Zweiten Weltkrieges." Zeitschrift für Geschichtswissenschaft, 7(1959), 755-96.

See too her "Great Britain in European Affairs, March 15 to August 21, 1939," Historica, 3(1961), 239-336.

1671.   USSR, Ministerstvo Inostrannikh Del. SSSR v borbe za mir nakanune vtoroi mirovoi voiny, sentiabr 1938g. -avgust 1939g.: Dokumenty i materialy. Edited by A.A. Gromyko et al. Moscow, 1971.

Almost 450 documents from Soviet archives and foreign sources; condensed translation in Soviet Peace Efforts on the Eve of World War II (Moscow, 1973); more in USSR, Ministerstvo Inostrannikh Del, Dokumenty i materialy kanuna vtoroi mirovoi voiny, 1937-1939, edited by A.P. Bondarenko, 2 vols. (Moscow, 1981); and USSR and Czechoslovakia, Ministerstvo Inostrannikh Del, Dokumenty po istorii Munkhensogo sgovora, 1937-1939 (Moscow, 1979).

1672.   Watt, Donald Cameron. How War Came: The Immediate Origins of the Second World War, 1938-1939. London, 1989.

A very detailed and widely documented account of events from the Munich agreement to the outbreak of war.

1673.   Wehner, Gerd. Grossbritannien und Polen, 1938-1939: Die britische Polen-Politik zwischen München und dem Ausbruch des Zweiten Weltkrieges. Frankfurt/M., 1983.

With some Polish-language sources; see also his "Die militärischen Verhandlungen im Anschluss an die britisch-polnische Garantie vom 31. März 1939," Militargeschichtliche Mitteilungen, 44(1988), 51-59; and "Die britisch-polnischen wirtschaftsverhandlungen vor dem ausbruch des Zweiten Weltkrieges," Vierteljahrschrift für Sozial- und Wirtschaftsgeschichte, 74(1987), 549-64.

H. THE SECOND WORLD WAR, 1939-1945

1. Origins and Conduct of the War

1674.   Adamthwaite, Anthony P. The Making of the Second World War.
2nd ed. London, 1977.

Introductory essay with 81 documents; similar in format is his The
Lost Peace: International Relations in Europe, 1918-1939
(London, 1980); and R.J. Overy, The Origins of the Second World
War (London, 1987).

1675.   André, Gianluca, and Pastorelli, Pietro. La seconda guerra
mondiale. 2 vols. Milan, 1964-67.

1676.   Aster, Sidney. " 'Guilty Men': The Case of Neville Chamberlain,"
in Paths to War: New Essays on the Origins of the Second
World War. Edited by Robert Boyce and Esmonde M.
Robertson. London, 1989.

A wide-ranging collection, including, on specific British aspects,
Steven Morewood, "Anglo-Italian Rivalry in the Mediterranean
and the Middle East, 1935-1940"; and Ritchie Ovendale, "Why the
British Dominions Declared War."

1677.   Baumont, Maurice. The Origins of the Second World War. New
Haven, CT, 1978.

Abr. trans. of La faillite de la paix, 1918-1939, 2 vols. (Paris,
1945).

1678.   Bell, P.M.H. The Origins of the Second World War in Europe.
London, 1986.

Including ideological, economic and strategic issues; with analysis
up to 22 June 1941; see also Akira Iriye, The Origins of the Second

World War in Asia and the Pacific (London, 1987); with extensive use of Japanese sources.

1679.   Bullock, Alan. Hitler and the Origins of the Second World War. London, 1967.

A synthesis of the evidence to that date.

1680.   Calvocoressi, Peter, et al. Total War. 2nd ed. London, 1989.

See also the essays in The Second World War as a National Experience, edited by Sidney Aster (Ottawa, Ontario, 1981).

1681.   Carr, William. Poland to Pearl Harbour: The Making of the Second World War. London, 1985.

Which the author terms "a truly global war" (Preface).

1682.   Eubank, Keith. The Origins of World War II. New York, 1969.

A companion volume is his The Road to World War II: A Documentary History (New York, 1973).

1683.   Gilbert, Martin. Second World War. London, 1989.

Massively researched analysis from a global perspective; concluding chapter entitled "Unfinished Business, 1953-"; other fiftieth anniversary accounts include Experience of World War II, edited by John Campbell (London, 1989); John Keegan, The Second World War (London, 1989); Lloyd E. Lee, The War Years: A Global History of the Second World War (London, 1989); Richard Overy and Andrew Wheatcroft, The Road to War (London, 1989); R.A.C. Parker, Struggle for Survival (London, 1989); and H.P. Willmott, The Great Crusade: A New Complete History of the Second World War (London, 1989).

1684.   Girault, René, and Frank, Robert, eds. La puissance en Europe, 1938-1940. Paris, 1984.

The results of a conference at Sèvres, in April 1982; with five essays on British aspects of the subject.

1685.   Hillgruber, Andreas. Zur Entstehung des Zweiten Weltkrieges: Forschungsstand und Literatur. Düsseldorf, 1980.

See also his Der Zweite Weltkrieg, 1939-1945: Kriegsziele und Strategie der grossen Mächte (Stuttgart, 1982).

1686. Israelian, Victor L. The Anti-Hitler Coalition: Diplomatic Co-operation between the USSR, USA and Britain during the Second World War, 1941-1945. Moscow, 1971.

See also V.G. Trukhanovskii, British Foreign Policy during World War II (Moscow, 1970).

1687. Jacob, Sir Ian. "The High Level Conduct and Direction of World War II." Journal of the Royal United Service Institution, 101(1956), 364-72.

See too his "The Turning Point: Grand Strategy, 1942-1943," Round Table, 62(1972), 529-35.

1688. Jacobsen, Hans-Adolf, and Smith, Arthur L. World War II, Policy and Strategy: Selected Documents with Commentary. Santa Barbara, CA, 1979.

A collection of 214 documents from numerous sources; see also Hans-Adolf Jacobsen, 1939-1945: Der zweite Weltkrieg in Chronik und Dokumenten (Darmstadt, 1959).

1689. Lafore, Laurence. The End of Glory: An Interpretation of the Origins of World War II. New York, 1970.

1690. Liddell Hart, Sir Basil H. History of the Second World War. London, 1971.

Other essentially military accounts by British historians include Philip Warner, World War II: The Untold Story (London, 1988); Michael Howard, History of the Second World War (London, 1971); Basil Collier, A Short History of the Second World War (London, 1967); Peter Young, World War, 1939-1945: A Short History (London, 1966); Cyril Falls, The Second World War: A Short History (London, 1950); and John F.C. Fuller, The Second World War, 1939-1945: A Strategical and Tactical History (London, 1948).

1691. Mandel, Ernest. The Meaning of the Second World War. London, 1986.

A Marxist interpretation; footnotes but no bibliography.

1692.   Medlicott, W.N. "The Coming of War in 1939," in From Metternich to Hitler: Aspects of British and Foreign History, 1814-1939. Edited by W.N. Medlicott. London, 1963.

1693.   Michel, Henri. The Second World War. London, 1975.

A comprehensive analysis; extensive bibliography; see too Pierre Miquel, La seconde guerre mondiale (Paris, 1986).

1694.   Niedhart, Gottfried, ed. Kriegsbeginn 1939: Entfesselung oder Ausbruch des Zweiten Weltkriegs? Darmstadt, 1976.

A collection of 18 previously published studies by historians; mainly on Anglo-German relations; see also Kriegsausbruch 1939: Beteiligte, Betroffene, Neutrale, edited by Helmut Altrichter and Josef Becker (Munich, 1989).

1695.   Parkinson, Roger. Peace for Our Time: Munich to Dunkirk, the Inside Story. London, 1972.

Continued in Blood, Toil, Tears, and Sweat: The War History from Dunkirk to Alamein; Based on the War Cabinet Papers of 1940 to 1942 (London, 1973); and A Day's March Nearer Home: The War History from Alamein to VE Day; Based on the War Cabinet Papers of 1942 to 1945 (London, 1974).

1696.   Pelling, Henry. Britain and the Second World War. London, 1970.

Essentially on foreign policy; useful bibliography.

1697.   Remak, Joachim. The Origins of the Second World War. Englewood Cliffs, NJ, 1976.

An introductory essay; with selected documents, 1915-41.

1698.   Robertson, Esmonde M., ed. The Origins of the Second World War: Historical Interpretations. London, 1971.

A collection of 13 previously published essays; none specifically on Britain, yet all are relevant.

1699.   Royal Institute of International Affairs. Chronology of the Second World War. London, 1947.

See also Andreas Hillgruber and Gerhard Hümmelchen, <u>Chronik des Zweiten Weltkrieges: Kalendarium militärischer und politischer Ereignisse, 1939-1945</u> (Düsseldorf, 1978).

1700. Snell, John, ed. <u>The Outbreak of the Second World War: Design or Blunder?</u> Boston, MA, 1962.

A collection of readings and documents; see also his <u>Illusion and Necessity: The Diplomacy of Global War, 1939-1945</u> (Boston, MA, 1963).

1701. Steinert, Marlis G. <u>Les origines de la seconde guerre mondiale</u>. Paris, 1974.

Introductory essay with supporting documents and selections from various historians.

1702. Taylor, A.J.P. <u>The Origins of the Second World War</u>. London, 1961.

To be read in conjunction with <u>The Origins of the Second World War Reconsidered: The A.J.P. Taylor Debate after Twenty-Five Years</u>, edited by Gordon Martel (London, 1986); <u>The Origins of the Second World War: A.J.P. Taylor and His Critics</u>, edited by William Roger Louis (New York, 1972); A.J.P. Taylor, <u>An Old Man's Diary</u> (London, 1984); and his <u>A Personal History</u> (London, 1983); with pieces from the <u>Listener</u> and the <u>London Review of Books.</u>

1703. Vidalenc, Jean. <u>Le second conflit mondial, mai 1939-mai 1945</u>. Paris, 1970.

1704. Woodward, Sir Llewellyn. "Diplomatic History of the Second World War," in <u>New Cambridge Modern History</u>, vol. 12, rev. ed. London, 1968.

See also his "Some Reflections on British Policy, 1939-1945," <u>International Affairs</u>, 31(1955), 273-90.

2. Refugees, Resistance and Peace Moves

1705. Beevor, J.G. <u>SOE: Recollections and Reflections, 1940-1945</u>. London, 1981.

The Special Operations Executive entrusted in July 1940 with executing plans for resistance, sabotage and subversion overseas; contributions from other participants include Ivor Porter, Operation Autonomous: With SOE in Wartime Romania (London, 1989); Nigel Clive, A Greek Experience, 1943-1948 (Salisbury, 1985); Douglas Dodds-Parker, Setting Europe Ablaze (London, 1983); Basil Davidson, Special Operations Europe (London, 1980); Special Operations (London, 1955), an anthology edited by Patrick Howarth; his Undercover (London, 1980); and Bickham Sweet-Escott, Baker Street Irregular (London, 1965).

1706.   Ben-Israel, Hedva. "Im Widerstreit der Ziele: Die britische Reaktion auf den deutschen Widerstand," in Der Widerstand gegen den Nationalsozialismus: Die deutsche Gesellschaft und der Widerstand gegen Hitler. Edited by Jürgen Schmädeke and Peter Steinbach. Munich, 1985.

See also his "Cross Purposes: British Reactions to the German Anti-Nazi Opposition," Journal of Contemporary History, 20(1985), 423-38.

1707.   Bennett, Jeremy. British Broadcasting and the Danish Resistance Movement, 1940-1945: A Study of the Wartime Broadcasts of the BBC Danish Services. London, 1966.

Based on British and Danish sources; similarly see Maura Piccialuti Caprioli, Radio Londra, 1939-1945 (Rome, 1979); Radio Londra, 1940-1945: Inventario delle trasmissioni per l'Italia, 2 vols., edited by the same author, (Rome, 1976); Jean-Louis Cremieux-Brilhac, Ici Londres, 1940-1945: Les voix de la liberté, 5 vols. (Paris, 1975); and André Gillois, Histoire secrète des français à Londres de 1940 à 1944 (Paris, 1973).

1708.   Bentwich, Norman. I Understand the Risks: The Story of the Refugees from Nazi Oppression Who Fought in the British Forces in the World War. London, 1950.

See too his The Refugees from Germany, April 1933 to December 1935 (London, 1936).

1709.   Clogg, Richard. "The Greek Government-in-Exile, 1941-1944." International History Review, 1(1979), 376-98.

See also his "The Special Operations Executive in Greece," in Greece in the 1940's: A Nation in Crisis, edited by John O. Iatrides (London, 1981).

1710.   Cookridge, E.H. Inside SOE: The Story of Special Operations in Western Europe, 1940-1945. London. 1966.

More in Nicholas Kelso, Errors of Judgement: SOE's Disaster in the Netherlands, 1941-1944 (London, 1988); Ian Trenowden, Operations Most Secret: SOE, the Malayan Theatre (London, 1978); and Josef Garlinski, Poland, SCE and the Allies (London, 1969).

1711.   Cruickshank, Charles. The Fourth Arm: Psychological Warfare, 1938-1945. London, 1977.

An analysis of the Political Warfare Executive; based on Public Record Office materials; see also his The German Occupation of the Channel Islands (London, 1975).

1712.   Deakin, F.W.D. The Embattled Mountain. London, 1971.

Seconded to SOE, 1941; led first British military mission to Tito, May 1943; first secretary, British embassy, Belgrade, 1945-46.

1713.   Deroc, Milan. British Special Operations Explored: Yugoslavia in Turmoil, 1941-1943 and the British Response. New York, 1988.

With multinational documentation; see also Michael McConville, A Small War in the Balkans: British Military Involvement in Wartime Yugoslavia, 1941-1945 (London, 1986); Tito-Churchill: Strogo tajno, edited by Dusan Biber (Zagreb, 1981); and British Policy towards Wartime Resistance in Yugoslavia and Greece, edited by Phyllis Auty and Richard Clogg (London, 1975); proceedings of a conference at the School of Slavonic and East European Studies held in July 1973; contains 10 papers, several by former SOE officials.

1714.   Douglas-Hamilton, James. Motive for a Mission: The Story behind Hess's Flight to Britain. London, 1971.

By the son of the Duke of Hamilton onto whose estate Hess parachuted; see also Peter Allen, The Crown and the Swastika: Hitler, Hess and the Duke of Windsor (London, 1983); Wulf Schwarzwäller, Rudolph Hess: The Last Nazi (Bethesda, MD, 1988); J. Bernard Hutton, Hess: The Man and His Mission (London, 1970); and James Leasor, Rudolf Hess: The Uninvited Envoy (London, 1962).

1715.   Fieldhouse, H.N. "The Anglo-German War of 1939-1942: Some Movements to End It by a Negotiated Peace." Transactions of the Royal Society of Canada, 9(1971), 285-312.

1716.   Foot, M.R.D. SOE: An Outline History of the Special Operations Executive, 1940-1946. London, 1984.

By another participant; see also his Resistance: An Analysis of European Resistance to Nazism (London, 1976); "L'Aide à la résistance en Europe," Revue d'histoire de la deuxième guerre mondiale, 23(1973), 39-52; "Special Operations, Parts 1 and 2," in The Fourth Dimension of Warfare, vol. 1, edited by Michael Elliott-Bateman (Manchester, 1970); and "Reflections on SOE," Manchester Literary and Philosophical Society: Memoirs and Proceedings, 111(1968), 87-96.

1717.   Fox, John. "The Jewish Factor in British War Crimes Policy in 1942." English Historical Review, 92(1977), 82-106.

See also his "Great Britain and the German Jews, 1933," Wiener Library Bulletin, 26(1972), 40-46.

1718.   Gilbert, Martin. Auschwitz and the Allies. London, 1981.

Including British attitudes and policy; documented with new material from numerous archives worldwide; and for the wider background see his The Holocaust: A History of the Jews of Europe during the Second World War (London, 1985).

1719.   Gilchrist, Sir Andrew. Bangkok Top Secret. London, 1970.

Joined Siam branch of consular service, 1933; served in British legation, Bangkok, 1933-36, 1938-41; on service in Siam with Force 136, 1944-46.

1720.   Gillman, Peter and Leni. "Collar the Lot!": How Britain Interned and Expelled Its Wartime Refugees. London, 1980.

With more in Miriam Kochan, Britain's Internees in the Second World War (London, 1983); Ronald Stent, A Bespattered Page? The Internment of His Majesty's "Most Loyal Aliens" (London, 1980); and Aaron Goldman, "Defence Regulation 18B: Emergency Internment of Aliens and Political Dissenters in Great Britain during World War II," Journal of British Studies, 12(1973), 120-36.

1721. Glees, Anthony. Exile Politics during the Second World War: The German Social Democrats in Britain. London, 1982.

See also Werner Röder, Die deutschen sozialistischen Exilgruppen in Grossbritannien, 1940-1945, 2nd ed. (Bonn, 1973).

1722. Graham-Murray, James. The Sword and the Umbrella. Isle of Man, 1964.

On the peace moves by the German opposition to Hitler.

1723. Gubbins, Major-General Sir Colin. "SOE and the Co-ordination of Regular and Irregular War," in The Fourth Dimension of Warfare. Edited by Michael Elliott-Bateman. Vol. 1. Manchester, 1970.

See also his "Resistance Movements in the War," Journal of the Royal United Service Institution, 93(1948), 210-23.

1724. Hauser, Oswald. "England und der deutsche Widerstand im Spiegel britischer Akten," in Weltpolitik, Europagedanke, Regionalismus: Festschrift für Heinz Gollwitzer zum 65. Geburtstag. Edited by Heinz Dollinger et al. Münster, 1982.

1725. Hillings, K.G.H. "The Danish Resistance Movement and Its Relations with Great Britain." Revue internationale d'histoire militaire, 53(1982), 105-12.

1726. Hirschfeld, Gerhard, ed. Exile in Great Britain: Refugees from Hitler's Germany. London, 1984.

An interdisciplinary collection of 11 essays dealing with both German and German-Jewish refugees; and of related interest, see Helene Maimann, Politik im Wartesaal: Oster reichische Exilpolitik in Grossbritannien, 1940-1945 (Vienna, 1975); and Austin Stevens, The Dispossessed: German Refugees in Britain (London, 1975).

1727. Hirszowicz, Lukasz. "The Soviet Union and the Jews during World War II: British Foreign Office Documents." Soviet Jewish Affairs, 3(1973), 104-19, 73-90.

1728. Hoffmann, Peter. The History of the German Resistance, 1933-1945. Cambridge, MA, 1977.

Massively documented analysis of the attempts to overthrow the regime or assassinate its leaders; a brief general introduction is his German Resistance to Hitler (Cambridge, MA, 1988); among much on the subject see also Michael Balfour, Withstanding Hitler in Germany, 1933-1945 (London, 1988); Hans Rothfels, The German Opposition to Hitler: An Assessment, 2nd ed. (London, 1987); and Hermann Graml et al., The German Resistance to Hitler (London, 1970).

1729. Kacewicz, George V. Great Britain, the Soviet Union and the Polish Government in Exile, 1939-1945. The Hague, 1979.

With Polish language sources.

1730. Kettenacker, Lothar. "Die britische Haltung zum deutschen Widerstand während des Zweiten Weltkriegs," in Das "Andere Deutschland" im Zweiten Weltkrieg: Emigration und Widerstand in internationaler Perspektive. Edited by Lothar Kettenacker. Stuttgart, 1977.

1731. King, F.P. "British Policy and the Warsaw Rising." Journal of European Studies, 4(1974), 1-18.

1732. Knight, Jonathan. "Churchill and the Approach to Mussolini and Hitler in May 1940: A Note." British Journal of International Studies, 3(1977), 92-96.

1733. Lampe, David. The Last Ditch: The Secrets of the Nationwide British Resistance Organization and the Nazi Plans for the Occupation of Britain, 1940-1944. London, 1968.

1734. Ludlow, Peter W. "The Unwinding of Appeasement," in Das "Andere Deutschland" im Zweiten Weltkrieg: Emigration und Widerstand in internationaler Perspektive. Edited by Lothar Kettenacker. Stuttgart, 1977.

Concentrates on British reaction to peace feelers in the "Phoney War" period; including relevant documents; see also his "Papst Pius XII, die britische Regierung und die deutsche Opposition in Winter 1939-1940," Vierteljahrshefte für Zeitgeschichte, 22(1974), 299-341; and "The Refugee Problem in the 1930s: The Failures and Successes of Protestant Relief Programmes," English Historical Review, 90(1975), 564-603.

1735. MacDonogh, Giles. A Good German: Adam von Trott zu Solz. London, 1990.

On the German resistance figure and his numerous British contacts; see also A Noble Combat: The Letters of Sheila Grant Duff and Adam von Trott zu Solz, 1932-1939, edited by Klemens von Klemperer (London, 1988); the latter's "Adam von Trott zu Solz and Resistance Foreign Policy," Central European History, 14(1981), 351-61; Henry O. Malone, Adam von Trott zu Solz: Werdegang eines Verschwörers, 1909-1938 (Berlin, 1986); Sheila Grant Duff, The Parting of the Ways: A Personal Account of the Thirties (London, 1982); David Astor, "Why the Revolt against Hitler Was Ignored: On the British Reluctance to Deal with German Anti-Nazis," Encounter, 32(1969), 3-13; his "Adam von Trott: A Personal View," in The Challenge of the Third Reich, edited by Hedley Bull (London, 1986); Christopher Sykes, Troubled Loyalty (London, 1968); and Hans Rothfels, "Trott und die Aussenpolitik des Widerstandes," Vierteljahrshefte für Zeitgeschichte, 12(1964), 300-323.

1736.   Marrus, Michael R. The Unwanted: European Refugees in the Twentieth Century. London, 1985.

See too his The Holocaust in History (London, 1989); and more generally Refugees in the Age of Total War, edited by Anna C. Bramwell (London, 1988).

1737.   Martin, Bernd. Friedensinitiativen und Machtpolitik im Zweiten Weltkrieg, 1939-1942. Düsseldorf, 1974.

A very detailed account based on German, American and British archives and private papers; mainly on Anglo-German contacts; see also his "Deutsche Oppositions- und Widerstandskreise und die Frage eines separaten Friedensschlusses im Zweiten Weltkrieg," in Der deutsche Widerstand, 1933-1945, edited by Klaus-Jürgen Müller (Paderborn, 1986); and "Britisch-deutsche Friedenskontakte in den ersten Monaten des Zweiten Weltkrieges: Ein Dokumentation über die Vermittlungsversuche von Birger Dahlerus," Zeitschrift für Politik, 19(1972), 206-21; Walter Lipgens, Europa-Föderationspläne der Widerstands-bewegungen, 1940-1945 (Munich, 1968); and Maxime Mourin, Les tentatives de paix dans la seconde guerre mondiale, 1939-1945 (Paris, 1959).

1738.   Mercuri, Lamberto. Guerra psicologica: La propaganda anglo-americana in Italia, 1942-1946. Rome, 1946.

See also Massimo de Leonardis, La Gran Bretagna e la resistenza partigiana in Italia, 1943-1945 (Milan, 1988); and his

"La Gran Bretagna e la monarchia italiana, 1943-1946," Storia contemporanea, 12(1981), 57-134.

1739. Pavlowitch, Stevan K.   "Out of Context: The Yugoslav Government in London, 1941-1945." Journal of Contemporary History, 16(1981), 89-118.

With more on the subject in his Unconventional Perceptions of Yugoslavia, 1940-1945 (New York, 1985).

1740. Rings, Werner. Life with the Enemy: Collaboration and Resistance in Hitler's Europe, 1939-1945. London, 1982.

A general introduction; still valuable are Jorgen Haestrup, European Resistance Movements, 1939-1945: A Complete History (London, 1981); his Kontakt med England, 1940-1943 (Copenhagen, 1954); Henri Michel, The Shadow War: Resistance in Europe, 1939-1945 (London, 1972); the ten essays by British academics in Resistance in Europe, 1939-1945: Based on the Proceedings of a Symposium at the University of Salford, March, 1973, edited by Stephen Hawes and Ralph White (London, 1975); and the essays of two international conferences held at Liège, 1958, and Milan, 1961, in European Resistance Movements, 1939-1945 (London, 1960, and New York, 1964).

1741. Schöllgen, Gregor. " 'Another' Germany: The Secret Foreign Office Contacts of Ulrich von Hassell during the Second World War." International History Review, 11(1989), 648-67.

See also James Lonsdale Bryans, Blind Victory: Secret Communications, Halifax-Hassell (London, 1951); and his "Zur britischen amtlichen Haltung gegenüber der deutschen Widerstandsbewegung," Vierteljahrshefte für Zeitgeschichte, 1(1953), 347-56.

1742. Schulz, Gerhard, ed. Geheimdienste und Widerstands-bewegungen im Zweiten Weltkrieg. Göttingen, 1982.

With two of six contributions relevant to British aspects; see also his "Zur englischen Planung des Partisanenkriegs am Vorabend des Zweiten Weltkriegs," Vierteljahrshefte für Zeitgeschichte, 30(1982), 322-58.

1743. Sebastian, Peter. I servizi segreti speciali britannici e l'Italia, 1940-1945. Rome, 1986.

An analysis with a documentary appendix of PRO materials.

1744.   Sherman, A.J. Island Refuge: Britain and Refugees from the Third Reich, 1933-1939. London, 1973.

Widely researched, with useful bibliography.

1745.   Simpson, Sir John Hope. The Refugee Problem: Report of a Survey. London, 1939.

MP, 1922-24; vice-president, Refugee Settlement Commission, Athens, 1926-30; mission to Palestine, 1930; director-general, National Food Relief Commission, China, 1931-33.

1746.   Stafford, David. Britain and European Resistance, 1940-1945: A Survey of the Special Operations Executive, with Documents. London, 1980.

"Concerned primarily with demonstrating how SOE and its activities related to the strategic and diplomatic objectives of the British government" (Preface); see also the same author's "SOE and British Involvement in the Belgrade Coup d'État of March 1941," Slavic Review, 36(1977), 399-419; "The Detonator Concept: British Strategy, SOE and European Resistance after the Fall of France," Journal of Contemporary History, 10(1975), 185-217; "Britain Looks at Europe, 1940: Some Origins of SOE," Canadian Journal of History, 10(1975), 231-48; and Jean Overton Fuller, The German Penetration of SOE: France, 1941-1944 (London, 1975).

1747.   Stein, Joshua B. "Britain and the Jews of Danzig, 1938-1939." Wiener Library Bulletin, 32(1979), 29-33.

See as well his "Great Britain and the Evian Conference, 1938," Wiener Library Bulletin, 29(1976), 40-52.

1748.   Tolstoy, Nikolai. Victims of Yalta. London, 1978.

On the forced repatriation of over three million Russians during 1944-47; more on the subject in his The Minister and the Massacres (London, 1986); Mark R. Elliot, Pawns of Yalta (London, 1982); and Nicholas Bethell, The Last Secret: Forcible Repatriation to Russia, 1944-1947 (London, 1974).

1749. Varsori, Antonio. "Italy, Britain and the Problem of a Separate Peace during the Second World War, 1940-1943." Journal of Italian History, 1(1978), 455-91.

See also his "Aspetti della politica inglese verso l'Italia, 1940-1941," Nuova antologia, 552(1983), 271-98; "L'antifascismo e gli alleati: Le missioni di Lussu e Gentili a Londra e Washington nel 1941-1942," Storia e politica, 19(1980), 457-507; and "La politica inglese e il Conte Sforza, 1941-1943," Rivista di studi politici internazionali, 43(1976), 31-57.

1750. Viault, Birdsall S. "Les démarches pour le rétablissement de la paix, septembre 1939-août 1940." Revue d'histoire de la deuxième guerre mondiale, 17(1967), 13-30.

See too his "Mussolini et la recherche d'une paix négociée, 1939-1940," Revue d'histoire de la deuxième guerre mondiale, 27(1977), 1-18.

1751. Wasserstein, Bernard. Britain and the Jews of Europe, 1939-1945. London, 1979.

Based on British, Israeli and Zionist archives.

1752. Watt, D.C. "Les alliés et la résistance allemande, 1939-1944." Revue d'histoire de la deuxième guerre mondiale, 9(1959), 65-86.

1753. Wendt, Bernd-Jürgen. München 1938: England zwischen Hitler und Preussen. Frankfurt/M., 1965.

On the German resistance of the time; see also his "Konservative Honoratioren - Eine Alternative zu Hitler? Englandkontakte des deutschen Widerstandes im Jahre 1938," in Deutscher Konservatismus im 19. und 20. Jahrhundert: Festschrift für Fritz Fischer, edited by Dirk Stegmann et al. (Bonn, 1983).

1754. Young, A.P. The "X" Documents: The Secret History of Foreign Office Contacts with the German Resistance, 1937-1939. Edited by Sidney Aster. London, 1974.

On the A.P. Young-Carl Goerdeler contacts, with an appendix by the editor analysing Foreign Office reaction; the revised German edition, Die "X" - Dokumente: Die geheimen Kontakte Carl Goerdelers mit der britischen Regierung, 1938-1939, edited by Sidney Aster (Munich, 1989), contains an epilogue by Helmut

Krausnick; on Goerdeler's further contacts with the British, see Gerhard Ritter, The German Resistance (London, 1958).

1755. Zayas, Alfred M. de. Nemesis at Potsdam: The Anglo-Americans and the Expulsion of the Germans, Background, Execution, Consequences. London, 1977.

On the transfer of 15 million Germans at the end of the second world war; with multilingual documentation.

3. Intelligence: Prewar and Wartime

1756. Aldrich, R. "Imperial Rivalry: British and American Intelligence in Asia, 1942-1946." Intelligence and National Security, 3(1988), 5-55.

1757. Andrew, Christopher. Secret Service: The Making of the British Intelligence Community. London, 1985.

Comprehensive analysis from the Victorian era to Elizabeth II; see also his "Churchill and Intelligence," in Leaders and Intelligence, edited by Michael I. Handel (London, 1989); "The Mobilization of British Intelligence for the Two World Wars," in Mobilization for Total War: The Canadian, American and British Experience, 1914-1918, 1939-1945, edited by N.F. Dreisziger (Waterloo, Ontario, 1981); "Governments and Secret Services: A Historical Perspective," International Journal, 24(1979), 167-86; "Whitehall, Washington and the Intelligence Services," International Affairs, 53(1977), 390-404; "The British Secret Service and Anglo-Soviet Relations in the 1920s: Part I, From the Trade Negotiations to the Zinoviev Letter," Historical Journal, 20(1977), 673-706; the sequel "British Intelligence and the Breach with Russia in 1927," Historical Journal, 25(1982), 957-64; and the essays he edited in Codebreaking and Signals Intelligence (London, 1986); and with Jeremy Noakes in Intelligence and International Relations, 1900-1945 (Exeter, 1987); with half the contributions on British aspects.

1758. Andrew, Christopher, and Dilks, David. The Missing Dimension: Governments and Intelligence Communities in the Twentieth Century. London, 1984.

Essays include codebreakers and Foreign Offices, British military and economic intelligence of Nazi Germany, the Foreign Office and the SIS before world war two, Enigma, and the Cambridge Comintern.

1759. Bazna, Elyesa. I Was Cicero. London, 1962.

Autobiography of the spy for Germany in the British wartime embassy in Ankara; see also Ludwig C. Moyzisch, Operation Cicero (London, 1950).

1760. Beesly, Patrick. Very Special Intelligence: History of the Admiralty's Operational Intelligence Centre, 1939-1945. London, 1977.

See also Donald McLachlan, Room 39: Naval Intelligence in Action, 1939-45 (London, 1968); the same author's "Naval Intelligence in the Second World War," Journal of the Royal United Service Institution, 112(1967), 221-28; and "Intelligence: The Common Denominator, Parts 1 and 2," in The Fourth Dimension of Warfare, edited by Michael Elliott-Bateman, vol. 1 (Manchester, 1970).

1761. Bennett, Ralph. Ultra and Mediterranean Strategy. London, 1989.

See too his Ultra in the West: The Normandy Campaign of 1944-1945 (London, 1979); and Jock Haswell, The Intelligence and Deception of the D-Day Landings (London, 1979).

1762. Bertrand, Gustave. Enigma ou la plus grande énigme de la guerre, 1939-1945. Paris, 1973.

By a member of French intelligence and a cipher expert.

1763. Best, Sigismund Payne. The Venlo Incident. London, 1950.

See too Johan P. Nater, Het Venlo incident (Rotterdam, 1984).

1764. Boyle, Andrew. The Climate of Treason. London, 1979.

Revelations about British spies Guy Burgess, Donald Maclean, Kim Philby and Anthony Blunt; among too much on the subject, see also John Costello, Mask of Treachery (London, 1988); Barrie Penrose and Simon Freeman, Conspiracy of Silence: The Secret Life of Anthony Blunt (London, 1988); Robert Cecil, A Divided Life: A Biography of Donald Maclean (London, 1988); Chapman Pincher, Their Trade Is Treachery (London, 1981); Douglas Sutherland, The Fourth Man (London, 1980); John Fisher, Burgess and Maclean (London, 1977); Hugh Trevor-Roper, The Philby Affair (London, 1968); and Tom Driberg, Guy Burgess: A Portrait with Background (London, 1956).

1765. Calvocoressi, Peter. Top Secret Ultra. London, 1980.

Memoir-history by a former RAF intelligence officer, stationed at Bletchley Park, which housed the Code and Cypher School, and where Enigma messages were decyphered; see also Gordon Welchman, The Hut Six Story: Breaking the Enigma Codes (London, 1982).

1766. Cecil, Robert. " 'C' 's War." Intelligence and National Security, 1(1986), 170-88.

1767. Clayton, Aileen. The Enemy Is Listening. London, 1980.

On the Y Service, the RAF intelligence branch responsible for interception of enemy communications.

1768. Collier, Basil. Hidden Weapons: Allied Secret or Undercover Services in World War II. London, 1982.

An assessment of intelligence from all sources.

1769. Cruickshank, Charles. Deception in World War II. 2nd ed. London, 1981.

On British attempts at tactical deception of the Germans in Europe and the Middle East; see also the seven essays in Strategic and Operational Deception in the Second World War, edited by Michael I. Handel (London, 1987); and Anthony Cave Brown, Bodyguard of Lies (New York, 1975).

1770. Evans, N.E. "Air Intelligence and the Coventry Raid." Journal of the Royal United Services Institute for Defence Studies, 121(1976), 66-74.

1771. Farago, Ladislas. The Game of the Foxes: The Untold Story of German Espionage in the United States and Great Britain during World War II. London, 1971.

1772. Foot, M.R.D., and Langley, J.M. MI9: Escape and Evasion, 1939-1945. London, 1979.

The intelligence section dealing with training in cases of capture and escape techniques; see also Airey Neave, Saturday at MI9: A History of Underground Escape Lines in Northwest Europe, 1940-1945 (London, 1969).

1773.   Funk, Arthur Layton.   "Churchill, Eisenhower and the French Resistance." Military Affairs, 45(1981), 29-33.

1774.   Garlinski, Josef. Intercept: The Enigma War. London, 1979.

Widely researched, with Polish sources and interviews.

1775.   Glees, Anthony. The Secrets of the Service: British Intelligence and Communist Subversion, 1939-1951. London, 1987.

On the "impact of secrets and intelligence" (Preface).

1776.   Handel, Michael I., ed.   Intelligence and Military Operations. London, 1989.

Includes three contributions on British military operations.

1777.   Hilton, Stanley E. Hitler's Secret War in South America: German Military Espionage and Allied Counter-Espionage in Brazil, 1939-1945. London, 1981.

Based on sources in Portuguese, German and English; see also Leslie B. Rout and John F. Bratzel, The Shadow War: German Espionage and United States Counterespionage in Latin America during World War II (Frederick, MD, 1986); with detailed documentation on activities in Mexico, Brazil, Argentina and Chile.

1778.   Hyde, H. Montgomery. Secret Intelligence Agent. London, 1982.

Another similar contribution is Richard Deacon, With My Little Eye: Memoirs of a Spy Hunter (London, 1982).

1779.   Irving, David, ed.   Breach of Security: The German Secret Intelligence File on Events Leading to the Second World War. London, 1968.

Analyses and reproduces intelligence reports of the Forschungsamt from October 1938 to September 1939; with some related subsequent material.

1780.   Jones, Reginald Victor.   Most Secret War: British Scientific Intelligence, 1939-1945. London, 1978.

Assistant director of scientific intelligence, Air ministry, 1941-46; based on his wartime reports; see also his Reflections on Intelligence (London, 1990); "Science, Intelligence and Policy," Journal of the Royal United Services Institute for Defence Studies, 124(1979), 9-17; Brian Johnson, The Secret War (London, 1978); and Gerald Pawle, The Secret War, 1939-1945, 2nd ed. (London, 1972).

1781.   Kahn, David. Hitler's Spies: German Military Intelligence in World War II. London, 1978.

See also his Kahn on Codes (New York, 1983); and The Codebreakers (London, 1967).

1782.   Kramer, Paul. "Nelson Rockefeller and British Security Coordination." Journal of Contemporary History, 16(1981), 73-88.

1783.   Langhorne, Richard, ed. Diplomacy and Intelligence during the Second World War: Essays in Honour of F.H. Hinsley. London, 1985.

Eight of 12 essays explore British aspects of the topic; including Vansittart and the Foreign Office, Anglo-Spanish, Anglo-Soviet and Anglo-Yugoslav relations, and the British decision to fight on in 1940.

1784.   Lewin, Ronald. Ultra Goes to War: The Secret Story. London, 1978.

A study based on the limited Ultra signals declassified in 1977; see also his complementary study of the war against Japan, The Other Ultra (London, 1982).

1785.   Masterman, Sir John C. The Double-Cross System in the War of 1939 to 1945. London, 1972.

Report, originally written in 1945, based on his work in section BIA of MI5, which dealt with double or ' turned round" agents.

1786.   May, Ernest R., ed. Knowing One's Enemies: Intelligence Assessment before the Two World Wars. Princeton, NJ, 1984.

Includes essays on British intelligence and the coming of the second world war, and the outbreak of the Pacific war.

1787.   Montagu, Ewen. Beyond Top Secret U. London, 1977.

"Top Secret U" being the highest designation of classified documents derived from deciphered enemy messages from the Enigma machine or other sources; headed section 17M of the Naval Intelligence Department, and its representative on the XX Committee, which controlled the traffic transmitted by double agents; see also his The Man Who Never Was: The Story of Operation Mincemeat (London, 1953).

1788.   Morris, L.P. "British Secret Missions in Turkestan, 1918-1919." Journal of Contemporary History, 12(1977), 363-79.

1789.   Mure, David. Master of Deception: Tangled Webs in London and the Middle East. London, 1980.

More on the subject in his Practise to Deceive (London, 1977).

1790.   Murray, Williamson. "Appeasement and Intelligence." Intelligence and National Security, 2(1987), 47-66.

1791.   Peis, Gunther. The Mirror of Deception. London, 1976.

An assessment of the double-cross system; largely based on interviews with former agents.

1792.   Robertson, K.G., ed. British and American Approaches to Intelligence. London, 1987.

Eleven conference papers, mainly British subjects, include intelligence in the 1930s, and world war two and its financing.

1793.   Rohwer, Jürgen, and Jäckel, Eberhard, eds. Die Funkkauflärung und ihre Rolle im Zweiten Weltkrieg. Stuttgart, 1979.

Papers of a 1978 conference on the role of signals intelligence.

1794.   Smith, B.F. "Admiral Godfrey's Mission to America, June-July 1941." Intelligence and National Security, 1(1986), 441-50.

1795.   Stafford, David. " 'Intrepid': Myth and Reality." Journal of Contemporary History, 22(1987), 303-17.

1796.   Stripp, Alan. Codebreaker in the Far East. London, 1989.

On Bletchley Park and Japanese codes; partly autobiographical.

1797.   Toscano, Mario. "Specific Problems in the History of World War II," in his <u>Designs in Diplomacy: Pages from European Diplomatic History in the Twentieth Century</u>. Baltimore, MD, 1970.

Specifically on several intelligence aspects.

1798.   Wark, Wesley K. <u>The Ultimate Enemy: British Intelligence and Nazi Germany, 1933-1939</u>. London, 1985.

See also his "Something Very Stern: British Intelligence, Moralism and Strategy in 1939," <u>Intelligence and National Security</u>, 5(1990), 150-70; "Three Military Attachés at Berlin in the 1930s: Soldier-Statesmen and the Limits of Ambiguity," <u>International History Review</u>, 9(1987), 586-611; "British Intelligence and Small Wars in the 1930s," <u>Intelligence and National Security</u>, 2(1987), 67-87; "In Search of a Suitable Japan: British Naval Intelligence in the Pacific before the Second World War," <u>Intelligence and National Security</u>, 1(1986), 189-211; "Baltic Myths and Submarine Bogeys British Naval Intelligence and Nazi Germany, 1933-1939," <u>Journal of Strategic Studies</u>, 6(1983), 60-81; and "British Intelligence on the German Air Force and Aircraft Industry, 1933-1939," <u>Historical Journal</u>, 25(1982), 627-48.

1799.   Watt, D.C. "Francis Herbert King: A Soviet Source in the Foreign Office." <u>Intelligence and National Security</u>, 3(1988), 62-82.

See too his "An Intelligence Surprise: The Failure of the Foreign Office to Anticipate the Nazi-Soviet Pact," <u>Intelligence and National Security</u>, 4(1989), 512-34; further information on John Herbert King in Gordon Brook-Shepherd, <u>The Storm Petrels</u> (London, 1977).

1800.   Wells, Anthony. "Naval Intelligence and Decision-Making in an Era of Technical Change," in <u>Technical Change and British Naval Policy 1860-1939</u>. Edited by Bryan Ranft. London, 1977.

1801.   West, Nigel. <u>The Sigint Secrets: The Signals Intelligence War, 1900 to Today.</u> London, 1990.

See also his <u>MI5: British Security Service Operations, 1909-1945</u> (London, 1981); <u>MI6: British Secret Intelligence Service Operations, 1909-1945</u> (London, 1983); <u>A Matter of Trust: MI5, 1945-1972</u> (London, 1982); Jock Haswell, <u>British Military</u>

Intelligence (London, 1973); Richard Deacon, A History of the British Secret Service (London, 1969); John Bulloch, MI5: The Origin and History of the British Counter-Espionage Service (London, 1963); and E.H. Cookridge, Secrets of the British Secret Service: Behind the Scenes of the Work of British Counter-Espionage during the War (London, 1948).

1802.   Whiting, Charles. The Battle for Twelveland: An Account of Anglo-American Intelligence Operations within Nazi Germany, 1939-1945. London, 1975.

1803.   Winterbotham, Frederick William. The Ultra Secret. London, 1974.

First details from the British side on Ultra.

1804.   Woytak, Richard A. On the Border of War and Peace: Polish Intelligence and Diplomacy in 1937-1939 and the Origins of the Ultra Secret. Boulder, CO, 1979.

Important for its use of Polish-language sources; see also his "The Origins of the Ultra-Secret Code in Poland, 1937-1938," Polish Review, 23(1978), 79-85; and Wladyslaw Kozaczuk, Enigma: How the German Machine Cipher Was Broken, and How It Was Read by the Allies in World War II, edited by Christopher Kasparek (Frederick, MD, 1984).

1805.   Young, Robert J. "Spokesman for Economic Warfare: The Industrial Intelligence Centre in the 1930s." European Studies Review, 6(1976), 473-89.

4. Diplomacy at War

General Wartime

1806.   Barker, Elisabeth. Churchill and Eden at War. London, 1978.

Principally based on Public Record Office material, and some Macedonian sources; see also her British Policy in South-East Europe in the Second World War (London, 1976).

1807.   Bittner, Donald F. The Lion and the White Falcon: Britain and Iceland in the World War II Era. Hamden, CT, 1983.

1808.   Callahan, Raymond. Churchill: Retreat from Empire. Wilmington, DE, 1984.

Other studies of Churchill's wartime leadership include Tuvia Ben-Moshe, Churchill: Strategy and History (Boulder, CO, 1991); Erich Schwinge, Churchill und Roosevelt aus kontinentaleuropäischer Sicht (Marburg, 1982); J.M. Lee, The Churchill Coalition, 1940-1945 (London, 1980); David Dilks, "Allied Leadership in the Second World War: Churchill," Survey, 21(1975), 19-29; Ronald Lewin, Churchill as Warlord (London, 1973); Patrick Cosgrave, Churchill at War, vol. 1, Alone, 1939-1940 (London, 1974-); R.W. Thompson, Generalissimo Churchill (London, 1973); Maxwell Philip Schoenfeld, The War Ministry of Winston Churchill (London, 1972); his "Winston Churchill as War Manager: The Battle of the Atlantic Committee, 1941," Military Affairs, 52(1988), 122-27; Brian Gardner, Churchill in His Time: A Study in a Reputation, 1939-1945 (London, 1968); Lewis Broad, The War That Churchill Waged (London, 1960); and the recollections of wartime colleagues in Action This Day: Working with Churchill, edited by Sir John W. Wheeler-Bennett (London, 1968).

1809. Chadwick, Owen. Britain and the Vatican during the Second World War. London, 1986.

See also Thomas Moloney, Westminster, Whitehall and the Vatican: The Role of Cardinal Hinsley, 1935-1943 (Tunbridge Wells, 1985); based in part on church archives; and John S. Conway, "The Vatican, Great Britain, and Relations with Germany, 1938-1940," Historical Journal, 16(1973), 147-67.

1810. Day, David. Menzies and Churchill at War. London, 1986.

On Menzies's "failure to topple Churchill in 1941" (Preface); see also his The Great Betrayal: Britain, Australia and the Onset of the Pacific War, 1939-1942 (London, 1988); "Promise and Performance: Britain's Pacific Pledge, 1943-1945," War and Society, 4(1986), 71-93; and Roland Quinault, "Churchill and Australia: The Military Relationship, 1899-1945," War and Society, 6(1988), 41-64.

1811. Feis, Herbert. Churchill, Roosevelt, Stalin: The War They Waged and the Peace They Sought. Princeton, NJ, 1957.

1812. Fisk, Robert. In Time of War: Ireland, Ulster and the Price of Neutrality, 1939-1945. London, 1983.

See also Bernard Share, The Emergency: Neutral Ireland, 1939-1945 (Dublin, 1978).

1813.   Goldman, Aaron. "Germans and Nazis: The Controversy over 'Vansittartism' in Britain during the Second World War." Journal of Contemporary History, 14(1979), 155-91.

1814.   Hachey, Thomas E., ed. Confidential Dispatches: Analyses of America by the British Ambassador, 1939-1945. Evanston, IL, 1974.

Reproduces 14 "Political Reviews" prepared under Lord Lothian and Lord Halifax; authors of individual reviews identified in principal persons' glossary.

1815.   Howard, Michael. The Mediterranean Strategy in the Second World War. London, 1968.

The Lees-Knowles lectures for 1966; see also his "La pensée stratégique," Revue d'histoire de la deuxième guerre mondiale, 23(1973), 1-9; Centre National de la Recherche Scientifique, La guerre en Méditerranée, 1939-1945 (Paris, 1971); Trumbull Higgins, "The Anglo-American Historians' War in the Mediterranean, 1942-1945," Military Affairs, 34(1970), 84-88; and his Soft Underbelly: The Anglo-American Controversy over the Italian Campaign, 1939-1945 (London, 1968).

1816.   Jedrzejewicz, Waclaw, ed. Poland in the British Parliament, 1939-1945. 3 vols. London, 1946-62.

1817.   Kersaudy, François. Churchill and de Gaulle. London, 1981.

A thoroughly documented study of the relationship; see also Jean-Paul Cointet, "Les relations entre de Gaulle et le gouvernement britannique durant la seconde guerre mondiale," Revue historique, 268(1982), 431-51; Douglas Johnson, "Le général de Gaulle et M. Winston Churchill," Etudes gaulliennes, 3(1975), 87-93; and Patrick Keatinge, "De Gaulle and Britain, 1940-1946," International Relations, 12(1965), 754-69.

1818.   Kettenacker, Lothar. "Preussen in der alliierten Kriegs-zielplanung, 1939-1947," in Studien zur Geschichte Englands und der deutsch-britischen Beziehungen: Festschrift für Paul Kluke. Edited by Lothar Kettenacker et al. Munich, 1981.

1819.   Keyserlingk, Robert H. Austria in World War II: An Anglo-American Dilemma. Montreal, Québec, 1988.

Argues that both countries recognised the Anschluss "not only in fact but also in law" (Conclusion); see also his "Arnold Toynbee's Foreign Research and Press Service, 1939-1943, and Its Post-War Plans for South-East Europe," Journal of Contemporary History, 21(1986), 539-58; "Austrian Restoration and Nationalism: A British Dilemma during World War II," Canadian Review of Studies in Nationalism, 9(1982), 279-96; and "Die deutsche Komponente in Churchills Strategie der nationalen Erhebungen, 1940-1942: Der Fall Otto Strasser," Vierteljarshefte für Zeitgeschichte, 31(1983), 614-45.

1820.   Killingray, David, and Rathbone, Richard, eds. Africa and the Second World War. London, 1986.

Ten essays, mainly on the war in anglophone Africa; see also Desmond Dinan, The Politics of Persuasion: British Policy and French African Neutrality, 1940-1942 (Lanham, MD, 1988); and Barbara Baer, "British Views of the Importance of French Africa to the Allied War Effort, 1940-1941," Proceedings of the French Colonial Historical Society, 2(1977), 16-23.

1821.   King, F.P. The New Internationalism: Allied Policy and the European Peace, 1939-1945. Newton Abbot, 1973.

Based on British and American documents.

1822.   Kitchen, Martin. British Policy towards the Soviet Union during the Second World War. London, 1986.

With British documentation only; see also his "Winston Churchill and the Soviet Union during the Second World War," Historical Journal, 30(1987), 415-36; P.M.H. Bell, John Bull and the Bear: British Public Opinion, Foreign Policy and the Soviet Union, 1941-1945 (London, 1990); and The Foreign Office and the Kremlin: British Documents on Anglo-Soviet Relations, 1941-1945, edited by Graham Ross (London, 1984).

1823.   Loewenheim, Francis L., et al., eds. Roosevelt and Churchill: Their Secret Wartime Correspondence. New York, 1975.

Extracts from more than 1,700 messages; extensive editorial notes; see also Churchill and Roosevelt: The Complete Correspondence, edited by Warren F. Kimball, 3 vols. (Princeton, NJ, 1984).

1824. Louis, William Roger. Imperialism at Bay: The United States and the Decolonization of the British Empire, 1941-1945. London, 1978.

As well as "a history of the origins of the trusteeship system of the United Nations" (Preface).

1825. Ludlow, Peter. "Britain and Northern Europe, 1940-1945." Scandinavian Journal of History, 4(1979), 123-62.

See also Edgar Anderson, "Die politische Einstelung Englands zu den baltischen Staaten, 1940-1946," Zeitschrift für Ostforschung, 30(1981), 559-87; Hermann Boehm, Norwegen zwischen England und Deutschland: Die Zeit vor und während des Zweiten Weltkrieges (Lippoldsberg, 1956).

1826. Nicholas, H.G., ed. Washington Despatches, 1941-1945: Weekly Political Reports from the British Embassy. London, 1981.

Introduction by Sir Isaiah Berlin, describing his role in the drafting of the reports; see also the latter's Mr. Churchill in 1940 (London, 1964); Against the Current (London, 1979); and Personal Impressions (London, 1980).

1827. Pawle, Gerald. The War and Colonel Warden. London, 1963.

Based on the recollections of Commander C.R. Thompson, personal assistant to Winston Churchill, 1940-45.

1828. Puto, Arben. From the Annals of British Diplomacy: The Anti-Albanian Plans of Great Britain during the Second World War According to Foreign Office Documents of 1939-1944. Tirana, 1981.

1829. Quinlan, Paul D. Clash Over Romania: British and American Policies toward Romania, 1938-1947. Los Angeles, CA, 1977.

See too Maurice Pearton, British Policy toward Romania (Iasi, 1986).

1830. Roskill, Stephen W. Churchill and the Admirals. London, 1977.

Critical of Churchill's wartime naval policy; see also Arthur J. Marder, Winston Is Back: Churchill at the Admiralty, 1939-1940 (London, 1972); an English Historical Review Supplement, number 5; the reply in Stephen W. Roskill, "Marder, Churchill and the Admiralty, 1939-1942," Journal of the Royal United Services Institute, 117(1972), 49-53; and the more general studies by Richard Hough, Former Naval Person: Churchill and the Wars at Sea (London, 1985); and Sir Peter Gretton, Former Naval Person: Winston Churchill and the Royal Navy (London, 1968).

1831. Sbrega, John J. Anglo-American Relations and Colonialism in East Asia, 1941-1945. London, 1983.

See also his "Determination versus Draft: The Anglo-American Debate over the Trusteeship Issue, 1941-1945," Pacific Historical Review, 55(1986), 256-80; " 'First Catch Your Hare': Anglo-American Perspectives on Indochina during the Second World War," Journal of Southeast Asian Studies, 14(1983), 63-78; and "Anglo-American Relations and the Selection of Mountbatten as Supreme Allied Commander, South East Asia," Military Affairs, 46(1982), 139-45.

1832. Thompson, R.W. Churchill and Morton. London, 1976.

Record of correspondence, from 1960-1962, between R.W. Thompson and Sir Desmond Morton.

1833. USSR, Ministry of Foreign Affairs. Correspondence between the Chairman of the Council of Ministers of the USSR and the Presidents of the USA and the Prime Ministers of Great Britain during the Great Patriotic War of 1941-1945. 2 vols. Moscow, 1957.

Vol. 1, for correspondence with Winston Churchill and Clement Attlee; see also USSR, Ministerstvo Inostrannikh Del, Sovetsko-angliiskie otnosheniia vo vremia velikoi otechest-vennoi voiny, 1941-1945gg.: Dokumenty i materialy, edited by G.P. Kynin et al., 2 vols. (Moscow, 1983).

1834. Voigt, Johannes H. Indien im Zweiten Weltkrieg. Stuttgart, 1978.

A widely documented study; see also Milan Hauner, India in Axis Strategy: Germany, Japan and Indian Nationalists in the Second World War (Stuttgart, 1980); and R.J. Moore, Churchill, Cripps and India, 1939-1945 (London, 1979).

1835. Weber, Frank G. The Evasive Neutral: Germany, Britain and the Quest for a Turkish Alliance in the Second World War. Columbia, MO, 1979.

The problem of Turkish neutrality based on non-Turkish archives; see also John Robertson, Turkey and Allied Strategy, 1941-1945 (New York, 1988); Selim Deringil, Turkish Foreign Policy during the Second World War: An "Active" Neutrality (London, 1989); and Edward Weisband, Turkish Foreign Policy, 1943-1945: Small State Diplomacy and Great Power Politics (Princeton, NJ, 1973), both with Turkish-language sources; Yosef Olmert, "Britain, Turkey and the Levant Question during the Second World War," Middle Eastern Studies, 23(1987), 437-51; Johannes Glasneck and Inge Kircheisen, Türkei und Afghanistan: Brennpunkte der Orientpolitik im Zweiten Weltkrieg (Berlin, 1968); and Nihat Erim Kocaeli, "The Development of the Anglo-Turkish Alliance," Asiatic Review, 42(1946), 347-51.

1836. Weinberg, Gerhard L. World in the Balance: Behind the Scenes of World War II. London, 1981.

Six essays, four previously published; good bibliography.

The Sole Belligerent

1837. Barclay, Glen St. J. Their Finest Hour. London, 1977.

A diplomatic and military analysis of the period June 1940 to June 1941; based on British, Australian and New Zealand archives; see also his "Singapore Strategy: The Role of the United States in Imperial Defense," Military Affairs, 49(1975), 54-58.

1838. Batowski, Henryk. "Polish-British Relations in September 1939: On the Basis of Foreign Office Archives." Polish Western Affairs, 13(1972), 108-16.

1839. Bayer, J.A. "British Policy towards the Russo-Finnish Winter War, 1939-1940." Canadian Journal of History, 16 (1981), 27-65.

See too Martti Häikiö, Maaliskuusta maaliskuuhun: Suomi Englannin politiikassa, 1939-1940 (Helsinki, 1976).

1840. Bédarida, François. La stratégie secrète de la drôle de guerre: Le conseil suprême interallié, septembre 1939-avril 1940. Paris, 1979.

The French records of the Supreme War Council, with an introduction and commentary; see also his "France, Britain and the Nordic Countries," Scandinavian Journal of History, 2(1977), 7-27.

1841.   Bell, P.M.H.   A Certain Eventuality: Britain and the Fall of France. London, 1974.

See also Eleanor M. Gates, End of the Affair: The Collapse of the Anglo-French Alliance, 1939-1940 (Berkeley, CA, 1981); Douglas Johnson, "Britain and France in 1940," Transactions of the Royal Historical Society, 22(1972), 141-57; John C. Cairns, "De Gaulle Confronts the British: The Legacy of 1940," International Journal, 23(1968), 187-210; and his "Great Britain and the Fall of France," Journal of Modern History, 27(1955), 365-409.

1842.   Bond, Brian.   "Leslie Hore-Belisha at the War Office," in Politicians and Defence: Studies in the Formulation of British Defence Policy, 1845-1970. Edited by Ian Beckett and John Gooch. Manchester, 1981.

His France and Belgium (London, 1975) is useful on Anglo-French strategy, 1939-40; see also A.J. Trythall, "The Downfall of Leslie Hore-Belisha," Journal of Contemporary History, 16(1981), 391-409.

1843.   Bosco, Andrea.   "Lothian, Curtis, Kimber and the Federal Union Movement." Journal of Contemporary History, 23(1988), 465-502.

See too Richard Mayne and John Pinder, Federal Union (London, 1990); and John Pinder, "Prophet Not Without Honour: Lothian and the Federal Idea," Round Table, 73(1983), 207-20.

1844.   Centre National de la Recherche Scientifique.   Français et Britanniques dans la drôle de guerre. Paris, 1979.

Proceedings of an Anglo-French conference, 1975; relevant essays on military problems, public opinion and diplomacy.

1845.   Curtright, Lynn H.   "Great Britain, the Balkans and Turkey in the Autumn of 1939." International History Review, 10(1988), 433-55.

See also Frank Marzari, "Western-Soviet Rivalry in Turkey, 1939," Middle Eastern Studies, 7(1971), 63-77, 201-20.

1846.   Davidson, Major-General F.H.N.   "My Mission to Belgium, 1940." Journal of the Royal United Service Institution, 94(1969), 80-82.

Director of military intelligence, War Office. 1940-44.

1847. Fair, John D. "The Norwegian Campaign and Winston Churchill's Rise to Power in 1940: A Study of Perception and Attribution." International History Review, 9(1987), 410-37.

For background, see François Kersaudy, Norway 1940 (London, 1990).

1848. Grace, Richard J. "Whitehall and the Ghost of Appeasement: November 1941." Diplomatic History, 3(1979), 173-91.

1849. Higham, Robin. "The Ploesti Ploy: British Considerations and the Idea of Bombing the Roumanian Oilfields, 1940-1941." War and Society, 5(1987), 57-71.

See also Günter Kahle, Das Kaukasusprojekt der Alliierten vom Jahre 1940 (Opladen, 1973).

1850. Kedourie, Elie. "Wavell and Iraq, April-May, 1941." Middle Eastern Studies, 2(1966), 373-86.

1851. Kent, George O. "Britain in the Winter of 1940-1941 as Seen from the Wilhelmstrasse." Historical Journal, 6(1963), 120-30.

1852. Kimball, Warren F. The Most Unsordid Act: Lend-Lease, 1939-1941. Baltimore, MD, 1969.

See too his "Lend-Lease and the Open Door: The Temptation of British Opulence, 1937-1942," Political Science Quarterly, 86(1971), 232-59; and " 'Beggar My Neighbour': America and the British Interim Finance Crisis, 1940-1941," Journal of Economic History, 29(1969), 758-72; Barbara Curli, "Keynes e il negoziato sul Lend-Lease, 1940-1941," Storia delle relazioni internationali, 3(1987), 267-94; Leon Martel, Lend-Lease, Loans and the Coming of the Cold War (Boulder, CO, 1979); Charles Smith, "Lend-Lease to Great Britain, 1941-1942," Southern Quarterly, 10(1972), 195-208; Philip Goodhart, Fifty Ships that Saved the World: The Foundation of the Anglo-American Alliance (New York, 1965); and Edward R. Stettinius, Lend-Lease: Weapon for Victory (New York, 1944).

1853. Kimche, Jon. The Unfought Battle. London, 1968.

On events in September 1939; see also Nicholas Bethell, The War Hitler Won: September 1939 (London, 1972).

1854.   Lash, Joseph P. Roosevelt and Churchill, 1939-1941:   The
        Partnership That Saved the West. New York, 1976.

        See too James Leutze, "The Secret of the Churchill-Roosevelt
        Correspondence: September 1939-May 1940," Journal of
        Contemporary History, 10(1975), 465-91.

1855.   Lowe, Peter.   "Winston Churchill and Japan, 1914-1942."
        Proceedings of the British Association for Japanese Studies,
        6(1981), 39-48.

        Mainly on events in 1940-41.

1856.   Lukacs, John.   The Last European War, September 1939-
        December 1941. New York, 1976.

        See also Hanson W. Baldwin, The Crucial Years, 1939-1941: The
        World at War (New York, 1976).

1857.   Mickelson, Martin L. "Another Fashoda: The Anglo-Free French
        Conflict over the Levant, May-September, 1941." Revue français
        d'histoire d'outre-mer, 63(1976), 75-100.

1858.   Nekrich, A.M. Vneshniaia politika anglii, 1939-1941gg. Moscow,
        1963.

        See also V.N. Yegorov, Politika anglii na dalnem vostoke,
        sentiabr 1939-dekabr 1941gg. (Moscow, 1960).

1859.   Nevakivi, Jukka. The Appeal That Was Never Made: The Allies,
        Scandinavia and the Finnish "Winter War," 1939-1940. London,
        1976.

        By a member of the Finnish foreign service and historian; based
        mainly on Finnish-language and British sources; see also R.A.C.
        Parker, "Britain, France and Scandinavia, 1939-1940," History,
        61(1976), 369-87; A.F. Upton, Finland, 1939-1940 (London, 1974);
        and Max Jakobson, The Diplomacy of the Winter War (Cambridge,
        MA, 1961).

1860.   Pankhurst, Richard. "The Ethiopian National Anthem in 1941: A
        Chapter in Anglo-Ethiopian Wartime Relations." Ethiopia
        Observer, 15(1972), 63-66.

1861.   Ponting, Clive. 1940: Myth and Reality. London, 1990.

Among the numerous accounts of this period, see also Roger Parkinson, Dawn on Our Darkness: The Summer of 1940 (London, 1977); Peter Fleming, Invasion 1940 (London, 1975); Laurence Thompson, 1940: Year of Legend, Year of History (London, 1966); Basil Collier, The Battle of Britain (London, 1962); and the sequel 1941: Armageddon (London, 1982).

1862. Reynolds, David. "Roosevelt, the British Left, and the Appointment of John G. Winant as United States Ambassador to Britain in 1941." International History Review, 4(1982), 393-413.

See also Bert R. Whittemore, "A Quiet Triumph: The Mission of John Gilbert Winant to London, 1941," Historical New Hampshire, 30(1975), 1-11.

1863. Rougier, Louis. Les accords Pétain-Churchill: Histoire d'une mission secrète. Montreal, Québec, 1945.

Vichy government emissary to London, 1940; see also his Les accords secrets franco-britanniques de l'automne 1940: Histoire et imposture (Paris, 1954); Prince Xavier de Bourbon, Les accords secrets franco-anglais de décembre 1940 (Paris, 1949); and General Gaston Schmitt, Les accords secrets franco-britanniques de novembre-décembre 1940: Histoire ou mystification (Paris, 1957).

1864. Salmon, Patrick. "Churchill, the Admiralty and the Narvik Traffic, September-November 1939." Scandinavian Journal of History, 4(1979), 305-26.

See also his "British Plans for Economic Warfare against Germany, 1937-1939: The Problem of Swedish Iron Ore," Journal of Contemporary History, 16(1981), 53-71; and more generally, Thomas Munch-Petersen, The Strategy of Phoney War: Britain, Sweden and the Iron Ore Question, 1939-1940 (Stockholm, 1981).

1865. Shlaim, Avi. "Prelude to Downfall: The British Offer of Union to France, June 1940." Journal of Contemporary History, 9(1974), 27-63.

On the same subject see also David Thomson, The Proposal for Anglo-French Union in 1940 (London, 1966); Max Beloff, "The Anglo-French Union Project of June 1940," in Mélanges Pierre Renouvin: Etudes d'histoire des relations internationales (Paris, 1966); and Léon Noël, "Le project d'union franco-britannique de juin 1940," <u>Revue d'histoire de la deuxième guerre mondiale</u>, 6(1956), 22-37.

1866.   Smyth, Denis. <u>Diplomacy and Strategy of Survival: British Policy and Franco's Spain, 1940-1941</u>. London, 1986.

Based on British and Spanish documentation; see too his "Screening 'Torch': Allied Counter-Intelligence and the Spanish Threat to the Secrecy of the Allied Invasion of French North Africa in November, 1942," <u>Intelligence and National Security</u>, 4(1989), 335-56.

1867.   Thomas, R.T. <u>Britain and Vichy: The Dilemma of Anglo-French Relations</u>. London, 1979.

1868.   Wanty, Emile. "Improvisations de la liaison belgo-britannique du 10 au 18 mai 1940." <u>Revue d'histoire de la deuxième guerre mondiale</u>, 14(1964), 29-50.

1869.   Wilson, Theodore A. <u>The First Summit: Roosevelt and Churchill at Placentia Bay, 1941</u>. Boston, MA, 1969.

1870.   Woolf, Stuart J. "Inghilterra, Francia e Italia, settembre 1939-giugno 1940." <u>Rivista di storia contemporanea</u>, 1(1972), 477-95.

Coalition Warfare and Diplomacy

1871.   Arcidianono, Bruno. "The 'Dress Rehearsal': The Foreign Office and the Control of Italy, 1943-1944." <u>Historical Journal</u>, 28(1985), 417-27.

See also Moshe Gat, "The Soviet Factor in British Policy towards Italy, 1943-1945," <u>The Historian</u>, 50(1983), 535-57; and Lamberto Mercuri, "La situazione dei partiti italiani vista dal Foreign Office, dicembre 1943," <u>Storia contemporanea</u>, 11(1980), 1049-60.

1872.   Armstrong, Anne. <u>Unconditional Surrender: The Impact of the Casablanca Policy upon World War II</u>. New Brunswick, NJ, 1961.

Of related interest is Raymond G. O'Connor, <u>Diplomacy for Victory: FDR and Unconditional Surrender</u> (New York, 1971); John L. Chase, "Unconditional Surrender Reconsidered," <u>Political Science Quarterly</u>, 70(1955), 258-79; and Lord Hankey, "Unconditional Surrender," <u>Contemporary Review</u>, 176(1949), 193-98.

1873.   Beaumont, Joan. <u>Comrades in Arms: British Aid to Russia, 1941-1945</u>. London, 1980.

Based mainly on Public Record Office materials and private papers; see also her "Great Britain and the Rights of Neutral Countries: The Case of Iran, 1941," <u>Journal of Contemporary History</u>, 16(1981), 213-28; and "A Question of Diplomacy: British Military Mission, 1941-1945," <u>Journal of the Royal United Services Institute for Defence Studies</u>, 118(1973), 74-77.

1874.   Beitzell, Robert. <u>The Uneasy Alliance: America, Britain and Russia, 1941-1943</u>. New York, 1972.

For an earlier account see David J. Dallin, <u>The Big Three: The United States, Britain, Russia</u> (New Haven, CT, 1945); no footnotes or bibliography.

1875.   Bernstein, Barton J. "The Uneasy Alliance: Roosevelt, Churchill and the Atomic Bomb, 1940-1945." <u>Western Political Quarterly</u>, 29(1976), 202-30.

1876.   Chan Lau Kit-Ching. "The Hong Kong Question during the Pacific War, 1941-1945." <u>Journal of Imperial and Commonwealth History</u>, 2(1973), 56-78.

See also his "Britain's Reaction to Chiang Kai-shek's Visit to India, February, 1942," <u>Australian Journal of Politics and History</u>, 21(1975), 52-61.

1877.   Charmley, John. "Harold Macmillan and the Making of the French Committee of Liberation." <u>International History Review</u>, 4(1982), 553-67.

See also Sydney H. Zebel, "Harold Macmillan's Appointment as Minister at Algiers," <u>Journal of the Rutgers University Library</u>, 41(1979), 79-103.

1878.   Danchev, Alex. <u>Very Special Relationship: Field-Marshal Sir John Dill and the Anglo-American Alliance, 1941-1944</u>. London, 1986.

More on the subject in his " 'Dilly-Dally,' or Having the Last Word: Field-Marshal Sir John Dill and Prime Minister Winston Churchill," <u>Journal of Contemporary History</u>, 22(1987), 21-44; and "A Special Relationship: Field-Marshal Sir John Dill and George C.

Marshall," Journal of the Royal United Services Institute for Defence Studies, 130(1985), 56-61.

1879. Deakin, William, et al., eds. British Political and Military Strategy in Central, Eastern and Southern Europe in 1944. London, 1988.

Proceedings of a conference in December 1984 organised by the British National Committee for the History of the Second World War.

1880. DeNovo, John A. "The Culbertson Economic Mission and Anglo-American Tensions in the Middle East, 1944-1945." Journal of American History, 63(1977), 913-36.

1881. Dobson, Alan P. U.S. Wartime Aid to Britain, 1940-1946. London, 1986.

See also his The Politics of the Anglo-American Economic Special Relationship, 1940-1987 (Brighton, 1983); " 'A Mess of Pottage for Your Economic Birthright?' The 1941-1942 Wheat Negotiations and Anglo-American Economic Diplomacy," Historical Journal, 28(1985), 739-50; and "Economic Diplomacy at the Atlantic Conference," Review of International Studies, 10(1984), 143-63; and the reply to the latter in L.S. Pressnell and Sheila V. Hopkins, "A Canard Out of Time? Churchill, the War Cabinet and the Atlantic Charter, August 1941," Review of International Studies, 14(1988), 223-35.

1882. Dunn, Walter Scott. Second Front Now - 1943. University, AL, 1980.

On the same subject see also V. Zolotarev and S. Lavrov, Vtoroi fronta - sorok let spystia (Moscow, 1987); Roger Beaumont, "The Bomber Offensive as a Second Front," Journal of Contemporary History, 22(1987), 3-19; Peter Böttger, Winston Churchill und die Zweite Front, 1941-1943: Ein Aspekt der britischen Strategie im Zweiten Weltkrieg (Frankfurt/M., 1984); John Grigg, 1943: The Victory That Never Was (London, 1980); George Bruce, Second Front Now: The Road to D-Day (London, 1979); Mark A. Stoler, The Politics of the Second Front: American Military Planning and Diplomacy in Coalition Warfare, 1941-1943 (London, 1977); Trumbull Higgins, Winston Churchill and the Second Front, 1940-1943 (New York, 1957); Igor N. Zemskov, Diplomaticheskaia istoriia otkritiia vtorogo fronta v Evrope, 1941-1944gg. (Moscow, 1980); and his "Diplomatic History of the Second Front," International Affairs (Moscow), 7(1961), 49-57.

1883.   Duroselle, Jean-Baptiste. "Le conflit stratégique anglo-américain de juin 1940 à juin 1944." Revue d'histoire moderne et contemporaine, 10(1963), 161-84.

1884.   Ellwood, David W. Italy, 1943-1945. Leicester, 1985.

A shorter and updated version of L'alleato nemico: La politica dell'occupazione anglo-americana in Italia, 1943-1946 (Milan, 1977); see also his "La politica anglo-americana verso l'Italia 1945: L'anno del trapasso del potere," in L'Italia dalla liberazione alla Repubblica: Atti del Convegno a Firenze il 26-28 marzo 1976 (Milan, 1977); and "Al tramonto dell'impero britannico: Italia e Balcani nella strategia inglese, 1942-1946," Italia contemporanea, 31(1979), 73-91.

1885.   Eshraghi, F. "Anglo-Soviet Occupation of Iran in August 1941." Middle Eastern Studies, 20(1984), 27-52.

Continued in "The Immediate Aftermath of Anglo-Soviet Occupation of Iran in August 1941," Middle Eastern Studies, 20(1984), 324-51; see also Jürg Meister, "Die britisch-sowjetische Intervention im Iran im August 1941," Marine-Rundschau, 79(1982), 647-54; and continued ibid., 80(1983), 25-35.

1886.   Eubank, Keith. Summit at Teheran. New York, 1985.

A comprehensive analysis, based on American and British sources; as is Paul D. Mayle, Eureka Summit: Agreement in Principle and the Big Three at Tehran, 1943 (London, 1987); see also Keith Eubank, The Summit Conferences, 1919-1960 (Norman, OK, 1966).

1887.   Filippone-Thaulero, Giustino. La Gran Bretagna e l'Italia: Dalla conferenza di Mosca a Potsdam, 1943-1945. Rome, 1979.

With an appendix of ten related documents from the Public Record Office.

1888.   Gandin, Robert. Darlan, Weygand, Cunningham: Artisans de la victoire, 1939-1944. Paris, 1977.

1889.   Gaunson, A.B. The Anglo-French Clash in Lebanon and Syria, 1940-1945. New York, 1987.

Detailed analysis, based on British documentation, especially the papers of Major-General Sir Edward Spears; see also his

"Churchill, De Gaulle, Spears and the Levant Affair, 1941," Historical Journal, 27(1984), 697-713; Aviel Roshwald, Estranged Bedfellows: Britain and France in the Middle East during World War II (London, 1990); his "The Spears Mission in the Levant, 1941-1944," Historical Journal, 29(1986), 897-919; and Anthony Mockler, Our Enemies the French: Being an Account of the War Fought between the French and the British, Syria 1941 (London, 1976).

1890.   Gorodetsky, Gabriel. Stafford Cripps' Mission to Moscow, 1940-1942. London, 1984.

With published Soviet sources; see also his "Churchill's Warning to Stalin: A Reappraisal," Historical Journal, 29(1986), 979-90; and "The Hess Affair and Anglo-Soviet Relations on the Eve of 'Barbarossa,' " English Historical Review, 101(1986), 405-20; more on Cripps in Harry Hanak, "Sir Stafford Cripps as British Ambassador in Moscow, May 1940 to June 1941," English Historical Review, 94(1979), 48-70; continued in "Sir Stafford Cripps as Ambassador in Moscow, June 1941-January 1942," English Historical Review, 97(1982), 332-44.

1891.   Herring, George C. "The United States and British Bankruptcy, 1944-1945: Responsibilities Deferred." Political Science Quarterly, 86(1971), 260-80.

1892.   Higham, Robin. Diary of a Disaster: British Aid to Greece, 1940-1941. Lexington, KY, 1986.

Further developments can be followed in E.D. Smith, The British in Greece, 1941-1946 (London, 1988); Procopis Papastratis, British Policy towards Greece during the Second World War, 1941-1944 (London, 1984); Anne Karalekas, Britain, the United States and Greece, 1942-1945 (New York, 1988); British Reports on Greece, 1943-1944 by J.M. Stevens, C.M. Woodhouse and D.J. Wallace, edited by Lars Baerentzen (Copenhagen, 1982); Henry Maule, Scobie, Hero of Greece: The British Campaign, 1944-1945 (London, 1975); George M. Alexander, The Prelude to the Truman Doctrine: British Policy in Greece, 1944-1947 (London, 1983); Heinz Richter, British Intervention in Greece: From Varkiza to Civil War, February 1945-August 1946 (London, 1986); and Stephen G. Xydis, Greece and the Great Powers, 1944-1947: Prelude to the "Truman Doctrine" (Thessaloniki, 1963); see also Martin van Creveld, "Prelude to Disaster: The British Decision to Aid Greece, 1940-1941," Journal of Contemporary History, 9(1974), 65-92; Sheila Lawlor, "Greece, March 1941: The Politics of British Military Intervention," Historical Journal, 25(1982), 933-

46; Alan J. Foster, "The Politicians, Public Opinion and the Press: The Storm over British Military Intervention in Greece in December 1944," Journal of Contemporary History, 19(1984), 453-94; and Elisabeth Barker, "Greece in the Framework of Anglo-Soviet Relations, 1941-1947," in Greece: From Resistance to Civil War, edited by Marion Sarafis (Nottingham, 1980).

1893.   Hughes, E.J. "Winston Churchill and the Formation of the United Nations Organization." Journal of Contemporary History, 9(1974), 177-94.

1894.   Johnson, Howard. "The Anglo-American Caribbean Commission and the Extension of American Influence in the British Caribbean, 1942-1945." Journal of Commonwealth and Comparative Politics, 22(1984), 180-203.

See too John Knape, "British Foreign Policy in the Caribbean Basin, 1938-1945: Oil, Nationalism and Relations with the United States," Journal of Latin American Studies, 19(1987), 279-94.

1895.   Kettenacker, Lothar. "The Anglo-Soviet Alliance and the Problem of Germany, 1941-1945." Journal of Contemporary History, 17(1982), 435-58.

1896.   Kirby, David. "Morality or Expediency? The Baltic Question in British-Soviet Relations, 1941-1942," in The Baltic States in Peace and War, 1917-1945. Edited by V. Stanley Vardys and Romuald J. Misiunas. London, 1978.

1897.   Kowalski, Hans-Günther. "Die 'European Advisory Commission' als Instrument alliierter Deutschland-Planung, 1943-1945." Vierteljahrshefte für Zeitgeschichte, 19 (1971), 261-93.

See also Bruce Kuklick, "The Genesis of the European Advisory Commission," Journal of Contemporary History, 4(1969), 189-201.

1898.   LaFeber, Walter. "Roosevelt, Churchill and Indochina, 1942-1945." American Historical Review, 80(1975), 1277-94.

Compare with Christopher Thorne, "Indochina and Anglo-American Relations, 1942-1945," Pacific Historical Review, 45(1976), 73-96.

1899.   Langer, John D. "The Harriman-Beaverbrook Mission and the Debate over Unconditional Aid to the Soviet Union, 1941." Journal of Contemporary History, 14(1979), 463-82.

1900.   McNeill, William Hardy. <u>America, Britain and Russia: Their Co-operation and Conflict, 1941-1946</u>. London, 1965.

Part of the Royal Institute of International Affairs wartime survey.

1901.   Miner, Steven Merritt. <u>Between Churchill and Roosevelt: The Soviet Union, Great Britain and the Origins of the Grand Alliance</u>. London, 1988.

Concentrates on the period January 1940-June 1942; with some Russian-language sources.

1902.   Nelson, Daniel J. <u>Wartime Origins of the Berlin Dilemma</u>. University, AL, 1978.

With special emphasis on the role of the European Advisory Commission; documentary annexes.

1903.   Neumann, William L. <u>Making the Peace, 1941-1945: The Diplomacy of the Wartime Conferences</u>. Washington, DC, 1950.

See also his <u>After Victory: Churchill, Roosevelt, Stalin and the Making of the Peace</u> (New York, 1967).

1904.   Sadkovich, James J. "Re-evaluating Who Won the Italo-British Naval Conflict, 1940-1942." <u>European History Quarterly</u>, 18(1988), 893-922.

1905.   Sainsbury, Keith. <u>The Turning Point: Roosevelt, Stalin, Churchill, and Chiang Kai-shek, 1943, the Moscow, Cairo, and Teheran Conferences</u>. London, 1985.

With limited use of American archives; see also his " 'Second Front in 1942': A Strategic Controversy Revisited," <u>British Journal of International Studies</u>, 4(1978), 47-58; and <u>The North Africa Landings, 1942: A Strategic Decision</u> (London, 1976).

1906.   Shai, Aron. <u>Britain and China, 1941-1947: Imperial Momentum</u>. London, 1984.

"A study of the very end of the British imperial decline in China" (Introduction).

1907.   Sharp, Tony. <u>The Wartime Alliance and the Zonal Division of Germany</u>. London, 1975.

Specifically on the relation between the negotiations and overall military strategy; based on British and American archives and interviews; see also his "The Origins of the 'Teheran Formula' on Polish Frontiers," Journal of Contemporary History, 12(1977), 381-93.

1908.   Siracusa, Joseph M.   "The Meaning of TOLSTOY: Churchill, Stalin and the Balkans, Moscow, October, 1944." Diplomatic History, 3(1979), 443-63.

A commentary, with the official British records; for more on the subject see his "The Night Stalin and Churchill Divided Europe: The View from Washington," Review of Politics, 43(1981), 381-410; P.G.H. Holdich, "A Policy of Percentages? British Policy and the Balkans after the Moscow Conference of October 1944," International History Review, 9(1987), 28-47; Warren F. Kimball, "Naked Reverse Right: Roosevelt, Churchill and Eastern Europe from TOLSTOY to Yalta - and a Little Beyond," Diplomatic History, 9(1985), 1-24; Procopis Papastratis, "The Anglo-Soviet Balkan Agreement and Greece," in New Trends in Modern Greek Historiography, edited by A. Lily Macrakis et al. (Hanover, NH, 1982); Albert Resis, "The Churchill-Stalin Secret 'Percentages' Agreement on the Balkans, Moscow, October 1944," American Historical Review, 83(1978), 368-87; and Stephen G. Xydis, "The Secret Anglo-Soviet Agreement on the Balkans of October 9th, 1944," Journal of Central European Affairs, 15(1955), 248-71.

1909.   Somerville, John.   "Die britische Strategie im Mittelmeer von Mitte 1941 bis Februar 1942," in Kriegswende Dezember 1941. Edited by Jürgen Rohwer and Eberhard Jäckel. Koblenz, 1984.

1910.   Thorne, Christopher.   Allies of a Kind: The United States, Britain and the War against Japan, 1941-1945. London, 1978.

Anglo-American relations in the context of the Far East conflict; well-researched with extensive bibliography; for the wider background see also his The Issue of War: States, Societies and the Far Eastern Conflict of 1941-1945 (London, 1985).

1911.   Tute, Warren.   The Reluctant Enemies: The Story of the Last War between Britain and France, 1940-1942. London, 1990.

See also Arthur Layton Funk, The Politics of Torch: The Allied Landings and the Algiers Putsch, 1942 (Lawrence, KS, 1974); his "Negotiating the 'Deal with Darlan,' " Journal of Contemporary History, 8(1973), 81-117; P.M.H. Bell, "War, Foreign Policy and

Public Opinion: Britain and the Darlan Affair, November-December 1942," Journal of Strategic Studies, 5(1982), 393-415; and Robert L. Melko, "Darlan between Britain and Germany, 1940-1941," Journal of Contemporary History, 8(1973), 57-80.

1912. USSR, Ministerstvo Inostrannikh Del. Sovietskii Soyuz na mezhdunarodnykh konferentsiiakh perioda velikoi otechestvennoi voiny, 1941-1945gg. 6 vols. Moscow, 1978-80.

A collection of documents; vol. 1 for the Moscow conference, 1943; vol. 2 for Tehran, 1943; vol. 3 for Dumbarton Oaks, 1944; vol. 4 for Crimea/Yalta, 1945; vol. 5 for San Francisco, 1945; and vol. 6 for Berlin/Potsdam, 1945.

1913. Wheeler, Mark C. Britain and the War for Yugoslavia, 1940-1943. Boulder, CO, 1980.

Based on British and Yugoslav archival sources; see also his "White Eagles and White Guards: British Perceptions of Anti-Communist Insurgency in Yugoslavia, 1945," Slavonic and East European Review, 66(1988), 446-61; Michael Lees, The Rape of Serbia: The British Role in Tito's Grab for Power, 1943-1944 (New York, 1990); Elisabeth Barker, "British Wartime Policy towards Yugoslavia," South Slav Journal, 2(1979), 3-9; and her "Fresh Sidelights on British Policy in Yugoslavia, 1942-1943," Slavonic and East European Review, 54(1976), 572-85; Stevan K. Pavlowitch, "Yugoslav-British Relations, 1939-1941, as Seen from British Sources," East European Quarterly, 12(1978), 309-39, 425-41; Walter R. Roberts, Tito, Mihailovic and the Allies, 1941-1945 (New Brunswick, NJ, 1973); which includes published Yugoslav sources; and F.W.D. Deakin, "Britanija i Jugoslavija, 1941-1945," Jugosolovenski istorijski casopis, 2(1963), 43-58.

1914. Williams, J. E. "The Joint Declarations on the Colonies: An Issue in Anglo-American Relations, 1942-1944." British Journal of International Studies, 2(1976), 267-92.

1915. Woodhouse, C.M. The Struggle for Greece, 1941-1949. London, 1976.

In command of allied military mission to Greek guerillas, 1943; see also his autobiographical Something Ventured (London, 1982); Apple of Discord (London, 1948); and "Early British Contacts with the Greek Resistance in 1942," Balkan Studies, 12(1971), 347-63; and of related interest, Nicholas Hammond, Venture into Greece (London, 1983).

1916.   Woods, Randall Bennett. A Changing of the Guard: Anglo-American Relations, 1941-1946. Chapel Hill, NC, 1990.

1917.   Zieger, Gottfried. Alliierte Kriegskonferenzen, 1941-1943. Hannover, 1964.

See also his Die Teheran-Konferenz, 1943 (Hannover, 1967); and Die Atlantik-Charter (Hannover, 1963).

1945: Before and After

1918.   Anderson, Terry H. The United States, Great Britain, and the Cold War, 1944-1947. Columbia, MO, 1981.

On "the evolution of Anglo-American relations toward the Soviet Union from wartime cooperation to the Truman Doctrine" (Preface).

1919.   Aronsen, Lawrence, and Kitchen, Martin. The Origins of the Cold War in Comparative Perspective: American, British and Canadian Relations with the Soviet Union, 1941-1948. London, 1988.

1920.   Balfour, Michael. The Adversaries: America, Russia and the Open World, 1941-1962. London, 1981.

An interpretive essay; bibliography but no footnotes.

1921.   Buhite, Russell D. Decisions at Yalta: An Appraisal of Summit Diplomacy. Wilmington, DE, 1986.

Of the numerous other studies, see also Siegfried Kogelfranz, Das Erbe von Jalta: Die Opfer und die Davongekommen (Hamburg, 1985); V.I. Sipols and I.A. Chelyshev, Krymskaia konferentsiia 1945 god (Moscow, 1984); Cyrus L. Sulzberger, Such a Peace: The Roots and Ashes of Yalta (New York, 1982); Floyd H. Rodine, Yalta: Responsibility and Response, January-March 1945 (Lawrence, KS, 1974); Diane Shaver Clemens, Yalta (New York, 1970), with extensive use of published Soviet sources; Arthur Conte, Yalta, ou le partage du monde (Paris, 1966); The Yalta Conference, edited by Richard F. Fenno, 2nd ed. (London, 1972); and for background, Stephen W. Stathis, "Malta: Prelude to Yalta," Presidential Studies Quarterly, 9(1979), 469-82.

1922.   Cairncross, Sir Alec. The Price of War: British Policy on German Reparations, 1941-1949. London, 1986.

Member, Economic Advisory Panel, Berlin, 1945-46.

1923.   Cox, Sir Geoffrey Sandford. The Road to Trieste. London, 1946.

Foreign and war correspondent, News Chronicle, 1935-37; Daily Express, 1937-40; served world war two, 1940-43; background in his Countdown to War (London, 1988).

1924.   Deighton, Anne, ed. Britain and the First Cold War. London, 1990.

See also her The Impossible Peace: Britain, the German Problem and the Origins of the Cold War (London, 1990); Joseph Foschepoth, "Britische Deutschlandpolitik zwischen Jalta und Potsdam," Vierteljahrshefte für Zeitgeschichte, 30(1982), 675-714; Die britische Deutschland- und Besatzungspolitik, 1945-1949, edited by Joseph Foschepoth and Rolf Steininger (Paderborn, 1985); and Hermann Graml, Die Alliierten und die Teilung Deutschlands: Konflikte und Entscheidungen, 1941-1948 (Frankfurt/M., 1985).

1925.   Edmonds, Robin. Setting the Mould: The United States and Britain, 1945-1950. London, 1986.

By a member of the British Foreign Service, 1945-77; with much on the situation in 1945.

1926.   Eisen, Janet. Anglo-Dutch Relations and European Unity. Hull, 1981.

A brief study, with Dutch sources and archives; background in Holland at War against Hitler: Anglo-Dutch Relations, 1940-1945, edited by M.R.D. Foot (London, 1990).

1927.   Farquharson, John E. "Hilfe für den Feind: Die britische Debatte um Nahrungsmittellieferungen an Deutschland, 1944-1945." Vierteljahrshefte für Zeitgeschichte, 37(1989), 253-78.

1928.   Garson, Robert. "The Atlantic Alliance, Eastern Europe and the Origins of the Cold War: From Pearl Harbor to Yalta," in Contrast and Contention: Bicentennial Essays in Anglo-American History. Edited by H.C. Allen and Roger Thompson. London, 1976.

1929. Harbutt, Fraser J. <u>The Iron Curtain: Churchill, America, and the</u> <u>Origins of the Cold War</u>. London, 1986.

Detailed analysis of Churchill's role during and immediately after the second world war; see also his "Churchill, Hopkins and the 'Other' Americans: An Alternative Perspective on Anglo-American Relations, 1941-1945," <u>International History Review</u>, 8(1986), 236-62.

1930. Hathaway, Robert M. <u>Ambiguous Partnership: Britain and</u> <u>America, 1944-1947</u>. New York, 1981.

1931. Kuniholm, Bruce R. <u>The Origins of the Cold War in the Near East:</u> <u>Great Power Conflict and Diplomacy in Iran, Turkey and Greece</u>. Princeton, NJ, 1980.

The historical context of the cold war from a regional perspective; based on American archives and interviews.

1932. Lewis, Julian. <u>Changing Direction: British Military Planning for</u> <u>Post-War Strategic Defence, 1942-1947</u>. London, 1988.

Thoroughly researched in Public Record Office files.

1933. Loth, Wilfred. <u>The Division of the World, 1941-1955</u>. New York, 1988.

A postrevisionist interpretation.

1934. Lukacs, John. <u>1945: Year Zero</u>. New York, 1978.

Essentially a collection of essays, including a study of Winston Churchill; no bibliography; see also Brian Gardner, <u>The Wasted</u> <u>Hour: The Tragedy of 1945</u> (London, 1963).

1935. Mee, Charles L. <u>Meeting at Potsdam</u>. New York, 1975.

Among numerous other studies see V. Beletskii, <u>Potsdam, 1945</u> <u>god</u> (Moscow, 1987); Ernst Deuerlein, <u>Deklamation oder</u> <u>Ersatzfrieden? Die Konferenz von Potsdam 1945</u> (Stuttgart, 1970); Jens Hacker, "Das Potsdamer Abkommen vom 2. August 1945," <u>Aus Politik und Zeitgeschichte</u>, supplement to <u>Das</u> <u>Parlament</u>, 61(1970), 1-30; Klemens Keplicz, <u>Potsdam: Twenty</u> <u>Years After</u> (Warsaw, 1965); Wenzel Jaksch, <u>Europe's Road to</u> <u>Potsdam</u> (New York, 1963); Alfons Klafkowski, <u>The Potsdam</u> <u>Agreement</u> (Warsaw, 1963); Helmut Sündermann, <u>Potsdam 1945:</u>

Ein kritischer Bericht (Leoni am Starnberger See, 1963); and Herbert Feis, Between War and Peace: The Potsdam Conference (Princeton, NJ, 1960).

1936. Miscamble, Wilson D. "Anthony Eden and the Truman-Molotov Conversations, April 1945." Diplomatic History, 2(1978), 167-80.

1937. Nagai, Yonosuke, and Iriye, Akira, eds. The Origins of the Cold War in Asia. Tokyo, 1977.

Sixteen papers presented at a symposium in Kyoto in 1975.

1938. Ovendale, Ritchie. "Britain, the U.S.A. and the European Cold War, 1945-1948." History, 67(1982), 217-35.

For background see The Foreign Policy of the British Labour Governments, 1945-1951, edited by Ritchie Ovendale (Leicester, 1984); and James Gormley, The Collapse of the Grand Alliance, 1945-1948 (London, 1987).

1939. Polonsky, Antony, ed. The Great Powers and the Polish Question, 1941-1945: A Documentary Study in Cold War Origins. London, 1976.

Introductory essay, with 149 documents, many from the Public Record Office; footnotes but no bibliography; see also his "Polish Failure in Wartime London: Attempts to Forge a European Alliance, 1940-1944," International History Review, 7(1985), 519-60; Edward J. Rozek, Allied Wartime Diplomacy: A Pattern in Poland (New York, 1958); and Roman Umiastowski, Poland, Russia and Great Britain, 1941-1945: A Study of Evidence (London, 1946).

1940. Rothwell, Victor. Britain and the Cold War, 1941-1947. London, 1982.

Mainly based on Foreign Office documents.

1941. Rubin, Barry. The Great Powers in the Middle East, 1941-1947: The Road to the Cold War. London, 1980.

Explores "the role of great power relations in the Middle East in the breakdown of the wartime alliance and in the origins of the Cold War" (Preface); see also his "Anglo-American Relations in Saudi Arabia, 1941-1945," Journal of Contemporary History,

14(1979), 253-67; William Roger Louis, The British Empire in the Middle East, 1945-1951: Arab Nationalism, the United States, and Postwar Imperialism (London, 1984); and Harold G. Marcus, Ethiopia, Great Britain and the United States, 1941-1974: The Politics of Empire (Berkeley, CA, 1983).

1942.   Ryan, Henry Butterfield. The Vision of Anglo-America: The US-UK Alliance and the Emerging Cold War, 1943-1946. London, 1987.

On the failure to create a new power, "Anglo-America," designed to arrest Britain's global decline (Introduction); see also his "Anglo-American Relations during the Polish Crisis in 1945," Australian Journal of Politics and History, 30(1984), 69-84; Anglo-American relations are further explored in Richard A. Best, Cooperation with Like-Minded People: British Influences on American Security Policy, 1945-1949 (Westport, CT, 1986).

1943.   Sainsbury, Keith. "British Policy and German Unity at the End of the Second World War." English Historical Review, 94(1979), 786-804.

1944.   Shlaim, Avi. Britain and the Origins of European Unity, 1940-1951. Reading, 1978.

Further analysis in John W. Young, Britain, France and the Unity of Europe, 1945-1951 (London, 1984).

1945.   Smith, Arthur L. Churchill's German Army: Wartime Strategy and Cold War Politics, 1943-1947. London, 1977.

See also his Churchill and the German Army, 1945: Some Speculations on the Origins of the Cold War (Los Angeles, CA, 1974).

1946.   Strang, Lord. "Prelude to Potsdam: Reflections on War and Foreign Policy." International Affairs, 46(1970), 441-54.

Other contributors to this issue on the twenty-fifth anniversary of Potsdam were historians Robert Cecil, André Fontaine and Walter C. Clemens.

1947.   Thomas, Hugh. Armed Truce: The Beginnings of the Cold War, 1945-1946. London, 1986.

Based on extensive research in archives and published sources; for additional background see Roy Douglas, From War to Cold War, 1942-1948 (London, 1981); Daniel Yergin, Shattered Peace: The Origins of the Cold War and the National Security State (Boston, MA, 1977); Martin J. Sherwin, A World Destroyed: The Atomic Bomb and the Grand Alliance (New York, 1975); George C. Herring, Aid to Russia, 1941-1946: Strategy, Diplomacy, the Origins of the Cold War (New York, 1973); John Lewis Gaddis, The United States and the Origins of the Cold War, 1941-1947 (New York, 1972); Gabriel Kolko, The Politics of War: The World and United States Foreign Policy, 1943-1945 (New York, 1968); Gar Alperovitz, Atomic Diplomacy: Hiroshima and Potsdam (New York, 1965); and Denna Frank Fleming, The Cold War and Its Origins, 1917-1960, 2 vols. (London, 1961).

1948. Watt, D.C. "Every War Must End: War-Time Planning for Post-War Security, in Britain and America in the Wars of 1914-1918 and 1939-1945." Transactions of the Royal Historical Society, 28(1978) 159-73.

See too John Baylis, "British Wartime Thinking about a Post-War European Security Group," Review of International Studies, 9(1983), 265-81.

1949. Wheeler-Bennett, John W., and Nicholls, Anthony. The Semblance of Peace: The Political Settlement after the Second World War. London, 1972.

1950. Wright, Michael. "British Foreign Policy in Europe." Annals of the American Academy of Political and Social Science, 240 (1945), 73-78.

Entered diplomatic service, 1926; served Washington, Paris and Cairo, 1926-43; counsellor, British embassy at Washington, 1943-46.

V. INDEX

This index covers authors, editors and compilers, both personal and institutional, as well as titles where there is no author. Numerical references are to serial numbers in the guide rather than to pages.

INDEX

INDEX

INDEX

Ritchie, A., 5
Ritchie, C., 707
Ritter, G., 1754
Roach, J., 114
Robbins, Baron (L. Robbins),
  596
Robbins, K., 203, 853, 890, 1049,
  1066, 1296, 1627
Roberts, Bechhofer, 829
Roberts, Brian, 753
Roberts, F.C., 206
Roberts, H.L., 1192
Roberts, R., 1573
Roberts, S., 59
Roberts, W.R., 1913
Robertson, E.M., 1474, 1515, 1543,
  1676, 1698
Robertson, J., 1835
Robertson, J.C., 1095, 1519, 1520
Robertson, J.H., 815, 876, 1116
Robertson, K.G., 1792
Robertson, W.R., 597
Robinson, K., 1174
Robson, W.A., 297, 1129
Rocholl, H., 1205
Rock, W.R., 766, 1296, 1585, 1658,
  1663,
Röder, W., 1721
Rodgers, F., 309, 315
Rodgers, H.I., 1323
Rodgers, W.T., 882
Rodine, F.H., 1921
Rohe, K., 1475
Rohn, P.H., 325
Rohwer, J., 1793, 1909
Roll, E., 598
Rolo, P.J.V., 1439
Rolph, C.H., 854
Ronaldshay, Earl of, 855
Rönnefarth, H.K.G., 1627
Rooke, M.J., 1134
Rooth, T.J.T., 1016
Rootham, J.St.J., 599
Rose, K., 748, 855, 856
Rose, N., 857, 1180, 1586
Rose, S., 1266
Rosecrance, R., 1635

Rosenof, T., 128
Rosenthal, J.A., 311
Roshwald, A., 1889
Roskill, S.W., 361, 858, 859, 972,
  975, 1830
Ross, G., 1135, 1822
Ross, M., 185
Rössler, H., 1325, 1440
Rostow, N., 1216
Rothermere, Viscount (H.S.
  Harmsworth), 600
Rothfels, H., 1728, 1735
Rothschild, R., 1627
Rothstein, A., 915, 1627
Rothwell, V., 1366, 1495, 1940
Rougier, L., 1863
Round Table, 300
Rout, L.B., 1777
Rowan-Robinson, H., 1522
Rowland, B.M., 1017
Rowland, J., 860
Rowland, P., 861
Rowse, A.L., 1297
Roy, I., 15d, 925, 1626
Royal Air Force Museum, 25
Royal Commission on Historical
  Manuscripts, 26, 76
Royal Commonwealth Society, 27
Royal Economic Society, 505
Royal Historical Society, 124
Royal Institute of International
  Affairs, 28, 221, 222, 1151,
  1171, 1251, 1262, 1522, 1544,
  1699
Rozek, E.J., 1939
Rubin, B., 1941
Ruby, E., 1545
Rueff, J., 708
Rupieper, H.J., 1410
Russell, T.W., 601
Russett, B.M., 1192
Rust, W., 1076, 1549
Ryan, A., 602
Ryan, H.B., 1942
Ryan, W.M., 862
Ryzhikov, V., 1235
Rzheshevskii, O.A., 1659, 1664